Personal Autonomy

New Essays on Personal Autonomy and Its Role in Contemporary Moral Philosophy

Autonomy has recently become one of the central concepts in contemporary moral philosophy and has generated much debate over its nature and value. This is the first volume to bring together original essays that address the theoretical foundations of the concept of autonomy, as well as essays that investigate the relationship between autonomy and moral responsibility, freedom, political philosophy, and medical ethics. Written by some of the most prominent philosophers working in these areas today, this book represents cutting-edge research on the nature and value of autonomy that will be essential reading for a broad range of philosophers as well as many psychologists.

James Stacey Taylor is Assistant Professor of Philosophy at The College of New Jersey.

Personal Autonomy

New Essays on Personal Autonomy and Its Role in Contemporary Moral Philosophy

Edited by
JAMES STACEY TAYLOR
The College of New Jersey

CAMBRIDGE
UNIVERSITY PRESS

CAMBRIDGE UNIVERSITY PRESS
Cambridge, New York, Melbourne, Madrid, Cape Town,
Singapore, São Paulo, Delhi, Mexico City

Cambridge University Press
The Edinburgh Building, Cambridge CB2 8RU, UK

Published in the United States of America by Cambridge University Press, New York

www.cambridge.org
Information on this title: www.cambridge.org/9780521732345

First published 2005
First paperback edition 2008
Reprinted 2008

A catalogue record for this publication is available from the British Library

Library of Congress Cataloguing in Publication Data

Personal autonomy: new essays on personal autonomy and its role in contemporary
moral philosophy I edited by James Stacey Taylor.
p. cm.
Includes bibliographical references and index.
ISBN 0-521-83796-0
1. Ethics, Modern. 2. Autonomy (Psychology) I. Taylor, James Stacey, 1970-
BJ324.A88T39 2004
170-dc22 2004045810

ISBN 978-0-521-83796-5 Hardback
ISBN 978-0-521-73234-5 Paperback

Contents

PART II. AUTONOMY, FREEDOM, AND MORAL RESPONSIBILITY

PART III. THE EXPANDING ROLE OF PERSONAL AUTONOMY

Contributors

Nomy Arpaly is Assistant Professor of Philosophy at Brown University.

Tom L. Beauchamp is Professor of Philosophy at Georgetown University.

Paul Benson is Professor of Philosophy at the University of Dayton.

Bernard Berofsky is Professor of Philosophy at Columbia University.

Michael E. Bratman is the Durfee Professor in the School of Humanities and Sciences and Professor of Philosophy at Stanford University.

John Christman is Associate Professor of Philosophy and Political Science at Pennsylvania State University.

Laura Waddell Ekstrom is the Robert F. and Sara M. Boyd Associate Professor of Philosophy at the College of William and Mary.

R. G. Frey is Professor of Philosophy at Bowling Green State University.

Ishtiyaque Haji is Professor of Philosophy at the University of Calgary.

Thomas May is Associate Professor of Bioethics at the Medical College of Wisconsin.

Michael McKenna is Associate Professor of Philosophy at Florida State University.

Alfred R. Mele is the William H. and Lucyle T. Werkmeister Professor of Philosophy at Florida State University.

Robert Noggle is Associate Professor of Philosophy at Central Michigan University.

Marina A. L. Oshana is Associate Professor of Philosophy at the University of Florida.

James Stacey Taylor is Assistant Professor of Philosophy at The College of New Jersey.

Susan Wolf is the Edna J. Koury Professor of Philosophy at the University of North Carolina–Chapel Hill.

Acknowledgments

As a glance at the list of contributors will show, I am the only unknown here; the others are among the most prominent writers on autonomy, moral responsibility, and applied ethics working today. My primary debt, then, is to those who have contributed chapters to this volume, all of whom have not only been extremely generous with their time in helping me to prepare this volume, but also the most agreeable contributors a fledgling editor could hope to work with. I also thank Terence Moore (of Cambridge University Press) and R. G. Frey (my Ph.D. supervisor) for all of their advice and encouragement during this project and Russell Hahn and Stephen Calvert for their editorial advice and assistance. Finally, I thank my wife, Margaret Ulizio, for her support during this project's progress.

Introduction

James Stacey Taylor

In recent years, the concept of autonomy has become ubiquitous in moral philosophy. Discussions of the nature of autonomy, its value, and how one should respect it are now commonplace in philosophical debates, ranging from the metaphysics of moral responsibility to the varied concerns of applied philosophy. All of these debates are underpinned by an increasingly flourishing and sophisticated literature that addresses the fundamental question of the nature of personal autonomy.

The concept of autonomy has, of course, been important for moral philosophy for some time, being central to the ethical theories of both Immanuel Kant and such contemporary Kantians as Thomas Hill and Christine Korsgaard.[1] However, recent interest in personal autonomy does not focus on the Kantian conception of autonomy on which a person is autonomous if her will is entirely devoid of all personal interests. Instead, it focuses on a more individualistic conception of this notion, whereby a person is autonomous with respect to her desires, actions, or character to the extent that they originate in some way from her motivational set, broadly construed.

Interest in this individualistic conception of autonomy was stimulated by the publication of a series of papers in the early 1970s, in which Harry Frankfurt, Gerald Dworkin, and Wright Neely independently developed "hierarchical" accounts of personal autonomy.[2] The shared core of these accounts is both simple and elegant: A person is autonomous with respect to a first-order desire that moves her to act (e.g., she wants to smoke, and so she smokes) if she endorses her possession of that first-order desire (e.g., she wants to want to smoke). This approach to analyzing autonomy has much to recommend it. First, it captures an important truth about persons: They have the capacity to reflect on their desires and to endorse or repudiate them as they see fit. Second, it is an explicitly naturalistic and compatibilist approach to analyzing autonomy. As such, it fits well with the currently dominant compatibilist analyses of moral responsibility, and it seems able to disavow the implausible claim that personal autonomy is incompatible with the truth of metaphysical determinism – a disavowal that is defended by Bernard Berofsky and Alfred Mele in their chapters in this volume.[3] Finally, this approach to analyzing autonomy is content neutral, for it does not require persons to hold any particular values in order for them to be autonomous. This enables it to be readily applicable to many debates within applied ethics where respect for autonomy is of primary concern and where this focus on autonomy is driven by the recognition that some means must be found to adjudicate between competing value claims in a pluralistic society.[4]

Yet despite the many advantages of the hierarchical approach to analyzing autonomy, it suffers from significant theoretical difficulties. In the light of these criticisms, some proponents of the hierarchical approach to analyzing autonomy (such as Stefaan Cuypers and Harry Frankfurt) have developed sophisticated defenses of it.[5] Other writers have developed a "second generation" of neohierarchical theories of autonomy that, while they move beyond the hierarchical approach to analyzing autonomy, acknowledge that the origins of their views lie in the original Frankfurt-Dworkin-Neely theory cluster. Two of the most prominent of these neohierarchical theories of autonomy are those developed by John Christman and Michael Bratman. Christman's historical approach retains the hierarchical analyses' requirement that the attitudes of the person whose effective first-order desire is in question are in some way autonomy conferring. However, rather than holding that this person must in some way endorse the desire in question for her to be autonomous with respect to it, Christman holds that she must not reject the *process* that led her to have this desire.[6] Bratman's analysis of autonomy – the key elements of which he outlines in the chapter "Planning Agency, Autonomous Agency" – combines his influential account of intention and planning agency with certain elements of the hierarchical approach to autonomy.[7] Such neohierarchical approaches to personal autonomy have also been joined by a number of diverse and original approaches to analyzing autonomy that depart from the hierarchical approach altogether. These new approaches to analyzing autonomy include, but are not limited to, the coherentist approach of Laura Waddell Ekstrom,[8] the "helmsman" approach of Thomas May,[9] the doxastic approach of Robert Noggle,[10] the sociorelational approach of Marina Oshana,[11] and the foundationalist approach of Keith Lehrer.[12] This debate over the nature of autonomy has led to a significant increase in the philosophical understanding of this concept, and so it is no longer correct that outside of the Kantian tradition autonomy "is a comparatively unanalyzed notion," as John Christman was truthfully able to write in 1988.[13] Moreover, the increasing attention that the concept of autonomy has recently received is not only of interest to autonomy theorists. This is because, as I outline in Section IV, which analysis of personal autonomy turns out to be the most defensible will have direct implications for all debates in moral philosophy in which this concept plays a major role.

These, then, are exciting times for both autonomy theorists and all who draw upon the concept of autonomy. The chapters in this volume, each original to it, represent the state of the art of the current discussion of autonomy and the roles that it plays in discussions of moral responsibility and applied philosophy. The purpose of this Introduction, thus, is to provide the theoretical background against which these chapters were written, by outlining the progress of the debate over the nature and role of autonomy as this has unfolded over the past three decades. As such, it can naturally be divided into four sections. The first will provide the theoretical background to this collection as a whole, through outlining Frankfurt's and Dworkin's hierarchical analyses of autonomy together with the major criticisms that have led to their modification. Despite these modifications, however, I will note that even in their most recent forms these analyses are both still vulnerable to serious theoretical objections.

The second section of this Introduction will outline three of the most prominent recent analyses of autonomy that have been developed to avoid the difficulties that beset the Frankfurt-Dworkin-Neely hierarchical approach: John Christman's historical approach, Michael Bratman's reasons-based view, and Laura Waddell Ekstrom's coherentist analysis. The second section of the Introduction will serve as a supplement to the first, as it provides an introduction to the most recent theoretical literature on autonomy. In so doing, it will serve as a useful backdrop to the discussions in the first part of this collection, "Theoretical Approaches to Personal Autonomy," in which Bratman and Ekstrom outline and develop their respective analyses of autonomy and in which the relationships among autonomy, free will, the "self," and the concept of "identification" are considered.

The third section of this Introduction will outline alleged connections between personal autonomy and moral responsibility. This will provide the theoretical background to the second part of this collection, "Autonomy, Freedom, and Moral Responsibility." Finally, the last section of this Introduction will indicate the various ways in which the concept of autonomy is invoked within areas of contemporary philosophy apart from discussions of moral responsibility. This section will provide a useful basis from which to approach the final part of this book, "The Expanding Role of Personal Autonomy," which focuses on the role that autonomy plays in political philosophy and in various fields of applied ethics.

I. THE HIERARCHICAL ANALYSES OF AUTONOMY

The core feature shared by Frankfurt's and Dworkin's analyses of autonomy and identification is that these concepts are to be analyzed in terms of hierarchies of desire. (For the sake of clarity, I henceforth take the phrase "is autonomous with respect to her desire *x*" to be synonymous with the phrase "identifies with her desire that *x*.")[14] More specifically, on Frankfurt's original analysis of autonomy a person is autonomous with respect to her first-order desire that moves her to act (her "will") if she *volitionally endorses* that desire. (A "first-order" desire is a desire that a particular state of affairs obtains.) That is to say, a person is autonomous with respect to her effective first-order desire that *x* if she both desired to have the desire that *x* (i.e., she had a *second-order desire* that she have her desire that *x*, where a "second-order" desire is a desire about a first-order desire) *and* she *also* wanted her desire that *x* to move her to act (i.e., she endorsed her desire that *x* with a second-order *volition*).[15] Similarly, on Dworkin's original analysis of autonomy an "autonomous person is one who does *his own* thing," where "the attitude that [the] person takes towards the influences motivating him . . . determines whether or not they are to be considered 'his.'"[16] That is to say, on Dworkin's view a person is autonomous with respect to the desires that motivate him if he endorses his being so moved. In addition to requiring that a person's motivations be "authentic" in this way, Dworkin also required that she enjoy both procedural independence and substantive independence with respect to her motivations. A person possesses procedural independence with respect to her motivations if her desire to be moved to act by them has not been produced by "manipulation, deception, the withholding of relevant information, and so on."[17] A person possesses substantive independence with respect to his motivations if he does not "renounce his independence of thought or action" prior to developing them.[18]

On both Frankfurt's and Dworkin's hierarchical analyses, then, a person's autonomy is impaired if she is moved to act by a desire that she does not volitionally endorse – if she has a second-order desire not to be moved by the first-order desire that is effective in moving her to act. In most cases, this is intuitively plausible. For example, if a person is subject to a constant neurotic compulsion to wash his hands from which he desires to be free, then his autonomy will be impaired if he is moved to act by a first-order desire to wash his hands that this neurosis causes him to have and by which he does not wish to be moved. Similarly, if a person is a "wanton," if he does not care which of his desires moves him to act, then it seems plausible to claim that he is not autonomous (he is not "self-directed"), either because his "self" is not engaged in directing his desires or actions or because he has no coherent "self" to play this role.

Yet despite their plausibility, these early hierarchical analyses of autonomy are subject to three serious objections. The first of these is the Problem of Manipulation.[19] Frankfurt's hierarchical analysis of autonomy is an *ahistorical* (or *structural, punctuate,* or *time slice*) account of autonomy, on which a person is autonomous with respect to his effective first-order desires *irrespective* of their historical origins, provided that he volitionally endorses them. The proponents of the Problem of Manipulation note that a third party (such as a nefarious neurosurgeon or a horrible hypnotist) could inculcate into a person both a certain first-order desire (e.g., the desire to smoke) and a second-order volition concerning this desire so that there is the pertinent sort of hierarchical endorsement. Because this inculcated first-order desire would satisfy Frankfurt's conditions for its possessor to be autonomous with respect to it, Frankfurt is committed to holding that she is autonomous with respect to it – but this ascription of autonomy to her with respect to this desire is suspect.[20]

Of course, Dworkin's analysis of autonomy is not directly subject to the Problem of Manipulation because it is blocked by his requirement that the process by which a person comes to have her desires be one that is procedurally independent – a condition that is clearly unsatisfied when a person's desires are inculcated into her through hypnosis or neurosurgery without her consent. Despite this, one can still use the Problem of Manipulation to develop an *indirect* objection to Dworkin's analysis of autonomy. Thus, although Dworkin's requirement of procedural independence enables him to avoid the Problem of Manipulation, it only does so by fiat, by simply ruling *ex cathedra* that a person is not autonomous with respect to those desires that he has been manipulated into possessing. And this is not enough for his analysis of autonomy to be theoretically satisfactory. This is because an acceptable analysis of autonomy should not merely list the ways in which it is intuitively plausible that a person will suffer from a lack of autonomy with respect to her effective first-order desires, but must also provide an account of *why* a person's autonomy would be thus undermined, so that influences on a person's behavior that do not seem to undermine her autonomy (e.g., advice) can be differentiated from those that do (e.g., deception).

Frankfurt's and Dworkin's analyses of autonomy also face the Regress-cum-Incompleteness Problem.[21] On these analyses, a person is autonomous with respect to her effective first-order desires if she endorses them with a second-order desire. Because this is so, the question arises as to whether this person is autonomous with respect to this second-order desire and, if she is, why this is so. If she is autonomous with respect to this second-order desire because it is, in turn, endorsed by a yet higher-order desire, then a regress threatens, for the question will then arise as to whether she is autonomous with respect to this *third*-order desire – and so on. If, however, this person is autonomous with respect to the second-order desire for a reason *other* than its endorsement by a higher-order desire, then the hierarchical approach to analyzing autonomy is incomplete.

Of course, the proponents of the hierarchical approach *could* avoid the Regress-cum-Incompleteness Problem simply by claiming that although the person in question is *not* autonomous with respect to her higher-order endorsing desire, she *is* autonomous with respect to her endorsed first-order desire, because autonomy is simply constituted by such an endorsement. Yet although Frankfurt and Dworkin could avoid the Regress-cum-Incompleteness Problem by adopting this line of response, neither of them does so, no doubt because they recognize that were they to do so they would encounter the equally troubling *Ab Initio* Problem: How can a person become autonomous with respect to a desire through a process with respect to which she was not autonomous? Or, in other words, how is it that a person's higher-order desires possess any authority over her lower-order desires?[22] When put in this way, the *Ab Initio* Problem is often termed the Problem of Authority and in this guise has been neatly encapsulated by Gary Watson: "Since second-order volitions are themselves simply desires, to add them to the context of conflict is just to increase the number of contenders; it is not to give a special place to any of those in contention."[23]

Faced with these three difficulties, both Frankfurt and Dworkin modified their original analyses. Recognizing that his analysis would be subjected to the Regress-cum-Incompleteness Problem, Frankfurt attempted to eliminate the possibility of such a problematic regress by claiming that a person's *decisive* identification with one of his desires would terminate it.[24] Frankfurt elaborated this decision-based version of his hierarchical analysis of autonomy in "Identification and Wholeheartedness," where he argued that a person is autonomous with respect to his effective first-order desire if he *decisively* endorses it with a second-order volition. Directly responding to the Regress Problem, Frankfurt claimed that if a person endorses his effective first-order desire "without reservation . . . in the belief that no further accurate inquiry would require him to change his mind," it would be pointless for him to continue to assess whether he was autonomous with respect to the first-order desire that was in question.[25] Furthermore, a person's decisive identification with his endorsing second-order volition also seems to circumvent the *Ab Initio* Problem/Problem of Authority, for through this decision the person in question will endow his volition with the authority that it previously lacked.

Unlike Frankfurt, Dworkin did not directly attempt to address criticisms of his analysis of what conditions must be met for a person to be autonomous with respect to her desires and actions. Instead, he clarified that his account was concerned *not* with the *local* conception of what conditions must be met for a person to be autonomous with respect to her actions (or desires), but, instead, with a more *global* conception of autonomy as a "second-order capacity of persons to reflect critically upon their first-order preferences, desires, wishes and so forth."[26] Dworkin argued that once it is understood that he was not trying to provide an account of what made a person autonomous with respect to her desires or actions, his conception of autonomy avoids the Regress-cum-Incompleteness Problem. This is because, he claimed, as long as a person enjoyed procedural independence with respect to her reflection upon her desires, there would be "no conceptual necessity for raising the question of whether the values, preferences at the second order would themselves be valued or preferred at a higher level. . . ."[27] Similarly, Dworkin held that his account of autonomy is unaffected by the *Ab Initio* Problem/Problem of Authority. Because on his view persons enjoy autonomy when they engage this capacity for reflection, the exercise of this second-order capacity for endorsement *just is* what is involved in being autonomous.

Yet even if Dworkin's more global approach to analyzing personal autonomy avoids the major problems that were outlined above, this is achieved at considerable cost. This is because in many discussions that concern the nature of autonomy the issue is *not* what psychological capacities a person must possess to have the *capacity* for autonomy, for it is generally accepted that to be autonomous an agent must possess the ability to engage in some form of second-order reflection of the sort that Dworkin outlines. Instead, what is really of interest in discussions of autonomy is the question of how the *exercise* of this psychological capacity for reflection results in persons being autonomous with respect to their desires and actions. Thus, in adopting this more global approach to autonomy Dworkin is no longer offering an analysis of autonomy that is congruent with the discussions in moral philosophy in which autonomy plays a major role, for these discussions focus on the more localized question of what makes a person autonomous with respect to her *particular* desires or her *particular* actions.

Once Dworkin's more recent aims in developing an analysis of autonomy have been clarified, then, they can be seen to be distinct from the primary aim of most autonomy theorists – namely, to provide an account of what it is for a person to be autonomous with respect to her desires and her actions. Yet this core aim of autonomy theorists is not satisfied by Frankfurt's decision-based analysis of autonomy either, for it fails as a successful response to three of the objections outlined above. First, the mere fact that a person has *decisively* identified herself with a particular first-order desire does not halt any possible problematic regress. This is because, as Frankfurt later recognized, the Regress-cum-Incompleteness Problem would still arise, given that one could still question whether the person in question was autonomous with respect to this decision. Furthermore, the Problem of Manipulation still poses difficulties for this account because such a decision could still be the result of the agent's succumbing to forces that are external to her. For example, she might have been hypnotized into decisively identifying with a given desire.[28] Finally, because a person can be manipulated into decisively identifying herself with a particular first-order desire, the proponents of the *Ab Initio* Problem/Problem of Authority can still question why such mental acts are authoritative for her.

Frankfurt recognized that his analysis of autonomy was beset by these three problems because it rested on the claim that a person became autonomous with respect to her desires through endorsing them with a "deliberate psychic event" – and one could always question whether the person in question was autonomous with respect to this event. To avoid these criticisms, Frankfurt developed a satisfaction-based analysis of identification.[29] On this analysis, a person need not engage in any "deliberate psychic event" for her to identify with her desires. Instead, on this analysis a person is autonomous with respect to a desire if he accepts it as his own – if he accepts it as indicating "something about himself."[30] In accepting a desire, a person will reflect on it to see if it is expressive of something about him. If it is, then he will form a higher-order attitude of acceptance toward it as part of himself. It is this *acceptance* of the desire that constitutes the person's *endorsement* of it, to use Frankfurt's "misleading" terminology from "The Faintest Passion."[31] The sense of endorsement that Frankfurt is using here, then, is the sense in which one might endorse the claim of an entity to be a member of a class, without thereby evaluating (either positively or negatively) the merits of the particular entity that is making the claim. Once a person has met the requirement that she reflectively endorse her first-order desires in this way, Frankfurt does not also require that she then reflectively endorse her attitude of endorsement, for, as he rightly notes, such a requirement would lead to a regress. Instead, Frankfurt holds that a person will identify with a first-order desire if she is *satisfied* with the higher-order attitude of endorsement (i.e., acceptance) that she has taken toward it. For Frankfurt, a person's being satisfied with his attitudinal set "does not require that [he] have any particular belief about it, or any particular feeling or attitude or intention.... There is nothing that he needs to think, or adopt, or to accept; it is not necessary for him to do anything at all." Instead, his being satisfied with his attitudinal set simply consists in his "having no interest in making changes" in it.[32] And this, notes Frankfurt, is important, for it explains why this analysis of identification as satisfaction is not subject to a problematic regress of the sort that beset his earlier analyses.[33] Here, then, a person will be autonomous with respect to his effective first-order desire if he is not moved to make changes in his motivational economy when he is moved to act by it, if he is *satisfied* with it.

Frankfurt's satisfaction-based analysis of autonomy is not subject to the Regress-cum-Incompleteness Problem for the reasons outlined above. Moreover, it is also not subject to the *Ab Initio* Problem/Problem of Authority. This is because Frankfurt has now clarified that a person's higher-order attitude of acceptance toward her lower-order desires does not possess any normative authority over them; instead, these attitudes are merely used by the person in question to assess whether her lower-order desires are to be regarded as being descriptively hers, whether they flow from her (broadly Lockean) self. However, this analysis of autonomy still faces the Problem of Manipulation. This is because a person could unwittingly be hypnotized into possessing a certain first-order desire in such a way that he believes that it originates from within him. Given this belief, he would then both endorse this first-order desire and be satisfied with it, in Frankfurt's senses of these terms. This person would thus meet all of Frankfurt's most recent criteria for him to identify with his hypnotically induced desire – yet surely such a desire is one with respect to which its possessor is paradigmatically heteronomous.

II. NEW APPROACHES TO AUTONOMY

Christman's Historical Analysis

From the previous discussion, it might seem that the hierarchical approach to analyzing personal autonomy is doomed to failure, in large part because it appears inevitably to succumb to the Problem of Manipulation. Yet this assessment of hierarchical theories of autonomy needs to be qualified, for the focus of the past discussion was on Frankfurt's explicitly *ahistorical* approach to analyzing autonomy. Recognizing the difficulties that such an approach would have when faced by the Problem of Manipulation, Christman developed an explicitly historically based version of the hierarchical approach to analyzing autonomy. For Christman, an agent P is autonomous relative to some desire (value, etc.) at time t if and only if

i. P did not resist the development of D (prior to t) when attending to this process of development, or P would not have resisted that development had P attended to the process;
ii. The lack of resistance to the development of D (prior to t) did not take place (or would not have) under the influence of factors that inhibit self-reflection;
iii. The self-reflection involved in condition i is (minimally) rational and involves no self-deception;[34]

and

iv. The agent is minimally rational with respect to D at t (where minimal rationality demands that an agent experience no manifest conflicts of desires or beliefs that significantly affect the agent's behavior and that are not subsumed under some otherwise rational plan of action).[35]

Unfortunately, as it stands, Christman's historical analysis of autonomy fails to provide either necessary or sufficient conditions for a person to be autonomous with respect to her desires. To see that this account does not provide necessary conditions for a person to be autonomous with respect to her desires, imagine a child at time t whose mother wished him to learn to play the piano and who beat him if he did not practice.[36] As time passes and the child grows more proficient at playing, he discovers (at time t1) that his mother's belief that piano playing suited him was right, and he comes to love playing – even though he still repudiates the means by which his mother brought him to this position. Thus, even though at t1 this person rejects the process by which he was brought to desire to play the piano, at t1 (and onward) he appears to be fully autonomous with respect to this desire.[37]

Furthermore, just as it is not necessary for a person to meet Christman's condition for autonomy for her to be autonomous with respect to her effective first-order desire, neither is it sufficient for this. To see this, one must note that Christman accepts that a person is autonomous with respect to a desire D even if she came to possess it under the influence of factors that inhibit self-reflection, provided that exposure to such factors was autonomously chosen.[38] Now consider the case of a man who wishes to join an order of monks who strictly follow the teachings of St. Ignatius of Loyola. It is a feature of the Ignatian tradition that its monks are required to subordinate their wills entirely to that of their abbots. No room at all should be left for the exercise of free choice or rational critical reflection, for these simply make the monk vulnerable to the temptation of Satan.[39] Knowing this, at time t this man decides to join the Ignatian order, thus autonomously choosing to subject himself to factors that inhibit self-reflection – namely, those that are required for him to subjugate his will to that of his abbot. If he is successful in his attempts to subjugate his will in this way, this man will (at time t1) only desire that which his abbot tells him to desire; he will, in effect, have reduced himself to the status of an automaton. However, he will still meet Christman's criteria for him to be held to be autonomous with respect to the desires that he has at time t1. This is because (since he had faith in his abbot) he would not have resisted the development of the desires he had at t1 had he attended to their generative process, the reflection-inhibiting factors that prevented him from reflecting on his desires were those that he autonomously chose, and he was minimally rational and not self-deceived at t1 also. However, because the *only* desires that he has are those that his abbot instructs him to have, this monk is a paradigm of heteronomy, rather than autonomy. And, because this is so, then even if a person's possession of his desires meets Christman's conditions, this does not suffice for him to be autonomous with respect to them.

Bratman's Approach

Christman's historical approach to analyzing autonomy was intended to be a development of the hierarchical approaches of Frankfurt and Dworkin. In a similar vein, Michael Bratman developed his reasons-based analysis of autonomy after he leveled what he took to be fatal objections to Frankfurt's satisfaction-based analysis.[40] At first approximation on Bratman's account, a person is autonomous with respect to a desire if she *decides* to treat it as being reason-giving (in the sense of being end-setting) in the relevant circumstances.[41] Bratman recognizes, however, that a person's decision to treat a desire as reason-giving is not sufficient for her to be autonomous with respect to it. This is because an unwilling drug addict might decide to give in to his craving and take drugs simply because it is becoming too painful for him to continue to resist his urges for them.[42] Here, the addict decides to treat his desire for drugs as being reason-giving in the relevant sense of being end-setting – and yet it seems that he is not autonomous with respect to it. To avoid this difficulty, Bratman argues that the key to understanding why the grudging addict is not autonomous with respect to his desire for drugs is that this desire is "incompatible with the agent's *other* standing decisions or policies concerning what to treat as reason-giving."[43] To be autonomous with respect to a desire, then, one must not only decide to treat it as being reason-giving but must also be *satisfied* with it. For Bratman, this satisfaction will consist in one not having "reached and retained a conflicting decision, intention or policy concerning the treatment of one's desires as reason-giving."[44]

As well as avoiding the Regress-cum-Incompleteness problem, Bratman's reasons-based analysis of autonomy also avoids the *Ab Initio* Problem/Problem of Authority. This is because he bases his account of what constitutes a person's standing decisions, intentions, and policies by reference to his broadly Lockean account of personal identity, on which an agent helps "ensure appropriate psychological continuities and connections [to retain her identity over time] by sticking with and executing [her] prior plans and policies, and by monitoring and regulating [her] motivational structures in favor, say, of [her] continued commitment to philosophy."[45] Because a person's standing decisions, intentions, and policies are constitutive of her self, they do indeed possess the authority to play the role in Bratman's analysis of assessing which of a person's first-order desires she is autonomous with respect to and which she is not. Furthermore, one need not ask whether the person is autonomous with respect to her standing decisions, intentions, and policies. This is because, on Bratman's account of autonomy, these cross-temporal mental states (at least partially) constitute her self, and so (for the reasons that Noggle outlines in his paper "Autonomy and the Paradox of Self-Creation," this volume) the question of whether she is autonomous with respect to them does not arise.

Yet although Bratman's reasons-based approach to analyzing personal autonomy avoids two of the primary difficulties that beset its hierarchical predecessors, it still appears to be subject to the Problem of Manipulation. To see this, consider again a person who has been hypnotized into both having certain desires and accepting these desires as his own. Just as this person satisfied Frankfurt's criteria for him to be autonomous with respect to his hypnotically inculcated desires, so, too, does he satisfy Bratman's criteria for him to identify with them. This is because, owing to his hypnosis, this person treats these desires as being reason-giving in the sense of being end-setting, and they do not conflict with any of his standing "decisions or policies concerning what to treat as reason-giving," for he has not formed any views concerning the status of any hypnotically inculcated desires that he might have. Bratman, then, is also committed to the view that this person is autonomous with respect to his hypnotically induced desires – and this view is false. However, given Bratman's broadly Lockean account of personal identity that undergirds his account of autonomy, he might have an answer to this – that in such cases, the person's desires do not flow from her self in the appropriate way.[46] To develop this line of response, Bratman would have to strengthen his criterion that a person's decision to treat a desire as being reason-giving not conflict with her standing decisions, policies, and intentions to the claim that it must be in accord with them, and also add in a historical component to Bratman's view to block any revised versions of the Problem of Manipulation that might be developed against this strengthened version of his account.[47] But this is certainly a promising line of inquiry to take.

Ekstrom's Coherentist Analysis

It appears from this discussion that the Problem of Manipulation is an especially difficult one to avoid, although Bratman's analysis of autonomy might be modified to do so. There is, however, an alternative approach to analyzing autonomy that is immune to this objection and that deserves wider attention. This is the coherentist approach Laura Waddell Ekstrom has developed and that she elaborates upon in her contribution to this volume, "Autonomy and Personal Integration." Ekstrom draws on the same insight that led Frankfurt and Bratman to develop their satisfaction- and reason-based analyses of autonomy: that a person is autonomous with respect to those conative states that move her to act if these flow from her self. Yet rather than analyzing what it is for a person to be autonomous with respect to her *desires*, Ekstrom is concerned with offering an account of what makes a person autonomous with respect to her *preferences*. For Ekstrom, a preference "is a very particular sort of desire: it is one (i) for a certain first-order desire to be effective in action, when or if one acts, and (ii) that is formed in the search for what is good."[48] Ekstrom's concept of a preference is thus like Frankfurt's concept of a second-order volition, except that Frankfurt allowed that a person might form a second-order volition for any reason at all, whereas for Ekstrom a person forms a preference for a first-order desire because he finds a certain first-order desire to be good.

In developing her original coherentist analysis of autonomy in her paper "A Coherence Theory of Autonomy," Ekstrom distinguished between a person's "self" and her "true or most central self." For Ekstrom, a person's "self" consists of her character together with the power for "fashioning and refashioning" that character, where a person S's character at time t is constituted by "the set of propositions that S accepts at t and the preferences of S at t."[49] A person's "true or most central self," however, consists of that subset of these acceptances and preferences that actually cohere. Ekstrom offers three reasons why such cohering preferences and acceptances are to be accepted as the elements of a person's core self. First, she notes that such elements are long-lasting; they are "guides for action that will likely remain, since they are well-supported by reasons." Second, the attitudes that constitute a person's core self are "fully defensible" against external challenges; they are those attitudes that one will fervently cling to through time. Third, those preferences that are elements of one's core self will be those that one is comfortable owning; they will be those that one will act on wholeheartedly. With this in place, Ekstrom argues that a person is autonomous with respect to her preferences (they "are *authorized* – or sanctioned as one's own") when "they cohere with [her] other preferences and acceptances" and thus can be recognized as members of her true self.[50] Thus, concludes Ekstrom, when a person acts on an authorized preference (i.e., one that coheres with her true self) she will act autonomously, not only because she will be able to give reasons for her action, but also because she will be acting in a way that is characteristic of her.

Ekstrom's coherentist analysis of autonomy was developed to avoid the standard problems that beset its hierarchical predecessors, and in this it appears to succeed. It is not faced with either the Regress-cum-Incompleteness Problem or the *Ab Initio* Problem/Problem of Authority. This analysis also appears to avoid the Problem of Manipulation, for Ekstrom requires that any preference that a person is autonomous with respect to be one that the person concerned can justify by appealing to his core preferences – and because these core preferences are, on Ekstrom's view, constitutive of the agent, any manipulation of them will result in a new agent and not in a loss of autonomy for their possessor.

Ekstrom avoids these three problems by basing her coherentist analysis of autonomy on the insight that if a person is to be autonomous with respect to a preference, that preference must originate from that person's self in a particular, objective way. Yet accepting this insight need not lead one to adopt a coherentist model of personal autonomy. Bratman, for example, draws on this insight to develop his reasons-based account of autonomy. Similarly, Robert Noggle also draws on it in his paper for this volume to show that neither the Regress-cum-Incompleteness Problem nor the *Ab Initio* Problem is as troubling as autonomy theorists (both coherentist and noncoherentist) take it to be – and he does so without committing himself to any particular approach to analyzing autonomy.

Of course, that a noncoherentist approach to analyzing autonomy might be able to avoid the Regress-cum-Incompleteness Problem and the *Ab Initio* Problem/Problem of Authority just as well as Ekstrom's coherentist analysis does, does not undermine the theoretical appeal of her approach. What might undermine its appeal, however, is the possibility that it fails to provide sufficient conditions for a person to be autonomous with respect to her preferences. To see this, consider again the case of the Ignatian monk who has subjected his will to that of his abbot. Because the preferences that this monk has through the operation of his abbot's will would (in the ideal situation) cohere (in Ekstrom's sense) with those that constitute this monk's "true or most central self," they will be "authorized" for him – and so when he acts on them, he would, on Ekstrom's account, act autonomously. But because this monk is a paradigm of heteronomy, rather than autonomy, Ekstrom's early coherentist analysis of autonomy fails to provide sufficient conditions for a person to be autonomous with respect to his actions.

However, it must be admitted that rather than providing a counterexample to Ekstrom's analysis, the example of the Ignatian monk might simply indicate that the relationship between the concepts of autonomy and authenticity is still unclear. If the property of "autonomy" is understood to apply to a person with respect to her desires and actions if they meet some criterion in addition to the negative criterion that she is not alienated from them, then, although one is likely to accept that the monk acts *authentically* when he is subject to the will of his abbot, one will deny Ekstrom's claim that he acts *autonomously*. Alternatively, if the property of "autonomy" is understood more broadly, such that a person will be autonomous with respect to her desires and actions if she is not alienated from them, then one is likely to accept, with Ekstrom, that the Ignatian monk acts autonomously. It is unlikely that the debate over the proper extensions of these two terms will be decided by etymology, for the concepts of both autonomy and authenticity require that in some way a person's desires or actions flow from her self. Instead, it would be better to settle this debate by asking whether any more precision could be brought to bear on discussions of autonomy by adopting either a broader or narrower construal of this term.[51]

III. AUTONOMY, FREEDOM, AND MORAL RESPONSIBILITY

Given the above litany of difficulties that face the various contemporary analyses of autonomy, one might worry that despite the considerable degree of attention the concept of autonomy has received in recent years, no real progress has been made toward developing a theoretically satisfying account of its nature. But this worry is unfounded for two reasons. First, by developing criticisms to current analyses of autonomy and thus seeing where their weaknesses lie, one can establish what features a theoretically satisfactory analysis of autonomy must possess. For example, the vulnerability of both ahistorical analyses and subjectively based analyses (i.e., those that rely on the subjective evaluation of the desires in question by their possessor to determine if she is autonomous with respect to them) to the Problem of Manipulation indicates that an acceptable analysis of autonomy should incorporate an *objective, historical* condition for a person to be autonomous with respect to her desires. That is, to avoid the Problem of Manipulation, an analysis of autonomy must require that for a person to be autonomous with respect to a desire, she must have come to possess that desire as a result of some particular historical process – and this process must not be one that is based on the person herself adopting a particular attitude toward the origins of the desire that is in question. Second, the more recent analyses of autonomy all share certain features in common that might indicate that they are starting to converge on a satisfactory analysis of autonomy. For example, in line with this first requirement, most contemporary analyses of autonomy require that a person's first-order desires must originate in some way from her "self" for her to be autonomous with respect to them, with this "self" often being given a distinctly Lockean gloss.[52]

Such progress in analyzing the concept of individual autonomy is not only of interest to autonomy theorists, but also to theorists of moral responsibility. As I noted above, one of the advantages that Frankfurt and Dworkin's individualistic conception of autonomy possesses is that it accords with the compatibilist analyses of moral responsibility developed in tandem with it. Yet, as well as being in accord with the compatibilist approach to moral responsibility, the individualistic approach to autonomy is also in accord with the plausible pretheoretical view that a necessary condition of a person's being morally responsible for an action is that he performed that action autonomously.

That the question of what it is for a person to be autonomous with respect to her actions is related to the question of what it is for her to be morally responsible for them is further demonstrated by the fact that there are, in John Martin Fischer's phrase, "parallel literatures" that discuss moral responsibility and autonomy.[53] For example, in both the literature on autonomy and the literature on moral responsibility, there has been considerable interest in utilizing a hierarchical approach to address their respective questions. Thus, writers in both areas often take Frankfurt's hierarchical analysis of what it is for a person to "identify with" her desires to be the starting point for their analyses[54] and question whether a purely structural analysis could adequately capture the concept of interest.[55] Moreover, just as it is intuitively plausible that a person is morally responsible for her actions only if she could have done otherwise, so, too, it is intuitively plausible that for a person to be autonomous she must have genuine options from which to choose. The plausibility of these views is undermined in this volume by both Marina Oshana, who argues in "Autonomy and Free Agency" that autonomy does not require that a person be free to do other than she did, and Ishtiyaque Haji, who argues in "Alternative Possibilities, Personal Autonomy, and Moral Responsibility" that there is reason to reject both the view that alternative possibilities are required for autonomy and the view that they are required for moral responsibility.

Yet despite the similarities between the contemporary discussions of autonomy and of moral responsibility, one should resist the temptation to collapse the two. This is because what actions a person is autonomous with respect to and what actions she is morally responsible for are not necessarily coextensive. Michael McKenna, for example, argues in his contribution to this volume, "The Relationship between Autonomous and Morally Responsible Agency," that morally responsible agency is not required for autonomous agency and that autonomous agency is not required for morally responsible agency. In a similar vein, Susan Wolf argues in her paper, "Freedom within Reason," that autonomy is not necessary for moral responsibility, where a person is understood to be autonomous if his actions are governed by his self. This is because, she argues, if moral responsibility requires autonomous action, then it is unlikely that persons are ever morally responsible for their acts, for persons' selves are not themselves free from governance by external factors and so might not be as autonomous as they first appear. However, she argues, if a person's self *is* free from such external influences and thus is a "spontaneous, undetermined entity," then it is difficult to see why a person should be responsible for the acts that flow from such a self. (Note that either Wolf is using a different conception of autonomy than are other contributors to this volume or else her conception of autonomy is open to challenge from the arguments offered in this volume by Berofsky, Mele, and Noggle.)[56] In place of this "autonomy view" of moral responsibility, Wolf argues that a person is morally responsible for her actions if she was not only free to govern her actions in accord with her values, but that she was able to revise her values in accord with reason and truth. Wolf terms this the "Reason View" of moral responsibility, and she defends it against several objections.

IV. THE EXPANDING ROLE OF PERSONAL AUTONOMY

Of course, progress in analyzing the concept of autonomy is not only of interest to those who work on moral responsibility. It is also of interest to those who work in the many areas of applied ethics and political philosophy where autonomy is now of central importance, because which account of autonomy turns out to be the most defensible will have important implications for these debates.

The concept of autonomy has risen to importance in applied ethics and political philosophy as a result of the recognition that the philosophical discussions that they encompass must take into account the deep pluralism of contemporary Western society and that employing a discursive framework that holds respect for autonomy to be one of its central tenets would achieve this. This is because to respect autonomy is to allow persons to form, revise, and pursue their own conceptions of the good. For example, there is a long tradition within political liberalism in which substantive liberal institutions such as freedom of expression, religious tolerance, and the freedom of association are primarily justified by appeal to the intrinsic value of autonomy. This appeal can be made in one of two ways. It could be argued on consequentialist grounds that persons will enjoy more autonomy under liberal political institutions and that this justifies liberalism.[57] Alternatively, it could be argued that liberal political institutions are required out of a duty to *respect* personal autonomy.[58] In addition to these attempts to justify political liberalism on the basis of the intrinsic value of personal autonomy, liberalism could also be justified by appeal to the *instrumental* value of autonomy. Proponents of this latter approach claim that if persons are allowed to exercise their autonomy, they will be able to pursue a form of life that is best suited to them.[59] Clearly, discussions in the autonomy literature that concern the nature and value of autonomy are of crucial importance for all of these strains of liberalism.[60] Moreover – and less obviously – the debates over the nature and value of autonomy are also important for political philosophy in general, insofar as aspects of this debate parallel similar discussions within political philosophy. For example, as John Christman argues in his contribution to this volume, "Procedural Autonomy and Liberal Legitimacy," the question of whether autonomy is to be understood as being a content-neutral or a substantive concept parallels the debate over whether the liberal state should adopt perfectionist policies.

Just as autonomy is an important concept within contemporary political philosophy, so, too, is it important within applied ethics – and for similar reasons. In medical ethics, for example, the Principle of Respect for Autonomy has emerged as a result of the recognition that in pluralistic societies healthcare workers and their patients might not share the same value systems.[61] To ensure that the patient receives treatment that is most appropriate for her, given both her physical condition and her values, she should be permitted to exercise her autonomy over her treatment by either giving or withholding her informed consent to it. The doctrine of informed consent is thus often based (albeit implicitly) on the instrumental value of personal autonomy in securing patient well-being. Similarly, the instrumental value of personal autonomy is also recognized in business ethics, where it is often argued that persuasive advertising is immoral on the grounds that it manipulatively subverts consumer autonomy and leads them to purchase goods that they would not have otherwise bought.[62]

Yet although recognition of the instrumental value of autonomy goes some way toward explaining the widespread use of this concept within applied ethics, many applied ethicists, like many political liberals, appeal directly to the intrinsic value of autonomy. For example, the doctrine of informed consent is often justified by appeal to the intrinsic value of personal autonomy,[63] as is the legal prohibition of markets in human kidneys.[64] More foundationally, some ethicists argue that the possession of autonomy is a necessary condition for a being to have moral standing, a view that both R. G. Frey and Tom L. Beauchamp debate in their chapters in this volume: "Autonomy, Diminished Life, and the Threshold for Use" and "Who Deserves Autonomy, and Whose Autonomy Deserves Respect?"

The question of whether the value of autonomy is primarily intrinsic or primarily instrumental cannot, of course, be settled apart from an adequate understanding of the nature of autonomy. It is for this reason, in part, that the theoretical progress that has recently been made in determining what it is for a person to be autonomous with respect to her desires and her actions is of interest to those who work in those areas of moral and political philosophy in which autonomy plays a major role. Yet in addition to influencing the answer to the question of how autonomy should be valued, the recent theoretical debates over the nature of autonomy also directly affect philosophical discussions in which it plays a central role. This is because the truth or falsity of many of the claims that the participants in these discussions proffer will be determined by which analysis of autonomy is the most defensible. For example, it is common for business ethicists to claim that manipulative advertising adversely affects consumer autonomy[65] and for medical ethicists to claim that a failure to secure a patient's informed consent to her treatment will compromise her autonomy.[66] But these claims are likely to be false if an *ahistorical* analysis of autonomy is correct. This is because on such an analysis of autonomy a person can still be autonomous with respect to those of her desires or actions that are in question provided that they possess certain structural relationships with her other desires and actions. Because this is so, even if the person whose desires (or actions) are in question was manipulated by avaricious advertisers or pernicious physicians into possessing (or performing) them, she could be held on such an analysis of autonomy to be autonomous with respect to them. Similarly, it is also common for social ethicists and certain political theorists to claim that violations of a person's privacy will violate her autonomy.[67] For this to be correct, however, the analysis of autonomy that is most defensible must be one that requires certain objective conditions to be met for a person to be autonomous with respect to her desires or actions. This is because if the most defensible analysis of autonomy is one that requires only *subjective* conditions to be met (i.e., it requires only that the person whose desires or actions are in question adopt certain attitudes toward them or toward their history), it is likely to be the case that if a person is placed under covert surveillance she will adopt the attitudes toward her desires (or their causal history) that would *satisfy* the conditions required by this analysis of autonomy for her to be autonomous with respect to them. More generally, the question of whether a content-neutral or substantive account of autonomy is the most defensible will, as Christman recognizes, have implications for liberal political theory, while the recurrent issue of whether a person can be coerced into acting by her economic situation can only be settled by appeal to an account of the relationship between autonomy and control.[68]

Yet although it is clear that if one holds personal autonomy to be the preeminent value within contemporary moral and political philosophy, one must take the theoretical debates over the nature of autonomy seriously, autonomy's preeminence within applied ethics (with the notable exception of environmental ethics) has not gone unchallenged. For example, some medical ethicists argue that insofar as autonomy has risen to prominence within applied ethics on the basis of its instrumental value, its primacy within medical ethics should be challenged in the light of empirical evidence that patient welfare could be better promoted by a return to a more paternalistic approach.[69] More generally, many feminists now challenge the primacy of autonomy within applied ethics on the grounds that it is based on an unrealistic ideal of personhood,[70] while communitarians similarly argue against what they perceive to be the excess respect that is currently accorded to the autonomous individual.[71]

These assaults on autonomy's status as the preeminent value within contemporary applied ethics have not gone unanswered. Both Paul Benson (in "Feminist Intuitions and the Normative Substance of Autonomy," this volume) and John Christman have, for example, responded to feminist criticisms of this focus on autonomy by arguing that once this concept is properly understood, it will be seen that it is one that feminists should embrace rather than reject.[72] Thomas May also defends the concept of autonomy from recent criticisms from feminist and communitarian perspectives. In his contribution to this volume, "The Concept of Autonomy in Bioethics: An Unwarranted Fall from Grace," May argues that the concept of autonomy that is invoked within medical ethics recognizes that individuals are socially located and so does not rest on an impoverished, atomistic view of the autonomous person in the way that some of its critics charge. Whether or not these defenses of autonomy are successful, the contemporary assaults upon it as the preeminent value within applied ethics do not detract from the importance of analyzing this concept. Instead, they serve to *reinforce* the importance of the philosophical discussion of the nature and value of autonomy. This is because the question of whether autonomy should be the preeminent value within applied ethics will turn on the answers to the questions of what constitutes autonomy and why it is valuable – and these questions are of interest to both the defenders and the detractors of autonomy alike.

Just as the debate over whether autonomy should retain its primacy within discussions of applied ethics reinforces the importance of the theoretical discussions of both the nature and value of autonomy, so, too, autonomy's importance within applied ethics has implications for the theoretical discussions of this concept. This is because autonomy's importance within applied ethics (and political philosophy) is a reminder that any analysis of this concept must meet what Gerald Dworkin termed the condition of "judgmental relevance."[73] (Or, if it does not, it must be explained why it is legitimate for it to fail to do so.) That is to say, an analysis of autonomy either must be in accord with standard pretheoretical intuitions concerning the concept (especially if these intuitions guide and direct the course of the debate that one is interested in) or else must provide the basis for an explanation of why these intuitions are mistaken.

The requirement that a theoretically satisfactory analysis of autonomy must be judgmentally relevant has two immediate implications for discussions of the nature of autonomy. First, this requirement indicates that it is likely that a successful analysis of autonomy will be either a content-neutral analysis or one that is very weakly substantive. That is, a person could be held to be autonomous without having to adopt any particular value system, or, if the adoption of certain values is a precondition for autonomy, then these values are widely held. This is because the less substantive an analysis of autonomy is, the more likely it is that more persons will be held to be autonomous, and, as Gerald Dworkin notes, "any feature that is going to be fundamental in moral thinking must be a feature that persons share."[74] In addition, the less substantive an analysis of autonomy, the easier it will be to justify its instrumental value as a means to securing the well-being of persons, irrespective of the values that they choose to pursue; for the more substantive one's analysis of autonomy becomes, the less one is able to claim that it is neutral between competing conceptions of the good. The respective merits of content-neutral and substantive analyses of autonomy are explored in Paul Benson's contribution to this volume, in which he argues in favor of a weakly substantive conception of autonomy that occupies the middle ground between the currently dominant content-neutral analyses of autonomy and the strongly substantive conceptions that some feminist writers (such as Natalie Stoljar) favor.[75]

In addition to privileging more content-neutral analyses of autonomy, the requirement that a fully satisfactory analysis of autonomy must be judgmentally relevant further undermines the plausibility of ahistorical approaches to autonomy, such as Frankfurt's. This is because it is generally accepted that a person's autonomy can be undermined if she is successfully manipulated or deceived by another. The view that manipulation and deception undermine the autonomy of those who are successfully subjected to them is not, however, based merely on raw intuition. Instead, it is often argued that through such practices the manipulator or deceiver is able to control what desires (and therefore what actions) her victim performs, thus undermining her autonomy through undermining her control in these areas.[76] And because, as I noted above, ahistorical approaches to autonomy focus solely on the structural relationships that hold between a person's mental states, they cannot recognize that a person who possesses her desires as a result of manipulation or deception suffers from the undermining of her autonomy.

Thus, just as those who work on applied philosophy should ensure that their use of the concept of autonomy is as well grounded in theory as possible, so, too, should autonomy theorists aim to develop analyses of autonomy that are judgmentally relevant. Rather than diverging, then, discussions of applied philosophy and autonomy theory should instead draw closer together – although Nomy Arpaly disputes this in her paper for this volume, "Responsibility, Applied Ethics, and Complex Autonomy Theories."

CONCLUSION

The concept of autonomy is clearly important in contemporary philosophy. Moreover, it has been subjected to sustained philosophical scrutiny only relatively recently. And this scrutiny is intensifying, both because autonomy theorists are starting to develop alternatives to the previously dominant hierarchical approach to analyzing autonomy and because writers in both moral responsibility and applied philosophy are respectively reexamining and reaffirming the role that autonomy should play within their respective discussions. All three of these factors result in this collection being a timely one, for the chapters not only represent the most recent work on the most prominent analyses of autonomy that are currently offered as alternatives to the hierarchical approach, but also the most recent work on the role that the concept of autonomy should play within discussions of moral responsibility and applied philosophy. Insofar as a firm understanding of autonomy is necessary to address successfully the diverse discussions in which it plays a key role, the focused attention that this concept receives in this volume is invaluable.

Notes

I thank Bernard Berofsky, Michael Bratman, John Christman, Stefaan Cuypers, John Davenport, Laura Waddell Ekstrom, R. G. Frey, Ishtiyaque Haji, Jonathan Malino, Marina Oshana, Mary Sirridge, Margaret Ulizio, and two anonymous readers for Cambridge University Press for their extremely helpful comments on earlier versions of this Introduction.

1. Thomas E. Hill, Jr., *Autonomy and Self-Respect* (Cambridge: Cambridge University Press, 1991); and Christine Korsgaard et al., *The Sources of Normativity* (Cambridge: Cambridge University Press, 1996).
2. Gerald Dworkin, "Acting Freely," *Noûs* 4 (1970): 367–383, and "Autonomy and Behavior Control," *Hastings Center Report* 6 (1976): 23–28; Harry Frankfurt, "Freedom of the Will and the Concept of a Person," in Harry Frankfurt, ed., *The Importance of What We Care About* (Cambridge: Cambridge University Press, 1988): 11–25; and Wright Neely, "Freedom and Desire," *Philosophical Review* 83 (1974): 32–54. In this Introduction, I focus on the work of Frankfurt and Dworkin because theirs has been the most influential.
3. Frankfurt was influential in this trend also; see his oft-cited "Alternative Possibilities and Moral Responsibility," in Frankfurt, ed., *The Importance of What We Care About*, 1–10.
4. See Janet Smith, "The Preeminence of Autonomy in Bioethics," in David S. Oderberg and Jacqueline A. Lang, eds., *Human Lives: Critical Essays on Consequentialist Bioethics* (New York: St. Martin's, 1997): 182–195.
5. See Stefaan E. Cuypers, "Autonomy Beyond Voluntarism: In Defense of Hierarchy," *Canadian Journal of Philosophy* 30 (2000): 225–256; and his *Self-Identity and Personal Autonomy: An Analytical Perspective* (Burlington, VT: Ashgate, 2001). See also Harry Frankfurt, "The Faintest Passion," in Frankfurt, ed., *Necessity, Volition, and Love* (Cambridge: Cambridge University Press, 1999): 95–107; his "Autonomy, Necessity, and Love," in Frankfurt, ed., *Necessity, Volition, and Love*: 129–141; and his "Reply to Richard Moran," in Sarah Buss and Lee Overton, eds., *Contours of Agency: Essays on the Philosophy of Harry Frankfurt* (Cambridge, MA: MIT Press, 2002): 218–225.
6. See John Christman, "Introduction," in Christman, ed., *The Inner Citadel: Essays on Individual Autonomy* (Oxford: Oxford University Press, 1989): 7–8; "Autonomy: A Defense of the Split-Level Self," *Southern Journal of Philosophy*

25 (1987): 281–293; and his "Autonomy and Personal History," *Canadian Journal of Philosophy* 21 (1991): 1–24.

7. See Michael Bratman, "Identification, Decision and Treating as a Reason," *Philosophical Topics* 24 (1996): 1–18; "Hierarchy, Circularity and Double Reduction," in Buss and Overton, eds., *Contours of Agency*: 65–85; "Valuing and the Will," *Philosophical Perspectives: Action and Freedom* 14 (2000): 249–265; "Reflection, Planning, and Temporally Extended Agency," *Philosophical Review* (2000): 35–61; and "Autonomy and Hierarchy," *Social Philosophy & Policy* 20 (2003): 156–176. The first of these papers is reprinted in Michael Bratman, ed., *The Faces of Intention: Selected Essays on Intention and Agency* (Cambridge: Cambridge University Press, 1999): 185–206.
8. Laura Waddell Ekstrom, "A Coherence Theory of Autonomy," *Philosophy and Phenomenological Research* 53 (1993): 599–616.
9. Thomas May, *Autonomy, Authority and Moral Responsibility* (Dordrecht: Kluwer Academic Publishers, 1997).
10. Robert Noggle, "Autonomy, Value, and Conditioned Desire," *American Philosophical Quarterly* 32 (1995): 57–69; and "The Public Conception of Autonomy and Critical Self-Reflection," *Southern Journal of Philosophy* 35 (1997): 495–515.
11. Marina A. L. Oshana, "Personal Autonomy and Society," *Journal of Social Philosophy* 29 (1998): 81–102.
12. Keith Lehrer, *Metamind* (Oxford: Clarendon Press, 1990): chap. 3; and "Reason and Autonomy," *Social Philosophy & Policy* 20 (2003): 177–198.
13. John Christman, "Introduction," 4. This change in the status of autonomy is owed in part to the success that *The Inner Citadel* had in stimulating interest in both the theory of autonomy and its wide-ranging applications. Moreover, four important book-length treatments of autonomy have been published since *The Inner Citadel*: Diana T. Meyers, *Self, Society, and Personal Choice* (New York: Columbia University Press, 1989); Bernard Berofsky, *Liberation from Self: A Theory of Personal Autonomy* (Cambridge: Cambridge University Press, 1995); Alfred Mele, *Autonomous Agents: From Self-control to Autonomy* (New York: Oxford University Press, 1995); and Marilyn Friedman, *Autonomy, Gender, Politics* (Oxford: Oxford University Press, 2003).
14. I argue for the legitimacy of treating these phrases as synonyms in my "Autonomy, Duress, and Coercion," *Social Philosophy & Policy* 20 (Summer 2003): 129 n. 5.
15. Frankfurt, "Freedom of the Will," 14–22.
16. Dworkin, "Autonomy and Behavior Control," 276.
17. Ibid.
18. Ibid.
19. A version of this problem was offered by Marilyn Friedman in "Autonomy and the Split-Level Self," *Southern Journal of Philosophy* 24 (1986): 19–35. See also Christman, "Introduction," 10.
20. Frankfurt reiterates his commitment to the view that such a manipulated individual does identify with, is autonomous with respect to, such an induced desire in his "Reply to Davenport," presented at the Eastern Division meeting of the American Philosophical Association, Atlanta, 1996. Quoted in John

J. Davenport, "Liberty of the Higher-Order Will: Frankfurt and Augustine," *Faith and Philosophy* 19 (2002): 453.

21. Frankfurt recognized that this would be a problem for his view in "Freedom of the Will," 21.
22. The *Ab Initio* Problem/Problem of Authority is neatly outlined in Laura Waddell Ekstrom, "Keystone Preferences and Autonomy," *Philosophy and Phenomenological Research* 49 (1999): 1061.
23. Watson, "Free Agency," *Journal of Philosophy* 72 (1975): 218.
24. Frankfurt, "Freedom of the Will," 21.
25. Frankfurt, "Identification and Wholeheartedness," in Frankfurt, ed., *The Importance of What We Care About*, 168–169.
26. Gerald Dworkin, *The Theory and Practice of Autonomy* (Cambridge: Cambridge University Press, 1988): 20
27. Ibid.
28. Christman, "Introduction," 10.
29. Frankfurt, "The Faintest Passion," in Frankfurt, ed., *Necessity, Volition, and Love*, 98–107.
30. Frankfurt, "Reply to Gary Watson," in Buss and Overton, eds., *Contours of Agency*, 160.
31. Frankfurt, "The Faintest Passion," 105. Frankfurt has admitted in his "Reply to Gary Watson" that his well-known claim that "inner freedom is a matter of whether or not a person 'endorses' the desires by which he is moved" was poorly phrased, for it "has naturally created a strong impression that 'an evaluative capacity' of some type figures essentially in my understanding of human agency, *but this impression is misleading*" (160, emphasis added). This is significant, for, as it is usually understood, Frankfurt's early analysis of identification was based on the person whose desires are in question making a *normative* judgment about them, whereas it now appears that his analysis of this concept is based on this person making a *descriptive* claim about his desires. Thus, either the basis of Frankfurt's recent account of identification is radically different from that of his early work (which, as Bernard Berofsky has pointed out to me in correspondence, leads to the question of whether the term "identification" can legitimately straddle both the earlier, normative account and the later, descriptive account), or else his early work has been widely misunderstood.
32. Frankfurt, "The Faintest Passion," 104–105.
33. However, the Regress Problem might not be as much of a problem for hierarchical analyses of autonomy as it is often taken to be, for it only shows that such theories might not be able to give a definitive answer to the question of whether a person is autonomous with respect to any given desire. It thus merely highlights the *epistemological* limitations of these theories; it does not show that they are mistaken as *ontological* analyses of autonomy. (I thank Michael Almeida and John Martin Fischer for pointing this out to me.) However, if a satisfactory analysis of autonomy is required to be judgmentally relevant (as I discuss below), then this epistemological drawback will serve to undermine the plausibility of those analyses of autonomy that are subject to it.

34. John Christman, "Defending Historical Autonomy: A Reply to Professor Mele," *Canadian Journal of Philosophy* 23 (1993): 288. See also Christman, "Autonomy and Personal History," 11.
35. Christman added this fourth condition in "Defending Historical Autonomy," 288, in response to objections from Alfred Mele, "History and Personal Autonomy," *Canadian Journal of Philosophy* 23 (1993): 271–280.
36. Ibid., 289 n. 5.
37. Christman might have a response to this objection, for in a recent paper he claims that a person is autonomous with respect to a desire if she reflects on it "*in light of* the processes by which it developed" – a claim that would increase the number of ways in which Condition 1 might be satisfied. "Liberalism, Autonomy, and Self-Transformation," *Social Theory and Practice*, 27 (2001): 201. Thus, even though this person might at t1 reject the process by which he comes to have his desire to play the piano, he might still, *all things considered*, prefer to have this desire and so endorse it in the light of the processes by which it was developed. In revising his account in this way, then, Christman is able to hold that the person in the above example is autonomous with respect to his desire to play the piano. Yet although modifying Condition 1 in this way enables Christman to avoid the above objection, it carries a considerable cost. This is because if Christman holds that a person can be autonomous with respect to a desire because he endorses it, *all things considered*, he will have abandoned his original claim that for a person to be autonomous with respect to a desire, then that desire must have a certain history. His view will thus no longer be a historical view, but a time slice view that is similar to Frankfurt's original account. For further discussion of these issues, see Christman's "Procedural Autonomy and Liberal Legitimacy," this volume.
38. Christman, "Autonomy: A Defense of the Split-Level Self," 288–289.
39. See, for example, St. Ignatius of Loyola, "To the Members of the Society in Portugal," in William J. Young, S.J., trans., *Letters of St. Ignatius of Loyola* (Chicago: Loyola University Press, 1959): 287–295. I thank Henry Richardson for bringing this to my attention.
40. Bratman argues that Frankfurt's account of identification as this is outlined in "The Faintest Passion" is unsatisfactory because it does not require that a person endorse (in some sense) those of his desires that he is said to identify with. Because this is so, Bratman argues, a person might meet Frankfurt's criterion for him to be satisfied with a desire (i.e., to identify with it) simply because he has not (yet) rejected it – and yet the mere failure to reject a desire does not mean that one identifies with it. "Identification, Decision and Treating as a Reason," 7.
41. Bratman, "Identification, Decision and Treating as a Reason," 9. Bratman recognizes that this account of what it is to treat a desire as reason-giving is only partially complete, for certain desires (such as a desire to favor a side constraint on action) might be reason-giving without being end-setting. However, he limits his attention to those reason-giving desires that are end-setting.
42. Bratman has a related discussion of the grudging drug addict in his "Reflection, Planning, and Temporally Extended Agency," 53.

43. Bratman, "Identification, Decision and Treating as a Reason," 11.
44. Ibid.
45. Bratman, "Reflection, Planning, and Temporally Extended Agency," 45.
46. In fairness to Bratman, it must be said that he explicitly notes that he has not (yet) tried to solve the Problem of Manipulation. See his "Autonomy and Hierarchy," *Social Philosophy & Policy* 20 (2003): 175–176; and his "Planning Agency, Autonomous Agency," this volume. Yet although Bratman has not yet tried directly to solve this problem, he does seem, as I indicate here, to have the conceptual resources to do this.
47. Bratman has recently made several remarks in the same spirit as my suggestive comments here. See his "A Desire of One's Own," *Journal of Philosophy* 100 (2003): 222 n. 3
48. Ekstrom, "A Coherence Theory of Autonomy," 603.
49. Ibid., 606.
50. Ekstrom's definitions of "coherence" and "authorization" are given in "A Coherence Theory of Autonomy," 611, 612.
51. In my "Review of Harry G. Frankfurt, *Necessity, Volition, and Love*," *Philosophical Quarterly* 51 (2001): 116; I indicate that such precision might be achieved by recognizing (with Frankfurt) a tripartite taxonomy of desire, such that a person might be autonomous with respect to her desires, that they might be authentically hers, or she might be alienated from them.
52. Bratman explicitly gives his analysis of autonomy this gloss in "Reflection, Planning and Temporally Extended Agency." See also Frankfurt's discussion of the need for a person's volitions to originate from "the essential character of his will" for him to be autonomous with respect to the actions that they lead him to perform in "Autonomy, Necessity and Love," 132; Ekstrom, "A Coherence Theory of Autonomy"; and Robert Noggle, "Kantian Respect and Particular Persons," *Canadian Journal of Philosophy* 29 (1999): 457–467.
53. John Martin Fischer, "Recent Work on Moral Responsibility," *Ethics* 110 (1999): 98.
54. See, for example, Susan Wolf's discussion in "Sanity and the Metaphysics of Responsibility," in John Christman, ed., *The Inner Citadel*: 138–140.
55. The autonomy literature that addresses this has already been outlined. For similar discussions in the philosophical literature on moral responsibility, see, e.g., John Martin Fischer and Mark Ravizza, *Responsibility and Control: A Theory of Moral Responsibility* (Cambridge: Cambridge University Press, 1998): 170–206.
56. In fact, the former is the case. Wolf's conception of "autonomy" is such that for a person to be "autonomous" with respect to her desires is for her to have performed them from her libertarian free will, whereas the conception of autonomy that Berofsky, Mele, and Noggle adopt is not connected to metaphysical libertarianism.
57. See Joseph Raz, *The Morality of Freedom* (Oxford: Clarendon Press, 1986).
58. This approach to justifying political liberalism will admit of widely divergent accounts of what form liberalism should take. See, e.g., Robert Nozick, *Anarchy, State, and Utopia* (New York: Basic Books, 1974); and John Rawls, *A Theory of Justice*, rev. ed. (Cambridge, MA: Belknap Press, 1999).

59. See J. S. Mill, *On Liberty* (Indianapolis: Hackett Publishing, 1978); and Stephen Wall, "Freedom as a Political Ideal," *Social Philosophy & Policy* 20 (2003): 307–334.
60. For an excellent overview of the role that autonomy plays in contemporary political philosophy, see John Christman, "Autonomy in Moral and Political Philosophy," *The Stanford Encyclopedia of Philosophy* (http://plato.stanford.edu/contents.html; accessed November 10, 2003).
61. Tom L. Beauchamp and James F. Childress, *Principles of Biomedical Ethics*, 5th ed. (New York: Oxford University Press, 2001): 77.
62. Richard Lippke, "Advertising and the Social Conditions of Autonomy," *Business and Professional Ethics Journal* 8 (1989): 35–58.
63. See *Nathanson v. Kline*, 186 Kan. 393 at 406.
64. Paul M. Hughes, "Exploitation, Autonomy, and the Case for Organ Sales," *International Journal of Applied Philosophy* 12 (1998): 89–95.
65. Richard Lippke, "Advertising and the Social Conditions of Autonomy," 35–58.
66. Beauchamp and Childress, *Principles of Biomedical Ethics*, 77.
67. Joseph Kupfer, "Privacy, Autonomy, and Self-Concept," *American Philosophical Quarterly* 24 (1987): 81–89.
68. For an example of the claim that a person's economic situation might undermine her autonomy by coercing her into performing an action that she did not really want to perform (here offered in the context of an argument against allowing markets in human transplant organs), see Nancy Scheper-Hughes, "Keeping an Eye on the Global Traffic in Human Organs," *Lancet* 361 (May 10, 2003): 1645.
69. Carl E. Schneider, *The Practice of Autonomy: Patients, Doctors and Medical Decisions* (Oxford: Oxford University Press, 1998).
70. See Carolyn Ells, "Shifting the Autonomy Debate to Theory as Ideology," *Journal of Medicine and Philosophy* 26 (2001): 417–430.
71. See Willard Gaylin and Bruce Jennings, *The Perversion of Autonomy: The Proper Uses of Coercion and Constraints in a Liberal Society* (New York: Free Press, 1996).
72. John Christman, "Feminism and Autonomy," in Dana E. Bushnell, ed., *"Nagging" Questions: Feminist Ethics in Everyday Life* (Lanham, MD: Rowman & Littlefield, 1995): 17–40.
73. Dworkin, *The Theory and Practice of Autonomy*, 9.
74. Ibid., 31.
75. Natalie Stoljar, "Autonomy and the Feminist Intuition," in Catriona Mackenzie and Natalie Stoljar, eds., *Relational Autonomy: Feminist Perspectives on Autonomy, Agency, and the Social Self* (New York: Oxford University Press, 2000): 94–111.
76. See Robert Noggle, "Manipulative Actions: A Conceptual and Moral Analysis," *American Philosophical Quarterly* 33 (1996): 43–55.

PART I

THEORETICAL APPROACHES TO PERSONAL AUTONOMY

1

Planning Agency, Autonomous Agency

Michael E. Bratman

I. PLANNING AND CORE ELEMENTS OF AUTONOMY

Humans seem sometimes to be autonomous, self-governed agents: Their actions seem at times to be not merely the upshot of antecedent causes but, rather, under the direction of the agent herself in ways that qualify as a form of governance by that agent. What sense can we make of this apparent phenomenon of governance by the agent herself?[1]

Well, we can take as given for present purposes that human agents have complex psychological economies and that we frequently can explain what they do by appeal to the functioning of these psychological economies. She raised her arm because she wanted to warn her friend; she worked on the chapter because of her plan to finish her book; she helped the stranger because she knew this was the right thing to do; he left the room because he did not want to show his anger. These are all common, everyday instances of explaining action by appeal to psychological functioning. In doing this, we appeal to attitudes of the agent: beliefs, intentions, desires, and so on. The agent herself is part of the story; it is, after all, her attitudes that we cite. These explanations do not, however, simply refer to the agent; they appeal to attitudes that are elements in her psychic economy. The attitudes they cite may include attitudes that are themselves about the agent and her attitudes – desires about desires, perhaps. But what does the explanatory work is, in the end, the functioning of (perhaps in some cases higher-order) attitudes. These explanations are, I will say, nonhomuncular.

When we come to self-governance, however, it is not clear that we can continue in this way. The image of the agent directing and governing is, in the first instance, an image of the agent herself standing back from her attitudes and doing the directing and governing. But if we say that this is, in the end, in what self-governance consists, we will be faced with the question whether the agent who is standing back from these attitudes is herself self-governing. And it is not clear how such an approach can answer that question. Further, if this is, in the end, what we say constitutes self-governance, then it will be puzzling how self-governing human agents can be part of the same natural world as other biological species. Granted, there is already a problem in understanding how the kind of psychological functioning cited in ordinary action explanation can be part of that natural world. But here I assume that we can, in the end, see such explanatory appeals to mind as compatible with seeing ourselves as located in this natural order. But if, in talking of self-governance, we need to see the agent as playing an irreducible role in the explanation of action, we have yet a further problem in reconciling our self-understanding as autonomous with our self-understanding as embedded in a natural order.[2]

These reflections lead to the question of whether there are forms of psychological functioning that can be characterized without seeing the agent herself as playing an irreducible role and that are plausible candidates for sufficient conditions for agential governance. It is also an important question, of course, whether certain forms of functioning are necessary for self-governance. But given the structure of the problem as I have characterized it, the basic issue is one about sufficient conditions for autonomy; and we should be alive to the possibility that there are, at bottom, several different forms of functioning, each of which is sufficient, but no one of which is necessary for self-governance.[3]

In response to this question, the first thing to say is that relevant psychological functioning will involve, but go beyond, purposive agency. Autonomous agents are purposive agents, but they are not simply purposive agents. Many nonhuman animals are purposive agents – they act in ways that are responsive to what they want and their cognitive grasp of how to get it – but are unlikely candidates for self-governance. A model of our autonomy will need to introduce forms of functioning that include but go beyond purposiveness.

In earlier work, I have emphasized that it is an important feature of human agents that they are not only purposive agents; they are also planning agents.[4] Planning agency brings with it further basic capacities and forms of thought and action that are central to our temporally extended and social lives. Indeed, our concept of intention, as it applies to adult human agents, helps track significant contours of these planning capacities.

I call my efforts to characterize these features of human agency, and the associated story of intention, the "planning" theory."

As important as it is, however, the step from purposive to planning agency is not by itself a step all the way to self-government. After all, one's planning agency may be tied to the pursuit of ends that are compulsive or obsessive or unreflective or thoughtless or conflicted in ways incompatible with self-government.

This may suggest that though the step from purposive to planning agency is an important step, it is a side step: It does not help us provide relevant sufficient conditions for self-governance. I believe, however, that this suggestion is mistaken, that important kinds of self-governance involve planning attitudes and capacities in a fundamental way.

J. David Velleman once remarked that "an understanding of intention requires an understanding of our freedom or autonomy." And he argued that my 1987 planning theory of intention "falls short in some respects because [it] tries to study intention in isolation from such questions about the fundamental nature of agency."[5] On one natural interpretation of these remarks, the claim is that a theory of intention needs itself to be a theory of autonomy. And this seems too strong to me. There can be intending, planning agents who are not autonomous. A theory of intention should not suppose that only autonomous agents have the basic capacities involved in intending and planning. Nevertheless, I do think that the planning theory of intention has a significant contribution to make to a theory of autonomy.

Let me try to articulate more precisely the kind of contribution I have in mind.[6] We seek models of psychological structures and functioning that, in appropriate contexts, can constitute central cases of autonomous agency. We should not assume there is a unique such model, but we can consider it progress if we can provide at least one such model. Further, to make progress in this pursuit we do well, I think, to focus initially on psychological structures and forms of functioning that are more or less current at the time of action, broadly construed. In the end, we will want to know whether there are further constraints to be added, constraints on the larger history of these structures and forms of functioning. Perhaps, for example, certain kinds of prior manipulation or indoctrination need to be excluded. But before we can make progress with that question of history, we need plausible models of important and central structures and functioning on (roughly) the occasion of autonomous action. I will call a model of such important and central structures and functioning a "model of core elements of autonomy." A model of core elements need provide neither necessary nor fully sufficient conditions for autonomy. It need not provide necessary conditions, for it may be that there is more than one way to be autonomous. And it need not provide fully sufficient conditions, for it may be that to ensure autonomy we need also to impose conditions on the larger history. Nevertheless, a plausible model of core elements would help us understand autonomy and its possible place in our natural world.[7] And I want to argue that the planning theory has an important contribution to make to a plausible model of core elements of autonomy.

My argument will take the following form. I will examine two prominent models of relevant forms of psychological functioning: (1) hierarchical models that highlight responsiveness to higher-order conative attitudes; and (2) value-judgment-responsive models that highlight responsiveness to judgments about the good. Although each of these models points to an important form of functioning, each faces problems when offered as a model of core elements of self-governance. My proposal will be that we solve these problems by drawing on the planning theory.

II. THE HIERARCHICAL MODEL AND WATSON'S THREE OBJECTIONS

Let's begin with hierarchy. Here the idea is that the basic step we need to get from mere purposiveness to self-government is the introduction of higher-order conative attitudes about the functioning of first-order motivating attitudes. One main source of this idea is a complex series of papers by Harry Frankfurt.[8] In his classic early essay, Frankfurt wrote that "[i]t is in securing the conformity of his will to his second-order volitions, then, that a person exercises freedom of the will."[9] Here, by "will" Frankfurt means, roughly, 'desire that motivates action'; and a second-order volition is a second-order desire that a certain desire motivate. When the effective motivation of action (the "will") conforms to and is explained by[10] an uncontested second-order volition, the agent exercises freedom of the will. And when Frankfurt later turns explicitly to autonomy and self-government (which he sees as the same thing), it seems fairly clear that something like this hierarchical story is built into his approach.[11]

Now, we have observed that self-government seems to involve the agent's standing back and doing the governing. The hierarchical model acknowledges the power of this picture, a picture that highlights the agent's reflectiveness about her motivation. But the model goes on to understand such reflectiveness by appeal to certain higher-order attitudes – in the simplest case that Frankfurt initially emphasized, an uncontested second-order volition. In this way, it tries to see self-governance as involving reflectiveness without a homunculus.

Note that the theory need not claim that the very same higher-order attitude is involved in all cases of hierarchical self-governance. It need only claim that all cases of hierarchical self-governance involve some such higher-order conative attitude.

This basic idea has been developed in a number of different ways in recent years both by Frankfurt and by others, and I will later advert to some elements from this literature. But enough has been said about the hierarchical model to see the force of an important trio of objections that were proffered by Gary Watson in response to Frankfurt's initial paper.[12]

Watson's first objection begins with an idea that is central to the hierarchical model, the idea that when a relevant, uncontested higher-order conative attitude favors a certain first-order motivation, the *agent* endorses, or identifies with, that motivation. In the terms of Frankfurt's early version of hierarchy, my uncontested second-order volition in favor of my desire to turn the other cheek constitutes my endorsement of, or identification with, that desire. That is why it is plausible to say that when that desire motivates action, in part because of my second-order volition, *I* am directing my action. But, Watson observes, the hierarchical model does not seem to have the resources to explain this. After all,

> [s]ince second-order volitions are themselves simply desires, to add them to the context of conflict is just to increase the number of contenders; it is not to give a special place to any of those in contention.[13]

We can express the point by saying that there is nothing in the very idea of a higher-order desire that explains why it has authority to speak for the agent, to constitute where the agent stands. For all that has been said, when action and will conforms to a higher-order desire, it is simply conforming to one attitude among many of the wiggles in the psychic stew. The hierarchical model does not yet have an account of the *agential authority* of certain higher-order attitudes.[14] But it needs such an account in order to provide a nonhomuncular model of agential governance. And that is Watson's first objection.[15]

Watson's second objection is built into the alternative model he offers, a model that highlights responsiveness to judgments of the good. Watson sees such judgments as an "evaluational system" that "may be said to constitute one's standpoint."[16] If we are looking for attitudes that speak for the agent, that constitute where the agent stands, then the natural candidates are not higher-order volitions, but evaluative judgments about what "is most worth pursuing."[17] I will call this idea, that the agent's standpoint is constituted by evaluative judgment rather than by higher-order conative attitude, the "Platonic challenge" to the hierarchical model.

Watson's third objection draws on but goes beyond this. He writes:

> [Agents] do not (or need not usually) ask themselves which of their desires they want to be effective in action; they ask themselves which course of action is most worth pursuing. The initial practical question is about courses of action and not about themselves.[18]

Here Watson is emphasizing his Platonic model; but he is also pointing to a further objection, one that involves a claim about the structure of ordinary deliberation. The basic idea is that ordinary deliberation is first-order deliberation about what to do, not higher-order reflection about one's desires. And the objection is that the hierarchical model misses this point and mistakenly sees deliberation as primarily a matter of higher-order reflection on motivating attitudes. Let us call this the "objection from deliberative structure."

So we have a trio of objections to the hierarchical model: the objection about agential authority, the Platonic challenge, and the objection from deliberative structure. Taken together, these constitute a serious challenge to the hierarchical model.

III. THE PLATONIC MODEL AND UNDERDETERMINATION BY VALUE JUDGMENT

I want to give the hierarchical model something to say in response to this challenge. My strategy is to do this by bringing together elements from the hierarchical model with elements from the planning theory. Before proceeding with this strategy, however, I want to reflect on the Platonic alternative that Watson sketches, one that highlights responsiveness to judgments about the good.

An initial observation is that it seems possible for one to judge that, say, turning the other cheek is best, but still be alienated from that judgment in a way that undermines its agential authority.[19]

We can clarify one way this can happen by turning to one of Frankfurt's later developments of the hierarchical model. In response to concerns about what I have called "agential authority," Frankfurt introduced an important idea: satisfaction.[20] Satisfaction is not a further attitude but rather a structural feature of the psychic system. For me to be satisfied with my higher-order desire in favor of my desire to turn the other cheek is not for me to have an even-higher-order desire. It is, rather, for my higher-order desire to be embedded in a psychic system in which there is no relevant tendency to change: "Satisfaction is a state of the entire psychic system – a state constituted just by the absence of any tendency or inclination to alter its condition."[21] Frankfurt's idea – expressed in the terms I have introduced here – is that such a higher-order desire has agential authority when the agent is satisfied with it.

I have elsewhere noted that satisfaction with such a desire may be grounded in depression, and in such cases satisfaction with desire does not seem to be enough to guarantee agential authority.[22] Nevertheless, I think that this idea of satisfaction is important in two ways. First, a version of it will be of use later, as one part of a more adequate account of agential authority. Second, it helps us see that one may be dissatisfied with, and for that reason alienated from, one's evaluative judgment in a way that undermines its agential authority. This is one way in which the Platonic proposal is faced with a problem of agential authority.

However, a defender of the Platonic proposal can, in response, focus on evaluative judgments with which the agent is, in an appropriate sense, satisfied. She may then propose that it is such evaluative judgments that constitute the agent's standpoint. A full defense of this proposal would need to say more about the roles of such evaluative judgments in our agency and why these help establish agential authority. Nevertheless, this does show how the Platonic model can, like the hierarchical model, draw on the idea of satisfaction.

But now we need to consider a different kind of alienation from value judgment, one that was emphasized by Watson himself in a later essay.[23] One might have a settled judgment that turning the other cheek would be best, might be satisfied with that as one's settled evaluative judgment, but nevertheless be fully committed, rather, to revenge. As Watson says, "I might fully 'embrace' a course of action I do not judge best." Watson calls such situations "perverse cases." In such cases, the agent's "standpoint" is not captured by his evaluative judgment but rather by his "perverse" commitment.

However, while Watson was right to emphasize such cases, a defender of the Platonic model does have a response. She can say that such cases involve a rational breakdown and that in the absence of rational breakdown an agent's standpoint consists of relevant evaluative judgments. Because we are seeking conditions for self-government and because the kind of rational breakdown at issue can plausibly be seen as blocking self-governance, this proposal keeps open the idea that self-governance consists primarily of rational responsiveness to relevant evaluative judgments.

This takes me to a third concern – namely, that even in the absence of rational breakdown, the agent's evaluative judgments frequently underdetermine important commitments. Faced with difficult issues about what to give weight or significance to in one's life, one is frequently faced with multiple, conflicting goods: Turning the other cheek is a good, but so is an apt reactive response to wrongful treatment; resisting the use of violence by the military is good, but so is loyalty to one's country; human sexuality is a good, but so are certain religious lives of abstinence. In many such cases, the agent's standpoint involves forms of commitment – to draft resistance, say – that have agential authority but go beyond his prior evaluative judgment. This may be because the agent thinks that, though he needs to settle on a coherent stance, the conflicting goods are more or less equal. Or perhaps he thinks he simply does not know which is more important. (He is, after all, like all of us, a person with significant limits in his abilities to arrive at such judgments with any justified confidence.) Or perhaps he thinks that the relevant goods are in an important way incommensurable.[24] In such cases, there need not be a rational breakdown but rather a sensible and determinative response to ways in which one's value judgments can underdetermine the "shape" of one's life.[25] One may be committed to building into the fabric of one's own life some things one judges good, but not others. And even in a case in which one judges that, say, a life of helping others is strictly better than one in which one does not help others, one's judgment will typically leave in its wake significant underdetermination of the exact extent to which this value is to shape one's life, the exact significance this value is to have in one's deliberations.

In these cases of underdetermination by prior value judgment, the hierarchical model seems to be in a better position than the Platonic model. The hierarchical model has room for the view that these elements of the agent's standpoint – elements of commitment in the face of underdetermination by prior value judgment – are constituted by relevant higher-order conative attitudes.[26] Granted, we are still without a full account of the agential authority of those higher-order attitudes. But that is not a defense of the Platonic model. Rather, it is an observation that, so far, neither model solves the problem of agential authority.

It is here that we do well to turn to the planning theory.

IV. PLANNING, TEMPORALLY EXTENDED AGENCY, AND AGENTIAL AUTHORITY

A basic feature of adult human agents is that they pursue complex forms of cross-temporal and social organization and coordination by way of planning. They settle on – commit themselves to – prior and typically partial and hierarchically structured[27] plans of action, and this normally shapes later practical reasoning and action in ways that support cross-temporal organization, both individual and social. Such planlike commitments can involve settling matters left indeterminate by prior evaluative judgment, as when one decides on one of several options no one of which one sees as clearly superior. Indeed, one can be settled on certain intentions, plans, or policies without reflecting at all on whether they are for the best or making an explicit decision in their favor.[28]

According to the planning theory, our planning agency brings with it distinctive norms of plan consistency, plan coherence, and plan stability. To intend to do something in the future or to have a policy concerning certain recurring types of circumstances is to have an attitude that is to be understood in terms of such planning capacities and norms. Such intendings and policies are importantly different from ordinary desires. But they are no more mysterious than the familiar phenomena and norms involved in planning. In this way, the planning theory is a modest, nonmysterious theory of the will.[29]

An agent's planlike attitudes support cross-temporal organization of her practical thought and action, and they do this in a distinctive way. Prior plans involve reference to later ways of acting; and in filling in and/or executing prior plans one normally sees oneself in ways that refer back to those prior plans. Such plans are, further, typically stable over time. So planning agency supports cross-temporal organization of practical thought and action in the agent's life in part by way of cross-temporal referential connections and in part by way of continuities of stable plans over time. So it supports such organization in part by way of continuities and connections of a sort that are highlighted by Lockean accounts of personal identity over time.[30] And this is no accident: It is a characteristic feature of the functioning of planning in our temporally extended lives.

This opens up an approach to agential authority. The problem of agential authority is the problem of explaining why certain attitudes have authority to constitute the agent's practical standpoint. So far, we have been thinking of this as a problem about the agent at a particular time. But the human agents for whom this problem arises are ones whose agency extends over time: They begin overlapping and interwoven plans and projects, follow through with them, and (sometimes) complete them. Such temporal extension of agency involves activities at different times performed by the very same agent. A broadly Lockean story of that sameness of agency over time will emphasize relevant psychological connections and continuities. In particular, our planning agency constitutes and supports the cross-temporal organization of this temporally extended agency by way of Lockean connections and continuities – by way of Lockean ties. And this gives relevant plan-type attitudes a claim to speak for the temporally persisting agent. As I once wrote, the idea is that "[W]e tackle the problem of where the agent stands *at a time* by appeal to roles of attitudes in creating broadly Lockean conditions of identity of the agent *over time*."[31] And central among the relevant attitudes are plan-type attitudes.

If this is right, then it is good news for the hierarchical theorist. She can see the relevant higher-order conative attitudes – those that constitute the agent's practical standpoint – not merely as desires but rather as plan-type attitudes. She can then cite the Lockean roles of these plan-type attitudes to explain their agential authority. Or, at least, this will be the basic step in such an explanation. In this way, the planning theory can give the hierarchical theorist something more to say in response to the objection from agential authority. And given that intentions and plans are sometimes formed in the face of underdetermination by prior value judgment, such plan-type attitudes are natural candidates to respond to the issues raised by such cases of underdetermination.

V. SELF-GOVERNING POLICIES

But what plan-type attitudes are these? Given the role they need to play within the theory we are developing, they need to be higher-order planlike attitudes. And they need to be higher-order planlike attitudes that speak for the agent because they help constitute and support the temporal extension of her agency. They will do this in large part by being plan-type attitudes whose primary role includes the organization of practical thought and action over time by way of Lockean ties. This makes it plausible that in the clearest cases the relevant attitudes will be policy-like: They will concern, in a more or less general way, the functioning of relevant conative attitudes over time, in relevant circumstances.[32]

What the hierarchical theorist will primarily want to appeal to, then, are higher-order policy-like attitudes. Which higher-order policy-like attitudes? Here we need to reflect further on the very idea of self-governance.

Autonomous actions, I have said, are under the direction of the agent in ways that qualify as a form of governance by that agent. But what forms of agential direction constitute agential governance? Well, the very idea of governance brings with it, I think, the idea of direction by appeal to considerations treated as in some way legitimizing or justifying. This contrasts with a kind of agential direction or determination that does not involve normative content. And this means that the higher-order policy-like attitudes that are cited by the hierarchical theorist should in some way reflect this distinctive feature of self-governance.

Recall Frankfurt's notion of a second-order volition: a desire that a certain desire motivate. The content of such a second-order volition concerns a process of motivation, not – at least not directly – a process of reasoning that appeals to legitimizing, justifying considerations. So such a higher-order attitude does not seem to reflect the way in which self-governance is a kind of governance, not a kind of direction that involves no normative content.

Consider now a higher-order policy concerning a desire for X. One such policy will say that this desire is to influence action by way of practical reasoning in which X, and/or the desire for X, is given justifying weight or significance. Call such a higher-order policy – one that favors such functioning of the desire in relevant motivationally effective practical reasoning – a *self-governing policy*. Our reflections about self-governance – in contrast with nonnormative self-direction – suggest that self-governing policies can play a basic role in hierarchical theories of self-governance.[33] For reasons we have discussed, such policies have a presumptive claim to agential authority, to speaking for the temporally persisting agent. And such policies will concern which desires are to be treated as providing justifying considerations in motivationally effective practical reasoning. They will in that sense say which desires are to have for the agent what we can call "subjective normative authority"; and they will constitute a form of valuing that is different from, though normally related to, judging valuable.[34]

Can the hierarchical theory, then, simply appeal to such self-governing policies in its model of self-governance? Well, if the guidance by these policies is to constitute the agent's governance, then we should require that the agent knows about this guidance.[35] Does that suffice? Not quite. Although such policies have a presumptive claim to agential authority, it still seems possible to be estranged from a particular self-governing policy. This is a familiar problem for a hierarchical theory. But we have already noted a further resource available to such a theory: a version of the Frankfurtian idea of satisfaction. To have agential authority, we can say, a self-governing policy must be one with which the agent is, in an appropriate sense, satisfied.[36]

But what if the satisfaction is grounded in depression? Depression might substantially undermine the normal functioning of these self-governing policies. Such a case would not challenge the present account. But what if these self-governing policies continue to play their characteristic roles in Lockean cross-temporal organization – by way of shaping temporally extended deliberation and action – but the absence of pressure for change in those policies is due to depression? Well, in this case the self-governing policies remain settled structures that play these central, Lockean roles in temporally extended, deliberative agency, and they do that in the absence of relevant pressure for change. So it seems to me that they still have a presumptive claim to establish the (depressed) agent's standpoint.

Can we stop here? Can we say that in a basic case self-governance consists primarily in the known guidance of practical thought and action by self-governing policies with which the agent is satisfied? Well, there does remain a further worry: Does self-governance require not just that the agent know about this functioning of the self-governing policy and be satisfied with it, but, further, that the agent *endorse* it in a way that is not just a matter of being satisfied with it? But what could such further endorsement be? Some yet further, distinct, and yet-higher-order attitude? But that way lies a familiar regress.

I think that a natural move for the hierarchical theorist to make at this point is to appeal to reflexivity: The self-governing policies that are central to the model of autonomy that we are constructing will be in part about their own functioning.[37] Such a policy will favor treating certain desires as reason-providing as a matter of this very policy.[38] The idea is not that such reflexivity by itself establishes the agential authority of the policy. Agential authority of such attitudes is, rather, primarily a matter of Lockean role and satisfaction. But in a context in which these conditions of authority are present, a further condition of reflexivity ensures, without vicious regress, the endorsement of self-governing policy that seems an element in full-blown self-governance.

The proposed model, then, appeals to practical reasoning and action that are appropriately guided by known, reflexive, higher-order self-governing policies with which the agent is satisfied. By combining the resources of the hierarchical and the planning theories in this way, we arrive at a nonhomuncular model of core elements of autonomy.

VI. REPLIES TO WATSON'S THREE OBJECTIONS

How does this proposed model respond to the cited trio of objections to the hierarchical theory? Well, the response to the objection from agential authority has already been front and center. Higher-order self-governing policies have an initial claim to speak for the temporally persisting agent given their systematic role in constituting and supporting the cross-temporal organization of practical thought and action by way of Lockean ties. This claim is relevantly authoritative when the agent is satisfied with these policies and they have the cited reflexive structure.

What about the Platonic challenge? Here the answer is that we need to be able to appeal to a central and important kind of commitment that goes beyond prior value judgment, given phenomena of underdetermination of the shape of one's life by such judgments. We need to be able to appeal to commitments in the face of judgments of roughly equal desirability or of incommensurability; and we need to be able to appeal to commitments in the face of reasonable inability to reach, with confidence, a sufficiently determinative judgment of value. Indeed, such commitments may arise even in an agent who does not much go in for value judgment. The appeal to self-governing policies provides for such commitments – commitments that will normally have a kind of stability over time that is characteristic of such attitudes.[39]

One way to see what is going on here is to suppose, with a wide range of philosophers, that evaluative judgments are in some important sense subject to intersubjectivity constraints. In contrast, the commitments that constitute an agent's own standpoint need not be subject to such constraints.[40] In cases of underdetermination by value judgment, the agent may sensibly arrive at further commitments that he does not see as intersubjectively directed or accountable in ways characteristic of value judgment. This leaves open the idea that self-governance precludes a severe breakdown between evaluative judgments with which the agent is satisfied and the commitments that constitute the agent's standpoint. Such a breakdown – as in a Watsonian "perverse" case – is a significant kind of internal incoherence. So it is plausible to say that there is not the kind of unity of view that is needed for self-governance. Nevertheless, and contrary to the Platonic challenge, a model that appeals only to evaluative judgment does not yet provide the resources to characterize forms of agential commitment that are central to self-governance.

What about the objection from deliberative structure? Should our hierarchical model reject Watson's suggestion that "[t]he initial practical question is about courses of action"? Well, sometimes in deliberation one does reflect directly on one's motivation. Nevertheless, I think that Watson is right that frequently in deliberation what we explicitly consider is, rather, what to do. But this need not be an objection to our hierarchical model. We can understand that model as one of background structures that bear on an agent's efforts to answer this "initial practical question": When a self-governing agent grapples with this question, her thought and action are structured in part by higher-order self-governing policies.[41] Or, at least, this is one important case of self-governance.

Those, anyway, are the basic responses to the three objections. But these responses do point to a further issue. We have seen why appeal to higher-order conative attitudes need not be incompatible with the typically first-order structure of ordinary deliberation. We have seen how to explain why certain kinds of higher-order conative attitudes can have agential authority. And we have seen reason for a model of central cases of self-governance to include forms of commitment, to modes of practical reasoning and action, that go beyond evaluative judgment. But none of these points as yet fully explains the basic philosophical pressure for the introduction of hierarchy into the model. They do show that once hierarchy is introduced we can respond to challenges concerning agential authority and the structure of deliberation. And they do show that appeal to hierarchical conative attitudes is one way to resolve issues raised by underdetermination by value judgment. But they do not yet fully clarify why we should appeal to such hierarchical attitudes in the first place. Perhaps, instead, we should appeal only to certain first-order planlike commitments that resolve the problems raised by underdetermination by value judgment, guide first-order deliberation, and also allow for a story of agential authority.

We might respond by reminding ourselves that our fundamental concern is with nonhomuncular sufficient conditions for self-governance. So we need not claim that hierarchy is necessary for self-governance. And this response is correct as far as it goes. But even after noting the availability of this response, there is an aspect of the objection to which we need to respond directly. We need to explain why we should see conative hierarchy as even one among perhaps several different models of core elements of autonomy; and to do that, we need to say more about the pressures for introducing such hierarchy.

This is a salient issue in part because it may seem that the account of self-governance as so far developed lends itself to a modification that leaves the account pretty much intact, but in which conative hierarchy drops out.[42] The idea here would be to appeal to policies simply to give weight or significance to consideration X in one's motivationally effective practical reasoning. Such policies seem to be first-order: Their target is a certain activity of reasoning. But in other respects, it seems they could have the features of self-governing policies that have been exploited by the model: Lockean role in cross-temporal organization, targets of self-knowledge and satisfaction, agential authority, and commitments concerning subjective normative authority that do not require determination by value judgment. So we may wonder why hierarchy should be built into the account. Why not throw away the ladder?

VII. REASONS FOR HIERARCHY

We can begin by recalling one reason we have already seen for introducing a kind of conative hierarchy into a model of autonomy: Relevant policies about practical reasoning will reflexively support themselves. This is a kind of conative hierarchy. But it is only a limited form of hierarchy, one that does not yet include the idea that such policies are generally about further, distinct forms of first-order motivation. In contrast, hierarchical theories of the sort we have been discussing involve these broader hierarchies of conative attitudes about conative attitudes.[43] So we are still faced with the question of why we should see such broader hierarchies as central to our model of core elements of autonomy.[44]

In at least one strand of his work, Frankfurt's appeal to conative hierarchy is driven by what he takes to be a reflective agent's project of self-constitution. Frankfurt seeks a notion of "internal" that fits with Aristotle's idea that "behavior is voluntary only when its moving principle is inside the agent." And Frankfurt's idea is that "[w]hat counts . . . is whether or not the agent has constituted himself to include" a certain "moving principle."[45] The reflective agent's effort at self-constitution is a response to the question, "with respect to each desire, whether to identify himself with it or whether to reject it as an outlaw and hence not a legitimate candidate for satisfaction."[46] In this way, conative hierarchy is seen as involved in the kind of self-constituted internality that is basic to reflective agency.

A second pressure in the direction of conative hierarchy comes from a picture of deliberation as reflection on one's desires, reflection aimed at choosing on which desire to act.[47] Such a model of deliberation, coupled with a search for a nonhomuncular story, can lead straightway to conative hierarchy.

Granted, these two different pressures can interact. Given such a model of deliberation, one may be led to think of deliberation as concerned with self-constitution. And given a Frankfurtian, hierarchical story of self-constitution, one may want to extend it to a model of deliberation.[48] Nevertheless, it is useful to keep these two ideas apart.

One reason this is useful is that these different approaches interact differently with Watson's objection to a model of deliberation as higher-order reflection. Here my strategy has been to argue that – though some deliberation does have this higher-order structure – the hierarchical model of self-governance need not see this as the central case of deliberation. Does this mean that our basic reason for building hierarchy into our model of self-governance should be a metaphysical concern with internality and self-constitution?

Although the issues are complex, I believe that if we stop here we may miss an important practical pressure in the direction of conative hierarchy.

An initial point – from Agnieszka Jaworska – is that the Lockean model of agential authority points to an account of internality (in the sense relevant to the cited Aristotelian idea) that does not make hierarchy essential.[49] There can be important attitudes – a child's love for her father, say – that do not involve conative hierarchy but nevertheless play the kind of Lockean roles in cross-temporal organization of thought and action that establish internality. So the concern with internality does not, on its own, provide sufficient philosophical pressure for conative hierarchy.

A Frankfurtian response would grant the point but insist that, *for agents who are sufficiently reflective to be self-governing*, internality of first-order motivation is (normally?) the product of higher-order reflection and higher-order endorsement or acceptance. And this brings with it conative hierarchy. So, while conative hierarchy need not be involved in all cases of internality, internality within the psychology of reflective self-governance needs conative hierarchy.

But now consider an alternative model of reflectiveness. This model highlights first-order policies about what to treat as a reason in one's motivationally effective practical reasoning; and it says that such policies are reflectively held when they are appropriately tied to (even if underdetermined by) evaluative reflection. Here we have a central role for plan-type commitments concerning practical reasoning (to which we can extend our account of agential authority); and we have a kind of reflectiveness; but we do not yet have conative hierarchy.

What this alternative model fails fully to recognize, however, is that human agents have a wide range of first-order motivating attitudes in addition to such first-order policies about practical reasoning, and that these other motivating attitudes threaten to undermine these policies. The point is related to an aspect of Aristotle's moral psychology that has been highlighted by John Cooper. Cooper emphasizes that a central Aristotelian theme is that human agents are subject to significant motivational pressures that do not arise from reflection on what is worth pursuing.[50] For our purposes here, what is important is the related idea that human agents are subject to a wide range of motivational pressures that do not arise primarily from their basic practical commitments. Indeed, as we all learn, these motivational pressures may well be contrary to those commitments. The clearest cases include (but are not limited to) certain bodily appetites and certain forms of anger, rage, humiliation, indignation, jealousy, resentment, and grief. It is an important fact about human agents – one reflected in our commonsense self-understanding – that such motivating attitudes are part of their psychology and that human agents need a system of self-management in response to the potential of these forms of motivation to conflict with basic commitments. In the absence of such self-management, human agents are much less likely to be effectively guided by their basic commitments.[51]

Once our model of reflective, self-governing agency explicitly includes these further, wide-ranging, first-order motivating attitudes, however, there is pressure for higher-order reflectiveness and conative hierarchy. After all, we can suppose that a self-governing agent will know of these first-order attitudes and of her need for self-management. And we can suppose that she will, other things being equal, endorse forms of functioning that serve this need. So it is plausible to suppose that her basic commitments will themselves include a commitment to associated management of relevant first-order desires and thus include such self-management as part of their content. And that means these commitments will be higher-order. In particular, given the centrality of practical reasoning to self-governed agency, we can expect that these commitments will include policy-like attitudes that concern the justifying significance to be given (or refused) to various first-order desires, and/or what they are for, in her motivationally effective practical reasoning. Such policies will say, roughly: Give (refuse) justifying significance to consideration X in motivationally effective practical reasoning, in part by giving (refusing) such significance to relevant first-order desires and/or what they are for (and do this by way of this very policy).[52] Such policies will help shape what has subjective normative authority for the agent.[53]

This means that a basic pressure for conative hierarchy derives from what is for human agents a pervasive practical problem of self-management. In particular, reflective, self-governing agents will have a wide range of first-order motivating attitudes that will need to be managed in the pursuit of basic commitments. This practical problem exerts pressure on those commitments to be higher-order. And once we recognize this point, we can go on to see such higher-order commitments as potential elements in a Frankfurtian project of self-constitution. If, in contrast, we were to try to model reflectiveness, internality, and self-government without appeal to conative hierarchy, we would be in danger of failing to take due account of this pervasive practical problem.

The idea is not that individual agents reflectively decide to introduce conative hierarchy into their psychic economies in response to the need for self-management.[54] Rather, we can agree with Frankfurt that human agents are in fact typically reflective about their motivation in ways that involve conative hierarchy. Our question is: What can we say to ourselves to make further sense to ourselves of this feature of our psychic lives? This question is part of what T. M. Scanlon calls our "enterprise . . . of self-understanding."[55] And the claim is that we can appeal here to the role of higher-order reflection and conative hierarchy as part of a reasonable response to fundamental, pervasive, and (following Cooper's Aristotle) permanent human needs for self-management in the effective pursuit of basic commitments.

This is not to argue that self-governance *must* involve conative hierarchy. It is, rather, to argue that there is a pervasive and permanent practical problem that human agents face and with respect to which conative hierarchy is a reasonable and common human response, at least for agents with relevant self-knowledge. The claim is, further, that when the hierarchical response to this pervasive and permanent practical problem takes an appropriate form – one we have tried to characterize – we arrive at basic elements of a central case of self-governance. Because the cited form of hierarchy essentially involves plan-type attitudes – in particular, self-governing policies – we arrive, as promised, at a model of core elements of human autonomy that involves in basic ways structures of planning agency. And because the planning theory is, as I have said, a modest theory of the will, this is a model of central roles of the will in autonomy.[56]

VIII. SOME FINAL QUALIFICATIONS

In discussing Watsonian "perverse" cases, I indicated that self-governance precludes certain kinds of severe incoherence between evaluative judgment and basic commitments. This does not entail that self-governance requires evaluative judgment; nor does it entail that self-governance requires that the agent who does make such evaluative judgments gets them right. Indeed, I think that it is not essential to the basic commitments I have emphasized – those that take the form of self-governing policies and have agential authority – that they derive from intersubjectively accountable value judgments. But it still might be urged that there is a further demand specifically on autonomy, that relevant self-governing policies be to some extent grounded in evaluative judgment – though they may also be underdetermined by, and go beyond, such judgments. And it might also be urged that there is a further demand specifically on autonomy, that the agent at least have the ability to arrive at evaluative judgments that get matters right.[57] These are not, however, issues I will try to adjudicate here. For our present purposes, it suffices to note that whatever we say on these further proposals is compatible with, and could be added to, the proposed model of core elements of autonomy.

Finally, there are traditional and perplexing issues about the compatibility of autonomy and causal determination. The features of agency I have highlighted here as core elements seem to me to be ones that could be present in a deterministic world, which is not to deny that certain forms of causal determination (for example, as the argument frequently goes, certain forms of manipulation) can undermine self-governance. Nevertheless, whether there is a persuasive reason for insisting that autonomy preclude any kind of causal determination of action (because, as the argument might go, causal determination of action is incompatible with self-determination of action) is a matter of great controversy, one that I also will not address here.[58]

Notes

This chapter is to a significant extent an overview of themes I have discussed in a recent series of essays. For further details, see "Identification, Decision, and Treating as a Reason," as reprinted in my *Faces of Intention* (New York: Cambridge University Press, 1999): 185–206; "Reflection, Planning, and Temporally Extended Agency," *Philosophical Review* 109 (2000): 35–61; "Valuing and the Will," *Philosophical Perspectives: Action and Freedom* 14 (2000): 249–265; "Hierarchy, Circularity, and Double Reduction," in S. Buss and L. Overton, eds., *Contours of*

Agency: Essays on the Philosophy of Harry Frankfurt (Cambridge, MA: MIT Press, 2002): 65–85; "Nozick on Free Will," in David Schmidtz, ed., *Robert Nozick* (New York: Cambridge University Press, 2002): 155–174; "Two Problems About Human Agency," *Proceedings of the Aristotelian Society* 101 (2001): 309–326; "Autonomy and Hierarchy," in Ellen Frankel Paul, Fred D. Miller, Jr., and Jeffrey Paul, eds., *Autonomy* (New York: Cambridge University Press, 2003): 156–176; "Shared Valuing and Frameworks for Practical Reasoning," in R. Jay Wallace et al., eds., *Reason and Value: Themes from the Moral Philosophy of Joseph Raz* (Oxford: Oxford University Press, 2004); "A Desire of One's Own," *Journal of Philosophy* (2003): 221–242; "Three Forms of Agential Commitment: Reply to Cullity and Gerrans," *Proceedings of the Aristotelian Society* 104 (2004): 327–35; and "Temptation Revisited," in Michael E. Bratman, ed., *Structures of Agency: Essays* (New York: Oxford University Press, 2007): 257–82. The present chapter benefited from written comments from Alfred Mele and Manuel Vargas, and from extremely helpful discussion in a meeting of the Stanford Social Ethics and Normative Theory discussion group and in a colloquium at the University of Miami. It was completed while I was a Fellow at the Center for Advanced Study in Behavioral Sciences. I am grateful for financial support provided by the Andrew W. Mellon Foundation.

1. As indicated, I understand self-governance of action to be a distinctive form of self-direction or self-determination (I do not distinguish these last two) of action. Autonomy – that is, personal autonomy – is self-direction that is, in particular, self-governance. Or anyway, that is the phenomenon that is my concern here. (See my "Autonomy and Hierarchy," 156–157, 168.) Autonomy is related in complex ways to moral responsibility and accountability, but I do not consider these further issues here.
2. See J. David Velleman, "What Happens When Someone Acts?" in his *The Possibility of Practical Reason* (Oxford: Oxford University Press, 2000): 123–143; and R. E. Hobart, "Free Will as Involving Determination and Inconceivable Without It," as reprinted in Bernard Berofsky, ed., *Free Will and Determinism* (New York: Harper & Row, 1966): 63–95, esp. 65–66.
3. As for the provision of fully sufficient conditions, though, see my qualifications below in remarks about core elements of autonomy. Alfred R. Mele also pursues a strategy of seeking sufficient (but perhaps not necessary) conditions for certain forms of autonomy. And Mele addresses issues about the historical background of autonomy, issues that, as I explain below, I put aside here. See Mele, *Autonomous Agents: From Self-Control to Autonomy* (New York: Oxford University Press, 1995): 187.
4. See my *Intention, Plans, and Practical Reason* (Cambridge, MA: Harvard University Press, 1987; reissued by CSLI Publications, 1999); and my *Faces of Intention.*
5. See his review of my *Intention, Plans, and Practical Reason* in *Philosophical Review* (1991): 283.
6. See my "Autonomy and Hierarchy," 157.
7. And it would be a model of what I have called "core features of human agency." See my "Reflection, Planning, and Temporally Extended Agency," 35–36. I point to a similar idea in talking about "strong forms of agency" in "A Desire of One's Own," 222 n. 3.

8. See Harry Frankfurt, *The Importance of What We Care About* (New York: Cambridge University Press, 1988); and *Necessity, Volition, and Love* (New York: Cambridge University Press, 1999). For related ideas, see also Gerald Dworkin, "Acting Freely," *Noûs* 4 (1970): 367–383; Wright Neely, "Freedom and Desire," *Philosophical Review* 83 (1974): 32–54; and Keith Lehrer, "Reason and Autonomy," in Paul, Miller, and Paul, eds., *Autonomy*, 177–198.
9. Frankfurt, "Freedom of the Will and the Concept of a Person," in his *The Importance of What We Care About*, 20. (It is interesting to note that in this passage Frankfurt appeals to something the agent is doing – namely, securing the cited conformity.)
10. Frankfurt points to this condition of explanatory role in his "Identification and Wholeheartedness," in *The Importance of What We Care About*, 163.
11. See esp. Frankfurt's "Autonomy, Necessity and Love" in his *Necessity, Volition, and Love*, 129–141. For a helpful discussion of some issues of Frankfurt interpretation that I am skirting over here, see James Stacey Taylor, "Autonomy, Duress, and Coercion," in Paul, Miller, and Paul, eds., *Autonomy*, 129 n. 5.
12. Gary Watson, "Free Agency," *Journal of Philosophy* 72 (1975): 205–220. R. Jay Wallace endorses similar objections in his "Caring, Reflexivity, and the Structure of Volition," in Monika Betzler and Barbara Guckes, eds., *Autonomes Handeln* (Berlin: Akademie Verlag, 2000): 218–222.
13. Watson, "Free Agency," 218.
14. Talk of agential authority comes from my "Two Problems About Human Agency"; talk of wiggles in the psychic stew comes, I admit, from my "Reflection, Planning, and Temporally Extended Agency," 38.
15. Watson notes that there are elements in Frankfurt's essay – in particular, Frankfurt's talk of an agent who "identifies himself *decisively* with one of his first-order desires" – that suggest that it is not conative hierarchy that is doing the main theoretical work but, rather, the idea of decisive identification. But, Watson remarks, if "notions of acts of identification and of decisive commitment . . . are the crucial notions, it is unclear why these acts of identification cannot themselves be of the first order. . . ." (The quote from Frankfurt is in Watson's "Free Agency," at 218, while the quote from Watson is at 219.) I discuss this exchange between Frankfurt and Watson in "Identification, Decision, and Treating as a Reason," in my *Faces of Intention*, 188–190.
16. Watson, "Free Agency," 216.
17. Ibid., 219.
18. Ibid.
19. Frankfurt made this point in conversation. Also see Velleman, "What Happens When Someone Acts?" 134.
20. Frankfurt, "The Faintest Passion," in his *Necessity, Volition, and Love*, 103–105.
21. Frankfurt, "The Faintest Passion," 104.
22. Bratman, "Identification, Decision, and Treating as a Reason," 194–195. And see Bratman, "Reflection, Planning, and Temporally Extended Agency," 49, for my strategy for avoiding this difficulty within my own account.
23. Watson, "Free Action and Free Will," *Mind* 96 (1987): 150. Also see my "A Desire of One's Own," 227.

24. For this last point, see Joseph Raz, "Incommensurability and Agency," as reprinted in his *Engaging Reason* (Oxford: Oxford University Press, 1999): 46–66. I discuss this trio of possibilities in "A Desire of One's Own."
25. See, for example, Robert Nozick, *Philosophical Explanations* (Cambridge, MA: Harvard University Press, 1981): 446–450. Talk of the shape of a life comes from Charles Taylor, "Leading a Life," in Ruth Chang, ed., *Incommensurability, Incomparability, and Practical Reason* (Cambridge, MA: Harvard University Press, 1997): 183.
26. For a somewhat similar view, see Keith Lehrer, *Self Trust: A Study of Reason, Knowledge, and Autonomy* (Oxford: Oxford University Press, 1997): chap. 4.
27. The hierarchies I allude to here are, roughly, ones of ends and means, not the conative hierarchies on which I have so far been focusing.
28. In a version of this sort of case emphasized by Nadeem Hussain, an agent in a strongly traditional society unreflectively internalizes certain general policies passed down by the tradition.
29. See my "Introduction," *Faces of Intention*, 5.
30. See Derek Parfit, *Reasons and Persons* (New York: Oxford University Press, 1984): 206–208; and my "Reflection, Planning, and Temporally Extended Agency," 43–45.
31. Bratman, "Reflection, Planning, and Temporally Extended Agency," 46.
32. Granted, there will be cases in which a relevant intention-like attitude will be a "singular commitment" to treat a certain desire in a relevant way on *this* occasion. (See my "Hierarchy, Circularity, and Double Reduction," 78–79.) Such intention-like attitudes will have some claim to agential authority. Given the singularity of the commitment, however, these intention-like attitudes will have a less extensive tie to temporally extended agency and thus a lesser claim to authority. Because our concern is primarily with sufficient conditions for autonomy, I will here put such cases to one side.
33. There will also be room for attitudes that play the higher-order policy-like roles in one's temporally extended agency that I have been emphasizing, though they are not general intentions. I call these "quasi-policies." See my "Reflection, Planning, and Temporally Extended Agency," 57–60.
34. For the point about valuing, see my "Valuing and the Will" and "Autonomy and Hierarchy." For the idea of subjective normative authority, see my "Two Problems about Human Agency." (In Section 7, I will be extending this notion of subjective normative authority.) Note that these policies concern the agent's practical *reasoning*. So we need to understand the reasoning that is the focus of these policies in a way that does not reintroduce worries about a homunculus. See my "Hierarchy, Circularity, and Double Reduction," 70–78; and "Two Problems about Human Agency," 322–323.
35. See Garrett Cullity and Philip Gerrans, "Agency and Policy," *Proceedings of the Aristotelian Society* 104 (2004): 317–27, and my "Three Forms of Agential Commitment: Reply to Cullity and Gerrans," pp. 329–337. This self-knowledge requirement is doubly motivated, by the way. It is a straightforwardly plausible condition on self-governance that the agent know what higher-order policies are guiding her thought and action. But, as Agnieszka Jaworska has noted, it is also unlikely that an unknown policy will have the

kinds of referential connections to prior intentions and later action that are central to our Lockean account of agential authority.

36. My efforts to spell out an appropriate sense appear in my "Reflection, Planning, and Temporally Extended Agency," 49–50, 59–60.
37. I think there is also another reason for such reflexivity, one associated with the concern about reasoning to which I allude in note 34 and the essays cited there.
38. A closely related idea is in Keith Lehrer, *Self-Trust,* 100–102; and also in his "Reason and Autonomy," 187–191. For the basic idea of seeing intentions as reflexive, see Gilbert Harman, *Change in View* (Cambridge, MA: MIT Press, 1986): 85–88. However, my appeal here to reflexivity is not part of a view that, like Harman's, sees *all* "positive" intentions in this way. Further, because my appeal to reflexivity is against a background of a Lockean story of agential authority, together with a Frankfurtian appeal to satisfaction, the job of such reflexivity within my account of autonomy is considerably more limited than its job within Lehrer's.
39. I should emphasize that the relevant notion of stability here is in part a normative one: It will involve norms of reasonable stability. It is an important question how exactly to understand such reasonable stability. For some efforts in this direction, see my "Toxin, Temptation, and the Stability of Intention," reprinted in Michael E. Bratman, ed., *Faces of Intention: Selected Essays on Intention and Agency* (Cambridge: Cambridge University Press, 1999): 58–90; and "Temptation Revisited." Note that the appeal to reasonable stability is *not* an appeal to "volitional necessities" in the sense invoked by Frankfurt in his "Autonomy, Necessity, and Love," 138.
40. For references and further discussion, see my "A Desire of One's Own."
41. In seeing deliberation as primarily first-order, but also seeing the valuings that enter into deliberation as involving conative hierarchy, my view is in the spirit of certain aspects of Simon Blackburn's approach to these matters. (I provide a different treatment of the relevant hierarchy, however. And my view remains neutral with respect to the basic debate between cognitivist approaches and expressivist approaches of the sort championed by Blackburn.) See Blackburn, *Ruling Passions: A Theory of Practical Reasoning* (Oxford and New York: Clarendon/Oxford University Press, 1998). (Blackburn's remarks about a "staircase of practical and emotional ascent" are at 9; his remarks about valuing are at 67–68; and his remarks about deliberation are at 250–256.)
42. As Samuel Scheffler and others have noted in correspondence and conversation.
43. Gilbert Harman argues that (1) "positive intentions are self-referential," so (2) all creatures who have positive intentions have higher-order conative attitudes, and so (3) "Frankfurt's appeal to second-order volitions is not the key to distinguishing autonomy from nonautonomy." Though I would not defend a simple appeal to second-order volitions as this "key," my remarks in the text do point to a response on Frankfurt's behalf to this criticism. Frankfurt can say that what provides the key is the capacity for *broad* conative hierarchy, a capacity that goes beyond the hierarchy built into the purported reflexivity of positive intentions. See Gilbert Harman, "Desired Desires," as

reprinted in his *Explaining Value and Other Essays in Moral Philosophy* (Oxford: Oxford University Press, 2000): 122–126.

44. For ease of exposition, in the discussion to follow of reasons for broad hierarchy I will simply speak of hierarchy where I mean broad hierarchy. Also, I do not claim that the pressures to be discussed exhaust the field. There may be other pressures for conative hierarchy that would need to be considered in a more extensive discussion.
45. Frankfurt, "Identification and Wholeheartedness," 171.
46. Frankfurt, "Reply to Michael E. Bratman," in Sarah Buss and Lee Overton, eds., *Contours of Agency* (Cambridge, MA: MIT Press, 2002): 88.
47. Though Christine Korsgaard shares with Frankfurt an interest in self-constitution, she also embraces such a model of deliberation when she writes: "When you deliberate, it is as if there were something over and above all your desires, something which is *you,* and which *chooses* which desire to act on" (*The Sources of Normativity,* 100). For Korsgaard's concerns with self-constitution, see her "Self-Constitution in the Ethics of Plato and Kant," *Journal of Ethics* 3 (1999): 1–29.
48. Though Frankfurt himself does not seem so inclined. (See his "Reply to Michael E. Bratman," 89–90.)
49. See her "Caring and Internality," unpublished manuscript. The example to follow comes (with a change in gender) from that paper.
50. John Cooper, "Some Remarks on Aristotle's Moral Psychology," reprinted in his *Reason and Emotion: Essays on Ancient Moral Psychology and Ethical Theory* (Princeton: Princeton University Press, 1999): 237–252. As Cooper puts the view, "non-rational desires will be desires no part of the causal history of which is ever any process (self-conscious or not) of investigation into the truth about what is good for oneself" (242). Cooper notes that this is compatible with holding, as Aristotle did, that "non-rational desires carry with them value judgments framed in (at least some of) the very same terms of good and bad, right and wrong, etc., that also reappear in our rational reflections about what to do and why" (247). (In contrast, I would want to allow for some nonrational desires that do not involve such value judgments.) What is central, Cooper indicates, is "the permanence in human beings and the independence from reason . . . of the nonrational desires" (249).
51. For a similar focus on this practical problem – though not in the service of a hierarchical model – see Martha C. Nussbaum, *The Fragility of Goodness: Luck and Ethics in Greek Tragedy and Philosophy* (Cambridge: Cambridge University Press, 1986): chap. 4. Note that the commitments that need to be supported by self-management will include shared commitments – for example, our shared commitment to a certain project.
52. See my "Autonomy and Hierarchy." Note that I do not claim that these are the only policies that may be relevant here. For example, as Alfred Mele has noted, the agent may also have a policy in favor of simply trying to remove a certain desire.
53. In including in some such policies a direct concern with X, as well as with associated desires and what they are for, I am extending (as anticipated earlier) what it is that is accorded subjective normative authority.

54. Though we, as theorists, can reason in this way, as part of what Paul Grice called "creature construction." See Grice's "Method in Philosophical Psychology (from the Banal to the Bizarre)" (Presidential Address), in *Proceedings and Addresses of the American Philosophical Association* (1974–75): 23–53. I pursue such a methodology in "Valuing and the Will" and in "Autonomy and Hierarchy," In "Autonomy and Hierarchy" I see self-governing policies as a solution to a pair of pervasive human problems: the need for self-management and the need to respond to underdetermination by value judgment.
55. T. M. Scanlon, "Self-Anchored Morality," in J. B. Schneewind, ed., *Reasons, Ethics, and Society: Themes from Kurt Baier with His Responses* (Chicago: Open Court, 1996): 198. As I see it, one use of Gricean creature construction is to help us achieve such self-understanding. Note that in locating this question about conative hierarchy within the enterprise of self-understanding, I do not suppose that the basic concern to which our answer to this question appeals must be a concern with self-understanding. Indeed, the relevant concern to which my answer appeals is a concern with the effective pursuit of basic commitments. For a view that sees this basic concern as, in contrast, a concern with self-understanding, see J. David Velleman, "Introduction," *The Possibility of Practical Reason*, 1–31.
56. These roles are multiple and interconnected: They include the organization of thought and action over time, related forms of agential authority, and roles in shaping what has subjective normative authority. This contrasts with a thin conception of the will as primarily a matter of deciding what to do in present circumstances.
57. See, e.g., Susan Wolf, *Freedom within Reason* (Oxford: Oxford University Press, 1990); Nozick, *Philosophical Explanations*, 317–332; and Gideon Yaffe, "Free Will and Agency at Its Best," *Philosophical Perspectives* 14 (2000): 203–229. We need to be careful, though, to remember that our concern here is with autonomy and not directly with moral accountability. (For a related caveat, see Gary Watson, "Two Faces of Responsibility," *Philosophical Topics* 24 (1996): 240–241.)
58. Though see my "Nozick on Free Will."

2

Autonomy without Free Will

Bernard Berofsky

Discussions of personal autonomy often proceed as if the free-will problem does not exist. Yet an incompatibilist – one who regards determinism as a genuine threat to free will – may wish to argue that an account of autonomy or self-government is severely compromised by the discovery that the self in question is a deterministic product of heredity and environment. Such a discovery would entail, in her eyes, that, even if I am judged autonomous through, say, a capacity for uncoerced and rational review of my deepest commitments (plus the ability to make appropriate adjustments), the failure in a deterministic world to control the origination of my desires and values, elements that explain my commitments, renders my self-governance seriously inauthentic.

Yet compartmentalization is an essential tool for the avoidance of intellectual paralysis. Perhaps then we ought not to worry simultaneously about both the conditions of autonomous decision making and the possibility that determinism will render our results a sham. If autonomy is our concern, we can let the other philosophical fellow raise the specter of enslavement of self arising from the domination exerted by heredity and environment over the elements that manifest our autonomy. Although no one can object to this pillar of intellectual practice, I would like to try to accommodate that peculiarly philosophical mindset that drives us to excess, that demand to be in good faith that, we suppose, fails to be met by a shallow theory that refuses to face the implications of our immersion in a controlling, hostile world.

I. AUTONOMOUS DECISION MAKING

Consider the capacities that enable an agent to exercise control over his or her life. Control can be exercised over actions, the world (via one's actions), or mental states. We need this control in the case of mental states most obviously when we are displeased with what we find and wish to bring our mental life into line. Consider beliefs, for example. Although we can often survive quite well with inconsistency within the corpus of our beliefs, we surely need the power to restore consistency upon the discovery that it is absent. The same ideal reigns over the relations between our beliefs and the principles to which we adhere concerning the proper way to acquire and assess beliefs. That is, we need to control the formation and re-formation of our beliefs to ensure adherence to these principles. We have motivations and emotions that we judge in acts of evaluation. Again, we must be able to modify motivations and emotions in accordance with our evaluations to attain control over our mental lives. Notice that these conditions do not presuppose the soundness, rationality, or even sanity of the principles and evaluations that do the controlling. Because they can be met by a psychotic, slave, or otherwise thoroughly heteronomous individual – for example, one in whom daft principles have been implanted by a fiend – they are merely necessary conditions, and pretty weak ones at that. They desperately need supplementation with the capacity to submit values (evaluations) and principles themselves to critical or rational review and to change them in light of the results of this review. The use of the terms "critical" and "rational" introduce a sorely needed element of external control over judgments of autonomy, about which we shall have more to say later.

It is reasonable to believe that an autonomous adult must be in a position to exercise control in the above ways. But an apparently insuperable barrier to the prospect of genuine autonomy is posed by the need to operate the most sophisticated control capacities from some perspective or other. A judgment is made about a particular state from the perspective of principles, strategies, beliefs, desires, and values that are provided to and, therefore, unchallenged in the context. Thus, we confront the very real possibility that the perspective from which evaluation takes place might itself be maintained heteronomously, thereby transmitting its heteronomy to the state under review. The perspective may be implanted in us by a powerful demon, for example. But we cannot then demand that each perspective be maintained autonomously if that requires actual submission to review, for because every review is conducted relative to a perspective, some perspective or other must always remain untouched. And if we imagine a scenario in which, say, perspective A (a principle, evaluation, belief, value, or desire) is endorsed relative to perspective B and then perspective B is endorsed relative to perspective A, we will never be able to secure an ungrounded judgment of autonomy. Call the argument that these considerations indeed make autonomy impossible the infinite regress/perspectives argument.

The picture we are presenting supposes that an individual decision may be judged autonomous or not, depending essentially on some sort of certification of its origin. Thus, if all other conditions on autonomy are in place, one decision may and another may not be judged autonomous based on etiological facts about a relevant perspective. Some philosophers prefer to think of autonomy as a characteristic of agents, resting on the possession of capacities for critical reflection (on desires, values, etc.), the readiness to take steps to adjust one's life in accordance with the results of reflection, and perhaps the capacity and willingness to identify with the values or reasons that guide decisions.[1] Of course, because one may possess such capacities in certain spheres and not in others, the difference between the two approaches may not be that stark. In any event, the incompatibilist worry may easily extend to these more generalized conceptions, because deterministic accounts of the origin of a capacity or disposition may be judged just as autonomy undermining as similar accounts of the elements that enter into a specific deliberation.

II. OBJECTIVELY GROUNDED STATES

Fortunately, the situation is not as hopeless as it appears. The infinite regress/perspectives problem can be shown to dissolve for most elements of a perspective. For my autonomy is not undermined by a failure to have submitted to an actual review those elements I am justified in adopting for use in decision making should I possess a merely tacit appreciation of their credentials. The clearest example is that of belief. Even if I had been manipulated by teachers with sinister motives long before I reached the age of reason, I am fortunate that their inculcation incorporated the correct multiplication table. Perhaps in the ensuing years, I never considered the possibility that 6×7 was other than 42 and never, therefore, submitted this belief to critical evaluation. But I used this knowledge in decision making and was justified in so doing by dint of its truth, together with the fact that I surely would have considered it more carefully if the need had arisen through techniques I have the competence to employ successfully. I can track the truth in these cases.

In the case of beliefs like this one, I am aware that the origin of my acceptance is not the appropriate sort of appeal should the belief be challenged. Because the belief is sustained through the recognition of the grounds of its acceptance, the manner of inculcation becomes irrelevant and the bogeyman of determinism is dealt a serious blow.[2]

This recognition is often tacit because an occasion for reconsideration of the product of 6 and 7 has never arisen. But it is there because experience would have given rise to problems had I been taught badly, and I would then have looked not at origins, but rather at the relevant facts. For this reason, it does not even matter that my evil (and incompetent) math teacher believed that $6 \times 7 = 43$ and was trying to deceive me by telling me that $6 \times 7 = 42$. I inadvertently learned the truth and, more importantly, became justified in continuing to believe it.

It is not enough, of course, that we possess the truth. But it is also not enough that we know how to defend the proposition were it challenged. We may in addition demand for knowledge or autonomous belief possession that the belief be *sustained* by me in virtue of its truth conditions and that condition will not obtain if I continue to believe a proposition just because I learned it. So the persistence of my belief that Sacramento is the capital of California must depend in part on the fact that it is. At some point in my history, that fact had to have, directly or indirectly, an abiding cognitive impact.[3]

I have no intention of embarking on a full-blooded discussion of the nature of knowledge. I want simply to highlight the possibility that tainted origins need not threaten the autonomous character of a decision. A belief invoked by a person engaged in autonomous decision making may, therefore, have been implanted in a way that bypassed the person's critical control mechanisms. If this specific form of determination does not undermine the person's autonomy, then a fortiori the simple fact that the appearance of the belief is determined (in some way or another) cannot render the agent heteronomous. The unselfconscious use of the belief as an assumption in decision making is not an automatic barrier to the autonomy of the process should the agent accept the (true) belief because of its basis.

I believe that we have a right to extend this conclusion to elements of a perspective that cannot be counted straightforwardly true or false. The key question again is whether the evaluation, principle, value, or desire is adopted or held in virtue of the grounds that would justify its adoption to any rational agent, should such grounds exist.

Of course, profound debates surround questions concerning the justification of evaluations and values. I believe that I am justified in evaluating Beethoven as a great composer, as greater than Bruckner, for example. If I am right in thinking that the "facts" warrant this judgment, then my autonomy is not threatened by my uncritical use of this evaluation in a decision-making process resulting in the purchase of a ticket to hear Beethoven rather than Bruckner. Again, if my judgment were challenged and I could produce a solid justification of my preference, my failure to have engaged earlier in an explicit critical comparison of the two composers does not threaten my autonomy. No more need be asked of an autonomous agent.

How do these thoughts square with the familiar psychological model of autonomous development according to which one enters into maturity through reflection on transmitted values that had hitherto been taken for granted and must now be certified through a critical process that, should it lead to identification, will permit the agent to regard the values as genuinely her own, as now arising out of personal and independent reflection rather than inculcation from without?

We must not lose sight of the fact that the goal of this maturation process is not just an independent adult – one can be independent and utterly mad. And if we describe the goal as the achievement of critical competence, we must then not lose sight of the fact that the exercise of critical competence is designed to elicit truths we are justified in believing because our competence has enabled us to ferret out the grounds of the truth. So if we are possessed of the outcome – we believe for the right reasons and are in a position to defend and, if necessary, modify our beliefs in a rational way – the demands of autonomy have already been met without the explicit performance. God, the ideally autonomous agent, does not need to engage in acts of critical competence – He already believes for the right reasons. The contrary position that leads to the demand for an infinite regress of actual evaluations is grounded on a picture of self-rule that I have tried elsewhere to undermine. The replacement model I have advocated sees an autonomous agent as one who is in the right relation to the world rather than her metaphysical origins.[4] To demand origination in the self, given a world in which no self is an island, is to invite defeat at the gate and for no good reason. A decision is under the control of the agent in the relevant sense when the perspective from which it is issued is maintained by that agent for the reasons that ground its acceptability.

III. CONTINGENCIES

The truly difficult cases, therefore, are those in which no objective grounding exists for the adoption of a particular perspective. Often, there is no (completely) objective justification for those commitments that express the deepest values of an agent: religion, profession, personal ideals, lifestyle, personal relationships. We have preferences and are prepared to concede that the distinct preferences of others are no less securely grounded in the nature of things. Indeed, our insistence that each truly autonomous agent undergo an actual personal review of her deepest commitments is testimony to the strength of the conviction that the world (or Reason) is not in a position to deliver the judgment on its own. We commend a person for using her reason to render a judgment on values hitherto taken for granted in a case in which we would characterize the judgment as objectively sound, as one no rational agent could fail to have made. But in other cases, we suppose that reason reaches a dead end and all we can do in the way of justifying a decision is to cite a personal, nonuniversalizable preference. Relative to that preference, a decision can be rational or irrational. It is rational for *him*, but not for *her*, a person with different desires and values, to make such and such a decision.

For example, it may be rational for one smitten by a love of rugby to have and act on various desires and values; but the core love of rugby, unlike the belief that $6 \times 7 = 42$, cannot itself be objectively grounded in the nature of things. Many important preferences and values appear as givens, products of our interactions with the world many crucial instances of which took place long before we attained critical maturity. Insofar as these enter into important deliberations, either in the form of assumptions functioning as premises of or forces operating to direct practical reasoning, the strategy outlined above for dealing with states that have not undergone critical scrutiny is inapplicable. In abandoning rugby, I would not be making the same sort of error that I would if I reverted to the belief that $6 \times 7 = 43$. Again, rationality is not entirely out of place. There are intelligent people who would argue that rugby is a worthless, even harmful, enterprise, and they must be heard. And the pursuit of the sport, especially as a player, requires the acceptance of certain sacrifices and risks the merits of which can be rationally debated. I am simply saying that, after reason has had its full turn at bat, in many such cases we are still left with decisions to be made, and we do so by consulting or by permitting the operation of those desires and values we shall now call "contingencies."

IV. INFINITE REGRESS/PERSPECTIVES ARGUMENT UNDERMINED

Thus, the infinite regress/perspectives argument runs afoul of two considerations: (1) concern about autonomy arising from the necessity of perspectives can be mitigated by the thought that many perspectives – those that are objectively grounded – may remain unquestioned without threatening the agent's autonomy; and (2) the other perspectives, the contingencies, may undermine autonomy not because they have not been critically assessed from a perspective that presupposes further perspectives, but rather because they *cannot* be (completely) critically assessed. They just are: I happen to prefer certain sorts of friends, jobs, places to live, amusements, lifestyles, activities, etc. To seek an account of autonomy that is immune from these contingencies is to seek an account of the autonomy of creatures very different from you and me. They would be purely rational creatures, bereft of the plethora of complex states that make us interestingly different from one another. In order to be perfect trackers of the world, these creatures must forgo the varied interests, tastes, and strong emotions that drive most of us in our daily doings. In fact, if ethical objectivism is false and moral outlooks are ultimately also expressions of preference, these creatures would be further denuded – reason cannot adjudicate moral disputes – and one begins to wonder what they would do with their time! My concern is the possible autonomy of human beings, creatures rich in contingencies, many of which have been set, more or less firmly, long before they became critically competent.

Thus, if the fact of contingency undermines our autonomy, the reason is not to be found in the infinite regress/perspectives argument. And we must, indeed, pay homage to the most rudimentary facts of human existence, according to which no actual human beings are as autonomous as we can easily imagine them to be. Enormous numbers of matters of great concern to us remain forever outside the domain of our choice, autonomous or otherwise. This truism obliges us to adopt as a constraint on a reasonable theory of autonomy that it construe autonomy as an intelligible ideal that all of us approximate only to a certain degree. The ideality of autonomy is even more manifest if we use "autonomy" (as most people do) to include "proficiency," the power to effect one's decisions.[5] Armed with this concession, we may on the one hand reject the infinite regress/perspectives argument's principled appeal to the ungrounded character of these contingencies, charging it with an unreasonable constraint on a theory of autonomy. On the other hand, we extract a cogent core from that appeal by conceding the need to rank people in terms of the extent to which they have indeed been limited by early environment and heredity.

Although rational grounding of all our values, desires, and principles is impossible for the creatures for whom we seek an account of autonomy, there are differences in the extent to which people can exercise control over contingencies. There are two important dimensions here. First, there is the range of items that has been set prior to the age of critical reflection; and second, there is the strength of the embedding. I may have been brought up to appreciate rock music only; but because my tastes change as I mature, the embedding can be undone. But some limits are either unalterable or sufficiently resistant to change to count as an obstacle to our emerging autonomy.

Strength is a function of technology. We used to have to accept physical limitations that we can now overcome; for example, it may soon become commonplace to change the color of one's eyes. To keep matters relatively simple, we shall restrict our concern to the autonomous acquisition and possession of states like values, preferences, desires, and principles. (I call these collectively "Motivational Input States," whether or not they motivate as bases of premises of practical reasoning or as forces operating to direct the course of practical reasoning.) Although it is evident that we would choose to perform many actions that we are just unable to perform, it is also evident that we are unable to alter many Motivational Input States that are genetically based or were environmentally induced before the age of reason.

Thus, when repeated challenges to an agent's perspective ultimately drive her to identify the contingencies of her existence, we may see these as *potential barriers to full autonomy* rather than *barriers to the conceptual possibility of an account of autonomy.* For each actual person, it is unnecessary to complete an infinite regress before reaching an autonomy-limiting perspective.

That we are not ideally autonomous is not a conclusion that should be resisted by compatibilists on the free-will question. Whether our early lives proceed along deterministic or indeterministic lines, we cannot have a free will before we have a will. When an agent begins to perform self-conscious intentional, voluntary actions, the desires, cognitive states, abilities, and character traits that enter into the intention-forming process have not been formed freely and are not to be charged against the person. No one wants to attribute freedom of will to young children. As I begin to mature, to be sure, I can rationally reflect upon and reconstruct my motivational repertoire. But early on, I am not responsible for what I find there. And should any of these states remain unalterable, they cannot be said to be freely possessed. I see no reason for a compatibilist to object.

This conclusion does not depend on whether the laws governing the earlier psychological processes are deterministic or merely statistical. Compatibilists may rightly seek differences that bear on freedom among socialization, indoctrination, pervasive nonconstraining control and determination by natural causes without needing to challenge the brute fact that original inputs to early deliberative episodes were not freely acquired. All parties to the free-will dispute should agree that neither freedom nor autonomy is part of the picture when little Johnny clings to his mother out of fear of abandonment.

If contingencies are *potential* barriers to autonomy, when do they *actually* limit autonomy? In other words, how serious a threat to our actual autonomy is posed by our inability to exercise control over all the contingencies of our lives? And what is the connection to the free-will problem?

V. CONTINGENCIES AS AUTONOMY LIMITING

As we have seen, all parties should agree that many contingencies just are out of our control, whether the world is deterministic or not. An unalterable state, implanted or not, that appears prior to the time when a person can exercise critical control over his life and that plays a role in decision making limits the freedom of any agent. The controversy must then concern contingencies that would normally be regarded as alterable and are relevant to our action-guiding ideals. Libertarians and other incompatibilists regard these as disturbing in a deterministic world. For, on their view, no control can be exercised over them in a way that allows us to think that that control really originated in the agent, even in cases in which an agent changes a contingency in accordance with her ideals and values. Incompatibilists insist that a decision giving rise to resolute and successful steps to quit smoking is an expression of freedom or genuine self-control only if the world is indeterministic. Compatibilists, on the other hand, would insist that some contingent states can be freely altered by us as we mature, even in a deterministic world, thereby permitting differences in freedom among people even in such a world. Can reflections on autonomy help us either overcome this deepest of impasses or at least reduce its sting?

VI. DETERMINISM AS A THREAT TO FREE WILL AND AUTONOMY

What, precisely, is the threat posed by determinism to the freedom of the will? Determinism can only pose a threat if freedom is construed as power. Determinism is certainly harmless if we adopt a hierarchical conception of freedom; surely, freedom as hierarchical theorists see it – some sort of internal harmony grounded in an identification with one's state of being – can exist in a deterministic world.[6] Nor can determinism threaten freedom understood negatively, that is, as the absence of constraints or potential interference, as the classical compatibilists like Hobbes and Hume pointed out.

These classical compatibilists and their successors would certainly invoke the time-honored distinction between determination and compulsion (coercion) should an incompatibilist regress to a bygone era by conflating these notions as the basis of the worry. This can happen if negative freedom is expanded to embrace as well the effects of any (sufficient) cause. Sophisticated incompatibilists from C. A. Campbell[7] at mid-twentieth century to Robert Kane[8] at the end of that century eschew the appeal of this conflation by seeking ways to argue for the freedom-undermining character of sufficient causes that do not require us to view them as coercive or compelling.

Sadly, however, the appeal is perennially tempting. For example, incompatibilists who wish to challenge Harry Frankfurt's celebrated claim that the mere fact that an agent lacks alternative possibilities does not imply that the agent is not morally responsible naturally seek a responsibility-defeating feature of determination other than the elimination of alternative possibilities. Here is Laura Waddell Ekstrom's attempt to do this: "Moral responsibility requires indeterminism so that an agent is not *pushed* by previous events. . . . A free act is one done deliberately from a preference of the agent's such that the preference was not *coercively* imposed. . . . It is primarily this "pushing" or *compelling* feature of determinism, in my view, that rules out morally responsible agency [italics mine]."[9]

I cannot improve on the many objections to this conflation found throughout the compatibilist literature.[10]

Some incompatibilists view determinism as a threat to moral responsibility independently of its implications for freedom or power. Advocates of the so-called direct argument infer nonresponsibility from determinism without resting their case on the assumption that determinism annuls power or control. In a thoughtful review of such efforts, Michael McKenna concludes that the best version of the direct argument bases the incompatibility of determinism and responsibility on the fact that we would not be the ultimate sources of our own actions in a deterministic world.[11] This argument would presumably be congenial to those incompatibilists like Kane who worry about the fate of self-formation or ultimate responsibility. But Kane himself is not sympathetic with the direct argument just because he sees ultimate responsibility as at least requiring the power to choose, a power he supposes is jeopardized by determinism.

I believe that Kane's repudiation of the direct argument is justified. Here is the direct argument that McKenna views as the best an incompatibilist can produce:

1. *p* and no one is or ever has been even partly responsible for the fact that *p*.
2. i. *p* is part of the actual sequence of events *e* that gives rise to *q* at *t*3.
   ii. *p* is causally sufficient for the obtaining of *q* at *t*3 and any other part of *e* that is causally sufficient for *q* either causes or is caused by *p*.
   iii. no one is or ever has been even partly responsible for 2.i. and 2.ii.
3. Therefore, no one is or ever has been even partly morally responsible for the fact that *q* obtains at *t*3.[12]

In essence, I am not responsible for an action in a deterministic world because I am responsible neither for facts concerning the distant past nor for the fact that those facts are causally sufficient for *q*.

If *q* is the fact that I raise my arm at *t*3, then we may suppose that I possess all the compatibilist freedoms – for example, the absence of compulsion, coercion, mental illness, irrationality, duress, ignorance, the presence of all skills including critical competence relevant to bringing about $\sim q$, as well as, individuality, dignity, and maturity. We may suppose as well that I fulfill the sort of criteria of responsibility embodied in the theory of John M. Fischer and Mark Ravizza – that is, I was guiding my action in a reasons-responsive way.[13]

As David Widerker has argued, it is difficult to see how a defender of McKenna's version of the direct argument could respond to someone who is sufficiently impressed by the array of compatibilist freedoms that she simply denies that determinism entails that I must have raised my arm at *t*3.[14] A classical compatibilist who concedes the premises of this argument, but who does not see that those premises establish the unavoidability of *q*, will not infer the conclusion and will instead, in light of the facts about me, conclude that I *am* responsible for *q*. The defender of the argument will have no recourse but to *abandon* the direct version in favor of one that reverts to the familiar complaint about determinism, to wit, that it narrows options to the actual.

Later, we shall be in a better position to examine the worry that determinism is troublesome not because it nullifies power, but rather because it undermines genuine "authorship" of decisions and actions.

But if freedom is power, it is clearly different from autonomy. The absence of many powers (and the presence of others) is simply irrelevant to autonomy. I may not care at all – indeed, I may be delighted – that I lack certain abilities, including the ability to make a specific decision. The development or expression of my self as I conceive it may be in no way frustrated by the presence of these limitations. My decision making is unaffected because no feasible options are closed to me. There are, of course, logically possible scenarios under which any action type would become an urgency; but my autonomy now and for any remotely plausible future does not embrace the ability now and for any remotely plausible future to (decide to) become a jockey or (decide to) say "waffle" twenty times in succession. And if my autonomy has been compromised by a subtle conditioning process conducted by the nefarious Anti-Jockey Society in which my natural desire to become a jockey had been quashed, then just assume that this or any other autonomy-reducing episode had not occurred. As long as an autonomous agent is one for whom not every option is a live one, we can easily drive a wedge between freedom (power) and autonomy.

Might these conclusions allay concerns raised by the specter of determinism? If freedom is not power, determinism is no threat and the free-will problem may be ignored in a discussion of autonomy. And if freedom is power, its diminution is not automatically a threat to autonomy. And we don't, therefore, have to worry if compatibilist efforts to find power in a deterministic world fail. But the situation is more complicated.

VII. INDEPENDENT FORMATION OF ACTION-GUIDING IDEALS

Some, perhaps many, Motivational Input States are embedded in me prior to the time I can critically form a life plan, hierarchy of values, or ego ideal. The possibility that later reflection may in fact be influenced by the very limits imposed by the world must be conceded. Indeed, some individuals unknowingly form preferences adaptively – that is, they "adjust their preference rankings on the basis of their beliefs about the feasibility of the options . . . in order to ensure against frustration."[15] But we need not highlight extreme cases to recognize that the formation of an ego ideal is colored by facts about ourselves, including our limitations. It appears, then, that we really cannot say in these cases in which a self-conception is yet to be formed that the limitations on freedom can be shown *not* to affect autonomy. The agent's indifference to some inability may disguise a case of covert conditioning leading up to this outcome. If autonomy is the power over options of interest and interest is determined in part by the power we in fact have, then we cannot dismiss as irrelevant the specter raised by a doctrine that challenges the very possibility of power that transcends the actual.

The situation may not be as irremediable as it appears. Consider a simple case. Mel, a New Yorker, grows up as a loyal Knicks fan and is unable to shift his preference to the Bulls when he moves to Chicago. We can compare this to a possible scenario in which either these loyalties are easily changed or are actually formed on the basis of critical reflection. If we ask Mel whether he would have preferred either of the latter arrangements, especially in light of the fact that they would most likely have led to a result that renders life more pleasant in certain ways – as a Bulls fan, he can feel closer to his new community – he is likely to answer in the negative because the installation of this new freedom will alter in adverse ways the very character of this engagement. It is a curious fact that some of the most important activities in life are the very ones in which we happily lose a great deal of control to the other. The most compelling example is love, for we prefer *not* to choose to engage in the activities and undergo the emotions and patterns of thinking intrinsic to loving. If I had been presented with the opportunity to choose, I would have the power to exercise a degree of control that would undermine the nature and special quality of my involvement. One *falls* in love. One finds oneself bound to a person, an ideology, a movement, or a job and are happy to be swept along by the rhythm and demands of the relationship. The same is true of rooting for a team. We don't want this to become one of the spheres of our autonomy. If team allegiance were under the domain of the voluntary, its attractiveness as a life form would be seriously compromised. Again, we want to *find* ourselves under a constraint to root for a certain team, and we want for the most part not to be able to alter that fact.[16]

But how autonomous is Mel's conservative predilection concerning this aspect of his life? Even if all our specific preferences are rooted deterministically in our backgrounds, the specific preference to omit team preference from the domain of the voluntary is not itself dependent upon the same factors that determine our specific allegiances. We are not asking about Mel's allegiance to the Knicks, but rather about his general attitude – what it is like to be a fan – toward rooting, toward feeling disappointment or joy at the fate of some team. Human beings are sufficiently complex so as often to permit or demand critical reflection on the generic that is not in any simpleminded way determined by the same elements that fix the specific configurations. Evidently, there are forms of life that, unlike this one, we would readily submit to our control if we could. The vast majority of us would love to be able to exercise greater control over our physical limitations, our moods, our fears, our addictions. There is nothing like adaptive preference formation on a grand scale.

If we are to dismiss incompatibilist concerns about limitations to our power over matters that are irrelevant to our action-guiding ideals, we must ensure that the formation of those ideals is itself autonomous and that result would be undermined by the discovery that these very limitations have influenced the construction of our ideals. It is important, then, to note that the latter concern can be assuaged without addressing the generic incompatibilist worry. For it is a broadly empirical question as to whether two matters are causally connected. If Mel's ideals in general are causally divorced in the appropriate way from the contingencies of his life – for example, his unalterable love of the Knicks – we can use this fact as a wedge between autonomy and freedom so as to preserve Mel's autonomy vis-à-vis fandom in spite of his unfreedom vis-à-vis his love of the Knicks.

But surely the fact that Mel enjoys rooting for the Knicks has something to do with his endorsement and pursuit of such activities. So we must here rely on the fact that Mel would feel the same way about team loyalty even if he were a Bulls fan. The sort of causal independence we are looking for then would involve the capacity to adopt operative principles for the formulation of action-guiding ideals (from desires and values) that are causally independent of the utilities of the desires and values themselves. If such principles can be objectively grounded, autonomy demands that they be held for the reasons that ground them. Otherwise, autonomy at least demands that there be grounds for a principle independent of the satisfaction of fulfilling a specific desire or value. The principle is supposed to enter to adjudicate competing claims on the assumption that each claimant has some sort of case already. So even if the principle itself rests on contingent circumstances, they must be different from the contingency of the desire-satisfaction itself.

Consider a simple case. Jones desires A and desires B. He desires A more than B and can certainly secure either if he wishes. There is no other relevant consideration. Jones has a principle of action that dictates that he choose to act on the stronger desire, other things being equal. The use of this principle in favor of A does not depend on the greater utility assigned to A because the principle would survive a reversal of preferences.

Another way to understand independence is to see the adoption of the principle for adjudicating disputes among conflicting values as determined not by the specific content of those values. One chooses to act on the stronger desire, not because it happens to be A, but rather because it is the stronger; one chooses to return the money, not because it is a transfer of money, but rather because it is an act of honesty.

We spoke above about an initial assignment of utility to each value realization antecedent to rational appraisal. But it is simplistic to suppose that these ends receive an initial assignment based on their raw attractiveness and that is then adjusted in light of other considerations. For at any level, these assignments already depend upon whether other values of the agent are realized. For example, the value to Mel of his bond to the Knicks may depend in part on other features of the social context. Mel prizes the liberal atmosphere that repudiates the conferral of official status on a particular team, exclusive rooting for which would then be socially required. If he lived in a more repressive society, he would not enjoy the status of a fan as much. That this sort of freedom is realized, therefore, enhances the quality of his appreciation of his life as a fan, and it may be impossible to isolate something called the intrinsic value of fandom – that is, its value antecedent to its interconnections with other elements of value. People generally enjoy smoking less when they are ostracized by people they respect. At any level, therefore, utility assignments to some outcome are made relative to larger perspectives that identify the social setting and other contextual features bearing on the value of the outcome.

A smoker may come to value smoking less either as a result of a revulsion induced by repeated displays of the harmful effects of tobacco or as the result of having adopted principles regarding the primacy of health. In the latter case, if the adoption of the principle depends upon the fear of smoking-induced illness, the principle is adopted heteronomously. To be sure, the fear of ill health, like the pleasure of smoking, is entitled to be fed into the calculations. But we must avoid double entries. We cannot base the autonomy of the decision to quit smoking on a principle of decision making whose adoption or use is itself determined by a desire certified by that very principle.

Thus, even in a deterministic world, an agent who forms a set of action-guiding ideals without the undue influence of her Motivational Input States may be counted autonomous.

Of course, it could turn out that Mel's general views about the life of a fan have been nonautonomously acquired even if the manner of acquisition is independent of the way he became a Knicks fan. An incompatibilist may concede that, because the causal source of Mel's indifference or hostility to the power to change team loyalty is different from that of his specific loyalty to the Knicks, his inability to change team loyalty does not per se undermine his autonomy. But the very fact that his general views are determined at all is sufficient, in the eyes of the incompatibilist, to nullify his autonomy.

A response to the incompatibilist, who is unhappy about *any* sort of deterministic story, requires us to step back and look more carefully at the nature of ideal autonomy.

VIII. IDEAL AUTONOMY

I do not want to argue for a conception of ideal autonomy. But we will be in a better position to respond to the incompatibilist worry by attempting to construct a plausible conception. We begin with the stipulation that an (ideally) autonomous agent be bereft of any unalterable (or even difficult to alter) Motivational Input traits when he reaches the point at which he is able to begin to exercise critical control over his life. The capacity to alter any trait will then nullify concerns about the autonomy-reducing character of its origin.

A standard rejection of the inclusion of this feature in a definition of autonomy rests on the familiar fact that decision making for humans demands fixed parameters against which answerable questions can be raised. When everything is up for grabs, we cannot formulate a coherent problem. To decide on a school, I have to take my interests in (or distaste for) certain subjects for granted. If I can alter them at will, I have to consider my personality and my fundamental preferences and principles. But then, those are not fixed either, ad infinitum.

But the fact that an assumption in a decision-making context *can* be challenged by one with the resources to alter it does not imply that autonomy demands that it actually *be* challenged. Decision making, by its nature, requires assumptions, and it is incoherent to demand that all assumptions be questioned at once.

So what is wrong with providing possibilities for our autonomous agent that he can avail himself of should the need arise, even though the nature of decision making and the incoherence of universal doubt restricts the conceivable application of this power? Why not imagine a maximal level of freedom (power) as we forge ahead to form a self-conception? Why worry needlessly about the undue influence of limitations in the construction of a sense of self? We can always modify the account along more realistic lines later to permit the rest of us to be counted *a little* autonomous.

We also need to provide our budding autonomous agent with a disposition to submit any matters to rational criticism if circumstances warrant. Aware of her enormous power, she must question the perpetuation of states when alteration might be advantageous. Some people who can make improvements in their lives suffer from character defects: lethargy, dispiritedness, weakness of will. So we must also posit in our autonomous agent self-knowledge (already implicit in the recognition that autonomy requires relevant knowledge), an alertness to opportunities for improvement, and an appropriately strong will. Thus, even if the roots of the self are external, uprooting by the self is always an option, and one that will be exercised if deemed appropriate. For full autonomy, we posit, at least at first, full freedom.

But even if we suppose that our autonomous agent is a purposive creature averse to massive frustration who must, therefore, rank her purposes and desires so as to be able to act intelligently, she needs to have some way to choose among all those consistent sets of mutually supporting desires or lifestyles that, given the nature of the world, do not result in massive frustration. She cannot do this in a purely quantitative way because a life of many fulfilled and few unfulfilled desires may be inferior to one in which the few achievements that have been reached are sufficiently profound or worthy so as to offset all the minor nuisances and frustrations.

We may suppose that, because this individual will be as autonomous as possible, she will rule out purposes – for example, slavery – that severely limit the perfect autonomy with which she begins. I say "severely," because in a sense all purposes are autonomy-limiting, even to an Übermensch. To act on a desire is to enter a commitment that restricts future possibilities. One cannot act on the desire to make someone his friend while planning to betray the individual. One cannot act on the desire to be a good soldier while planning to skip shooting practice. Here, again, however, we confront an analogous dilemma: How can such decisions be made on a quantitative basis? Is a tyrant who makes life-or-death decisions lacking in much autonomy because he has relegated the numerous day-to-day decisions regarding choice of clothing, food, etc. to his underlings? Is a "slave" more autonomous because he makes a greater number of decisions (red or blue shirt, chicken or beef stock, and the like) than the tyrant? Clearly not.

Thus, without a set of values that would enable the autonomous individual to order her desires, nonarbitrary choice among the set of consistent purposes is impossible. Without a starting point from which to view one's possible values, no priorities can be constructed and no directed action can be taken. Thus, the assumptions required to initiate decision making will include significant personal commitments reflecting the agent's sense of importance and revealing what she truly cares about.

The sting of this methodological demand is assuaged somewhat by the recognition that the adoption of those assumptions that admit of objective grounding is autonomous so long as they are held in virtue of their ground. But then there are the contingencies. Many preferences are just not grounded in the nature of things. One may dispute the status of religious preference and character training; but choices of occupation, mate, friends, locale, food, dress, recreation, etc., are not objectively grounded. So even if some decisions of value are objective, many questions about significance cannot be so construed. That is, I need a set of values to make decisions under the superhuman conditions now being envisaged; but no basis exists for choosing a set in the absence of a perspective that already incorporates a hierarchy of values and principles. To be sure, given the preferences, arbitrary as they may be, decisions regarding action can be perfectly rational. If I love broccoli, I should buy some. But if autonomy is incompatible with arbitrary choice, and choice is arbitrary if its basis is, then even our Übermensch falls short.

If we cannot annul the arbitrary character of an assumption, we may still impose significant necessary conditions on its autonomous possession. We can demand of each unexamined state that (1) the failure to have been examined not be explained by cognitive incapacity, emotional deficit, or preclusion by an outside agency; (2) the state not conflict seriously with other values and principles of the agent; and (3) the state would have been endorsed had it been submitted to critical review.[17] For example, a person goes through life never questioning the desirability of acting on the desire to quench her thirst. It does not actually conflict with any of her desires, values, or principles and would have been endorsed wholeheartedly had an occasion for reflection arisen. Moreover, she could have taken steps to control it (through temporary suppression or elimination or just not acting on it) if, as in an example of Joseph Raz,[18] an occasion arose for her to fulfill a powerful desire to supply medical aid to a distant community by embarking on a journey during which drinking water would be unavailable. If we cannot certify that the agent is fully autonomous, we can at least demand that these conditions be met.

If then we suppose that human agents are de facto barred from attaining full autonomy by the contingencies of their existence, it appears that that de facto barrier cannot be entirely removed even for a being free of limits. Herein lies the moral of this tale of the Übermensch. For even he needs a starting point that, as arbitrary, cannot be certified as autonomously possessed. But perhaps this concession is premature. Perhaps the contingencies are not barriers to autonomy in the first place.

IX. ARE CONTINGENCIES REALLY AUTONOMY LIMITING?

Imagine a child on whom a Motivational Input State has been imposed prior to the age of reason. If this state is to play a role in her later decision making, and if it can be objectively grounded, then she need not have diminished autonomy so long as the state is maintained in virtue of its ground. But what if it is a contingency and lacks a ground? If the state is unalterable and later circumstances make it desirable (in her eyes) to change it, the agent's live options will be narrowed and her autonomy will suffer. But suppose, unlike Mel, who moved to Chicago, this will not happen. Imagine, in fact, that God has arbitrarily dispensed various sets of mutually supporting contingencies in a Garden of Eden from which humans will not be expelled. So Harry wants to be a barber, and there is plenty of work for barbers. He loves broccoli, and it is always plentiful. He loves the beach, and there are ample sites just east of Eden at reasonable prices. He prefers brashness, bawdy humor, basketball, beer, bassoons, blondes, benevolent human beings, bowler hats, and Braque collages, and the Garden is replete with them. Frank has a different set of tastes, just as readily satisfiable. Why should it matter that any of these states cannot be changed *given that there is no reason to do so*? If we all need starting points and none is better than another, is it not a mistake to view Frank and Harry as disadvantaged in autonomy?

In the real world, we often need to change the contingencies, for, as in Mel's case, circumstances change. There is scarcity, growth, or internal conflict. So it is important to autonomous agents in the real world that alteration be possible. A poor person who inherits a penchant for champagne tastes is less able to choose her life than a rich person with peasant tastes. And although the effect of this initial distribution of contingencies is most clearly seen on proficiency (the power to effect choices), there is also an impact on decision making. For example, a knowledge of the likelihood of achieving one's goals affects the manner in which one attains a preference ordering among goals and an environment that persistently frustrates the realization of one's fondest dreams can eventually take an emotional toll on one's decision-making capacities.[19] So there is a powerful de facto effect on autonomy of the manner of distribution of the contingencies. But might the importance be of an extrinsic character only? What possible value can there be in changing *ab initio* sets of desires that are of equal value? Suppose, for example, that we control the selection of contingencies by making it beforehand, behind a veil of ignorance. Mel is an avid sports fan for whom life would be much duller without his passionate involvement in the fate of the Knicks. And, of course, from his perspective, it is unthinkable that he convert to the Bulls. But were he to choose *ab initio*, he would have no a priori reason to prefer the Knicks to the Bulls. Assuming he does not move to Chicago and has no other extrinsic reason to shift loyalties, the option of conversion is of no interest to him, and his inability to change is, therefore, not a barrier to autonomy.

Might it then be that our earlier conclusion that the contingencies surely limit our autonomy even *in principle* was premature? If one were lucky to have inherited contingencies that mesh perfectly with the world one happened to inhabit, why would one not have the capacity for perfect autonomy? Because said mesh can obtain in a deterministic world, our autonomy may be fortuitous, but no less real. Or, in the event that one is not quite this fortunate, is one not as (potentially) autonomous if blessed with the power to make suitable alterations in the initial distributions so as to attain the same perfect mesh?

The mesh I have in mind here is a match between the world and the realization of values, not the world and contentment (or happiness). Thus, we are not imposing any limits on the selection of ultimate values or ideals. An autonomous agent may choose a fundamental ideal – say, useful work – that results in an unhappy life under certain circumstances. His world is safe for autonomy should it permit useful work regardless of the effect on his happiness.

Might we now have a response to the conceptual problem posed by the necessity for valuational assumptions? For the arbitrary character of the ultimate valuational posits can now be seen to be matters of indifference in principle. May we then say that an omnipotent agent whose valuational assumptions fulfill the aforementioned necessary conditions of autonomous possession is *fully* autonomous in the sense that he has all the freedom that is worth having?

To be sure, a person who bemoans the prospect of membership in a deterministic world may look at his endowments and come to believe that "the grass is greener on the other side," that he would have a richer and more fulfilling life had he been invested with a different set of starting points. He is jealous of those who can appreciate the finer things of life. So he comes to have second-order desires to replace the first-order package, not for extrinsic reasons – they are just as mutually supporting and easy to satisfy as those in the contemplated exchange set – but for genuinely intrinsic ones; namely, they would, he supposes, be more satisfying in the way that matters to him, say, in terms of fulfillment. These new, second-order desires and beliefs appear as part of a new perspective, for they may affect his decision making.

If his belief is false, then his autonomy is adversely affected not because of determinism, but because he is under an illusion that distorts his reasoning and his emotions. If his belief is true, then he recognizes that he is less fortunate in the way anyone born with a handicap is less fortunate. Perhaps, by dint of a dearth of variety, he is getting bored, and cannot, for that reason, find fulfillment. He cannot realize his values. Again, the fault does not lie with determinism – he might be living in an indeterministic world and lack the power to alter a condition that impairs his capacity for fulfillment. So we repeat the question: What possible nonextrinsic benefit can there be in changing sets of desires that are *really* of equal value?

If the answer is "none," then what disadvantage to autonomy per se is suffered by one who is born into a deterministic rather than an indeterministic world?[20]

In an effort to find one, the incompatibilist can retreat to the following position.

> Perhaps I must concede that so-called 'de facto autonomy' is genuine autonomy. There are people who establish their autonomy by managing (rationally, independently, etc.) to realize their values, whether the world is deterministic or indeterministic. But if the world is deterministic, no one who fails to attain de facto autonomy really possesses the capacity for it at all. Since people have more real options in an indeterministic world, there is likely to be more autonomy in such a world.

This admission constitutes an abandonment of an incompatibilist stance vis-à-vis autonomy (for it allows autonomy in a deterministic world) and narrows the sphere of controversy a great deal. Call this position "diluted incompatibilism (DI)."

X. AUTONOMY WITHOUT FREE WILL

We have been able to some extent to face down the skeptic about free will. For worries arising from the deterministic origin of Motivational Input States can be combated by the following simple argument: The etiology of states that admit of objective grounding is irrelevant, whereas the etiology of contingencies bears on one's luck, a feature of all worlds, deterministic or indeterministic.

With respect to the former, we have argued for the irrelevance to autonomy of the origin, possibly deterministic, of the desires, values, and beliefs that, as objectively grounded, permit an agent to retain them in virtue of the reasons for doing so.

With respect to the latter, the world does not confer objective merit on a Knicks' victory over the Bulls or vice versa. To a committed fan, there may be enormous significance to the outcome of a game; but that tells us about his preferences after the fact. In the state of nature, behind a veil of ignorance, there is nothing to choose between the Knicks and the Bulls. Hence, one should be indifferent to these endowments from the point of view of initial autonomy. If God had asked me at the time to make the choice, I would have been unable to make a rational, nonarbitrary (autonomous) decision, and I cannot, therefore, care that God never did.

Thus, there are both autonomous and nonautonomous agents in a deterministic world, including many who never in fact attain a satisfactory adjustment of their desires and values. Proponents of DI believe in addition that, in such a world, *no one* who fails to attain this adjustment is autonomous.

XI. THE INCOMPATIBILIST DEMAND FOR SELF-CREATION

Before abandoning the prospects for undiluted incompatibilism, we ought in fairness to consider the charge that we are overlooking a fundamental value relevant to autonomy that is lost in a deterministic world. In accusing the incompatibilist of possibly harboring a yen for power – a feature that would appear to have no intrinsic worth in the case of contingencies – we ought to recognize that the yen in question may rather be for one of a set of closely related features linked to, but not identical with, power. One might put the complaint in the following way:

> I want more options (power) for I want the determination of my future to rest with me. If my decision is determined, I am not its real author; and if I am not its real author, I have forgone the opportunity to take responsibility for what I become, for the values I live by. Even in the case of the contingencies, I want to make the choice in spite of the absence of good reasons for so doing. I want to put my mark on my life so that it is an expression of my individuality.[21] If I am "ultimately responsible" for my nature and my values (Kane), I can take credit or blame for the results and that is what makes me fully human.

In this chapter, we are not taking the incompatibilist head on, but are rather conceding the case to him, just so that we can see how detrimental to our autonomy is such a concession. But our charitableness goes just so far. Yes, we will allow that determinism entails that we can only decide and act in the way we do decide and act. But that means just that, that the subject of decision and action is the agent, the self. There is a robust sense – one that survives incompatibilist worries – according to which it is a fact that *I* decide and that *I* act antecedent to the project of explaining decisions and actions even if it is concluded that I had to decide and act as I did. And agents can, in a deterministic world, take responsibility for their decisions and actions (even if an incompatibilist deems them foolish for so doing). And if it is I who decide, then the decision that is made reflects me, my individuality. I have put my mark on the world even if someone else who is like me in all relevant respects would put the same sort of mark. (Even in a deterministic world, there may be no other person like me in all relevant respects.)

An incompatibilist may retort that I am begging the question by assuming a compatibilist conception of the self, one that in a sense reduces the self to a set of mental states and processes. Without directly responding to this charge, I think it can be dismissed in the context for the following reasons.

If the incompatibilist envisages this self antecedent to the emergence of a real human being (who would, of course, be limited in all sorts of ways long before the emergence of a sense of self), there is nothing in this pre-immersion state that makes this being an individual, different from every other self. (These conclusions obtain whether or not the incompatibilist accepts the theory of agency, the view that the self is capable of exerting causal influence directly rather than through the states and processes of the self.) How are two identical selves confronting decisions that can only be made in completely arbitrary ways to assert their individuality, to make their distinctive mark on the world? (If each tosses a coin, both coins might end up heads!) So much for our alleged disregard of individuality.

Although in the real world we do not construct a system of preferences from scratch, the failure to find an objective basis from which to complain about the distribution of the contingencies shows that we humans are not at an a priori disadvantage in the development of our autonomy over these hypothesized creatures we have been contemplating. Foundationalism founders as much here as it does in epistemology. Some of us are disadvantaged by the imposition in childhood of distorted value systems; but the problem lies in the distortions, not in the imposition. For we must begin from somewhere. Thus, even a concept of ideal autonomy cannot rest on the idea of autonomous construction of self, for that is incoherent. The self is, of necessity, formed from without – the self is not yet there to do it – and that fact cannot diminish autonomy if the latter is a coherent idea. Of course, infants can have some of the tools of autonomy – perhaps innate knowledge of certain things. But it would be incoherent to object to arbitrary, initial perspectives in the case of the contingencies, for they are, of necessity, both arbitrary and required for the sort of decision-making creatures that we are.

Therefore, we reject the extreme incompatibilist position that contends that no human being is autonomous because no human being has ever been in a position to create himself or herself *ex nihilo*.

We look then to incompatibilists who confront the implications of our actual immersion in the world and do not bemoan our inability to confront real choices with the freedom of one picking from a deck of fifty-two cards. Here, Robert Kane's self-forming actions are a case in point.[22] They represent instances of self-formation that take place as we mature and confront decisions in the context of psychological and situational givens. We approach these situations with reasons provided by our mental constitution and with limitations provided by our physical and emotional makeup, so that any decision that emerges is under the causal influence of these elements. But in Kane's eyes, only if our wills are capable of an indeterministic decision may we be judged ultimately responsible for that decision.

When Kane talks of these self-forming actions (or acts of will) as value experiments, he highlights a type of choice that may be difficult to make for two reasons: First, it may concern a contingency, that is, a choice among options that does not admit of objective grounding; and second, the limited ways in which reason may be brought to bear are hampered in one way or another – for example, a dearth of relevant information.

Harry must decide whether to ask Sally to marry him. The wisdom of this decision depends upon future facts unavailable to Harry. Without a sufficient reason to do so, he performs a value experiment and pops the question anyway. Twenty years later, he concludes that he was right to do so.

Although Harry lacked a sufficient *reason* at the time of the proposal, there may have been a sufficient *cause*. But if there had been a sufficient cause, Harry would have had to do what he did, or so we are conceding. Kane concurs and concludes that the inability to decide otherwise nullifies Harry's ultimate responsibility.

Now, if the sufficient cause did not include Harry's reasons, insufficient as they were as reasons, then clearly Harry lacked freedom. All parties to disputes about freedom and autonomy must agree that a necessary condition of the very possibility of freedom *and* autonomy is that we act as we do for the reasons we cite. The verdict of the compatibilist regarding the implications of a discovery that neurophysiological laws govern human behavior in general or that a particular occurrence was brought about by neurophysiological processes should be the same as that of the incompatibilist. Both ought to be driven by the thought that free and autonomous agents are responsive to reasons in a sense that precludes an account of behavior in terms of neurophysiological processes that *displace* the one in terms of reasons. Compatibilists must pin their hopes on the existence of (possibly deterministic) laws that mirror the intentionality of decision making, that reflect our status as reason-giving creatures. Only such beings can be conceived as free, autonomous, and responsible.[23]

Thus, we suppose that, even if there were a sufficient cause and Harry could not have decided otherwise, he decided as he did for the (insufficient) reasons he had. Harry is just as rational in a deterministic world as he is in an indeterministic one. Of course, because the reasons were insufficient, there must have been distinct nonrational causal factors leading to Harry's decision. But this is true whether or not Harry's decision is indeterministic. Kane wisely rejects the extreme libertarian position according to which the self is the sole causal factor in a free, undetermined decision. So even though it is perhaps logically possible in a self-forming action for the reasons to constitute all the causally relevant factors, it is wildly implausible to believe that the agent is not to a certain extent influenced by other considerations. (Obviously, when the decision is undetermined, these influences only change the probabilities.)

In limiting Harry's decision to an instance of *self*-formation only if it is undetermined, Kane thereby expresses sympathy for the incompatibilist complaint we are currently addressing. Determinism, he supposes, destroys authorship in spite of the fact that it is *superior or equal* to indeterminism in terms of the following criteria of freedom: (1) the capacity for action from *sufficient* reason;[24] (2) control; (3) freedom from luck; and (4) freedom from arbitrariness.

Why introduce the elusive notion of authorship if the real complaint is loss of power, a complaint we have already addressed? That is, if an agent blessed with all the compatibilist freedoms (noncoercion, rationality, knowledge, mental health, etc.) makes a decision in which he is under the causal influence of a variety of factors (including factors that render the decision reasonable), then Kane is tentatively prepared to regard the agent as having free will in the sense that he is ultimately responsible for that decision. But should we discover further that the causal information adds up to a deterministic account, then Kane would insist that we withdraw that judgment *not because of the inference that the agent could not have decided otherwise.* That is implausible. If Kane could be convinced that determinism does not imply that we cannot act otherwise, what conceivable basis would he have for this demand? Why would he believe that the decision was not self-forming? He is clearly driven by a picture in which agents *choose* from reasons even when their choices fall under statistical causal laws until those laws become deterministic. At that point, the causes magically become the agents and they do the choosing. And the reason for this transition is presumably *not* that determination tells us that the causes "made me do it," for that is to complain about loss of power. (It cannot be the complaint that causes literally compel for Kane is too sophisticated to revert to that old charge.)[25] So, although much more needs to be said about the precise nature of the threat posed by determinism, we may conclude that DI's belief that no one who lacks autonomy in a deterministic world could have possessed it is based on a concern about power, not authorship, individuality, or the prospects for self-formation.

We have been addressing two distinct problems pertaining to the contingencies, a historic one and a conceptual one. Historically, each of us is bound to trace our development back to a precritical time in which contingencies became rooted. We have addressed that problem by conceding the importance to our de facto autonomy of the power to make changes in light of circumstances and our developing ideals, but denying any further significance in this context in virtue of the fact that the arbitrariness of preference here reveals at best a lust for power rather than autonomy. The conceptual problem, the demand for assumptions, including important assumptions about personal priorities, inherent in the very nature of decision making, is solved in exactly the same way. Those priorities express the contingencies of our existence, and the worry that they may not be autonomously held can be assuaged by acknowledging that it would indeed be better under special circumstances to be in a position to alter some of them, while also acknowledging that otherwise it does not matter.

So if we are reasonable concerning our expectations, we can have a decent amount of real autonomy even in a world without free will. If the incompatibilist is right, determinism annuls free will, but it is not per se a barrier to autonomy.

Notes

1. See, e.g., Gerald Dworkin, "The Nature of Autonomy," in *The Theory and Practice of Autonomy* (Cambridge: Cambridge University Press, 1988): 3–20.
2. It might be useful here to invoke Alfred Mele's distinction between autonomous origination and autonomous possession, in *Autonomous Agents: From Self-Control to Autonomy* (Oxford: Oxford University Press, 1995): 138–139. That sinister mathematics teacher inculcated the multiplication table by bypassing my critical capacities; but the significance of heteronomous origination should begin to pale once it is recognized that I come to hold these beliefs for the right reasons and can make adjustments if called for.
3. I might have inadvertently learned the truth about some matter such that, were the proposition in question to be false, my experience would *not* have revealed this to be so. Thus, an occasion for reconsideration would not arise. Here again, the key question concerns the grounds on which I continue to hold the belief. If the explanation of the belief's remoteness is that it concerns some exotic fact of theoretical physics, then I might still be justified in uncritically using the proposition in decision making on the basis of the fact that the belief is sustained in virtue of its grounds. For, although its grounds are utterly remote from me personally, I might have good reason to believe that such is not the case for the source of my belief: an expert. Indeed, even the mundane fact about Sacramento can become known, not simply believed, if the belief comes to rest on some sort of reliable source.
4. Bernard Berofsky, *Liberation from Self: A Theory of Personal Autonomy* (Cambridge: Cambridge University Press, 1995). One of the central goals of this book is to reorient the way in which philosophers approach the subject of autonomy. Taking a clue from etymology ("autonomy" is "rule by self"), philosophers are prone to direct their attention to the difference between origination (of decision or action) in the self and origination outside the self. I argue that the focus of certain psychologists on the connection of the agent to the world rather than to origins leads to a preferable account. Autonomous agents are ones who manage to *transcend* their origins to establish a flexible, spontaneous, and objective relation to the world.

5. In order not to beg questions about the desirability of autonomy, "ideality" simply means "practical unrealizability."
6. Michael McKenna correctly pointed out to me that hierarchical theorists are committed to some sort of control (or power) condition, for a freely willed action must be one whose source is the endorsement of the will. Contented slaves are still slaves. But, of course, determinism still does not pose a problem for the hierarchical theorist for she sees that, because determinism is not fatalism, it allows for the possible control of actions by the will; and even if it precludes counterfactual control, the hierarchical theorist does not care about that.
7. C. A. Campbell, "Is 'Freewill' a Pseudo-Problem?" *Mind* 60 (1951): 446–465.
8. Robert Kane, *The Significance of Free Will* (Oxford: Oxford University Press, 1996): 67–69.
9. Laura Ekstrom, *Free Will: A Philosophical Study* (Boulder, CO: Westview Press, 2000): 190, 194.
10. See, e.g., R. E. Hobart, "Free Will as Involving Determination and Inconceivable Without It," *Mind* 43 (1934): 1–27; Moritz Schlick, "When Is a Man Responsible?" in David Rynin, trans., *Problems of Ethics* (Englewood Cliffs, NJ: Prentice Hall, 1939): 143–156; A. J. Ayer, "Freedom and Necessity," *Philosophical Essays* (New York: Macmillan, 1954): 271–284; Paul Edwards, "Hard and Soft Determinism," in Sidney Hook, ed., *Determinism and Freedom in the Age of Modern Science* (New York: New York University, 1958): 104–113; and Kai Nielsen, "The Compatibility of Freedom and Determinism," *Reason and Practice* (New York: Harper & Row, 1971): 55–64.
11. Michael McKenna, "Source Incompatibilism, Ultimacy, and the Transfer of Non-Responsibility," *American Philosophical Quarterly* 38 (2001): 37–51.
12. Ibid., 45.
13. John Martin Fischer and Mark Ravizza, *Responsibility and Control: A Theory of Moral Responsibility* (Cambridge: Cambridge University Press, 1998).
14. David Widerker, "Farewell to the Direct Argument," *Journal of Philosophy* 99 (2002): 316–324.
15. Berofsky, *Liberation from Self*, 204.
16. But not necessarily. Having grown up a Yankee fan and then become disenchanted by the antics of George Steinbrenner, I did not like finding myself rooting for the Yankees.
17. To be sure, the approval might have been contingent on an assumption with heteronomous origins. But that tells us only that this condition is not sufficient for autonomy.
18. Joseph Raz, *The Morality of Freedom* (Oxford: Clarendon Press, 1986): 296.
19. See Berofsky, *Liberation from Self*, 68.
20. We will soon consider the worry that determinism renders genuine creativity by the self impossible.
21. The capacity to make a distinctive mark on the world plays a central role in the conception of autonomy of Lawrence Haworth, *Autonomy: An Essay in Philosophical Psychology and Ethics* (New Haven: Yale University Press, 1986). See, e.g., 88.
22. Kane, *The Significance of Free Will*, 32–37.

23. For further discussion, see Bernard Berofsky, "Classical Compatibilism: Not Dead Yet," in David Widerker and Michael McKenna, eds., *Moral Responsibility and Alternative Possibilities* (Aldershot, England: Ashgate Press, 2003): 107–126.
24. Timothy O'Connor objects to the claim that undetermined actions cannot be performed with sufficient reason, pointing out that, in an indeterministic world, one agent might and another might not perform an action each has sufficient reason to perform. The point is that the other, nonrational causal influences might work indeterministically. Both Joe and Moe should quit smoking, and they are each prone to weakness of will. Although they are equally tempted to continue, Joe finally quits; but Moe does not, and there is no way to account for the difference. I think O'Connor is right and would, not, therefore, view this criterion of freedom as favoring the compatibilist. See his "Agent Causation" in O'Connor, ed., *Agents, Causes, and Events: Essays on Indeterminism and Free Will* (Oxford: Oxford University Press, 1995): 173–200.
25. For further discussion, see Bernard Berofsky, "Ultimate Responsibility in a Deterministic World," *Philosophy and Phenomenological Research* 60 (January 2000): 135–140.

3

Autonomy and the Paradox of Self-Creation

Infinite Regresses, Finite Selves, and the Limits of Authenticity

Robert Noggle

INTRODUCTION

The political state of autonomy has proven to be a compelling metaphor for the condition in which a person is under his or her own control, master of his or her own destiny. The political metaphor suggests that personal autonomy is a condition in which one is not ruled over by external forces. However, there is another dimension to personal autonomy. This is the idea of government *by the legitimate authority*. A usurper takes power from within the state, rather than conquering it from the outside. Likewise, psychological forces can usurp power from a person. Just as a person can lose control to *external* forces such as coercion or peer pressure, so, too, can s/he lose control to *internal* forces.

Apparent examples of internal forces that may threaten to usurp control from its rightful locus include addictions, obsessive-compulsive disorder, pathological gambling, kleptomania, and strong phobias. For those who prefer more-fanciful examples, the philosophical literature on autonomy also includes scenarios involving desires implanted through psychological conditioning, hypnosis, brainwashing, futuristic psychosurgery, and (that old favorite) supernatural intervention. Such forces may seem "alien" or "ego dystonic" because they do not issue from the person's goals, values, and beliefs. Although they come from inside her own head, so to speak, they are not experienced as being part of "who she really is." She seems to be the victim whom they afflict rather than their author. This sense of affliction or alienation is often expressed in more everyday language by a certain special use of the term "self." Thus, a person in the grip of an addiction might explain his behavior by saying that "he is not himself." Philosophers reflect this usage when they say that such forces are not part of the true or real self of the person who is afflicted by them. This sense of the term "self" refers to an especially significant *subset* of the person's psychology. According to this usage, the person's self does not include those internal but phenomenologically alien forces that may afflict her and threaten her personal autonomy. The adjective "authentic" is commonly applied to elements of the person's psychology that are part of or produced by this true or real self.[1] Thus, to say that an impulse is not authentic is to say that it does not lie within that part of a person's psychology that must be in charge if she is to be genuinely autonomous (or that must be the source of her actions if they are to count as autonomous). Depending on how we fill out the theory of autonomy, it is possible that a person's behavior could be caused by authentic elements of her psychology without her being autonomous. For example, coercion may be thought to rob an agent of autonomy, even though the coerced agent's behavior may be caused by authentic desires (e.g., to avoid harm). On most accounts, acting from authentic motivations is a necessary but not sufficient condition for personal autonomy.

I. THE QUESTION OF AUTHENTICITY

A theory of authenticity will determine what must be true of an element of a person's psychology (typically a desire) in order for it to be true that, if that element is in control of the person's activity, the activity may count as autonomous. Thus, a theory of authenticity can be seen as beginning with the following base clause:

Element (or set of elements) E_1 of the psychology of person S is authentic if . . .

Such a theory will then add at least one condition to fill in the antecedent. A great many specific theories about how to do this have emerged. Most propose conditions that fit one of three schemata:

Structural Condition Schema: E_1 is related in the right way to E_2, where E_2 is some other element (or group of elements) of S's psychology.
Historical Condition Schema: E_1 arose in the right way.
Substantive Condition Schema: E_1 has the right content or causes S to believe, desire, intend, or do the right things.

II. AUTHENTICITY AND THE REGRESS PROBLEM

In this section, I will discuss the three types of conditions for authenticity and their susceptibility to the most pervasive objection in the philosophical literature on personal autonomy. Although I will treat them as separate conditions, a particular theory of authenticity may include more than one of them. This possibility should not affect the substance of my remarks, however.

Structural Conditions

Structural conditions define the authenticity of one element of a person's psychology in terms of its relationship to some other element of that same person's psychology. Two forms of structural condition have been prominent in the literature: higher-order desire conditions and partitioning conditions.

Higher-Order Desires. The higher-order desire (HOD) approach to authenticity arose from seminal work by Gerald Dworkin and Harry Frankfurt in the early 1970s.[2] Its basic idea can be illustrated by one of Frankfurt's favorite examples, the unwilling addict. Such an addict suffers a lack of autonomy because he acts upon a desire that he desires to be rid of. The desire to use the drug is a first-order desire, while the desire not to have that desire is a second-order desire. When a person has both a first-order desire and a second-order desire not to have the first-order desire, Frankfurt writes, this repudiated first-order desire is properly regarded as "a force other than his own."[3] By contrast, when an agent endorses, or desires to have, a particular desire, he thereby makes that desire "more truly his own" and "identifies himself" with it.[4] In other words, a desire that is repudiated by a higher-order desire is inauthentic, while a desire that is either endorsed by a higher-order desire or at least not repudiated by one is authentic. Thus, for example, my desire to write a book on autonomy is authentic because it is a desire that I *want* to have. In contrast, my desire to take a nap right now is inauthentic because I want it to go away.

Frankfurt noticed that just as we can ask whether an ordinary desire or impulse is authentic, we can ask the same question about a second-order desire. For second-order desires can themselves result from brainwashing, psychological conditioning, or mental disorders that seem inconsistent with authenticity. If a second-order desire is itself inauthentic, one naturally wonders how it could confer authenticity on a desire that it endorses. The natural response is to claim that a second-order desire must be authentic in order for it to determine the authenticity of a first-order desire. However, this response seems to require that we posit a *third*-order desire to determine whether the second-order desire is authentic. But, of course, nothing prevents us from raising the same question about the authenticity of this third-order desire and to settle it by positing a fourth-order desire, and so on ad infinitum. Frankfurt realized that this potential for an infinite regress was a problem. His proposal was to introduce a somewhat mysterious notion of a "decisive commitment" that " 'resounds' through the potentially endless array of higher order desires."[5]

Frankfurt's critics were quick to criticize this proposal. Collectively, their criticisms came to be known as the "regress problem." This problem first arises when we ask about the authenticity of the second-order desire that endorses (and thus authenticates) the first-order desire. If we answer that question in the same way we answered the question about the authentication of the first-order desire, we simply move the problem back a step; and if we keep doing this, the regress ensues. To avoid the regress, then, we seem to need a different way to ground the authenticity of the highest-order desire in the chain and thus to make it a fit candidate to authenticate the next highest desire, which can now authenticate the next highest desire, and so on down the line. This is what Frankfurt's notion of a decisive commitment was supposed to provide.

However, many critics found this proposal less than satisfying. Frankfurt's "decisive commitment" seemed either to be or to be caused by another desire.[6] Thus, it would seem that this commitment, or the desire that causes it, could be either authentic or inauthentic. If it is authentic, then the theory needs to explain what makes it authentic (and, of course, if the explanation makes reference to some other desire, then the regress threatens again). If it is inauthentic, then we have what John Christman calls the "*ab initio* problem."[7] This problem arises when we make the seemingly implausible claim that a psychological element or process that lacks authenticity can nevertheless impart authenticity to some other element or process.

The regress problem has played a major role in shaping philosophical work on autonomy from the early 1970s onward. Some philosophers attempted to modify the "pure" HOD theory by positing some additional condition that the highest-order desire could fulfill so that it would not need an even higher-order desire to confer authenticity on it. Others responded by rejecting the HOD theory outright. Early on, a partitioning condition – our next topic – was suggested as a potential replacement.

Partitions. Partitioning conditions for authenticity claim that a desire, decision, belief, or other mental element can be authentic in virtue of its being related in a certain way (to be spelled out by the theory) to some more or less distinct psychological structure within the person.

The most influential example of the partitioning approach to autonomy/authenticity was proposed by Gary Watson in 1985.[8] Watson partitions the "springs of actions" into two systems. A person's *motivational system* consists of "that set of considerations which move him to action."[9] The *evaluational system* "assigns values to states of affairs" and consists of "those principles and ends which he – in a cool and non-self-deceptive moment – articulates as definitive of the good, fulfilling and desirable life."[10] Watson links this evaluative system with what we are calling the "authentic self," writing that "one cannot coherently dissociate oneself from it in its entirety. . . ."[11] Normally, the desires produced by the motivational system are in "harmony" with the contents of the evaluational system. But it is possible for a desire produced by the motivational system to conflict with the contents of the evaluational system. When this happens, Watson says, the person is "estranged" from the desire; in our terms, this desire is inauthentic.

Given that Watson offered an early version of the regress argument against Frankfurt's theory, it is perhaps ironic to find that his own theory is susceptible to much the same problem. Just as we can imagine an inauthentic HOD, we can also imagine cases in which an element within the evaluative system seems inauthentic. For instance, a value implanted via surreptitious or involuntary processes like psychological conditioning by a mad scientist, brainwashing by a religious cult, or indoctrination by a totalitarian state would certainly seem inauthentic, especially if it is contrary to the agent's original values. We can even imagine cases in which a person's entire "evaluational system" arose from such processes.[12]

If we assume that elements of an evaluational system can authenticate a motive only if they are themselves authentic, then a regress seems to be in the offing. This regress is structurally isomorphic to the one confronting Frankfurt's theory. In both cases, the theory claims that a desire is authentic only if it bears a certain relation to some other psychological element, either a higher-order desire or an "evaluational system." The problem that makes the regress infinite is simply that the authenticator seems to need an authenticator.

This problem generalizes. For any attempt to locate a mental element or structure that can render other elements authentic, it seems possible to imagine that this new element or structure is as clearly inauthentic as any mental element ever is. At the very least, we can always imagine a science fiction scenario in which the new element or structure has been implanted by a nefarious neurosurgeon, cult, or demon against the wishes of the victim. The defender of the theory now faces a dilemma: She can either make the seemingly implausible claim that even an element or structure of *that* sort can impart authenticity; or posit some psychological element to confer authenticity, only to face the same kind of apparent counterexample as before.[13]

The Ab Initio *Requirement: The Regress Made Insoluble.* For both kinds of structural conditions, the regress problem begins when we ask whether the mental element (E_2) that is supposed to impart authenticity to some other mental element (E_1) is itself authentic. Evidently, we can always imagine a scenario in which the proposed authenticator (E_2) has features that make it seem to be *inauthentic.* If we regard it as implausible for an inauthentic element to impart authenticity to another element, then we will need to guarantee that this proposed authenticator (E_2) is itself authentic before we can be sure that it can impart authenticity to some other element (E_1). And this need will tempt us to posit yet another authenticator, the authenticity of which can then be questioned, and so on.

The force driving this regress is a seductive assumption about what must be the case if a psychological element is to impart authenticity to some other psychological element. In a passage laying out his version of the regress problem, John Christman characterizes one of the horns of the dilemma as "the *ab initio* problem," which he elucidates by asking, "[H]ow can a desire be autonomous [authentic] if it was formed or evaluated by a process that was not itself autonomous."[14] Of course, this could be a genuine request for an explanation, but the context of the question suggests that it may be meant as a rhetorical device to call attention to the apparent implausibility of an inauthentic process giving rise to an authentic product.

Similar suggestions appear throughout the literature on autonomy. Thus, Marilyn Friedman writes of "the old adage that like comes from like; autonomy is not expected to emerge out of processes which are not autonomous, not a person's 'own' to begin with."[15] Stefaan Cuypers writes, "How can there be autonomy without autonomous foundations?"[16] Laura Ekstrom either assumes or attributes to Frankfurt the claim that "the second-order desire can confer internality [authenticity] only if it is internal to the self [i.e., authentic]."[17] The general principle suggested in these passages seems to be that if a psychological element is to confer authenticity on some other psychological element, then it must be authentic. For convenience, we may label this the "*ab initio* requirement." It is a putative requirement on theories of authenticity that they not rest authenticity on inauthentic foundations or derive it from inauthentic sources.

Now, if we can always imagine a case in which it is implausible to regard a given psychological element as authentic, the question of the authenticity of an authenticating element can always be raised. If we accept the *ab initio* requirement, we must give an affirmative answer to that question if the element is to serve as an authenticator. Evidently, the attempt to define the authenticity of one psychological element in terms of its relationship to some other element, together with the *ab initio* requirement, generates a regress. No finite chain of authenticating elements can provide an account of how any element is made authentic, because no element can be the last member of the chain if every member must be authenticated by some other element.

The susceptibility of structural theories to the regress problem might suggest either that an otherwise structural theory will need to include a supplementary nonstructural condition or that we should abandon structural conditions altogether. Historical conditions – our next topic – have been popular both as supplements and as alternatives to structural conditions for authenticity.

Historical Conditions

Historical conditions claim that an element of a person's psychology is authentic if it arose in the right way – the nature of which will be spelled out by the particular theory. Gerald Dworkin offers the following example of a historical condition: The "right way" for an element to arise is under conditions of "procedural independence," which he characterizes by offering examples of conditions that do not count: "hypnotic suggestion, manipulation, coercive persuasion, subliminal influence, and so forth."[18] Christman offers a somewhat more subjective condition: A desire is authentic if it arose by a process to which the person did not object or would not have objected if she had attended to it.[19]

Although specific formulations vary somewhat, the motivating idea behind historical conditions seems to be that a psychological element is authentic if its history is free of the kinds of influences – especially external influences – that seem to undermine authenticity. Because historical conditions make the authenticity of an element depend on its *own* history, they seem to avoid the regress of authenticating elements. Without the requirement of another element to serve as an authentic authenticator, the regress seems to lack a place to get started.

However, I think that this appearance that historical conditions are regress-proof is illusory. To see why, we have to think more about the "right way" for an element to be generated. Most proponents of historical conditions attempt to characterize the "wrong way" for a psychological element to arise. They generally do this by ruling out certain kinds of external forces in the etiology of authentic elements, either by name or by description.

Although it is difficult to characterize these forces precisely, I think it is fair to say that they all involve processes in which the agent's own psychology is not involved at all, or at least not involved in a robust, controlling way. This suggests that, whatever the *right way* is, it will involve elements of the agent's own psychology. The underlying intuition behind this approach seems to be that, in the absence of external interference or other authenticity-undermining processes, a person's psychological elements are free to develop in such a way as to reflect the "real self."[20] If S herself was not involved in the right way in the generation of E_1, then it is difficult to see how E_1 could be plausibly regarded as authentic, given that the core notion of authenticity has to do with belonging to the self. The "right way" for E_1 to be created will evidently have to be some process that involves elements of S's own psychology. Thus, it seems that we can, without distortion, rewrite most, if not all, historical conditions for authenticity as follows:

Revised Historical Condition Schema: E_1 arose in the right way from E_2, where E_2 is one or more element(s) or configuration(s) of elements of S's psychology.

In this way, we can see that the historical condition preserves the idea that authenticity requires a psychological element to have the right relationship to some element of the person's own psychology, which we may take to be a more or less literal "real self." Thus, we might say that both historical and structural theories are, so to speak, "self-referential" in that they define the authenticity of an element by its connection to the self. On this view, the self is, by definition, the determiner of authenticity or inauthenticity, because the authenticity of a psychological element depends on its relationship to the self. In the context of a self-referential theory, this *authenticating self* – however exactly it may be conceived – is the source of authenticity.

When we express the historical condition in this fuller way, we can see how the *ab initio* requirement does, in fact, apply to it. For if authenticity can arise only from something that already has it, then in order for an element (E_1) to be authentic, any other element (E_2) involved in its genesis must also be authentic. And, of course, the *ab initio* requirement also implies that these earlier elements can be authentic only if the elements that caused *them* are also authentic. Thus, if the authenticity of any psychological element or configuration requires that it arise from authentic earlier elements or configurations, then we face an infinite regress of earlier and earlier elements or configurations, each of which must have arisen only from authentic elements or configurations. It is precisely because historical conditions, once unpacked, have the same "self-referential" form as structural conditions that they fall prey to the same regress problem. The *ab initio* requirement apparently guarantees a regress in any authenticity condition that requires one psychological element or configuration of elements to be authenticated by another, whether it is contemporaneous with it or temporally earlier.

In its "synchronic," or contemporaneous, form, such a regress is a problem because we do not have an infinite number of psychological elements ready to serve as authenticators to authenticators to authenticators. . . . In its "diachronic," or historical, form, the regress is a problem because of the obvious fact that we lack infinitely long psychological histories. As we move back in time, we eventually reach a point at which our psychological configurations no longer even exist. And well before then, we find psychological causes that involve processes (often lumped together under the broad heading of "socialization") like conditioning, role model imitation, the internalization of socially endorsed behavioral norms, and the acceptance of claims on the basis of adult authority. Such processes are paradigmatic of the kind of external manipulation, or "brainwashing," that normally seems to undercut autonomy and impart inauthentic attitudes.[21]

Substantive Conditions

As we saw in the previous section, the combination of self-referentiality and the *ab initio* requirement makes both structural and historical conditions susceptible to the regress problem. If we take this problem seriously, we might be tempted to abandon self-referential conditions in favor of a condition that proposes a more objective criterion for the authenticity of a mental element.[22] Such conditions make the authenticity of an element depend on its relationship to some substantive criterion, such as truth, goodness, appropriateness, etc.

Although I cannot mount a comprehensive critique of substantive conditions here, I do want to sketch briefly what I see as the most serious drawback with this approach.[23] As I see it, this approach risks conflating authenticity/autonomy with some other notion – such as moral agency, rationality, or some sort of mental health. Such an approach changes the question, I think, from one about the person's relation to one of her own psychological elements to the question of whether the element, in itself, exemplifies some other property that has nothing to do with the person to whom it belongs. In so doing, a substantive condition abandons the idea of authenticity as involving being a part or product of the person's own self rather than a usurping psychological force. I believe that we should have very compelling reasons before adopting an analysis of a concept that changes the concept into something else.

Of course, if self-referential conditions turn out to be incoherent or otherwise defective, that would count as a compelling reason. It may be thought that the regress problem renders the self-referential approach to authenticity conceptually incoherent. I will argue, though, that the regress problem is driven by an assumption – the *ab initio* requirement – that we have compelling reasons to reject.

III. THE PROBLEM WITH THE REGRESS PROBLEM

The problem with the *ab initio* requirement is that it requires a self-creating self that could never exist. Or, to put the point another way, if we accept that the self cannot be the cause of its own existence, then we must deny the *ab initio* requirement. And clearly we must accept that the self is not self-creating, if for no other reason than that complete self-creation is impossible. This is because complete self-creation would require the truth of two contradictory propositions: first, that the self-creating thing exists, which seems to be necessary for it to *do* anything, such as create something; and second, that the thing does not exist, which must be true in order for it to require to be created. Thus, barring backward causation and temporal loops, true self-creation seems to be a conceptual impossibility, except, perhaps, for God.

Now, if the self cannot be the cause of its own creation and it has not been around forever, then we know that the self must have arisen from something that is not the self. Thus, if a self is possible at all and it has a finite history, then it must at some point arise from materials and forces that are not the self and that are, therefore, inauthentic. Consequently, the *elements* of this initial self *also* must have arisen from something that was not authentic. Now, *ex hypothesi,* these elements are *parts of the initial self;* this fact, together with the core intuition that authenticity has to do with belonging to the self, implies that they are in fact authentic. This implies that a psychological element can be authentic even though it arises from nonauthentic sources. Thus, if the *ab initio* requirement is valid, then *either* the self is self-creating, *or* the self has an infinitely long history, *or* the existence of the self is simply impossible, *or* being an element of the self does not make that element authentic. Because none of the claims expressed in the disjuncts of the consequent are especially plausible, we have good reason to reject the antecedent, that is, the *ab initio* requirement.

IV. RECALCITRANT INTUITIONS

The familiar story has it that, after delivering a public lecture on cosmology, Bertrand Russell encountered an elderly woman who objected to the contemporary theory and offered an alternative: The surface of the earth, she asserted, is really the curved back of a giant turtle. When asked what the turtle was standing on, she replied that it was standing on the back of another, larger turtle. When asked what *that* turtle stands on, she replied, "You can't trick me, young man – it's turtles all the way down." The *ab initio* requirement generates an infinite regress of "turtles," for it requires each authentic turtle to stand on the back of another authentic turtle. To jettison the *ab initio* requirement is to realize that for finite beings like us, "all the way down" is a finite distance and there is a bottom turtle that must stand on something that is not itself a turtle.

Ironically, most philosophers who have posed the regress problem in debates about autonomy recognize, and have often explicitly acknowledged, that ultimate self-creation is impossible. I suspect that the reason why regress arguments are so gripping is that the *ab initio* requirement – even when we do not consciously endorse it as a general principle – tends to drive our intuitions about specific theoretical proposals so as to produce much the same effect as it would if we did explicitly endorse it. To mix metaphors, any attempt to terminate the regress of elements within a self-referential theory will seem intuitively to be too much like pulling an authentic rabbit out of an inauthentic hat. For it will necessarily label at least one element (or configuration of elements) authentic despite the fact that it is not authenticated by any other authentic element(s) (or configurations of elements). Whatever condition is offered to authenticate this "bottom turtle," our knee-jerk intuition is likely to be that this is *really* the job for yet another turtle. And that intuition can only be strengthened by constructing fanciful brainwashing and supernatural intervention scenarios to manipulate the ground on which the bottom turtle stands, so as to make it seem too shaky to support any turtle at all. And imagining that the origin of the first authentic element must involve an *immediate and sudden* transition in which completely inauthentic causes give rise to a completely authentic element makes the intuition stronger still. If we trust *these* intuitions, we will end up rejecting any attempt to cut off the regress – perhaps without ever realizing that if we generalize these intuitions, we end up with an *ab initio* requirement that we have good reason to reject.

Marilyn Friedman calls the idea underlying the *ab initio* requirement an "old adage." I would be more inclined to label it a superstition, for I think that, like any robust superstition, this one may continue to influence our intuitions even when we recognize that it is bunk. As long as the *ab initio* superstition continues to exercise this covert influence, I suspect that we will continue to lack a convincing theory of authenticity, precisely because our intuitions will only be satisfied by something that nothing can possibly be.[24]

The foregoing is, of course, merely armchair psychology. And my "patients" (academic philosophers) are particularly challenging. So it is quite possible that the diagnosis I have sketched does not apply to my current patient. Be that as it may, it still seems to be a sufficiently dangerous syndrome to merit attention. It certainly would help to explain why philosophers working in this area have been so quick to dismiss as counterintuitive any proposed solution to the regress problem. In any case, I think that it shows that we must be suspicious of the feeling that an attempt to terminate the regress in a self-referential theory of authenticity is intuitively implausible – *simply because it derives the authentic from the inauthentic.*

V. WHO'S AFRAID OF THE BIG, BAD REGRESS?

As we saw, rejecting the *ab initio* requirement frees us from the need for an infinite regress of "turtles," that could never be instantiated by beings for whom "all the way down" is a finite distance. It is worth noting that just as we should reject the generalized *ab initio* requirement for an infinite "tower of turtles," so, too, we should reject any *particular* theory of authenticity that makes the same sort of infinite "tower of turtles" a requirement for authenticity. Hence, cutting off any regress that a theory of authenticity may generate should be a high priority for the theory's defenders. Had the *ab initio* requirement been valid, however, such a regress would be *inevitable* for any self-referential theory, and terminating it would render such a theory *implausible*. That would have put any self-referential theory into an insoluble catch-22. But once we reject the *ab initio* requirement (and the intuitions that it may covertly spawn), terminating the regress becomes more like trimming an unruly hedge than like defeating an invincible opponent – difficult, perhaps, but not one that requires a self that can somehow serve as the cause of its own creation. To avoid the regress problem, a theory must not make meeting a self-referential condition *necessary* for an element to be authentic, even if it claims that meeting such a requirement is a *sufficient* condition and the one that most authentic elements fulfill. Thus, a self-referential theory apparently must leave open the possibility of another means by which authenticity can arise besides having it be conferred by some other element that is already authentic. Of course, doing so raises new questions: Just how can authenticity arise from states or processes that cannot be plausibly regarded as being authentic already? If we accept that there is a bottom turtle standing on something that is not itself a turtle, the question becomes, "What is the bottom turtle standing upon?"

VI. THE AUTHENTICATING SELF'S INAUTHENTIC ORIGINS

So how does the authenticating self first arise? The smart-alecky answer is just "gradually." I'll elaborate: It seems clear to me that the self emerges gradually via incremental processes of psychological development during childhood. While the full details of these processes are the proper domain of psychology rather than philosophy, I will nevertheless exercise the philosophers' prerogative to do some armchair psychology.

I begin with what seems to be a near consensus among philosophers working on autonomy: the idea that whatever else the self must have, if it is to ground assertions of authenticity, it must have a stable, orderly, belief system and preference structure, and it must have the psychological mechanisms necessary to allow it to reflect upon and revise those beliefs and desires.

A person's beliefs and desires, I speculate, are structured around a core that consists of those beliefs that constitute her most basic cognitive organizing principles and fundamental assumptions and convictions, together with the desires that constitute her deepest, most significant goals, concerns, commitments, and values. Taken together, these core attitudes form a kind of skeleton for the rest of her psychological structure. In so doing, they form the basis and the ultimate court of appeal for the reflective self-adjustment that allows the self to react and develop in response to changing conditions, improved information, and increasing self-awareness. These core attitudes form a relatively stable framework for the agent's psychology; they play a key role in making the person who she is and giving shape to the rest of her psychological elements. Collectively, they determine what her life is all about and what is important to her; they give shape and contour to her way of looking at, and being in, the world. In a very significant sense, they make her who she is. They may be thought of as forming the wellsprings of higher-order desires, or the values of which Watson writes, or the "character system" of which Laura Ekstrom writes.[25]

In addition to a skeleton of core attitudes, the fully formed self has the ability to adjust and revise its own attitudes. Of course, it does not usually do this for no reason at all. When it alters its *beliefs*, it generally does so on the basis of perceptions and various kinds of reasoning processes (not all of which may be conscious, and not all of which may be sound). Generally speaking, the more peripheral a belief is, the more likely it is to be changed in light of new information, new reasoning, or conflicts with other beliefs. Changes to peripheral *desires* (especially when these are instrumental) are normally occasioned by changes in circumstances, new information, or new episodes of practical reasoning. Peripheral desires tend to be altered fairly easily, in part because they often rest on beliefs about means and ends that are themselves subject to revision. Peripheral attitudes, then, tend to be relatively flexible and to change fairly rapidly to reflect new situations and new information.

Core attitudes, on the other hand, tend to remain relatively stable over time. However, they are not necessarily permanent, nor do they form an "exclusive club." Over time, new attitudes can be admitted into their ranks, and current members can be expelled. Often, such changes are, to a large degree, "internally motivated" in such a way that they seem to be *intelligible reflections* of the contents of the core attitudes. Such changes resolve contradictions, inconsistencies, or other kinds of tension among core attitudes or between a core attitude and persistent information about oneself or the outside world. When changes to the core attitudes are of this kind, the self evolves according to its own internal logic – its own contents determine whether and how it is to change in response to new information, internal conflicts, and changing conditions. While outside forces or external circumstances may occasion such a change, its direction and nature are largely determined by the actual contents of the core attitudes.[26]

When psychological changes happen this way, it seems correct to say that the new configuration of the self is an authentic continuation of the previous configuration. On the other hand, a psychological change – especially a change to the core attitudes – that does not occur in this way produces a new configuration that is not an authentic continuation of the previous one. Such changes are not driven by the contents of the core attitudes and thus are not caused in the right way to count as internally motivated. Changes caused by sudden organic trauma, or by nefarious brain surgery, might fall into this category, for they might change the attitudes that form the core of the self in ways that do not reflect their contents. If the changes are radical enough, it might be proper to speak of the destruction of one self and its replacement by a new one.

How does such a first self arise? Infants and very young children do not yet have the two key psychological ingredients for the kind of self that we are supposing is the determiner of authenticity. The infant's cognitive structures and capacities are unformed, and her motivational system consists mainly of unstructured biological drives. As the child grows, she begins to develop cognitive structures around which she will organize her beliefs, as well as the stable concerns, attachments, and goals that will provide structure to her motivational system. Together, these will gradually coalesce to form the core of her self. The earliest core desires, as well as the initial elements of the child's cognitive conceptual scheme, arise via processes that would be considered authenticity undermining if they were used to implant beliefs and desires into an adult. Such processes apparently include operant, aversive, and classical conditioning; role model imitation; blind obedience to and subsequent internalization of behavioral norms; uncritical acceptance of propositions on the authority of parents and teachers; and so on. Out of a seemingly unpromising beginning – a sort of chaotic psychological "soup" – the child's self gradually emerges as her cognitive and motivational systems develop the kind of structure and stability and the rational and reflective capacities necessary for the existence of a coherent and stable self that can be the source of authenticity.[27]

If we think of the structure and origins of the authenticating self along these lines – and for our present purposes, the general outlines matter more than the details – then it becomes relatively easy to see how it could arise gradually from a psychological configuration that does not yet have the properties that are characteristic of the fully developed authenticating self. For the key features of the self – structure and capacity – are both features that can admit of degrees and that therefore can arise gradually.[28] As with all gradual processes, it will, of course, be difficult to know what to say while it is going on (just as it is difficult to know when a balding man has gone bald). But a theory that characterizes the authenticating self in this way will have no conceptual problem with the claim that the self develops gradually. In this way, we can see how an authentic rabbit gradually emerges from an inauthentic hat.

VII. SOOTHING BRUISED INTUITIONS

If we claim that authentic selves emerge from a disorganized and undeveloped psychological quagmire, helped along by processes that would otherwise count as subversive to authenticity, we may not derive much comfort from the fact that this is the kind of origin our own selves had. In addition, we have only to imagine cases in which such processes go awry to wonder whether we really can pull an authentic rabbit out of an inauthentic hat after all. I want to conclude by looking in some detail at the kinds of scenarios that pose the greatest intuitive hurdle for attempts to halt the regress that threatens self-referential theories of authenticity. The kind of example I have in mind involves manipulation that runs deep. How deep? All the way down, both temporally and structurally. Bottom turtle manipulation. Consider, then, two thought experiments, both of which are composites of several cases discussed in various places in the literature:

Edgar the Evil is the son of a crime boss who rears him to follow in his footsteps. Using standard child-rearing techniques, he encourages Edgar's more selfish and violent impulses and discourages empathy and compassion. As Edgar reaches adulthood, he is quite thoroughly evil.

Oppressed Olivia has been raised (using standard child-rearing techniques) to abide by and adopt the sexist attitudes of the patriarchal society in which she lives. Consequently, she shapes her ideals, aspirations, and activities in ways that reflect these attitudes. As Olivia reaches adulthood, her convictions include a belief in the naturalness of women's subservient role, and her deepest aspiration is to be a housewife.

Such cases attempt to undermine our willingness to allow the bottom turtle to stand on anything that is not itself a turtle. It is perhaps worth recalling that "standard child-rearing techniques" include such processes as operant, aversive, and classical conditioning; role model imitation; blind obedience to and subsequent internalization of behavioral norms; uncritical acceptance of propositions on the authority of parents and teachers; and so on. Given that such processes are the origins of their attitudes, we *might* ask: "How can we really say that the attitudes Edgar and Olivia have are authentic?"

If we ask the question *this* way, though, I think that we risk giving in to the temptation posed by the intuitions that arise from the *ab initio* superstition. Moreover, I think this way of asking the question misunderstands the logic of the concept of authenticity. We sometimes speak imprecisely of authenticity as though it were a simple one-place predicate. We must keep in mind, though, that it is really a two-place relation: Some element is authentic *to* a particular person. If we accept a self-referential condition of authenticity, an element is authentic to a person just in case it bears the right relation to her true self. Before the self initially arises, there is no other self for the initial self to bear any authenticity-grounding relation to. Viewed in this way, it is meaningless to ask whether the initial self that arises in Edward or Olivia is authentic. When that initial self forms, it is the only self that there is. Sadly, that initial self is the only game in town, so to speak. Now if we ask whether some *element* of that initial self is authentic, then the answer simply has to be "yes." After all, the element belongs, *ex hypothesi,* to the only self that exists. If the self is fully formed and the elements are related to it in the right way (with the right way depending on what theory of authenticity we finally adopt), then that is all there is to their being authentic. Hence, Edgar's evil life plans and Olivia's subservient aspirations are authentic.

We might be tempted to note that a different self *could* have emerged in each of these cases. Indeed, it is likely that better selves *would* have emerged in Edgar and Olivia but for the warped upbringing to which they were subjected. But while we can certainly posit such a counterfactual self, it is difficult to see how a self that, *ex hypothesi,* is nonexistent can be anyone's real self. Such a self does not now exist, *nor did it ever exist.* As I have told the stories, no other self ever emerged from their childhoods. Unfortunately, each of the selves that did emerge formed around a core that includes attitudes that are factually and morally defective. But if the question of authenticity is a question about what beliefs and desires are truly a person's own, then it is difficult to see any basis for the claim that these beliefs and desires do not belong to the self that arises from Edgar's and Olivia's childhoods.[29]

But isn't there something about these cases that just doesn't "sit well"? Haven't Edgar and Olivia been brainwashed into having evil or oppressive attitudes? Perhaps, but then the only real difference between them and us is that we were brainwashed into having less dysfunctional attitudes (or if not, then we have at least been better able to leave ours behind). We must keep in mind that acknowledging that these attitudes are authentic (*to* Olivia and Edgar) does not require us to abandon our moral outrage at the fact that they have warped, corrupted, and stifled the development of these two people. We simply need to articulate that outrage a bit more carefully. It is not that the earliest socialization of a child into an evil or oppressive worldview imprisons some better self. For there is no self at all before the socialization that initially creates it. But saying that evil or oppressive attitudes are authentic to someone who has them does not make them any less evil or oppressive.

Of course, these elements of the initial self did arise through processes that we normally think of as having the capacity to undermine authenticity. And certainly, if we were to use such processes to implant impulses or attitudes into a person who already *has* an existing authentic self, then it would make sense to ask whether those new impulses or elements are authentic to *that* self. And, depending on the details of the case, we may conclude that they are not.

In other words, it makes a great deal of difference whether such processes are being used to build an *initial* self, or whether they are being used to implant psychological elements into an *existing* self. For in the latter case, we can ask whether such implantation preserves the self that is already there. We can ask, in short, whether the self that results from the implantation is an authentic descendent of the earlier self. But when there is no earlier self, such questions are meaningless. To see the contrast, consider one final case:

Brainwashed Ben was raised Catholic; his upbringing is such that his religious beliefs help to define who he is. Craving a vegetarian meal, he attends a free dinner put on by a local cult. The cult slips psychoactive drugs into Ben's couscous, and these facilitate subsequent brainwashing. The techniques include many of the same processes used to socialize young children. These nonrational means root out Ben's Catholic worldview and replace it with that of the cult. This brainwashing is sufficiently radical to count as the replacement of Ben's earlier core self with a new one.

Now, what are we to say about the new elements of Ben's psychology? Are they authentic or not? That depends on what self we are talking about. If we assume that the brainwashing has been sufficiently thorough to count as the implantation of a new self into Ben's psychological make-up, then it would be accurate to say that the elements of the cult worldview are authentic *to* this new self. Of course, these elements are *not* authentic *to* Ben's prior self. Suppose, on the other hand, that a few of the old Catholic habits remain. Despite the cult's commitment to vegetarianism, Ben gets an irresistible craving for fish on Fridays. Presumably, this craving was authentic to Ben's original, Catholic self. However, it might be properly regarded as inauthentic to his new, cult self.

The contrast between Ben's case and the cases of Olivia and Edgar reveals something important. There is, it seems, a big difference between the application of brainwashing and related techniques to a person with a fully formed self and the application of very similar techniques during the early stages of child rearing. In both cases, we create a self. But in the former case, we create a self by destroying an already existing one.

Cases like Ben's raise interesting moral questions about child rearing, so-called deprogramming, and the tactics of political or religious groups that seek to produce major conversions in the worldviews of potential members. While I have no remaining space to get into these interesting questions, one moral principle that suggests itself is that if we do care about autonomy and authenticity, then we should adopt at least a prima facie norm against simply "assassinating" any existing self, even if we wish to make that self less stunted or less evil. We should prefer, instead, means of influencing the growth and development of existing selves that make their (perhaps very different) end points authentic descendents of their starting points. If authenticity is something worth caring about, then we should seek to preserve it when we can, even if the attitudes that possess it are sufficiently defective or evil that we are morally compelled to try to change them. This won't answer all of our moral questions about such issues, but perhaps it is a start.

Notes

I am grateful to James Stacey Taylor for feedback on this chapter and for arranging its presentation at Louisiana State University in September 2003, as well as to that audience for insightful comments. I am also grateful to Central Michigan University for a Research Professorship award that supported this work.

1. Commonly but not universally. Some philosophers refer to what I am calling "authentic desires" as "internal desires." Sometimes, the phrase "autonomous desire" is used to mean the same thing (but see Al Mele, "History and Personal Autonomy," *Canadian Journal of Philosophy* 23 [1993]: 271–280, for other uses of this phrase). When discussing other people's theories, I will substitute

"authenticity" and "inauthenticity" when it seems clear to me that this does not distort the theory in question. Those who think I have erred in any such judgment are welcome to treat my intended exegesis as the construction of a parallel theory. For a useful recent discussion of authenticity, see Insoo Hyun, "Authentic Values and Individual Autonomy," *Journal of Value Inquiry* 35 (2001): 195–208.

2. Gerald Dworkin, "Acting Freely," *Noûs* 4 (1970): 367–383; Harry Frankfurt, "Freedom of the Will and the Concept of a Person," *Journal of Philosophy* 68 (1971): 829–839, reprinted in Harry Frankfurt, *The Importance of What We Care About* (Cambridge: Cambridge University Press, 1988): 11–25; and John Christman, ed., *The Inner Citadel: Essays on Individual Autonomy* (New York: Oxford University Press, 1989): 63–76 (subsequent page references to this edition).
3. Frankfurt, "Freedom and Concept," 69.
4. Ibid. This theme is amplified in "Identification and Externality," in Amelie Rorty, ed., *The Identities of Persons* (Los Angeles: University of California Press, 1976): 239–251; reprinted in Frankfurt, *The Importance of What We Care About,* 58–68.
5. Frankfurt, "Freedom and Concept," 71; Frankfurt characterized this as "wholehearted identification" in "Identification and Wholeheartedness," in Ferdinand Schoeman, ed., *Responsibility, Character, and the Emotions* (New York: Cambridge University Press, 1987): 27–45; reprinted in Frankfurt, *The Importance of What We Care About,* 159–176.
6. Later work by Frankfurt suggests a more complex understanding of decisive commitment. See "Identification and Wholeheartedness" and "The Importance of What We Care About," in his *The Importance of What We Care About,* 80–94; and "Autonomy, Necessity, and Love," in his *Necessity, Volition, and Love* (Cambridge: Cambridge University Press, 1999): 129–141. For an interesting reconstruction of Frankfurt's recent work, see Stefaan Cuypers, "Autonomy Beyond Voluntarism: In Defense of Hierarchy," *Canadian Journal of Philosophy* 30 (2000): 225–256.
7. John Christman, "Introduction," *The Inner Citadel,* 10. See also his "Autonomy: A Defense of the Split-Level Self," *Southern Journal of Philosophy* 25 (1987): 281–293; and Marilyn Friedman, "Autonomy and the Split-Level Self," *Southern Journal of Philosophy* 24 (1986): 19–35.
8. Gary Watson, "Free Agency," *Journal of Philosophy* 72 (1975): 205–220; reprinted in Christman, ed., *The Inner Citadel* (subsequent page references to latter edition).
9. Ibid., 117.
10. Ibid., 116.
11. Ibid., 117.
12. See, e.g., Robert Lifton, *Thought Reform and the Psychology of Totalism* (Chapel Hill: University of North Carolina Press, 1961); and Jonathan Bennett, "The Conscience of Huckleberry Finn," *Philosophy* 49 (1974): 123–134.
13. *Contra* Laura Waddell Ekstrom, "A Coherence Theory of Autonomy," *Philosophy and Phenomenological Research* 53 (1993): 599–616, I think that a coherence theory of authenticity faces the same regress. Roughly, such a theory

claims that an element (E_1) is authentic if it coheres with either the entire psychology of S or a fairly large subset of it. But now S's entire psychology (or a subset of it) simply fills the E_2 slot in the structural condition schema. The possibility of global manipulation suggests that E_2 could seem inauthentic even if it is the totality of the agent's psychology. In such scenarios, the defender of a coherence theory of authenticity must posit some other condition to make E_2 authentic or make the seemingly counterintuitive claim that mental elements can be rendered authentic in virtue of their coherence with elements that seem inauthentic. (Later, I shall argue that the latter claim is not as implausible as it may at first seem.)

14. Christman, "Introduction," *Inner Citadel*, 10
15. Friedman, "Autonomy and the Split-Level Self," 24, 26.
16. Cuypers, "Autonomy Beyond Voluntarism," 230.
17. Ekstrom, "A Coherence Account of Autonomy," 602.
18. Gerald Dworkin, *The Theory and Practice of Autonomy* (Cambridge: Cambridge University Press, 1988): 18.
19. John Christman, "Autonomy and Personal History," *Canadian Journal of Philosophy* 21 (1990): 1–24, esp. 11.
20. Ibid., 12, 16.
21. James Stacey Taylor has suggested (personal communication) that construing the regress problem as a problem about theories of authenticity might neglect a separate regress problem for theories of autonomy. While I suspect that he might be right about this, I think that if there is a separate regress problem about autonomy, then it is likely to be either parasitic upon, parallel to, or less difficult than the regress problem about authenticity.
22. A substantive theory of autonomy that rejects the self-referential approach to authenticity is developed by Bernard Berofsky in *Liberation from the Self: A Theory of Personal Autonomy* (Cambridge: Cambridge University Press, 1995). Susan Wolf also rejects a self-referential approach to autonomy/authenticity in "Sanity and the Metaphysics of Responsibility," in Schoeman, ed., *Responsibility, Character, and the Emotions*, 46–62, reprinted in Christman, ed., *The Inner Citadel*, 137–151; and in *Freedom within Reason* (New York: Oxford University Press, 1990). The work of both philosophers suggests substantive conditions for authenticity.
23. Isaiah Berlin offers classic objections to such accounts in *Two Concepts of Liberty* (Oxford: Clarendon Press, 1958). My own worries apply only to theories that make meeting a strong substantive condition the only or main determiner of authenticity. For a defense of a weaker substantive condition, see Sigurdur Kristinsson, "The Limits of Neutrality: Toward a Weakly Substantive Account of Personal Autonomy," *Canadian Journal of Philosophy* 30 (2000): 257–286. I argue that, at least for certain purposes, we should favor a thin conception of autonomy in "The Public Conception of Autonomy and Critical Self-Reflection," *Southern Journal of Philosophy* 35 (1997): 495–515.
24. These intuitions resemble those that make libertarian freedom seem like the only kind of freedom worth wanting. My approach to issues discussed in the preceding paragraphs is parallel to and influenced by Daniel Dennett's

Elbow Room: The Varieties of Free Will Worth Wanting (Cambridge, MA: MIT Press, 1984).

25. See Ekstrom, "A Coherence Account of Autonomy," and Watson, "Free Agency." Frankfurt's later work (e.g., "Identification and Wholeheartedness," "The Importance of What We Care About," and "Autonomy, Necessity, and Love") suggests such a view about the origin and significance of HODs and the decisive commitment discussed above. See Cuypers, "Autonomy Beyond Voluntarism," for more on this matter.
26. This basic picture of the self – which evokes Otto Neurath's famous metaphor of a ship being rebuilt piecemeal as it sails – is quite common among philosophers. A few examples include Charles Taylor, *Sources of the Self* (Cambridge: Cambridge University Press, 1989); Marya Schechtman, *The Constitution of Selves* (Ithaca, NY: Cornell University Press, 1996); Henry Richardson, *Practical Reasoning about Final Ends* (Cambridge: Cambridge University Press, 1977); Stanley Benn, "Freedom, Autonomy, and the Concept of a Person," *Proceedings of the Aristotelian Society* (1976): 109–130; Friedman, "Autonomy and the Split-Level Self"; Richard H. Dees, "Moral Conversions," *Philosophy and Phenomenological Research* 56 (1996): 531–550; and my "Kantian Respect and Particular Persons," *Canadian Journal of Philosophy* 29 (1999): 449–477.
27. I expand on this in "Special Agents: Children's Autonomy and Parental Authority," in David Archard and Colin MacLeod, eds., *The Moral and Political Status of Children* (Oxford: Oxford University Press, 2002): 97–117.
28. James Stacey Taylor (personal communication) asks whether the authenticating self must have the capacities to reflect and revise. While we could require such capacities for autonomy rather than authenticity, I prefer to include them in a characterization of the authenticating self because they allow for authenticity-preserving growth necessary for the self to be a temporally extended entity.
29. Of course, if authenticity is necessary but not sufficient for autonomy, then Olivia and Edgar may fail to be autonomous despite their authentic attitudes.

4

Agnostic Autonomism Revisited

Alfred R. Mele

Autonomy, as I understand it, is associated with a family of *freedom* concepts: free will, free choice, free action, and the like. In much of the philosophical literature discussed in this chapter, issues are framed in terms of freedom rather than autonomy, but we are talking about (aspects of) the same thing. Libertarians argue that determinism precludes autonomy by, for example, precluding an agent's being ultimately responsible for anything.[1] Some compatibilist believers in autonomy argue that libertarians rely on indeterminism in a way that deprives us of autonomy-level control over our decisions.[2] Theorists who contend that no human being is autonomous can benefit from arguments on both sides, alleging that libertarians decisively reveal the ordinary person's notion of autonomy, an incompatibilist notion, and that compatibilist critics of libertarianism show that the notion is incoherent or unsatisfiable. Is there a way to use the resources both of libertarianism and of compatibilism in defending the following thesis: The claim that there are autonomous human beings is more credible than the claim that there are none?

I believe that the answer is "yes." I defended that answer in *Autonomous Agents*.[3] Part of my strategy was to develop an account of an ideally self-controlled agent (where self-control is understood as the contrary of *akrasia* [roughly, weakness of will]), to argue that even such an agent may fall short of autonomy, and to ask what may be added to ideal self-control to yield autonomy. I offered two answers, one for compatibilists and another for libertarians. I then argued that a certain disjunctive thesis involving both answers (identified in Section 4 below) is more credible than the thesis that there are no autonomous human beings.

I. A HISTORY-SENSITIVE COMPATIBILISM

Control is a major topic in the literature on autonomy. Sometimes, it is claimed that agents do not control anything at all if determinism is true. That claim is false. When I drive my car (in normal conditions), I control the turns it makes even if our world happens to be deterministic. I certainly control my car's turns in a way in which my passengers and others do not. A distinction can be drawn between compatibilist, or "nonultimate," control and a species of control that might be available to agents in some indeterministic worlds – "ultimate" control.[4] I exert the former kind of control of my car's normal turns, and I might exert the latter kind as well. Ultimate control might turn out to be remarkably similar to the control that many compatibilists have in mind; the key to its being *ultimate* control might be its indeterministic setting.[5] Certain kinds of manipulation pose an apparent problem for compatibilists. Incompatibilists sometimes argue that compatibilists cannot find a difference relevant to autonomy between cases of manipulation (often featuring external intelligent controllers) in which an agent clearly acts nonautonomously and cases of causally determined action that involve no monkey business.[6] They conclude, of course, that compatibilism is false.

Here is a case of manipulation from my *Autonomous Agents.*[7] Ann is an autonomous agent and an exceptionally industrious philosopher. She puts in twelve solid hours a day, seven days a week; and she enjoys almost every minute of it. Beth, an equally talented colleague, values many things above philosophy, for reasons that she has refined and endorsed on the basis of careful critical reflection over many years. She identifies with and enjoys her own way of life – one which, she is confident, has a breadth, depth, and richness that long days in the office would destroy. Their dean wants Beth to be like Ann. Normal modes of persuasion having failed, he decides to circumvent Beth's agency. Without the knowledge of either philosopher, he hires a team of psychologists to determine what makes Ann tick and a team of new-wave brainwashers to make Beth like Ann. The psychologists decide that Ann's peculiar hierarchy of values accounts for her productivity, and the brainwashers instill the same hierarchy in Beth while eradicating all competing values – via new-wave brainwashing, of course. Beth is now, in the relevant respect, a "psychological twin" of Ann. She is an industrious philosopher who thoroughly enjoys and highly values her philosophical work. Indeed, it turns out – largely as a result of Beth's new hierarchy of values – that whatever upshot Ann's critical reflection about her own values and priorities would have, the same is true of critical reflection by Beth. Her critical reflection, like Ann's, fully supports her new style of life.

Naturally, Beth is surprised by the change in her. What, she wonders, accounts for her remarkable zest for philosophy? Why is her philosophical work now so much more enjoyable? Why are her social activities now so much less satisfying and rewarding than her work? Beth's hypothesis is that she simply has grown tired of her previous mode of life, that her life had become stale without her recognizing it, and that she finally has come fully to appreciate the value of philosophical work. When Beth carefully reflects on her preferences and values, she finds that they fully support a life dedicated to philosophical work, and she wholeheartedly embraces such a life and the collection of values that support it.

Ann, by hypothesis, is autonomous; but what about Beth? In important respects, she is a clone of Ann – and by design, not by accident. Her own considered preferences and values were erased and replaced in the brainwashing process. Beth did not consent to the process. Nor was she even aware of it; she had no opportunity to resist. By instilling new values in Beth and eliminating old ones, the brainwashers gave her life a new direction, one that clashes with the considered principles and values she had before she was manipulated. Beth's autonomy was violated, we naturally say.[8] And it is difficult not to see her now, in light of all this, as heteronomous to a significant extent. If that perception is correct, then given the psychological similarities between the two agents, the difference in their current status regarding autonomy would seem to lie in how they *came* to have certain psychological features that they have, hence in something *external* to their here-and-now psychological constitutions. That is, the crucial difference is *historical*; autonomy is in some way history-bound.

In *Autonomous Agents*, I argued that this last sentence is true in a version of the story that involves some relevant "unsheddable" values.[9] (I discuss such values shortly.) Thus, I faced an apparent problem. Richard Double contends that once agents' histories are allowed to have a relevance of the sort mentioned here to their autonomy, their having *deterministic* histories is relevant, as well, and in a way that undermines compatibilism.[10] It may be thought that if instances of manipulation of the sort present in the Ann/Beth story block psychological autonomy, they do so only if they *deterministically cause* crucial psychological events or states and that determinism consequently is in danger of being identified as the real culprit.[11]

This worry is exaggerated. Even compatibilists who embrace determinism are in a position to distinguish among different causal routes to the collections of values (and "characters") agents have at a time. They are also in a position to provide principled grounds for holding that distinct routes to two type-identical collections of values may be such that one and only one of those routes blocks autonomy regarding a life lived in accordance with those values. An analog of the familiar compatibilist distinction between *caused* and *compelled* (or constrained) *behavior* may be used here.[12] Perhaps in engineering Beth's values, her brainwashers *compelled* her to have Ann-like values. Even so, a true and complete causal story about Ann's having the values she has might involve no compulsion. If Beth was compelled to possess her Ann-like values whereas Ann was not, there are some apparent grounds, at least, for taking the latter alone to be responsible for the pertinent aspects of her character and for value-guided actions of the pertinent sort and to have performed those actions autonomously.

In this connection, I argued in *Autonomous Agents* for the relevance of a notion of agents' (perhaps relatively modest) capacities for control over their mental lives being *bypassed.*[13] In ideally self-controlled agents, these capacities are impressive. Such agents are capable of modifying the strengths of their desires in the service of their normative judgments, of bringing their emotions into line with relevant judgments, and of mastering motivation that threatens (sometimes via the biasing of practical or theoretical reasoning) to produce or sustain beliefs in ways that would violate their principles for belief acquisition and retention. They are capable, moreover, of rationally assessing and revising their values and principles, of identifying with values of theirs on the basis of informed, critical reflection, and of intentionally fostering new values and principles in themselves in accordance with their considered evaluative judgments. Presumably, most readers of this chapter have each of these capacities in some measure. All such capacities are bypassed in cases of value engineering of the sort at issue. In such cases, new values are not generated via an exercise or an activation of agents' capacities for control over their mental lives; rather, they are generated despite the agents' capacities for this.

It is time to discuss a complication I alluded to earlier. Even effective manipulation as severe and comprehensive as Beth's might not thwart autonomy. To the extent to which one can successfully counteract the influence of brainwashing, having been a victim of it does not necessarily render one nonautonomous. Agents may be able (at least in a compatibilist sense of "able") to "shed" many attitudes produced by brainwashing – that is, to eliminate the attitudes or to attenuate them significantly. In *Autonomous Agents*, I argued that agents can autonomously possess attitudes that they are "practically unable" to shed and that "psychological twins," owing to different histories, may be such that although one of them is autonomous regarding a practically unsheddable attitude, the other is not.[14] The issue is complicated. I lack the space to do it justice here, but I will say a bit more about it.

Imagine an agent, Pat, who autonomously developed deep and admirable parental values. In some robust sense of "can," it may be true that, given how deeply entrenched Pat's parental values are, he can neither eradicate nor attenuate them during *t* (a certain two-week span, say) – that is, Pat's shedding those values during *t*, given his psychological constitution in his world, is not a psychologically genuine option. Of course, there might be conditions beyond Pat's control such that, were they to arise, he would shed these values. He might become hopelessly insane, for example. Or CIA agents might use his parental values as a lever to motivate him to uproot those very values: They might convince him that the CIA will ensure his children's flourishing if he eradicates his parental values and that, otherwise, they will destroy his children's lives. Under these conditions (I will suppose), Pat would take himself to have a decisive reason for shedding his parental values; and if he thought hard enough, he might find a way to shed them. (Once he sheds the values, he might not care at all how his children fare; but that is another matter.) However, if, in fact, conditions such as these do not arise for Pat in the next two weeks, he will not shed his parental values during that period. Insofar as (1) the conditions that would empower Pat to shed these values are beyond his control – that is, insofar as his psychological constitution precludes his voluntarily producing those conditions – and (2) the obtaining of those conditions independently of Pat's voluntarily producing them is not in the cards, he is apparently "stuck" with the values. Any agent who is stuck in this sense with a value (during *t*) may be said to be *practically unable* to shed it (during *t*), and values that one is practically unable to shed may be termed *practically unsheddable*. In Chapter 9 of *Autonomous Agents*, I argued that although an agent like Pat may autonomously possess (during *t*) his parental values, this is not true of a current psychological twin, Paul, who had been among the most uncaring parents imaginable, until, last night, brainwashers instilled unsheddable parental values like Pat's in him.

Tentatively assuming the truth of compatibilism, I also defended a compatibilist set of sufficient conditions for autonomous agency.[15] To being an ideally self-controlled and mentally healthy agent, I added the following: The agent has no compelled or coercively produced attitudes; the agent's beliefs are conducive to informed deliberation about all matters that concern her; and the agent is a reliable deliberator.

Daniel Dennett evaluates my history-sensitive compatibilist proposal in his recent book.[16] Toward the end of the book, he writes: "Austin's putt, Kane's faculty of practical reasoning, and Mele's autonomy . . . have come in for the sort of detailed attention philosophers expect."[17] However, inattention to detail has led Dennett astray. He observes that in cases like that of Ann and Beth, there is, in addition to the difference that only one member of the pair was brainwashed, the difference that only one is mistaken about whether she has been brainwashed (assuming that they have beliefs about this); and he suggests that the latter difference is the important one between autonomous agents and brainwashed, nonautonomous ones. However, Dennett ignores unsheddable values in this connection. If Paul were informed before brainwashing that it would result in his having the admirable unsheddable parental values that Pat has and were reminded of this afterward, would that render him autonomous with respect to his possession of those values? I do not see how.[18]

II. A PROBLEM ABOUT LUCK FOR LIBERTARIANS

Libertarians have the option of endorsing either a stronger, nonhistorical requirement on autonomous action or a weaker, historical requirement.[19] They can hold that an agent autonomously *A*-ed at a time *t* only if, at *t*, he could have done otherwise than *A* then. Alternatively, they can maintain that an agent who could not have done otherwise at *t* than *A* then may nevertheless autonomously *A* at *t*, provided that he earlier performed some relevant autonomous action or actions at a time or times at which he could have done otherwise than perform those actions. Actions of the latter kind may be termed "basically autonomous actions." Libertarians can hold that basically autonomous actions of an agent that are suitably related to his subsequent *A*-ing can confer autonomy on his *A*-ing and that he autonomously *A*-s even though he could not have done otherwise than *A* then. Some libertarians may hold that the only autonomous actions are what I am calling basically autonomous actions, and other libertarians may disagree. This issue may be sidestepped entirely for the purposes of this section by framing the discussion in terms of basically autonomous actions. That is what I will do. Exactly parallel options are open on morally responsible action. Framing discussion of moral responsibility in terms of basic moral responsibility will sidestep these issues. The simplest way to implement the framing is simply to say that henceforth in this section by "autonomous" I mean "basically autonomous" and by "morally responsible" I mean "basically morally responsible."

Now for luck. Agents' *control* is the yardstick by which the bearing of luck on their autonomy and moral responsibility is measured. When luck (good or bad) is problematic, that is because it seems significantly to impede agents' control over themselves.[20] It may seem that to the extent that it is causally undetermined whether, for example, an agent intends in accordance with a better judgment that he made, the agent lacks some control over what he intends, and it may be claimed that a positive deterministic connection here would be more conducive to autonomy. Weakness of will is bad enough; an indeterministic connection between better judgments and intentions that allows, in addition, for "random" failures to intend as one judges best seems problematic.

I illustrate this worry with a fable. Suppose you are a libertarian demigod in an indeterministic world who wants to build rational autonomous human beings capable of being very efficient agents. You believe that proximal decisions – decisions to *A* straightaway – are causes of actions that execute them, and you see no benefit in designing agents in such a way that even given that they have decided to *A* straightaway, and even given the persistence of the intention to *A* formed in that act of deciding and the absence of any biological damage, there is a chance that they will not even try to *A*. Fortunately, the indeterministic fabric of your world allows you to build a deterministic connection between proximal decisions and attempts, and you do. Now, because you are a pretty typical libertarian, you believe that autonomous decisions cannot be deterministically caused, even by something that centrally involves a considered judgment that it would be best to *A* straightaway. However, you do think that agents can make autonomous decisions on the basis of such judgments. So you design your agents in such a way that, even given that they have just made such a judgment and the judgment persists in the absence of biological damage, they may decide contrary to it. You build an indeterministic connection between judgments of the kind at issue and proximal decision making.

Given your brand of libertarianism, you believe that whenever agents perform an autonomous action of deciding to *A*, they could have *autonomously* performed some alternative intentional action.[21] You worry that the indeterministic connection that you built might not accommodate this. If the difference between the actual world, in which one of your agents judges it best to *A* straightaway and then decides accordingly, and any world with the same past and laws in which while the judgment persists he makes an alternative decision is just a matter of luck, you worry that he does not autonomously make that decision in that possible world, *W*. You suspect that his making that alternative decision rather than deciding in accordance with his best judgment – that is, that difference between *W* and the actual world – is just a matter of bad luck (or, more precisely, of worse luck in *W* for the agent than in the actual world). This leads you to suspect that, in *W*, the agent should not be blamed for making the decision he makes there.[22] And that he should not be blamed, you think, indicates that he did not autonomously make it.

This is a typical worry for libertarians. It is a worry about whether, on typical libertarian views, according to which one autonomously *A*-ed only if one could have autonomously done otherwise at the time, one was able to *A* autonomously. All libertarians who hold that *A*'s being an autonomous action depends on its being the case that, at the time, the agent was able to do otherwise autonomously then should tell us what it could possibly be about an agent who autonomously *A*-ed at *t* in virtue of which it is true that, in another world with the same past and laws, he autonomously does something else at *t*. Of course, they can *say* that the answer is free will. But what they need to explain is how free will, as they understand it, can be a feature of agents – or, more fully, how this can be so where "free will," on their account of it, really does answer the question. Some libertarians have tried to explain this. Although I have not been persuaded by their proposals, I would not infer from this that the worry cannot be laid to rest.

III. A MODEST LIBERTARIAN PROPOSAL

Suppose that Ann, on the basis of careful, rational deliberation, judges it best to *A*. And suppose that, on the basis of that judgment, she decides to *A* and then acts accordingly, intentionally *A*-ing. Suppose further that Ann has not been subjected to autonomy-thwarting mind control or relevant deception, that she is perfectly sane, and so on. To make a long story short, suppose that she satisfies an attractive set of sufficient conditions for *compatibilist* autonomy regarding her *A*-ing.[23] Now add one more supposition to the set: While Ann was deliberating, it was not causally determined that she would come to the conclusion that she did.

In principle, an agent-internal indeterminism may provide for indeterministic agency while blocking or limiting our (nonultimate) control over what happens only at junctures at which we have no greater control on the hypothesis that our world is deterministic.[24] Ordinary human beings have a wealth of beliefs, desires, hypotheses, and the like, the great majority of which are not salient in consciousness during any given process of deliberation. Plainly, in those cases in which we act on the basis of careful deliberation, what we do is influenced by at least some of the considerations that "come to mind" – that is, become salient in consciousness – during deliberation and by our assessments of considerations. Now, even if determinism is true, it is false that, with respect to *every* consideration – every belief, desire, hypothesis, and so on – that comes to mind during our deliberation, we are in control of its coming to mind; and some considerations that come to mind without our being in control of their so doing may influence the outcome of our deliberation. Furthermore, a kind of internal indeterminism is imaginable that limits our control only in a way that gives us no less nonultimate control than we would have on the assumption that determinism is true, while opening up alternative deliberative outcomes. (Although, in a deterministic world, it would never be a matter of genuine chance that a certain consideration came to mind during deliberation, it may still be a matter of luck relative to the agent's sphere of control.) As I put it in *Autonomous Agents*, "Where compatibilists have no good reason to insist on determinism in the deliberative process as a requirement for autonomy, where internal indeterminism is, for all we know, a reality, and where such indeterminism would not diminish the nonultimate control that real agents exert over their deliberation even on the assumption that real agents are internally deterministic – that is, at the *intersection* of these three locations – libertarians may plump for ultimacy-promoting indeterminism."[25]

A short chapter precludes much elaboration, but I will point out that the modest indeterminism at issue allows agents ample control over their deliberation. Suppose a belief, hypothesis, or desire that is relevant to a deliberator's present practical question comes to mind during deliberation, but was not deterministically caused to do so (perhaps unlike the great majority of considerations that come to mind during this process of deliberation).[26] Presumably, a normal agent would be able to *assess* this consideration. And upon reflection, she might rationally reject the belief as unwarranted, rationally judge that the hypothesis does not merit investigation, or rationally decide that the desire should be given little or no weight in her deliberation. Alternatively, reflection might rationally lead her to retain the belief, to pursue the hypothesis, or to give the desire significant weight. That a consideration comes to mind indeterministically does not entail that the agent has no control over how she responds to it.

Considerations that indeterministically come to mind (like considerations that deterministically come to mind) are nothing more than input to deliberation. Their coming to mind has at most an indirect effect on what the agent decides, an effect that is mediated by the agent's own assessment of them. They do not settle matters. Moreover, not only do agents have the opportunity to assess these considerations, they also have the opportunity to search for additional relevant considerations before they decide, thereby increasing the probability that other relevant considerations will indeterministically come to mind. They have the opportunity to cancel or attenuate the effects of bad luck (e.g., the undetermined coming to mind of a misleading consideration or an undetermined failure to notice a relevant consideration). And given a suitable indeterminism regarding what comes to mind in an assessment process, it is not causally determined what assessment the agent will reach.

Compatibilists who hold that we act autonomously even when we are not in control of what happens at certain specific junctures in the process leading to action are in no position to hold that an indeterministic agent's lacking control at the same junctures precludes autonomous action. And, again, real human beings are not in control of the coming to mind of everything that comes to mind during typical processes of deliberation. If this lack of perfect nonultimate control does not preclude its being the case that autonomous actions sometimes issue from typical deliberation on the assumption that we are deterministic agents, it also does not preclude this on the assumption that we are *indeterministic* agents.

Is a modest indeterminism of the kind I have sketched useful to libertarians? Elsewhere, I have suggested that what at least some libertarians might prize that compatibilist autonomy does not offer them is a species of agency that gives them a kind of independence and an associated kind of explanatory bearing on their conduct that they would lack in any deterministic world.[27] The combination of the satisfaction of an attractive set of sufficient conditions for *compatibilist* autonomy, including all the nonultimate control that involves, and a modest agent-internal indeterminism of the sort I have described would give them that. Agents of the imagined sort would make choices and perform actions that lack deterministic causes in the distant past. They would have no less control over these choices and actions than we do over ours, on the assumption that we are deterministic agents. And given that they have at least robust *compatibilist* responsibility for certain of these choices and actions, they would also have *ultimate* responsibility for them. These choices and actions have, in Robert Kane's words, "their ultimate sources in" the agents, in the sense that the collection of agent-internal states and events that explains these choices and actions does not itself admit of a deterministic explanation that stretches back beyond the agent.[28]

Now, even if garden-variety compatibilists can be led to see that the problem of luck is surmountable by a libertarian, how are theorists of other kinds likely to respond to the libertarian position that I have been sketching? There are, of course, philosophers who contend that moral responsibility and autonomy are illusions and that we lack these properties whether our world is deterministic or indeterministic.[29] Elsewhere, I have argued that the impossible demands this position places on moral responsibility and autonomy are *unwarranted* demands.[30]

Modest libertarians can also anticipate trouble from traditional libertarians, who want more than the modest indeterminism that I have described can offer. Randolph Clarke, a libertarian, criticizes modest libertarianism on the grounds that it adds no "positive" power of control to compatibilist nonultimate control, but simply places compatibilist control in an indeterministic setting.[31] However, traditional libertarians need to show that what they want is coherent. That requires showing that what they want does not entail or presuppose a kind of luck that would itself undermine moral responsibility.[32] The traditional libertarian wants both indeterminism and significant control at the moment of decision. That is the desire that prompts a serious version of the worry about luck I sketched earlier. In the absence of a plausible resolution of that worry, it is epistemically open that a modest libertarian proposal of the sort I sketched is the best a libertarian can do. Of course, even if that is the best libertarian option, it does not follow that all believers in free and morally responsible action should gravitate toward it – as long as compatibilism is still in the running.

IV. HOW TO ARGUE FOR AGNOSTIC AUTONOMISM

Must one choose between compatibilism and incompatibilism about autonomy? No. One can be agnostic about the issue. Moreover, consistently with agnosticism, one can make a case for the existence of autonomy. In *Autonomous Agents,* I defended what I dubbed "agnostic autonomism," the conjunction of the agnosticism just identified with the belief that there are autonomous human beings.[33] This position can draw on the resources both of compatibilism and of libertarianism. It can offer both a robust, satisfiable set of sufficient conditions for compatibilist autonomy and a coherent set of conditions for incompatibilist autonomy that, for all we know, is satisfied by real human beings. It has the resources to resolve alleged, determinism-neutral problems for compatibilist accounts of autonomy, to conquer (along lines sketched earlier in this chapter) the problem about "luck" or control that libertarianism traditionally faces, and to show that *if* compatibilism is true, belief in the existence of human autonomy is warranted. Furthermore, agnostics have the advantage of not having certain disadvantages. Agnostics do not insist that autonomy is compatible with determinism; nor need they insist that we are internally indeterministic in a way useful to libertarians. But if it were discovered that we are not suitably indeterministic, they would have compatibilism to fall back on.

I claimed then, and still believe, that agnostic autonomism is more credible than the view that no human being is autonomous (nonautonomism). Consider the following propositions:

a. Some human beings are autonomous, and determinism is compatible with autonomy (compatibilist belief in autonomy).
b. Some human beings are autonomous, and determinism is incompatible with autonomy (libertarianism).
c. Either *a* or *b* (agnostic autonomism).
d. No human beings are autonomous (nonautonomism).

Imagine that each proposition has a probability between 0 and 1. Then *c* has a higher probability than *a* and a higher probability than *b*, because *c* is the *disjunction* of *a* and *b*.[34] So what about *d*? I argued that nonautonomism, at best, fares no better than *a* and no better than *b*.[35] If that is right, then because *c* has a higher probability than each of *a* and *b*, *c* has a higher probability than *d*: Agnostic autonomism beats nonautonomism! The nature of the claimed victory is such as to call for further work on all sides. Part of my aim in *Autonomous Agents* was to motivate such work.[36]

Notes

1. Robert Kane, *The Significance of Free Will* (New York: Oxford University Press, 1996).
2. Bernard Berofsky, *Liberation from Self: A Theory of Personal Autonomy* (Cambridge: Cambridge University Press, 1995).
3. Alfred R. Mele, *Autonomous Agents: From Self-Control to Autonomy* (New York: Oxford University Press, 1995).

4. See Fischer's distinction between "guidance control" and "regulative control" in John Martin Fischer, *The Metaphysics of Free Will* (Oxford: Blackwell, 1994): 132–135.
5. Mele, *Autonomous Agents*, 213.
6. Kane, *The Significance of Free Will*; and Derk Pereboom, *Living Without Free Will* (Cambridge: Cambridge University Press, 2001).
7. Mele, *Autonomous Agents*, 145.
8. This use of "autonomy" is adequately captured by Joel Feinberg's gloss on it: "the sovereign authority to govern oneself." *Harm to Self* (New York: Oxford University Press, 1986): 28.
9. For another compatibilist view of *moral responsibility* that is explicitly history sensitive, see John Martin Fischer "Responsiveness and Moral Responsibility," in Ferdinand Schoeman, ed., *Responsibility, Character, and the Emotions* (Cambridge: Cambridge University Press, 1987): 81–106. (Fischer does not there endorse the compatibility of determinism with freedom to do *otherwise*, but compatibilists about determinism and free action need not be compatibilists about determinism and freedom to do otherwise.) Fischer's historicism is developed further in his *Metaphysics of Free Will*; John Martin Fischer and Mark Ravizza, "Responsibility and History," *Midwest Studies in Philosophy* 19 (1994): 430–451; and John Martin Fischer and Mark Ravizza, *Responsibility and Control: A Theory of Moral Responsibility* (Cambridge: Cambridge University Press, 1998).
10. Richard Double, *The Non-Reality of Free Will* (New York: Oxford University Press, 1991): 56–57.
11. Roughly, this idea is a theme in various "mind control" arguments against compatibilism, as David Blumenfeld observes in "Freedom and Mind Control," *American Philosophical Quarterly* 25 (1988): 215–227.
12. See, e.g., Robert Audi, *Action, Intention, and Reason* (Ithaca, NY: Cornell University Press, 1993): chaps. 7, 10; A. J. Ayer, "Freedom and Necessity," in Ayer, ed., *Philosophical Essays* (London: Macmillan, 1954): 271–284; A. Grünbaum, "Free Will and the Laws of Human Behavior," *American Philosophical Quarterly* 8 (1971): 299–317; John Stuart Mill, *An Examination of Sir William Hamilton's Philosophy and of the Principal Philosophical Questions Discussed in His Writings*, in J. M. Robson, ed., *Collected Works of John Stuart Mill* (Toronto: University of Toronto Press, 1979): chap. 26, esp. 464–467; and M. Schlick, *Problems of Ethics*, D. Rynin, trans. (New York: Dover, 1962): chap. 7. Also see David Hume's remarks on the liberty of spontaneity versus the liberty of indifference in L. Selby-Bigge, ed., *A Treatise of Human Nature* (Oxford: Clarendon Press, 1975): bk. II, pt. III, sec. 2.
13. Mele, *Autonomous Agents*, 168–172, 183–184. For a useful discussion of bypassing, see Blumenfeld, "Freedom and Mind Control," 222–223.
14. Mele, *Autonomous Agents*, 149–173.
15. Ibid., chaps. 9–10.
16. Daniel Dennett, *Freedom Evolves* (New York: Viking Press, 2003): 281–284.
17. Ibid., 307.
18. Dennett's readers may find it interesting to compare the "Default Responsibility Principle" he says I propose and his explication of it (*Freedom*

Evolves, 281) with Mele, *Autonomous Agents*, 168–169, and to compare his presumption about Beth's beliefs about her past (*Freedom Evolves*, 283) with Mele, *Autonomous Agents*, 145.

19. Mele, *Autonomous Agents*, 207–209.
20. For recent versions of this worry, see Istiyaque Haji, "Indeterminism and Frankfurt-Type Examples," *Philosophical Explorations* 2 (1999): 42–58; Mele, *Autonomous Agents*, 195–204; Mele, "Ultimate Responsibility and Dumb Luck," *Social Philosophy and Policy* 16 (1999): 274–293; Galen Strawson, "The Impossibility of Moral Responsibility," *Philosophical Studies* 75 (1994): 5–24; and Bruce Waller, "Free Will Gone out of Control," *Behaviorism* 16 (1988): 149–167.
21. Kane, *The Significance of Free Will*, 109–114, 134–135, 143, 179–180, 191.
22. You toy with the thought that the agent may be blamed for the decision if past autonomous decisions of his had the result, by way of their effect on his character, that there was a significant chance that he would decide contrary to his best judgment. But it occurs to you that the same worry arises about past autonomous decisions the agent made.
23. See Mele, *Autonomous Agents*, 186–191.
24. Mele, *Autonomous Agents*, chap. 12. See also Daniel Dennett, *Brainstorms* (Montgomery, VT: Bradford Books, 1978): 294–299; Laura Waddell Ekstrom, *Free Will* (Boulder, CO: Westview Press, 1999): 103–129; and Robert Kane, *Free Will and Values* (Albany, NY: SUNY Press, 1985): 101–110.
25. Mele, *Autonomous Agents*, 235. On the relative theoretical utility of internal versus external indeterminism, see *Autonomous Agents*, 195–204.
26. Regarding the parenthetical clause, bear in mind that not all causally determined events need be part of a deterministic chain that stretches back even for several moments, much less to near the Big Bang.
27. Mele, "Soft Libertarianism and Frankfurt-Style Scenarios," *Philosophical Topics* 24 (1996): 123–141; and "Ultimate Responsibility and Dumb Luck."
28. Kane, *The Significance of Free Will*, 98.
29. See, e.g., Richard Double, *The Non-Reality of Free Will*; and Galen Strawson, *Freedom and Belief* (Oxford: Clarendon Press, 1986). For a more recent defense of this view, see Pereboom, *Living Without Free Will*. And see my "Review of Pereboom," *Mind* 112 (2003): 375–378.
30. Mele, *Autonomous Agents*, chap. 12–13.
31. Randolph Clarke, "Modest Libertarianism," *Philosophical Perspectives* 14 (2000): 35. See also Pereboom, *Living Without Free Will*, 39.
32. Just as I distinguished between ultimate and nonultimate control, one may distinguish between ultimate and nonultimate *luck*. Perhaps millions of years ago, in a deterministic universe, conditions were such that today Karl would be an exceptionally kind person, whereas Carl would be a ruthless killer. Here we have ultimate luck – good and bad. Libertarians have been much more impressed by it than by nonultimate luck.
33. In Mele, "Soft Libertarianism," 123–141; and "Ultimate Responsibility and Dumb Luck." I developed a related view as a possibility: "soft libertarianism." A soft libertarian leaves it open that autonomy and moral responsibility are

compatible with determinism, but maintains that the falsity of determinism is required for *more desirable* brands of these things.

34. This is not to say that every disjunction of propositions with probabilities between 0 and 1 has a higher probability than each of the disjuncts. Consider the disjunction "*p* or *p*." My claim is about the propositions at issue here.
35. Mele, *Autonomous Agents*, chap. 13.
36. Parts of this essay derive from Mele, *Autonomous Agents*; and Mele, "Autonomy, Self-Control, and Weakness of Will," in Robert Kane, ed. *The Oxford Handbook of Free-Will* (New York: Oxford University Press, 2002): 529–548; and, more directly, from "Agnostic Autonomism," which I wrote in 2002 for Ted Honderich's "Determinism and Freedom Philosophy website" (http://www.ucl.ac.uk/~uctytho/dfwIntroIndex.htm).

5

Feminist Intuitions and the Normative Substance of Autonomy

Paul Benson

The concept of personal autonomy has become a matter of considerable contention among feminists. For quite some time, many feminists disowned the concept for purposes of ethical and social theory, arguing that the notion of personal autonomy harbors dangerous masculinist implications.[1] However, over the past decade it has become clear that autonomy is too useful for both critical and constructive purposes for feminists to abandon the concept altogether. If autonomous agency is intuitively a matter of claiming ownership of what one does and one's reasons for doing it, then some conception of autonomy, suitably "refigured,"[2] would seem to be indispensable for feminist projects of personal, institutional, and social critique and transformation.[3]

Among feminists seeking to reconceive autonomous agency, there has arisen considerable contention about how normatively robust a conception of autonomy must be to underwrite feminist projects of ethical and social criticism and reconstruction. This has come at a time when the issue of autonomy's normative content has also been the subject of much debate among a wider circle of theorists.[4] To put the matter (too) simply, some feminists argue that only a conception of autonomy that incorporates *substantive* normative commitments can adequately explain how oppressive modes of gender socialization can impair women's and men's autonomy.[5] Other feminists argue that such substantive accounts of autonomy are intolerably restrictive because they clash with the fundamental conviction that autonomous agents must be self-directing or self-ruling in a manner that leaves them free to adopt or act upon normative commitments other than those that substantive theories prescribe. This second camp urges various *procedural, content-neutral* conceptions of autonomy. Procedural views set out constraints on the processes or volitional structures through which persons come to form their motives, make decisions, and initiate actions. Such views describe the purportedly value-neutral capabilities by which women can claim authority for the interpretation and direction of their own lives in the midst of oppressive social practices and institutions.[6] Thus, one feminist writer pits "latitudinarian" conceptions of the latter sort against "restrictive, value-saturated" conceptions of autonomy.[7]

This chapter begins with an examination of Natalie Stoljar's recent attempt to show that feminist politics demand some strong substantive theory of autonomy – a theory, in other words, that places normative restrictions on the preferences or values that persons can form or act upon autonomously.[8] I argue that feminists need not accept the intuition on which Stoljar founds her position. I also present general objections against the type of substantive theory Stoljar favors. In the course of these arguments, I sketch part of an alternative conception of autonomy that incorporates normative content but does not constrain directly the types of actions agents might autonomously perform or the content of the motives or values that lead them to act. Such conceptions are weak substantive conceptions. In the account I propose, autonomy's normative substance resides in agents' attitudes toward their own authority to speak and answer for their decisions. This proposal occupies a largely neglected middle ground between strong substantive theories and content-neutral conceptions of autonomy. I maintain that this account is well suited for feminist efforts to analyze possibilities for women's autonomy within oppressive social arrangements. The chapter concludes by discussing the significance of weak substantive conceptions for autonomy theory in general.

I. STOLJAR'S "FEMINIST INTUITION"

Natalie Stoljar has recently argued that feminists should reach a certain verdict about the implications of oppressive feminine socialization for women's autonomy and that this verdict favors a strong substantive account of personal autonomy. A strong substantive account is one that directly imposes normative restrictions on the contents of the preferences or values that agents can form or act upon autonomously.[9] For example, a strong substantive conception might hold that persons can only autonomously prefer or value what accords with the value of autonomy itself.[10] Strong substantive conceptions may take a positive form, requiring that autonomous agents value certain things, or a negative form, excluding at least one desire or value from an autonomous agent's motives or commitments.[11]

Purely procedural theories, by contrast, understand autonomy to rest entirely in the structure of agents' motives or in the processes by which their motives and decisions are formed, independently of the specific content of the desires or values that lead agents to act.[12] For instance, many procedural theories maintain that agents' reflective endorsement of their effective intentions or of the ways in which those intentions were formed secures autonomy regardless of the substance of the beliefs, preferences, and evaluative attitudes that inform those intentions.[13] Procedural theories that grant a central place to reflective endorsement vary along many dimensions. Some demand actual endorsement; others require only counterfactual endorsement. Some require merely the absence of reflective rejection or feelings of alienation, instead of positive endorsement. Some focus on formal, structurally defined relations among motives; others consider the historical routes through which an agent's attitudes were formed. Some procedural theories posit preferences or preference formation as the primary locus of autonomy, while others see autonomy as residing in decisions or in deeper features of a person's character or the broader contours of her life.

Stoljar grants that procedural conceptions have been fruitful for feminist theory. They have done much to unseat the long-held presumption that autonomy depends upon "masculinist ideals of substantive independence and self-sufficiency."[14] Because agents can reflectively embrace attitudes and decisions that favor forms of personal interdependence involving care, vulnerability, trust, and love, procedural theories need not implicitly valorize Marlboro men over maternal thinkers. Furthermore, as Stoljar observes, procedural conceptions of autonomy can draw attention to the ways in which some personal relationships and social practices nourish or erode persons' capacities for autonomy. Procedural theories also permit respect for differences among the myriad ethical and cultural positions out of which persons can act autonomously.[15] In short, procedural theories appear to be responsive to some of the relational dimensions of autonomous agency that many feminists would want to highlight.

Nevertheless, Stoljar contends that procedural conditions alone cannot suffice for autonomy, as feminists should hold "the feminist intuition," according to which attitudes and decisions directly produced by women's internalization of false and oppressive norms of femininity cannot yield autonomous action, regardless of whether these agents would reflectively endorse their attitudes or the oppressive forms of socialization by which they came to have them.[16] Stoljar claims, in other words, that the internalization of incorrect and harmful norms as part of ordinary feminine socialization disrupts some women's autonomy because of the contents of the preferences it leads them to have, even when these women act for reasons or due to influences that they would not reject upon reflection.

Stoljar elucidates and seeks to support the feminist intuition by discussing Kristin Luker's research into the decision-making processes of a group of women who decided to take contraceptive risks, which led eventually to pregnancies and then to elective abortions, because they had internalized norms for women's sexuality that are plainly oppressive and misguided.[17] Among the norms that seem to have motivated these women are the following:

> [I]t is inappropriate for women to have active sex lives; it is unseemly for women to plan for and initiate sex; it is wrong to engage in or be seen to engage in premarital sex; pregnancy and childbearing promote one's worthiness by proving one is a "real woman"; it is normal for women to bargain for marriage by, for instance, proving their fertility to their partners or their partners' families; and women are worthwhile marriage partners only if they are capable of childbearing.[18]

Stoljar contends that, even if Luker's subjects did try to make rational decisions about running contraceptive risks, in light of the norms they had internalized they nonetheless failed to act autonomously when they decided to refrain from contraception. These women are not autonomous, Stoljar urges, because "they are overly influenced in their decisions about contraception by stereotypical and incorrect norms of femininity and sexual agency. Unlike risk takers in other domains, such as those who smoke or fail to wear safety belts in a car, Luker's subjects are motivated by oppressive and misguided norms that are internalized as a result of feminine socialization."[19] It is crucial for Stoljar's eventual argument about normative substance that, to the degree that the influence of such norms on Luker's subjects impairs their autonomy, this occurs because of the content of the preferences or values that feminine socialization presses them to form, not simply because of the kinds of psychological or social process through which such socialization influences them.

Stoljar's discussion of the women in Luker's study is nuanced and perceptive. She observes that some of these women's choices violate common procedural conditions of autonomy that rule out substantial barriers to self-knowledge or manifestly inconsistent attitudes.[20] She also shows, however, that many of the decision-making processes Luker describes satisfy all common procedural conditions for autonomy, including self-knowledge, internal coherence, reflective endorsement, and absence of reflection-inhibiting factors.[21] Hence, if the so-called feminist intuition that Luker's subjects cannot have acted autonomously is to be sustained, then procedural conditions, by themselves, must not be adequate to explain autonomy.[22] Stoljar concludes, "It is the content of these norms [regarding women's sexuality] that can be criticized from a feminist point of view, not the way in which Luker's subjects engage in the bargaining process. To vindicate the feminist intuition that the subjects are not autonomous, therefore, feminists need to develop a strong substantive theory of autonomy."[23]

II. OTHER FEMINIST INTUITIONS[24]

A central difficulty with Stoljar's argument is that it supposes that feminists will (or should) widely share a resolute conviction that none of the many women Luker discusses, in none of the various modes of reflection and practical reasoning in which they engage, can act autonomously upon decisions that are influenced by misogynist norms. Many feminists are likely to regard some of Luker's subjects differently, however.

Among the subjects of the contraception study who meet standard procedural conditions of autonomy,[25] let us distinguish, in what should be an intuitive way, those women whose reflexive attitudes toward their own agency indicate that they really do take agential ownership of their decisions from those whose attitudes manifest marked disengagement or dissociation from their conduct. This is not an exhaustive distinction; some subjects of the study will not belong to either group. In the former group will be women who know well enough their reasons for omitting to use contraception and who confidently affirm those reasons, upon reflection, along with the motivational influences that contribute to their acceptance of those reasons. Women in this first group also have no serious doubts about their competence to recognize or construct reasons for their actions or about their authority to speak and answer for their conduct, should others criticize it. Finally, these women are not systematically prevented access to practically germane information about the effectiveness, safety, and availability of contraception.[26]

The women in this first group may well be as autonomous in their decisions and actions as more progressively socialized women usually are, if not more so in some cases. Notwithstanding the influence upon them of harmful conventions regarding the sexual activities purportedly characteristic of "real womanliness," those conventions do not prevent them from reflecting critically on their motives and decisions or from modifying their intentions on the basis of reflection. As stipulated above, these women have a degree of self-awareness and access to relevant information that precludes their being literally brainwashed or subsumed by some form of Orwellian mind control.[27] Most importantly, the effects of their social training have not, *ex hypothesi*, diminished these women's regard for their own competence and worth as persons appropriately positioned to present their reasons for acting and to speak with authority in support of their decisions, should others question them. These women not only act upon what they reflectively stand for,[28] they also can properly view themselves as having the social authority to stand by their decisions, in virtue of being in a position to speak and answer for them in the face of potential criticism.[29]

Women in the first group make decisions to take contraceptive risks that bear their own authority as agents, notwithstanding their deplorably misdirected understanding of women's (and men's) social roles and the basis of their value as persons. They treat themselves as fit and worthy to identify adequate grounds for their decisions, to translate those decisions appropriately into conduct, and to answer for themselves should others challenge their reasons. Furthermore, there is nothing in their circumstances or constitution that indicates that it is inappropriate for them to claim for themselves the authority to scrutinize, stand by, and speak for their reasons for acting.[30] Nor would claiming such authority be incompatible with the demeaning norms they endorse. These women will not present reasons for their contraceptive risk taking that most feminists would accept. They may not be capable of justifying their decisions in terms that most feminists would find adequate. By itself, however, this circumstance merely reflects these women's evaluative distance from mainstream feminism. It does not diminish their ability to authorize their decisions and fully inhabit what they do in the sense that autonomy requires.[31]

Women in the second group of Luker's subjects also meet standard procedural conditions for autonomy. In contrast with the first group, however, these women are so unsure or distrustful of themselves that they feel unfit to articulate or answer for the reasons for their decisions to refrain from contraception. The women in this group will be uncertain about what their reasons are or unable to stand by their reasons as their own, although not in ways that would run afoul of procedural requirements of self-knowledge or reflective endorsement. For instance, when asked why she didn't use more effective contraception, one of Luker's subjects replies, "I always thought about it, but never did anything about it. I used to think about the pill, but my sister used it, she's married now and stuff, and my mother used to tell me she'd die. She's really Catholic. But it seems as if most of my friends are on it."[32] When women who in other arenas of their lives could present reasons for their actions with clarity and competence respond in such an inchoate, halting manner, this is good evidence that they do not treat themselves as having the authority to construct good reasons for their sexual conduct or to speak for their reasons. Stoljar grants that the failures of these subjects "are closer to failures of confidence or trust in one's ability to make claims than to flaws in the capacity for critical reflection. . . . [Many of] Luker's subjects lack confidence in asserting their sexual agency and, as a result, do not have a robust sense of their own authority in asserting their claims."[33]

Women in this second group may accept the same misguided, harmful views of their sexuality as women in the former group. The difference with respect to their autonomy is that they do not claim for themselves the authority to identify and speak for the reasons for their conduct. Their profound self-doubt leaves them alienated from what they do and their reasons for doing it, even though they would not be inclined to repudiate those reasons upon reflection.[34] These women inhabit in a passive, disengaged way their choices not to use contraception. Because they do not claim authority for themselves to speak for these choices, the choices do not bear their agential authority, and thus the women fail to act autonomously in carrying them out.

I have appealed to some widely shared convictions about the significance of agents' attitudes toward their authority as potential answerers for their actions in order to challenge Stoljar's intuition that agents burdened by internalized, oppressive social norms cannot act autonomously with respect to those norms. These convictions cohere with many forms of feminism, for reasons I indicate below. Many people who have no particular commitment to feminism will also accept these convictions. Three additional considerations count against Stoljar's case for some strong substantive conceptions of autonomy and against such conceptions more generally.

First, the critical analyses of social and psychological oppression that inform much feminist theorizing and politics suggest that the reach of oppressive practices and institutions is broad and that the socialization that transmits them runs deep. More generally, honest thinkers of all stripes recognize that the compass of human fallibility is great. We underestimate these elements of human life at our peril. As a result, we should grant that autonomous agency is compatible with making some seriously mistaken or unwarranted normative judgments, embracing some harmful values, or maintaining some attitudes that are inimical to agents' own interests. The price of refusing to grant this would be far-reaching skepticism about our ordinary prospects for autonomy. Conceptions of autonomy's normative substance that directly restrict the contents of agents' preferences or values must pay this price and tolerate some fairly radical skepticism about autonomy. Without independent reasons to favor such skepticism, I find this implication unacceptable. Many feminists will also be reluctant to embrace this skeptical posture, in part for the political reasons presented in the following argument.

It has been commonplace in the critical study of oppression to note the importance of identifying arenas for some autonomy within the evaluative, psychological, and political frameworks that undergird relations of domination and subordination. In the absence of such spaces for autonomy, limited though they may be, the agency of persons weighed down by those relations – as well as much of the agency of those who reap unfair advantage in them – vanishes. Critical examination of and resistance to oppression often arise from within. Yet internal resistance requires more room for autonomy than strong substantive accounts such as Stoljar's can permit. Diana Meyers presses a similar point, arguing that "an autonomy-friendly environment" is not a prerequisite for autonomy and that "multiply oppressed individuals are in some respects better positioned . . . to exercise autonomous moral and political agency . . . than multiply privileged individuals are."[35] Elsewhere, Meyers contends that strong substantive theories that would count many women as devoid of autonomy based on the cultural values they have internalized "deny existing opportunities for choice and . . . erase the real, sometimes courageous choices women have actually made."[36] A second charge against strong substantive conceptions is, therefore, political: Such conceptions seriously underestimate possibilities for autonomous agency within oppressive social relations and consequently fail to discern valuable opportunities for internal criticism and resistance.

Notice that we can recognize prospects for autonomous action within the scope of false or harmful norms without having to erase impairments of autonomy from the catalog of injuries that oppressive practices perpetuate. That is, we can hold off the skepticism about autonomy that Stoljar's position implies without going to the opposite extreme and finding an implausible wealth of autonomy within oppressive social systems. Misogynist conceptions of women's sexuality, for example, often assail women's autonomy by underwriting coercion of women's choices, by denying many women access to the material, cognitive, and emotional resources they need to participate meaningfully in the development of social policies affecting women's sexual health and freedom and by interfering with some women's reflective capabilities or with their sense of their own trustworthiness and authority as agents within a community of moral equals.

A third objection to strong substantive requirements on autonomy is that they conflate the power to *take ownership* of one's actions with something quite different, the power to *get things right*, or the ability to adopt the preferences or values one ought to have (or at least avoid those one ought not to have). Stoljar's central worry about many of the women in Luker's study is that they accept a false view of their worth as women and cannot uncover this falsehood because of the ways in which they have internalized their gender socialization.[37] If these women have been impaired in this manner – a possibility I cannot reject out of hand – then this is unquestionably a serious matter. Its gravity arises, however, from the ideal of right rule, or "orthonomy,"[38] not the standard of self-rule, or self-direction, that comprises autonomy. That self-rule is distinct from right rule can be seen by recalling the observation above that we can autonomously take ownership of our mistakes and limitations and act autonomously when bounded by them, even when we are not entirely capable of doing precisely the right thing for just the right reasons. The conceptual confusion between autonomy and orthonomy in strong substantive accounts parallels, then, the skeptical leanings of those accounts. The tendency to confuse orthonomy and autonomy may stem in part from the fact that both capabilities appear to be necessary for some sorts of moral accountability, or responsibility.[39]

This third objection also coheres with a dominant strand of much feminist thought. One of feminism's guiding commitments is to take women's experiences and perspectives seriously. Stoljar's argument seeks to do this by attending to the damage that social training in compulsory femininity can inflict on women's decision making. My proposal also aims to take women's perspectives seriously, but in a more immediate manner than Stoljar's and in a way that seems more germane to women's capabilities for self-direction. The distinction I have drawn between women who act autonomously despite their misguided view of women's sexual roles and those women whose agency is impaired by the way they have internalized this gender training attends to women's experience of themselves as agents. In particular, this distinction focuses on women's attitudes toward their own socially situated authority to construct, stand by, and speak for their reasons for acting. I have proposed that such reflexive attitudes provide a key to determining whether oppressive socialization impedes the agential authority necessary for autonomy. In the next section, I argue that the modest way in which this proposal incorporates normative substance does not leave it vulnerable to the criticisms I have leveled against substantive conceptions like Stoljar's.

III. WEAK NORMATIVE CONTENT

Before discussing how the conception of autonomy I have begun to assemble in this chapter incorporates normative content, it will be useful to step back and survey various types of substantive conception. This survey will reveal why some objections commonly brought against (what appear to be) strong substantive theories miss their mark. More importantly, it will show that a wide theoretical space lies between strong substantive conceptions and content-neutral accounts. By considering where my proposal falls within this space, I hope to illustrate some of the promise of weak substantive theories of autonomy.

Up to this point, I have defined strong substantive accounts of autonomy in the generally received way, as those in which the contents of the preferences or values that agents can form or act upon autonomously are subject to direct, normative constraints. At a minimum, this means that, for any strong substantive account, there must be some things that autonomous agents cannot prefer or value without sacrificing some autonomy, where this restriction depends immediately on the substance of such preferences or values. Some contemporary theorists have defended conceptions that meet this criterion, but they are far less common than one would suppose from the literature.[40] Many well-known theories of autonomy that are regarded as strong substantive accounts fail to satisfy this criterion.[41] These theories incorporate normative substance by way of agents' *competence* to recognize and appreciate various norms that apply to their actions. The normative content of these theories issues from the values or reasons that autonomous agents must be capable of detecting and responding to in appropriate ways. The normative competencies these theories describe, however, need not entail any direct, normative restrictions on the contents of autonomous agents' preferences or values. These theories typically allow that normatively competent persons can choose what is unreasonable or wrong or value what is bad, because competence lies some distance short of perfect evaluative perception or responsiveness.

The distinction between substantive theories that conceive of autonomy as consisting in normative competence and other types of substantive accounts is rarely appreciated.[42] In particular, it is seldom understood that, because normative competence theories do not constrain directly the content of autonomous agents' preferences or values, they do not necessarily succumb to the difficulties that plague genuinely strong substantive conceptions. A brief examination of Diana Meyers's latest objections to "restrictive, value-saturated" accounts of autonomy amply illustrates the point.

Meyers objects that nonneutral views of autonomy mistakenly "insist on the need to distinguish real from apparent desires and authentic values from spurious ones . . . by placing constraints on what people can autonomously choose."[43] She also argues that substantive theories "homogenize authentic selves and autonomous lives" and, in doing so, paradoxically "*deindividualize* autonomy" [Meyers's emphasis].[44] Meyers contends, finally, that substantive theories ignore subtle features of history and context when assessing ways in which cultural norms can disrupt autonomy and so tend to exaggerate the effect of oppressive socialization.[45] These criticisms represent well some of the most common objections raised against strong substantive theories.

None of Meyers's criticisms fare well against normative-competence theories, however. For, as we have seen, requiring some robust, normative competence for autonomy does not entail restricting agents' preferences or values directly. Yet Meyers's objections target just such restrictions. Normative-competence accounts demand that agents' capabilities of perception, reasoning, and motivation be connected in the right sorts of ways to what is really valuable or reasonable for them. But this demand neither mandates a distinction between real and apparent desires nor forces autonomous selves and lives into an oppressively uniform, impersonal mold. Normative-competence theories can readily allow that desires to do other than the right things for the right reasons are just as "real," for purposes of understanding autonomy, as desires for truth and goodness. Similarly, there is no reason to think that persons who share similar normative competence must lead the same sort of life or that their lives must lack individual distinctiveness. Only very narrow conceptions of the normative "facts," supplemented by implausibly strong claims about internal relations between judgment and motivation, would tend toward the implications Meyers fears.[46] Meyers is correct that substantive theories of autonomy have too often been insensitive to historical or other contextual particularities that structure the choices that agents face and inform the meanings of those choices in specific cultural settings. Nothing stands in the way, however, of bringing greater historical sophistication and contextual nuance to conceptions of normative competence.[47]

Perhaps it is not surprising that Meyers's objections do not succeed against substantive conceptions that center upon agents' normative competence, because Meyers herself favors a skills- or competency-based theory of autonomy. According to Meyers,

> autonomous people have well-developed, well-coordinated repertoires of agentic skills and call on them routinely as they reflect on themselves and their lives and as they reach decisions about how best to go on. When a woman speaks in her own voice, then, she is articulating what she knows as a result of exercising these skills.[48]

The agentic skills that Meyers has in mind include skills in introspection, communication, memory, imagination, analytical reasoning, "self-nurturing," resistance to pressures to conform, and political collaboration.[49] Meyers asserts that a skills-based view of autonomy stands apart from substantive accounts and content-neutral theories alike, but also exhibits some virtues of each. She holds that a skills-based conception can respect women's ability to make their own choices, even in social circumstances hostile to autonomy. At the same time, she believes that her approach can explain how internalized oppression may curtail women's powers of self-determination.

Much like the normative-competence theories discussed above, Meyers's competency-based theory is clearly not a strong substantive conception in the strict sense. But her position also does not appear to be purely procedural or content-neutral. The agentic skills she describes seem to import specific values into the account. For instance, Meyers defines the skills of "self-nurturing" in relation to the value of self-worth. She says that these skills enable agents "to appreciate the overall worthiness of their self-portraits and self-narratives" and to "sustain their self-respect."[50] Similarly, Meyers's description of educational programs designed to augment the autonomy of women within oppressive social practices adopts values such as interpersonal and community solidarity.[51] Therefore, although Meyers's approach eschews direct restrictions on what autonomous agents can prefer or value, it carries normative content indirectly, through the values subsumed in its descriptions of autonomy competencies.

We have seen that normative-competence theories may afford substantive conceptions of autonomy that fall short of being strong substantive accounts. Our discussion of Meyers's recent work likewise has shown that some common criticisms of substantive conceptions actually pertain to strong substantive theories alone. Meyers's own view now appears to fall somewhere within the potentially wide, largely unmapped expanse of theoretical terrain that stretches between strong substantive theories and strictly neutral ones. The approach I have suggested also lies within this intermediate region. In this approach, normative standards for agents' authority to construct and potentially answer for their reasons for acting enter into autonomy by way of the attitudes toward their own competence and worth through which agents claim such authority. Because the contents of persons' attitudes can lead them to distrust their own fitness or deny their worthiness to speak for their reasons and thereby diminish their autonomy, this approach is not content neutral. We have already found that this approach is not a strong substantive one. Hence, the account I have sketched to this point provides a *weak* substantive conception of autonomy.[52]

Until my proposal has been developed fully, it will be difficult to say how it might be related to normative-competence theories or to strong restrictions on what autonomous agents can choose to do. It is possible, in principle, that attitudinal conditions of the sort I have described might be joined to competence conditions that require some capability to recognize and respond to reasons. In turn, it is possible that arguments could be given that aim to show that these competence conditions are naturally supplemented with some strong substantive restrictions.[53] However, in order to connect weak attitudinal conditions both to weak normative-competence requirements and to strong substantive constraints, it would be necessary to circumvent the objections raised in the preceding section to strong constraints, objections that apply as well to normative-competence theories. I do not see how to do this, especially for the kind of constraint that Stoljar proposes for actions influenced by false or harmful social norms.

A notable strength of the weak substantive account I favor is that it withstands the three objections I posed against Stoljar's case for normative content. Yet the proposed account also avoids the intuitive implausibility of purely procedural views for understanding autonomy within oppressive social circumstances. First, the attitudinal components of agents' claiming for themselves authority as potential answerers for their decisions do not imply wholesale skepticism about everyday prospects for autonomy. Nor do these conditions too readily affirm people's capacities to act autonomously, because oppressive stereotypes and power relations are well known to infect many persons' sense of their fitness or worthiness to speak for their decisions. Second, the proposed conditions make room for women to criticize and resist misogynist conventions even if they have internalized some aspects of traditional femininity that are hostile to their interests. So long as women are able to retain properly a sense of their authority as reasoning, potentially answerable agents, they may autonomously develop criticisms of sexism even while they endorse some sexist practices. Third, the proposed view suitably distinguishes autonomy from the more stringent demands of orthonomy or full accountability.

The results of this discussion reach beyond the prospects for Stoljar's defense of normative content or for my proposal for certain weak substantive conditions of autonomy. We have found, not surprisingly, that no single interpretation of women's agency within male-dominated social systems can claim the label "feminist" for itself alone. More interesting is our finding that the distinction between substantive and content-neutral theories of autonomy, which seemed so sharp and straightforward in earlier phases of contemporary writing on autonomy,[54] should be reconceived as a range of theories that impute varying kinds of normative substance, through disparate pathways, to autonomous agency. Despite the outpouring of important work on autonomy over the past thirty years, the middle ground between strong substantive conceptions and content-neutral accounts remains largely unexplored. Efforts to demarcate plausible positions within this territory would be likely to give rise to new ways of understanding autonomy's evaluative elements and, in turn, to new interpretations of autonomy's value. We have found, lastly, that close study of feminist work on autonomy's normative substance promises to bear fruit for autonomy theory in general.

Notes

I am grateful to an audience at the April 2002 Central Division Meetings of the American Philosophical Association for discussion of an early version of this chapter. I am especially indebted to James Stacey Taylor, Diana Meyers, Michael Root, and John Santiago for their written comments on a draft of this chapter.

1. For helpful surveys of feminist critiques of autonomy, see Marilyn Friedman, "Autonomy and Social Relationships: Rethinking the Feminist Critique," in Diana T. Meyers, ed., *Feminists Rethink the Self* (Boulder, CO: Westview Press, 1997): 40–61; Marilyn Friedman, *Autonomy, Gender, Politics* (New York:

Oxford University Press, 2003); and Catriona Mackenzie and Natalie Stoljar, "Introduction: Autonomy Refigured," in their *Relational Autonomy: Feminist Perspectives on Autonomy, Agency, and the Social Self* (New York: Oxford University Press, 2000): 3–31.

2. I borrow this term from Mackenzie and Stoljar, "Introduction," 3–4.
3. For defenses of this view, see, e.g., Paul Benson, "Feminist Second Thoughts about Free Agency," *Hypatia* 5 (1990): 47–64; Paul Benson, "Autonomy and Oppressive Socialization," *Social Theory and Practice* 17 (1991): 385–408; John Christman, "Feminism and Autonomy," in Dana Bushnell, ed., *Nagging Questions: Feminist Ethics in Everyday Life* (Lanham, MD: Rowman & Littlefield, 1995): 17–40; Friedman, "Autonomy and Social Relationships"; Friedman, *Autonomy, Gender, Politics*; Mackenzie and Stoljar, "Introduction"; Diana T. Meyers, *Self, Society, and Personal Choice* (New York: Columbia University Press, 1989); Diana T. Meyers, "Intersectional Identity and the Authentic Self? Opposites Attract!" in Mackenzie and Stoljar, eds., *Relational Autonomy*, 151–180; Diana T. Meyers, "Feminism and Women's Autonomy: The Challenge of Female Genital Cutting," *Metaphilosophy* 31 (2000): 469–491; Diana T. Meyers, *Gender in the Mirror: Cultural Imagery and Women's Agency* (New York: Oxford University Press, 2002): chap. 1; and Jennifer Nedelsky, "Reconceiving Autonomy: Sources, Thoughts and Possibilities," *Yale Journal of Law and Feminism* 1 (1989): 7–36.
4. For a useful survey of points of convergence between feminist discussions of autonomy and mainstream accounts, see Friedman, "Autonomy and Social Relationships." Also see Friedman, *Autonomy, Gender, Politics*, chap. 4.
5. Proponents of this sort of position include Benson, "Feminist Second Thoughts about Free Agency"; Benson, "Autonomy and Oppressive Socialization"; Sarah Buss, "Autonomy Reconsidered," *Midwest Studies in Philosophy* 19 (1994): 95–121; Sigurdur Kristinsson, "The Limits of Neutrality: Toward a Weakly Substantive Account of Autonomy," *Canadian Journal of Philosophy* 30 (2000): 257–286; Marina Oshana, "Personal Autonomy and Society," *Journal of Social Philosophy* 29 (1998): 81–102; Natalie Stoljar, "Autonomy and the Feminist Intuition," in *Relational Autonomy*, 94–111; Susan Wolf, "Sanity and the Metaphysics of Responsibility," in Ferdinand Schoeman, ed., *Responsibility, Character, and the Emotions* (New York: Cambridge University Press, 1987): 46–62; and Susan Wolf, *Freedom within Reason* (New York: Oxford University Press, 1990).
6. Diana Meyers has been the most influential feminist advocate of a procedural conception of personal autonomy. See her "Personal Autonomy and the Paradox of Feminine Socialization," *Journal of Philosophy* 84 (1987): 619–628; *Self, Society, and Personal Choice*; "Intersectional Identity and the Authentic Self?"; "Feminism and Women's Autonomy"; and *Gender in the Mirror*, chap. 1. I argue below, however, that Meyers's position is better understood as a substantive one. Marilyn Friedman has recently argued that content-neutral and substantive conceptions of autonomy should be thought of as marking different degrees of autonomy and that content-neutral views manage to establish an appropriate minimum threshold of autonomy. See *Autonomy, Gender, Politics*, 19–25.

7. Meyers, "Feminism and Women's Autonomy," 475–476; and *Gender in the Mirror*, 11.
8. Stoljar, "Autonomy and the Feminist Intuition."
9. See ibid., 95, 107–109. For general discussion of the distinctions between substantive and procedural, or content-neutral, theories, also see Mackenzie and Stoljar, "Introduction," 19–21; and Paul Benson, "Free Agency and Self-Worth," *Journal of Philosophy* 91 (1994): 650–668.
10. According to Friedman, all substantive conceptions of autonomy require that autonomous agents choose in accord with the value of autonomy. See her *Autonomy, Gender, Politics*, 19–20. This is incorrect, strictly speaking. The values that strong substantive theories require conceivably might not include or be limited to the value of autonomy. Also, some strong substantive theories will allow that agents can autonomously choose or act in ways that are incompatible with the value of autonomy. Furthermore, Friedman's claim leaves no room for weaker types of substantive accounts that do not constrain directly agents' motives or preferences. I argue for the importance of such accounts later in this chapter.
11. Kristinsson calls such negative accounts "weakly substantive" and the positive requirements "strongly substantive" (see "The Limits of Neutrality," 258–259). This terminology is misleading, as negative forms of normative requirement could prove to impose many demanding constraints on autonomous agents, whereas a positive normative requirement might involve nothing more than a single, relatively permissive value. For this reason, I regard the normative constraint that Kristinsson favors, namely that persons cannot autonomously embrace the value of self-effacement, or blind, unconditional obedience, as belonging to a strong substantive conception.
12. Although requirements of internal rationality concern relations among the contents of agents' beliefs and desires, procedural theories of autonomy are permitted to make such requirements. For discussion, see John Christman, "Autonomy and Personal History," *Canadian Journal of Philosophy* 21 (1991): 1–24, esp. 13–16.
13. The contemporary literature on the character of such reflective endorsement is vast. Much of it was inspired initially by Harry Frankfurt in *The Importance of What We Care About* (Cambridge: Cambridge University Press, 1988); and by Gerald Dworkin in *The Theory and Practice of Autonomy* (Cambridge: Cambridge University Press, 1988).
14. Stoljar, "Autonomy and the Feminist Intuition," 94. Stoljar's observation is somewhat ironic. Procedural theories criticized such masculinist views of autonomy in virtue of their being strong substantive views. Yet Stoljar herself defends a strong substantive conception, only one with more explicitly feminist substance.
15. Ibid., 95.
16. Ibid.
17. Kristin Luker, *Taking Chances: Abortion and the Decision Not to Contracept* (Berkeley: University of California Press, 1975). Stoljar credits Elizabeth Anderson's paper, "Should Feminists Reject Rational Choice Theory?" for drawing her attention to the significance for autonomy of Luker's examples.

Since the publication of Stoljar's essay, Anderson's paper has been published in Louise M. Antony and Charlotte Witt, eds., *A Mind of One's Own*, 2nd ed. (Boulder, CO: Westview Press, 2001): 369–397.

18. Stoljar, "Autonomy and the Feminist Intuition," 99.
19. Ibid., 98.
20. On self-deception, see Diana Meyers's description of the introspective skills necessary for autonomy in "Intersectional Identity and the Authentic Self?" 166; and in *Gender in the Mirror*, 20. Also see John Christman's treatment of self-deception and inconsistent attitudes in "Autonomy and Personal History," 13–18.
21. Stoljar, "Autonomy and the Feminist Intuition," 100–107. I would quarrel with some of Stoljar's interpretations of these conditions, especially with her interpretation of Calhoun's view of internal coherence (ibid., 104–105). But these disagreements are not germane here.
22. For an argument against merely procedural accounts of autonomy that is similar in form to Stoljar's, see Henry Richardson, "Autonomy's Many Normative Presuppositions," *American Philosophical Quarterly* 38 (2001): 287–303.
23. Stoljar, "Autonomy and the Feminist Intuition," 109.
24. Cf. Friedman's reply to Stoljar, in which she presents "*another* feminist intuition" (*Autonomy, Gender, Politics*, 25).
25. I am supposing only for the purposes of discussion that standard procedural conditions are necessary for autonomy. In fact, I think that some such conditions are too strong, as they rule out the autonomy of trivial acts and of actions that arise out of authentic ambivalence. For further discussion, see my "Taking Ownership: Authority and Voice in Autonomous Agency," in John Christman and Joel Anderson, eds., *Autonomy and the Challenges to Liberalism: New Essays* (Cambridge: Cambridge University Press, forthcoming).
26. Luker found that her subjects generally had access to contraception, knew how to use it, and had used it in the past.
27. I take these features to be implied by the characterization of these women's socialization as "ordinary" in its manner. However, if close analogs to brainwashing or Orwellian mind control are taken to be part of ordinary feminine socialization, then I would retract the claim that women in the first group can be autonomous agents. This would have no bearing on Stoljar's argument, though, because standard procedural elements of autonomy would be absent from scenarios of brainwashing and the like.
28. Even if there is disagreement about this, at least we can assume that women in this first group meet the relevant requirements for reflective endorsement in order to evaluate Stoljar's argument that strong substantive conditions are needed to assess these women's autonomy.
29. This does not mean that these women are fully answerable, or accountable, for what they do. It only means that they regard themselves as having the abilities and social standing that fit them to serve as potential "answerers" for their conduct. In fact, some of these women may lack certain sorts of knowledge or certain motivational capabilities that would be necessary for them to be fully accountable for their actions.

30. See my "Taking Ownership" for extended discussion and supporting argument. Among the conditions necessary for properly claiming this authority is the requirement that the agent not be systematically prevented from acquiring practically germane information. I have already assumed that women in the first group meet this condition.
31. Notice that, if the autonomy of women in the first group is marked by the ways they regard themselves as authorized to identify and present reasons for their decisions, then it would not necessarily matter if these women did not act upon the wills they reflectively most wanted, after all. For instance, they might have been ambivalent about running contraceptive risks without being significantly less autonomous in doing so. They still could properly treat themselves as having the authority necessary for their actions to belong fully to them, despite their failure to achieve unqualified volitional endorsement or wholeheartedness.
32. Luker, *Taking Chances*, 46; quoted in Stoljar, "Autonomy and the Feminist Intuition," 98.
33. Stoljar, "Autonomy and the Feminist Intuition," 97–98.
34. Elsewhere, I discuss in detail how such self-doubt can interfere with certain components of moral responsibility without disrupting agents' capacities for reflective self-control of their conduct. See my "Feeling Crazy: Self-Worth and the Social Character of Responsibility," in *Relational Autonomy*, 72–93.
35. Meyers, "Intersectional Identity and the Authentic Self?" 152.
36. Meyers, "Feminism and Women's Autonomy," 475.
37. Stoljar, "Autonomy and the Feminist Intuition," 109.
38. Philip Pettit and Michael Smith, "Freedom in Belief and Desire," *Journal of Philosophy* 93 (1996): 429–449, esp. 442–444. Also cf. Susan Wolf's account of her "reason view" of freedom and responsibility in *Freedom within Reason*, 70–71, 75–76.
39. Or perhaps, as Gary Watson has argued, we readily blur two "faces" of responsibility, namely, attributability and moral accountability, where the latter requires a strong form of normative competence. See Watson, "Two Faces of Responsibility," *Philosophical Topics* 24 (1996): 227–248.
40. For theories that do meet the criterion, see Susan E. Babbitt, "Feminism and Objective Interests: The Role of Transformation Experiences in Rational Deliberation," in Linda Alcoff and Elizabeth Potter, eds., *Feminist Epistemologies* (New York: Routledge, 1993): 245–264; Buss, "Autonomy Reconsidered"; Kristinsson, "The Limits of Neutrality"; Oshana, "Personal Autonomy and Society"; Richardson, "Autonomy's Many Normative Presuppositions"; and George Sher, *Beyond Neutrality: Perfectionism and Politics* (Cambridge: Cambridge University Press, 1997): chap. 3.
41. For instance, see Benson, "Autonomy and Oppressive Socialization"; Pettit and Smith, "Freedom in Belief and Desire"; Stoljar, "Autonomy and the Feminist Intuition"; and Wolf, "Sanity and the Metaphysics of Responsibility" and *Freedom within Reason*.
42. Stoljar comments, e.g., that there may be strong substantive conceptions that do not employ the notion of normative competence, but she gives no

examples of such theories and limits her discussion otherwise to normative-competence theories ("Autonomy and the Feminist Intuition," 111 n. 51).

43. Meyers, "Feminism and Women's Autonomy," 477; cf. her *Gender in the Mirror*, 13.
44. Meyers, "Feminism and Women's Autonomy," 480; cf. her *Gender in the Mirror*, 16.
45. Ibid.
46. Wolf makes a point of explaining that the normative competence her "reason view" requires is compatible with a wide range of metaethical positions, including various strains of relativism and normative pluralism (*Freedom within Reason*, chap. 6).
47. I have begun to do this in "Culture and Responsibility," *Journal of Social Philosophy* 32 (2001): 610–620, in which I respond to Michele Moody-Adams's claim that cultures cannot disable our moral capacities to know what is morally right or wrong.
48. Meyers, *Gender in the Mirror*, 21.
49. Ibid., 20–21. In "Feminism and Women's Autonomy," 485–489, Meyers also discusses empathy skills.
50. Meyers, *Gender in the Mirror*, 20.
51. Meyers, "Feminism and Women's Autonomy," 480–487.
52. For previous discussions of the distinction between weak and strong substantive theories, see Mackenzie and Stoljar, "Introduction," 19–21; Stoljar, "Autonomy and the Feminist Intuition," 107–108; and Benson, "Free Agency and Self-Worth," 663–665. I have departed from those discussions here by classifying normative-competence theories as weakly substantive.
53. The only work I know that aims to connect various weak and strong substantive conditions in this way is Richardson, "Autonomy's Many Normative Presuppositions," 295–299.
54. Recall, e.g., Dworkin's distinction between "purely formal" conceptions of autonomy, in which "what one decides for oneself can have any particular content," and substantive conceptions, in which "only certain decisions count as retaining autonomy where others count as forfeiting it" (*The Theory and Practice of Autonomy*, 12).

6

Autonomy and Personal Integration

Laura Waddell Ekstrom

One of the most intriguing aspects of the well-known exchange between Harry Frankfurt (1971) and Gary Watson (1975) concerning freedom of the will and the nature of the self is a shared insight, namely, that the autonomy of an action is decreased, perhaps even to the point of being nullified, by that action's springing from an attitude that conflicts with certain other elements of the agent's psychology.[1] Is this so? And if it is, then what type of internal conflict is inimical to autonomy: conflict between levels of desire, as on Frankfurt's early view, or tension between Reason and Appetite, as on Watson's original account, or conflict of some other sort? Frankfurt in later work highlights a notion of wholeheartedness as a crucial agential good.[2] The wholehearted agent is free of ambivalence, Frankfurt suggests, such that at least one of a pair of conflicting psychic elements is rejected "as an outlaw"; the element integrated into the self is the one with which the agent "identifies," and action on a motivation with which one identifies is autonomous.

Much philosophical discussion has centered on the difficult notion of identification. Yet there is no consensus on either the nature of that phenomenon or its importance to understanding agency in general or autonomous agency, in particular. On one approach, identification consists of decision and action of a particular sort: Michael Bratman, for instance, understands identification as a matter of an agent's deciding to treat, and treating, a certain desire as reason-giving for action and practical deliberation, adding that the decision must be one with which the agent is "satisfied."[3] This satisfaction, like Frankfurt's notion of wholeheartedness, might be understood in at least two distinct ways: one, as a kind of *feeling* that accompanies the decision to treat a certain desire as reason-giving, so that the satisfied agent decides (and treats) exuberantly, for instance, with gusto, or with contentment. On the other hand, satisfaction and wholeheartedness might be understood as *structural* requirements, such that the relevant deciding (and treating), or the relevant formation of desire, is done without mental reservation – in other words, it is not in conflict with other important items of the agent's psychology; and perhaps, even further, it is positively supported by the agent's other psychic elements. On the structural approach, the wholehearted or satisfied agent possesses cohesion among the significant items of his psychology. (It remains an open issue which items must cohere, to what degree and in what fashion.)

A coherence theory of autonomy such as the one I have developed in earlier work[4] takes the latter, structural, approach to wholeheartedness, rather than the former, sensational or emotive, approach. Motivated, in part, by reflection on particular cases and motivated, as well, by the problem of regress for hierarchical accounts, a coherence approach to autonomy specifies that the preference on which a person acts must cohere with other of his attitudes, in order for the act to be autonomously performed. I have found it striking that those working in moral psychology and action theory on the issues of agential identification and psychological integration have not made use of the rich conceptual resources of epistemology, especially the detailed accounts one finds there of coherence among mental states. Although Keith Lehrer, in particular, does not himself take a coherence approach to analyzing personal autonomy – rather, he takes what might be termed a foundationalist approach[5] – nonetheless, Lehrer's coherence theory of epistemic justification provides a useful springboard for developing an account of coherence among states of preference. If an autonomous agent needs to be wholehearted, and if wholeheartedness implies psychological integration, then it is only natural to look to the existing literature on coherence among mental items for help in understanding autonomous agency.

I. INTERNALITY AND AUTONOMY

To back up. Suppose we understand the idea of "living an autonomous life" as a matter of exercising an ability, often and in significant areas of one's life, to act autonomously. Then it is the autonomy of action that is of primary concern (rather than, for instance, the autonomy of desire). Because decisions are mental actions, an account of autonomous action is also an account of autonomous decision or choice. The autonomous *person* is able to make autonomous decisions and to perform other actions autonomously, and he exercises these abilities. (I leave as an open issue how often, and in which arenas, one must autonomously act in order to qualify as an autonomous person.)

One might begin with the thought that one autonomously does just plain whatever one does. But then, of course, we slip and fall not autonomously but accidentally, and we digest and sweat and grow in ways not normally under our control in any sense. We recognize good reason to distinguish mere behavior from action, where intentionality is part of the right analysis of the latter. But not everything we intentionally do is an autonomous action. Sometimes we are motivated by intentions so far below the level of consciousness (as in Freudian slips of the tongue) that some decline to call the results autonomous actions. (Velleman describes them as mere activities, falling short of what he calls "full-blooded human action.")[6] Some acts are done intentionally but under the force of coercive pressure, as when one hands money over to another with a gun in one's face, and many find such coerced acts nonautonomous. Perhaps, then, uncoerced (consciously?) intentional action is autonomous. If so, then an autonomous person is one who is often and in significant areas of her life able to act in ways that are (consciously?) intentional and not subject to coercion.

But coercion – understood to comprise a large category of external interference with agency, including brainwashing, science fiction neurological puppetry, and other forms of manipulation by outside persons and forces, including the use of threats, indoctrination, and posthypnotic suggestion – is not agreed by all to be in all cases autonomy undermining. Frankfurt maintains that what matters for autonomy and moral responsibility is that one is wholehearted with respect to the motivation that leads one to act; it is unimportant whether one had alternative possibilities for acting, and it matters not how one got to be the way one is.[7] Mele holds that coercion for which one has autonomously arranged – as in the case of a dieter who voluntarily seeks the hypnotic induction of certain food-avoidance desires – is an exception to its general autonomy undermining nature.[8] Thus, while various forms of external coercive pressure are widely recognized as threats to persons' power autonomously to author their choices and ways of life, they are not universally agreed to be in every case autonomy undermining.

If coercion is generally destructive of autonomy, it nonetheless is not the only way in which our intentional actions can fall short of the autonomy bar. Standard cases considered by action theorists include those of persons suffering from various compulsive disorders. Kleptomaniacs, for instance, can act intentionally as they steal and be uncoerced by others, yet their thefts are not paradigms of autonomous action. Compulsive gamblers likewise can be free from coercive pressures and intentionally place their bets, as alcoholics can intentionally order more rounds and heroin addicts can intentionally, not accidentally, shoot up. In all of these cases, it is not as if the problematic behavior "happens to" the persons involved. Rather, stealing, betting, drinking, and drug taking are actions that the addicts themselves are trying deliberately to accomplish. Furthermore, in all of these cases, it is not as if the problematic behavior is something that the persons involved are pushed into doing by some force or agent external to the addicts themselves, or at least this is apparently not so. The alcoholic whose brother forcefully pours drinks down his mouth clearly does not act autonomously in drinking. But neither does the self-loathing alcoholic who drinks on his own, without coercive pressure and with intention to take a drink, but in disgust and anguish over his condition.

It is precisely the difficult issue of settling which forces are external and which are internal to the agent himself (which are "truly his own") that is at the center of the discussion between Frankfurt and Watson and many others since. A threatening or manipulative person is clearly external, in a spatial sense, to another agent – in being outside of his head – but the desire to binge in a bulimic who hates and feels trapped by her condition seems external to her in a more subtle way. And there are less dramatic examples. One may in an episode of consternation want to end a certain relationship, but that desire may not represent who one really is in some important sense, albeit a sense that is in significant need of clarification.

The problem with regard to autonomous action on which I focus is that certain acts that we intentionally do frustrate rather than express the self, even when we have not been the victim of coercion or when our being the victim of coercion has played no role in the production of these acts. Another way to put the difficulty is in terms of personal alienation: One can be distanced from or revolted by the ways in which one acts, even when one acts intentionally and without external manipulation, where this revulsion shows alienation of the self from certain actions or motivations that otherwise might be thought to be internal to the self. Frankfurt's willing and unwilling addicts highlight the phenomenon of alienation: Although both are addicted, the unwilling addict loathes his condition and wishes he could be different; he is enslaved in a way that the willing addict is not. Because the willing addict is happy to "go along with" his addiction, he does not experience the kind of inner turmoil that the unwilling addict experiences. Inner turmoil, disharmony in the self, indicates lack of autonomy.

Hierarchical theories such as Frankfurt's original view account for this disharmony, of course, as a conflict between levels of desire.[9] Many have found hierarchical approaches to autonomy suggestive but problematic. They are insightful in highlighting a very special ability: to "rise above" or "step back from" our own attitudes, reflecting evaluatively upon them and forming (higher-level) attitudes concerning those attitudes. In exercising not only a power of observation of our own mental states, but also powers for forming and for acting in line with higher-order attitudes, we seem to achieve control over both who we are and the direction of our lives. But two problems are especially salient. First, the accounts generate an evaluative regress of endorsing states, each of which grants internality to the state at the prior level.[10] Second, it is difficult to explain why the true self should be identified with desires of the higher level, rather than with those of the lower level or with something else, instead.[11] Thus, we have been led to develop alternative approaches to autonomy.

II. WHOLEHEARTEDNESS AND IDENTIFICATION

We should not stray so far, however, that we neglect the insights in Frankfurt's "Freedom of the Will and the Concept of a Person." This work has been so influential in part because of the truth it elegantly expresses: We *are* able to form higher-level mental states, and this is important to an understanding of the human mind. Nonetheless, the central significance of this fact to autonomy is not in second-order volitions (in Frankfurt's sense) themselves, for it is not true that we act autonomously only when we act from a desire for another desire. It is not the order of the motivation that matters – not whether the desire has as its intentional object another desire, or the state of affairs of a particular desire's being effective in leading to action, rather than its having as its intentional object a particular course of action. Instead, what matters for autonomy is what we take to have been implicit in the formation of a higher-level attitude, namely, the activity of reflective endorsement. The reason this matters is that our ability mentally to draw away from our own mental states and to subject them to critical evaluation enables us to ensure that our desires do not automatically move us to act, making us the passive vehicles through which the strongest impulses hold sway. Our critical engagement with reasons, our evaluation of desires and courses of action with respect to worth, and our endorsement of some of these – these activities constitute the participation of the self.

Frankfurt himself does not require "positive endorsement" of our desires, but instead "acceptance." It is his intuition that one may "join oneself" to a desire for any variety of reasons and that an account requiring positive reflective endorsement is "excessively rationalistic."[12] On his view, there need be no particular standard against which desires are assessed, and one may act autonomously from higher-order volitions formed arbitrarily or capriciously. However, certain reasons for aligning oneself with one motivation and rejecting another as an "outlaw" are intuitively autonomy undermining. Through the warped view of depression, for instance, one might accept as one's own a desire to quit one's profession, even though one does not at the time view one's quitting as a good thing, and one has many reasons not to quit. ("I might as well accept it," says the voice of depression, Eeyore-style, "I am just a quitter.") After the fog has lifted, one might be startled by the attitudes with which one was earlier willing to be satisfied, grasping the extent to which one was then "not oneself" or not governed in one's higher-order attitudes by Reason.[13] Likewise, fatigue, boredom, and external manipulation – all allowed by Frankfurt as explanations of higher-order acceptance – seem not sufficiently authenticating states or processes to ground autonomous action.

Suppose, then, that we do not rely centrally on the Frankfurtian conception of a second-order volition or higher-order acceptance. Consider, instead, the notion of a "preference," understood not in the usual comparative sense ("I prefer this to that"), but rather, stipulatively, as a desire that has survived a process of critical evaluation – in particular, with respect to an individual's conception of the good. Some of our preferences are for having certain desires; others are for particular courses of action or for certain states of affairs. A preference is identified as such not by its type of intentional object, but rather by the process through which it was generated. Not everything that one wants counts as a preference: A fleeting morbid desire, for instance (depending on the rest of one's character), for many of us does not rise to the level of being an attitude that accurately describes *what one is like*, because it has not been formed by a process of evaluation as part of one's pursuit of the good. Just as one might adopt a belief out of convenience or for the sake of the argument, and not because one thinks it is true, so, too, one might form a desire from guilt or parental pressure or instinct, and not because one finds the desire or its object to be good.

I have elsewhere defended an account of free action as action on indeterministically and uncoercively formed preference.[14] And I have proposed that we understand one's (moral or psychological) self to be a certain ability, along with an aggregate of particular mental states: one's preferences and one's acceptance states – that is, beliefs formed with the aim of assenting to what is true.[15] Who I am, in this moral or psychological sense, is a character – a certain collection of acceptances and preferences – together with a power for fashioning and refashioning that character.[16] The account takes us to be moved to act not centrally by judgments but by desires and posits that certain of these (not all of them) help to define our characters. As Watson has emphasized, free agency requires both self-direction and alternative possibilities.[17] Because preferences are partially definitive of who one is, I have argued that the self-direction condition for a free act is met by that act's being nondeviantly caused by a deliberatively formed preference. And the alternative-possibilities condition is met, I have argued, by the indeterministic causation of the agent's preference by considerations of hers that enter into the deliberation process. The crucial causal openness preceding a free act is within the agent's decision process, which I describe as a decision concerning what to prefer (to desire or to do).

The question at issue here is whether the integration into the self accomplished by the process that turns a mere desire into a preference is integration of a sort sufficient for characterizing agent autonomy. Is a desire psychologically integrated in virtue of being formed through critically evaluative reasoning with an eye toward one's conception of the good? Or are there further conditions on psychological integration? In particular, must the conglomeration of one's evaluatively formed attitudes be related to each other in certain ways? That is, must there be a structural arrangement of coherence between them, and if so, how is that coherence to be characterized?

Notice that a preference is an appetite, in being a desire; it is a conative rather than cognitive attitude. But it is not a mere impulse, because it is formed by a process of critical evaluation and given a stamp of authenticity by the activity of reflective endorsement. Perhaps this marriage or integration between Appetite and Reason is sufficient for autonomous action. When an act springs (nondeviantly) from such a state, and in forming this state one was not the victim of coercion, then perhaps the act is self-directed, self-ruled. I think, in fact, that this is a plausible view concerning the autonomy of action.

III. A RICH ACCOUNT OF PERSONAL AUTHORIZATION

But one might devise a richer theory. Consider the reasons for doing so, beginning with the regress problem for hierarchical accounts. A regress is generated by supposing both that what it is to identify with a desire is to have a desire for (to have or to act on) that desire and that identification with a desire is required for the autonomy of action on it. But the authority of the second-level desire to stand as the view of the true self is in question without the self's identification with it, requiring a third-level desire, and so on. Likewise, when facing a choice concerning what to do and asking oneself, "Why would I do that?" one might reply, "Because I prefer it," but the authority of this preference may seem to require reasons, perhaps preferences of higher and higher orders, in its favor. One might follow Frankfurt in allowing boredom, stress, fatigue, or even external manipulation of one's attitudes to count as explanations of one's regress-ending satisfaction with what one decides to prefer. But, as I have said, this seems inappropriate for grounding autonomy, in that the supposed engagement of the self is explained ultimately by conditions of passivity and defeat.[18]

There is another way of responding to a regress of reasons, familiar in the epistemological literature: to view the structure of reasons as a loop, or an interweaving structure of mutual support. On an internalist view of epistemic justification, a believer is required to have reasons in support of the adoption or maintenance of a particular belief, in order for that belief to be justified. The justifying reasons might have a foundationalist structure, or they might form an interwoven, coherent network. Similarly, we might suppose that a desire to act in a particular way requires reasons in support of its authenticity, or its claim to represent what the agent really wants, and that these reasons, too, might form structures of various sorts, including foundationalist or coherentist ones.[19]

On the coherence theory of autonomy I have suggested,[20] coherence is understood not in a minimal sense of lack of conflict, but in a fuller sense of defensibility and mutual support. Lehrer's theory of epistemic justification provides a useful model, for it envisions justification centrally as a process: a game or contest with a skeptical interlocuter, who challenges one's beliefs (or, more specifically, one's states of acceptance). On the account, an acceptance state is justified just in case it coheres with what else the believer accepts, and an acceptance coheres just in case it can be defended against skeptical challenges by the believer's other acceptances, so that competitors to the acceptance are either beaten or neutralized by the elements of the believer's acceptance system.[21] Applying the structure of this theory to the issue of preference authorization yields a parallel account of the coherence of a preference with the other elements of one's character. Rather than resting on a basic notion of *reasonableness*, as is featured in Lehrer's account, I use as a base notion that a preference might be more or less *valuable* to have on the basis of a character system – that is, one's conglomeration of acceptances and preferences – at a time. To say that a preference is valuable to have according to a system means roughly that it is sensible to have it or that the preference is useful or worthy, according to that system.

On the coherence account, a preference P is *personally authorized* for a person at a time (or counts as "truly her own" or is representative of her "real self") if and only if the preference coheres with her character system at that time. A preference P *coheres* with the character system of a person at a time if and only if, for any competing preference, it is either more valuable for the person to have P than the competing preference on the basis of her character system at the time, or it is as valuable for her to have the competing preference and a neutralizing attitude, as it is for her to have the competing preference alone, on the basis of her character system at the time.[22] One preference *competes* with another preference for a person at a time just in case it is less valuable for that person to have the preference on the assumption that the object of the other is good than on the assumption that the object of the other is bad, on the basis of her character system at a time. One can meet the challenge of a competing preference either by defeating it or by neutralizing it. For instance, a preference for spending one's vacation in the Caribbean might cohere with one's character, in being supported by a network of supporting acceptances and preferences, such that a competing preference – to spend one's vacation in England instead – is defeated: One accepts that one needs to relax and that one relaxes better in a warm climate than in a chilly one; one prefers to snorkel and to read on the beach; one accepts that one would not be able to enjoy those activities in England; and so on. A desire to vacation in England might survive a process of reflective evaluation with respect to the good, so that it qualifies as a preference. Nonetheless, that preference might not cohere with one's character at a particular time, as its competitor does, given the overall considerations.[23]

Application to the matter of autonomy produces the following coherence account of autonomous action: An act is autonomous just in case it is nondeviantly caused by an uncoercively formed, personally authorized preference. A preference that is personally authorized for an individual has authority for speaking for her, for representing what she truly wants, in being well supported by a network of her considered attitudes; it is an attitude with respect to which she is wholehearted. Thus, action on such a preference is self-directed or self-ruled, rather than heteronomous. Regarding the problem of identification, on the coherence account, to "identify" oneself with a desire is for one to have a personally authorized preference for having or acting upon that desire. And to identify oneself with a particular course of action is for one to act in that way because one has a personally authorized preference for doing so.

Notice that I have presented what is not a purely structural account of either the self or of autonomy. There are procedural elements built into the notion of preference, because preferences to count as such must be formed by a process of critical reflection with regard to the agent's conception of the good. Furthermore, preferences must be uncoercively formed in order for the actions resulting from them to be autonomous. Hence, the account is one that, unlike Frankfurt's, affirms historical or procedural conditions for autonomous action.

IV. REAL SELVES DO NOT FLOAT

In this section, I address concerns over the plausibility of the coherence approach to autonomy. In the following section, I discuss the issue of its usefulness. First, one might object to the whole idea of a "real self" within the agent, whether that self is depicted as I have described or in any other of a variety of ways in which one might characterize it. Velleman's suggestion – that in a certain sort of case of explosive conflict with another, "it was my resentment speaking, not I"[24] – may be dismissed as a metaphorical expression. Of course, there is some sense in this reaction, as on a literal reading, resentment speaks (as it does not; if it was not the speaker speaking, then who was it?). A theorist may maintain, as Al Mele does, that we can describe what "self-directed" action is, without positing the existence of a self or a "real self" within the agent. A human agent, on Mele's view, is simply a human being who acts.[25] The task of action theorists is then to describe the various properties and capacities of human beings and their relation to the ability to act, where these abilities get exercised by various people at various times more and less impressively.

Some of the skepticism over a real-self approach to autonomy may owe to a misunderstanding.[26] None of the proponents of such an approach, as I understand them, including myself, intends to propose an ontological thesis, according to which, for instance, there is some sort of entity –

some item to be added to our metaphysics – floating around or somehow attached to the human being. A real-self approach to autonomy does not commit itself to the existence of nonmaterial souls, for instance, or to transempirical power centers or Cartesian egos. Frankfurt, for instance, is clear on this fact.[27] Rather, the idea is that certain of our attitudes are more central to who we are in a moral or psychological sense than are other of our attitudes, and that it is in acting on these more central attitudes that we exert special direction over our lives.

It is not implausible to view particular aspects of a person's psychology as more definitive of what he is like, or of his character, than are others. In our everyday interactions with others, we tend to overlook certain attitudes and actions, taking them as nonindicative of who another truly is. We say such things as, "She's not herself today; she is under a lot of stress" and, "Yes, he is subject to occasional impulses to overspend, but he is really quite a frugal and conservative person." We rely on certain of a person's attitudes remaining relatively constant in our relationship with her, viewing them as central to her identity, but we see other of her attitudes as peripheral. In the case of the title character in Charlotte Brontë's novel *Jane Eyre*, for instance, the desire for moral purity seems crucial to her real self, whereas her desire to be the lover of Mr. Rochester – whom she has discovered to be a married man – though strong, is not as central. Brontë conveys this impression through a rich depiction of Jane's mental life, her cares and concerns centering on moral uprightness and her disdain for personal indulgence and erotic gratification. In a pivotal, tortured night that is as much self-creation as self-discovery, Jane affirms the acceptances that support her fleeing her tempting situation at Thornfield, despite her love for its owner (that is, her acceptance of the importance of living by right moral principles, the relative unimportance of personal pleasure, the wrongness of adultery, a preference for being a good example to others, and so on). She decides on a preference to leave, and this preference is personally authorized for her in being well supported by a network of cohering attitudes. Jane does indeed accept that she would enjoy living as Mr. Rochester's lover, but that option in the end is not one with respect to which she can be wholehearted, as it is not supported by the bulk of what she accepts and prefers.

Now one might deem sensible a psychological notion of the self but object to the conception of it on the coherence theory, in particular. Are not people all full of conflicts, one might ask? And don't they act autonomously anyway, despite their inner turmoil, hesitation, and confusion? Why think that it is only the actions on well-integrated or cohering attitudes that are autonomous? Might not a single anomalous attitude represent "who one really is," while the bulk of one's personality is externally imposed by, say, extensive social conditioning or even by a manipulative neurosurgeon? It is difficult, on the face of it, to see what psychological integration as structural coherence has to do with self-rule.

Of course, we are all conflicted to some extent – some greater, some lesser – but we all live with ambitions, desires, and values that call us to develop our lives in different, sometimes conflicting, ways. It is difficult to achieve cohesion among the elements of one's inner life, and I do not deny the fact of our inner disorder. Moreover, it is certainly not my view that conflict within an individual prevents that individual from having the ability to act autonomously. We may see the (moral or psychological) self as comprised of *all* of a person's preferences and acceptances, together with the power for forming and altering these. Thus, there is room for conflicting attitudes within the self. What I am suggesting, as one inviting way to view autonomous action, is that a person acts autonomously only when acting from motivation of a certain sort: one that (1) has undergone critical evaluation with respect to his conception of the good, (2) was uncoercively formed, and (3) coheres with his other acceptance and preference states. It may be that we regularly live with internal conflict, but that we act autonomously only when acting on one of those attitudes that is central to who we are, where centrality to the self is established as I have described.

But why think that the cohering motivations are deeper or more central to true psychological identity than noncohering ones? There are several reasons: One, the cohering attitudes are abiding, relatively stable through time, because they support each other. Such attitudes are less likely to be discarded or changed, as parts of a consistent and supportive network. Altering one such attitude requires change in others, in order to restore consistency and justifiability in the face of external challenge or internal doubt, which is not the case for anomalous attitudes. We tend to view the more enduring aspects of a person's psychology as central rather than peripheral. Two, the cohering considered attitudes are fully defensible by the agent. They are not "oddball" attitudes that the agent cannot explain or defend. They fit with – in fact, constitute – the person's "party line." The cohering preferences and acceptances make sense to the agent, and others find one's having them understandable, given knowledge of the rest of one's considered attitudes. When the value of having a particular preference is challenged or the truth of a particular proposition one accepts is doubted, if that attitude coheres with one's other preferences and acceptances, then one can support it by citing other elements of one's character system. Three, coherent preferences and acceptances are attitudes with which the agent is for the most part comfortable. One tends not to be in distress over such attitudes, not to be agitated or frustrated by them, but rather to feel tranquil with having them, because they are consistent with, and positively supported by, one's other important attitudes. There may be other approaches to defining *depth* to the self, but the coherence approach is, for these reasons, one that I find natural and persuasive.

Suppose one were to grant the point concerning psychological depth. Is it a short step or a long one from here to the coherence theory of autonomous action? I think it is a short step. Here is why. We all agree that autonomy is to be understood as self-direction, self-command, or self-rule. It is opposed to rule-from-without, enslavement, and victimization. Christine Korsgaard comments that "autonomy is commanding yourself to do what you think it would be a good idea to do,"[28] and we recognize the sense in her remark, although it leaves open significant questions. (Who or what is doing the commanding, and who or what is being commanded? Who is the "you" who must think that the chosen action is a good idea to do?) An act is autonomous, we want to say, when it derives from the individual and is not controlled by anyone or anything external to the individual; the autonomous agent is not pushed about from the outside, but is, rather, self-governed. Consider a therapeutic context. A good therapist aims to facilitate change in a client's behavior or personality without forcing that change through methods that bypass the client's own will. The therapist endeavors, that is, to guide self-directed change in the client, and, in so doing, she respects the client's autonomy.

If "self-direction" means direction by the genuine or true self – and not the inauthentic or contrived or externally imposed self – then this is why psychological integration promotes autonomy or, in other words, what coherence among motivational states has to do with self-rule: One's action is self-governed when it is directed by the true self, and the true self is comprised of a cohering aggregate of preference and acceptance states, along with the capacity to form and re-form these.

The distinction between *autonomy* and *authenticity*, then, is in my view not so clear as some theorists – for instance, Velleman and Arpaly – make it out to be. Consider Velleman's case of a particular man who "laughs at what he thinks he is supposed to find amusing, shows concern for what he thinks he is supposed to care about, and in general conforms himself to the demands and expectations of others. The motives that his behavior is designed to simulate are motives that he doesn't genuinely have."[29] This case of manifesting a false self Velleman finds to be a case not lacking in self-governance or autonomy. "To be sure, he has a problem with autonomy," Velleman writes concerning the man, "but his problem is one of excess: he is overly self-controlled, overly deliberate; his grip on the reins of his behavior is too tight, not too loose. His failure to be motivated from within his true self makes him inauthentic, but it seems to result from his being all too autonomous." But Velleman's analysis strikes me as off the mark. The man in question is controlled, all right, in his ingratiating behavior. But is he really *self*-controlled? It seems not. He seems not guided by what he thinks it would be a good idea to do or by what he really prefers, but rather by a neurotic need to please others. He seems driven, not liberated. By discovering and creating a true self, and by directing what he does by that self rather than by a false one, he could increase the autonomy of his actions and so the autonomy of his life.

V. USEFULNESS AND EGO-SYNTONICITY

One may put the coherence theory of autonomy to use both in practical and theoretical contexts. In practice, for instance, one might need to make a medical treatment decision on behalf of a friend who is temporarily incapacitated.[30] In trying to discern what one's friend would autonomously decide, were he capable of making the decision for himself, one could take centrally into account the considered attitudes of one's friend – the various things that he prefers and accepts. If one saw these preferences and acceptances as pointing in different directions, not giving one clear guidance concerning how to decide in the circumstances, one might discern to the best of one's ability which preference regarding the current situation would best fit or cohere with the bulk of his considered attitudes – which would be best defended by them, or which would be the more valuable preference, on the basis of the elements of his character.

Consider theoretical applications: first, to a recent proposal concerning the conditions for praiseworthiness and blameworthiness of persons for their actions. On Nomy Arpaly's theory of moral worth, the moral worth of an action is the extent to which the agent deserves moral praise or blame for performing it, "the extent to which the action speaks well of the agent."[31] An action's moral worth depends in part on its moral desirability (whether it is right or wrong and to what extent). It also depends on the agent's reasons for doing the act and how "deep" these are to her psyche. People are praiseworthy for acts of good will and blameworthy for acts of ill will or the absence of good will, and the amount of praise or blame they deserve varies with the depth of their motivation or the extent of their indifference.[32] Good will is wanting, noninstrumentally, to perform actions that are right. Ill will is wanting, noninstrumentally, to perform actions that are wrong.[33] To hold that someone is blameworthy is "to hold that a certain attitude toward him is epistemically rational" or warranted or deserved.[34]

Arpaly's view of responsibility, then, closely connects responsibility with self-expression. Because the degree to which an agent is morally praiseworthy or blameworthy for an action varies with the depth of the concern motivating the action, Arpaly is committed to the claim that some desires (concerns) are deeper or more central to a person's moral or psychological identity than are others, and that depth is a matter of degree.[35] The theory of moral worth, that is, requires an account of the deep or real self and views persons as candidates for legitimate praise or blame when their actions derive from that self.[36]

I have explored here one account of psychological depth, a structural coherence view. One might attempt, then, to put the coherence theory of autonomy to use in moral responsibility theory.[37]

Consider, finally, a distinction between "ego-dystonic" and "ego-syntonic" desires. The former may be described as desires one might find oneself having, but about which one is disapproving or distressed – they seem to one repugnant, or not a reason for acting, or alien (so that one thinks, "That's not really me"). Ego-dystonic desires are "desires that do not fit with the agent's 'party line.'"[38] Actions on such desires are not the agent's own or "happen without the participation of the agent." Frankfurt might call them "outlaw desires." I have given one way of characterizing the distinction between ego-dystonicity and ego-syntonicity, according to which personally authorized preferences are ego-syntonic.

Arpaly raises the following problem concerning the identification of such desires: Sometimes, the agent has a perspective of estrangement toward certain desires (for instance, the Victorian lady toward her sexual desires or the nice Jewish boy toward his hostility toward his parents), yet we tend to see the very desires labeled as outlaw by the agent as truly his or her own, or part of his or her "real self." We think, in those cases, that the agent is "in denial" or has a false self-image.

This phenomenon can be explained by the coherence theory. A person might at some time feel estranged from a desire, for whatever reason (perhaps, out of situational embarrassment or in denial). But if that desire is a preference and it coheres with her character, then it is part of her real self, whether at any given moment she wishes to acknowledge that fact or not. A feeling of alienation or, conversely, a feeling of satisfaction does not by itself settle the matter of what is central to a person's psychological identity, on my account. The first-person perspective can be mistaken concerning the status of a preference as authorized or outlaw, because the status of a preference as coherent or incoherent with the character is a fact, which may or may not be apprehended from the first-person perspective. A third-person perspective, as well, may be mistaken concerning whether an attitude is part of someone's real self, depending on the extent of one's knowledge of the other's character. That is, one must have sufficient knowledge concerning another's collection of evaluatively formed attitudes, in order to know if a given preference coheres with them.

CONCLUSION

One aspect of the pursuit of moral decency is the attempt to care about the autonomy of others and to grant it respect as we make our own decisions and plans. One might take an interest in understanding autonomy's nature, then, out of concern for the promotion of others' autonomy. But there is another widespread and rather natural motivation: the desire to understand how to make one's life more "one's own." The thought is, the more self-directed one's life is, the more satisfying that life will be, as the less one will be pulled in different directions by external forces and unconscious drives and the less one will be plagued by inner tension, by confusion over what to do, and by alienation from certain of one's decisions and actions.

I have explored the idea that we could make our lives more autonomous or self-driven were we regularly to act on motivations that are well integrated into our personalities, rather than on anomalous or ego-dystonic motivations. In acting on an anomalous motivation, we frustrate our deeper or more central goals, and so acting from such motivation is a form of enslavement rather than liberated self-expression.

Notes

For comments on this chapter, I am grateful to Al Mele and the editor of this volume, James Stacey Taylor.

1. Harry Frankfurt, "Freedom of the Will and the Concept of a Person," *Journal of Philosophy* 68 (1971): 5–20; Gary Watson, "Free Agency," *Journal of*

Philosophy 72 (1975): 205–220. Frankfurt and Watson discuss freedom of action (and freedom of the will), rather than emphasizing the term "autonomy." I will use the terms "freedom" and "autonomy" for the most part interchangeably here, although, of course, there may be contexts in which it is useful to distinguish between the two. A central concern of free-will theory is the question of whether we can act freely if certain metaphysical doctrines are true, such as the thesis of causal determinism and the doctrines of divine providence and foreknowledge. In ordinary contexts, such as medical and legal ones, our concern to protect someone's autonomy is not sensitive to such metaphysical issues, although if pressed ("Has the patient *really* autonomously signed the consent form, if God determines our actions?") it might become so. Free-will theorists and autonomy theorists are commonly interested, at base, in the power of agents to direct their lives on their own.

2. Frankfurt, "Identification and Wholeheartedness," in *The Importance of What We Care About* (Cambridge: Cambridge University Press, 1988): 159–176.
3. Michael Bratman, "Identification, Decision, and Treating as a Reason," *Philosophical Topics* 24 (1996): 1–18.
4. Laura Waddell Ekstrom, "A Coherence Theory of Autonomy," *Philosophy and Phenomenological Research* 53 (1993): 599–616; "Keystone Preferences and Autonomy," *Philosophy and Phenomenological Research* 59 (1999): 1057–1063; and "Alienation, Autonomy, and the Self," unpublished manuscript.
5. Ekstrom, "Keystone Preferences and Autonomy."
6. J. David Velleman, "What Happens When Someone Acts?" *Mind* 101 (1992): 461–481; and Velleman, *The Possibility of Practical Reason* (New York: Oxford University Press, 2000).
7. Frankfurt writes: "It seems to me that if someone does something because he wants to do it, and if he has no reservations about that desire but is wholeheartedly behind it, then – so far as his moral responsibility for doing it is concerned – it really does not matter how he got that way." "Reply to John Martin Fischer," in S. Buss and L. Overton, eds., *Contours of Agency* (Cambridge, MA: MIT Press, 2002): 27.
8. Alfred Mele, *Autonomous Agents* (New York: Oxford University Press, 1995).
9. A willing addict acts freely in taking his drug, on the view, because he is positively inclined toward both that course of action and the desire for that course of action; in other words, he desires to take the drug and desires to desire to take it. An unwilling addict, by contrast, does want to take the drug (because of his addiction), but he desires to desire to refrain; and so when he takes the drug, he does not act freely or responsibly, on the hierarchical account; his taking the drug frustrates and does not give expression to his true self.
10. See Watson, "Free Agency"; Adrian Piper, "Two Conceptions of the Self," *Philosophical Studies* 48 (1985): 173–197; and Ekstrom, "A Coherence Theory of Autonomy."
11. See Watson "Free Agency"; Piper, "Two Conceptions of the Self"; and Eleonore Stump, "Sanctification, Hardening of the Heart, and Frankfurt's Concept of Free Will," *Journal of Philosophy* 85 (1988): 395–412.

12. Frankfurt, "Reply to Michael E. Bratman," 86–90.
13. One objection questions the rationalistic, evaluative approach to autonomy that I (and many others) have. Why think that we cannot act autonomously on passions, whims, and impulses? Is not the approach taken here excessively intellectualistic? It should not be startling, and it is certainly not unconventional, to view a person's Reason or Understanding as establishing his point of view, his take on the world, his mode of making sense of experiences and of putting his "stamp" on things. Perhaps most or all persons have a capacity to act autonomously. But it is not a strike against a theory of autonomous action that, according to it, it takes some work to exercise that capacity. In my view, we do not act autonomously in acting on passions, whims, and impulses because these overtake us; we are generally passive with respect to them; they do not engage our understanding or capacity for reflective evaluation. We make our lives more our own by examining such impulses and by acting in accordance with our evaluations. Call this a rationalistic, intellectualistic approach to autonomy if you like, but, as many theorists have emphasized, we are rational, intellectual creatures, enabling us to do things in ways that other creatures cannot.
14. Laura Waddell Ekstrom, *Free Will* (Boulder, CO: Westview Press, 2000); "Indeterminist Free Action," in Ekstrom, ed., *Agency and Responsibility* (Boulder, CO: Westview Press, 2001): 138–157; and "Free Will, Chance, and Mystery," *Philosophical Studies* 113 (2003): 153–180.
15. The notion of an acceptance state I use here is Keith Lehrer's, not Frankfurt's. Lehrer, *Theory of Knowledge* (Boulder, CO: Westview Press, 1990).
16. For discussion, see the Ekstrom papers cited above.
17. Gary Watson, "Free Action and Free Will," *Mind* 46 (1987): 145–172.
18. My complaint is that Frankfurt's current way of responding to the regress of practical reasons is akin to a certain response to the regress of theoretical reasons in the epistemic realm, according to which the chain of justifying beliefs ends in beliefs that are themselves unjustified.
19. For reasons to reject a foundationalist approach to autonomy, see Ekstrom, "Keystone Preferences and Autonomy."
20. Ekstrom, "A Coherence Theory of Autonomy"; and "Alienation, Autonomy, and the Self."
21. Lehrer, *Theory of Knowledge.*
22. For precise definitions of these notions and further discussion, see my "A Coherence Theory of Autonomy" and "Alienation, Autonomy, and the Self." A neutralizing attitude may work to make a preference that is initially competing, no longer a competitor.
23. For examples of the neutralization of competing preferences, see my "A Coherence Theory of Autonomy" and "Alienation, Autonomy, and the Self."
24. Velleman, "What Happens When Someone Acts?" 464–465.
25. Alfred Mele, *Motivation and Agency* (New York: Oxford University Press, 2003): chap. 10.
26. I do not attribute this misunderstanding to Mele.
27. Frankfurt, "Reply to J. David Velleman," 124–128.

28. She goes on to remark, "but that in turn depends on who you think you are." Autonomy is in part dependent on practical identity. Christine Korsgaard, *The Sources of Normativity* (Cambridge: Cambridge University Press, 1996): 107.
29. Velleman, "Identification and Identity," 97.
30. Ekstrom, "Alienation, Autonomy, and the Self."
31. Nomy Arpaly, *Unprincipled Virtue: An Inquiry into Moral Agency* (New York: Oxford University Press, 2003): 69.
32. Arpaly, *Unprincipled Virtue*, 115.
33. For elaboration, see ibid., 79.
34. Ibid., 144, 173.
35. On my definitions of coherence, competition, and personal authorization, authorization is not a matter of degree; a preference either coheres with a character system at a time or it does not. A project of interest would be to pursue modification of the definitions to allow for degrees of authorization, but I will not do that here.
36. Arpaly argues that it is not true that only agent-autonomous action is blameworthy or praiseworthy (*Unprincipled Virtue*, 132 ff.). She complains that attention has shifted among moral responsibility theorists from questions about praise and blame to questions about autonomy, suggesting that this has been an unhelpful development and that responsibility theorists would "be better off going back to investigating praiseworthiness and blameworthiness directly, ignoring intuitions regarding autonomy" (*Unprincipled Virtue*, 118). I find this suggestion puzzling. Autonomy and free-will theorists take up issues – including the natures of self-direction and agential control over action and the relevance and right understanding of alternative possibilities – crucial to the matter of an agent's praiseworthiness or blameworthiness for an act. Arpaly's dismissal of autonomy theory is particularly perplexing, given her own view of responsibility as tied to *self-expression*. This seems to me clearly to connect responsibility with self-direction, or autonomy. One might view the theory of moral worth, as Arpaly does, as connecting responsibility with "authenticity" and not autonomy. But, again, I do not see the clear distinction between the two that she and Velleman do. Arpaly describes "agent-autonomy" as "self-control" over action; but by "self-control," she apparently does not mean control by a true self (because she describes "authenticity" as being true to one's real self). By my lights, self-control (autonomy) implies control by the self – the genuine or authentic self – and so autonomy seems indistinct from, or at least very closely connected with, authenticity.
37. I leave this an open issue. One might reasonably question the coherence theory's depiction of the kind of control a person must have over his action in order to be morally responsible for performing that action. In particular, the account may seem too stringent as an account of the freedom condition of morally responsible action, because it requires coherence of the preference preceding action. Perhaps, instead, the coherence account depicts an ideal of agency or provides a plausible account of self-identification.
38. Arpaly, *Unprincipled Virtue*, 15.

7

Responsibility, Applied Ethics, and Complex Autonomy Theories

Nomy Arpaly

When I was kindly invited to contribute a chapter to this volume, the letter of invitation included the following sentence:

> *As you know, the twin concepts of autonomy and identification have become increasingly important within contemporary philosophy, especially in discussions of moral responsibility and applied ethics.*

Now, without wanting to seem ungrateful, I have to admit that I am not convinced that I *do* know this. Some things worthy of the name "autonomy" are clearly important in these domains; that much is clear. But when it comes to what philosophers in the Frankfurt-inspired moral psychological tradition have been working on, it is far from clear that the "twin concepts" of autonomy and identification have any relevance to either moral responsibility or applied ethics. I do not say that they have *no* relevance. Arguing for this strong thesis is not my intent. Instead, I will argue in this chapter for the somewhat weaker thesis that there is no trivial, or even obvious, argument for their relevance. The sentiment expressed in my letter of invitation is a prevalent one, but one that I think needs to be challenged. Although some broadly Frankfurtian theories of autonomy and identification may have major implications for moral responsibility and applied ethics, one cannot – perhaps, can no longer – assume uncritically that they do; and even in cases in which it is plausible to think there would be significant implications, it is often not clear exactly what these implications are. In arguing for this conclusion, I will focus on moral responsibility first and then say something about applied ethics afterward.

Let me explain what I mean by trivial or obvious relevance. Some views of autonomy, such as Fischer and Ravizza's view, are driven by the assumption that the class of deeds for which we are morally responsible and the class of deeds that are instances of autonomous agency are identical, or approximate each other quite closely.[1] Such theories can generally treat "autonomous action" and "action for which we are morally responsible" as interchangeable expressions. A philosopher advancing such a view will be guided by intuitions about moral responsibility in a fairly clear way: She will assume by default that if an agent would commonly be held responsible for an action, or praiseworthy or blameworthy for it, the action should, prima facie, be treated as an instance of that agent exercising autonomy, while if a person would commonly be exempt from moral responsibility, it would be prima facie counterintuitive to regard him as autonomous. In any case of an apparent clash between the author's definition of autonomy and common intuitions about moral responsibility, she will see it as her task to provide a satisfactory explanation of this apparent clash. Such philosophers generally make reference to the usual paradigmatic cases of people who are not morally responsible for things that one is usually responsible for – psychotics, victims of coercion, and so on – and explain why it is they lack autonomy. Within the framework of such a view, the claim that an action is or is not autonomous has a fairly obvious relevance to issues of moral responsibility: An autonomous action, for all or almost all intents and purposes, simply *is* an action for which we are morally responsible. This is how the theorist has intended the theory to work.

But things are more complicated with theories of autonomy or identification whose authors neither argue nor assume that the class of autonomous actions is identical (or near-identical) to the class of actions for which we are morally responsible. These theories are the subject of this chapter, and they are numerous. Consider first the *locus classicus*: Harry Frankfurt's early introduction of the idea of identification.[2] Early Frankfurt thinks of identification – and, we assume, of autonomy – in terms of acting on desires that one desires to act on; but he has no intention of arguing, strictly speaking, that I am exempt from moral responsibility if I desire to act on my desire to prepare my class but act instead on my "outlaw desire" to read *The Curious Incident of the Dog in the Nighttime.* Early Frankfurt holds that there is a significant connection between his notion of autonomy and responsibility, but unlike Fischer and Ravizza, he does not assume that the set of actions for which we are responsible and the set of actions that are autonomous are identical or near-identical: It is not his methodological starting point. So divorced is Frankfurt from this assumption that he sees no need to address at any length what may seem, to the old-fashioned free-will theorist, like an apparent conflict between intuitions about moral responsibility (that I am morally blameworthy for not preparing for my class) and implications of his view (that I am not autonomous if I akratically fail to prepare for my class). Later Frankfurt, who thinks of autonomous actions as wholehearted actions, clearly does not intend to argue that we are only responsible for wholehearted actions.[3] His work is driven not by intuitions about moral responsibility, but by intuitions about internal conflict and the disturbing sense that we sometimes get of being acted upon by our own minds.

To a greater or lesser degree, many theories of autonomy and identification follow Frankfurt in lacking a commitment to understanding autonomy and identification through intuitions about moral responsibility. Such theories generally seem to suggest that the set of autonomous actions is significantly smaller than the set of actions for which we are commonly held morally responsible. Although their authors are often inclined to hold that some connection exists between autonomy and moral responsibility, they do not simply assume that their account of autonomy must serve directly as an account of the necessary conditions for moral responsibility; and if an action appears nonautonomous by their lights but actionable by ordinary standards, they do not see it as a philosophical emergency requiring immediate action by way of in-depth explanation. Consider, for example, a claim advanced by Ekstrom in this volume:

> What I am suggesting, as one inviting way to view autonomous action, is that a person acts autonomously only when acting from motivation of a certain sort: one that (i) has undergone critical evaluation with respect to his conception of the good, (ii) was not coercively formed, and (iii) coheres with his other acceptance and preference states. It may be that we regularly live with internal conflict, but that we act autonomously only when acting on one of those attitudes that is central to who we are, where centrality to the self is established as I have described.[4]

These are fairly strict conditions for autonomy. If we "regularly live with internal conflict," it very well may be that autonomy, as Ekstrom defines it, is a bit like happiness or fitness: an eminently reasonable thing to which to aspire, but not the default condition of human beings. It may be even rarer, depending on the strictness of our interpretation of "critical evaluation with respect to his conception of the good" – something that even people whom we would not regard as particularly conflicted do not do very often. As Ekstrom herself admits in a footnote, her account of autonomy, if coupled with the assumption that autonomous actions are actions for which we are morally responsible, would yield an account of moral responsibility that is far too restrictive (for instance, it would probably excuse the torn Raskolnikov, from *Crime and Punishment*, from responsibility for the murder he commits). But this is not a problem for Ekstrom's view, because she does not argue that we are only responsible for actions that meet her conditions. The question of the precise relevance of the quoted view to moral responsibility is left open.

Let me refer to theories of autonomy that have not been derived to deal with intuitions about moral responsibility and so cannot easily dispense with the expression "autonomous action" and replace it with "action for which we are morally responsible," as "*Complex Autonomy Theories* (CATs)." As I said, I do not wish to argue that CATs in general, or any CAT in particular, is irrelevant to moral responsibility. My purpose is to make it clear, in a way it usually is not, that the clichés "autonomy grounds moral responsibility" and "autonomy is central to moral responsibility" are neither automatically true for CATs nor obvious upon simple reflection. Anyone who wishes to argue that a CAT is relevant to moral responsibility can be fairly asked to defend and clarify her view and can expect this task to be a substantial one, perhaps a research program of its own. (This is true however valuable the CAT may be in other ways not related to responsibility: A CAT can be valuable and interesting even if it has nothing to do with moral responsibility or, for that matter, with applied ethics, for of course there is more to the philosophical study of the vagaries of the human heart than what is contained in these subjects.)

That CATs are not *automatically* relevant to theories of moral responsibility follows directly from their nature, for CATs are not custom built to address problems in the theory of moral responsibility. By their very nature, they attribute autonomy and identification to fewer individuals than the number most philosophers would judge to be appropriately subject to moral praise and blame. The nonobviousness of their utility to the moral responsibility theorist is a more complex matter, however, and two objections come quickly to mind. First, an objector could claim that while she is not simply describing the class of actions for which we are morally responsible, her CAT clearly describes the class of actions for which we are *directly* morally responsible and therefore is linked to moral responsibility in a clear enough way. For example, if a theory implies that procrastinating against one's best judgment is not autonomous and is confronted with the intuition that such procrastinating can still be blameworthy, the theorist may explain that one is not directly responsible for the procrastinating, but one is blameworthy for autonomously taking a course of action that allowed the procrastination to happen. Second, an objector may claim that if a theory of autonomy successfully describes a property that is essential to being a person and is not shared by non-persons, it is thereby relevant to moral responsibility, which only persons have. In other words, instead of methodologically assuming an identity between the class of autonomous actions and the class of actions for which one is responsible, one can appeal to an identity between the class of autonomous *agents* and the class of agents that can be held morally responsible and say that this establishes a clear enough connection between autonomy and moral responsibility. Other objections might be possible, but these are two that I have encountered often enough to address. I will discuss them in order.

I. THE INDIRECT STRATEGY

A CAT theorist might claim that her CAT clearly describes the class of actions for which we are *directly* morally responsible and therefore is linked to moral responsibility in a clear enough way. I do not intend to argue that this is mistaken. But even if the CAT theorist is right, this does not mean that saying, offhandedly, something like "Of course you are responsible for procrastinating, but it is indirect responsibility – you should have controlled yourself more strictly" is enough to establish a clear connection between the CAT and moral responsibility. It takes arguments to show that every action a CAT deems nonautonomous, but for which we are apparently morally responsible, is one for which we are indirectly responsible. Beyond such intuitions as "You should have controlled your temper," it can also be difficult to clarify exactly what the meaning of such an indirect responsibility claim is, and it needs to be fleshed out theoretically rather than assumed.

In "What Happens When Someone Acts?" David Velleman gives us the following example of a failure of autonomy:

> I have a long-anticipated meeting with an old friend for the purpose of resolving some minor difference; but . . . as we talk, his offhand comments provoke me to raise my voice in progressively sharper replies, until we part in anger. Later reflection leads me to realize that accumulated grievances had crystallized in my mind, during the weeks before our meeting, into a resolution to sever our friendship over the matter at hand, and that this resolution is what gave the hurtful edge to my remarks. In short, I may conclude that desires of mine caused the decision, which in turn caused the corresponding behavior; and I may acknowledge that

> these mental states were thereby exerting their normal motivational force, unabetted by any strange perturbation or compulsion. But do I necessarily think that I made the decision or that I executed it? Surely, I can believe that the decision, though genuinely motivated by my desires, was thereby induced in me but not formed by me; and I can believe that it was genuinely executed in my behavior but executed, again, without my help. Indeed, viewing the decision as directly motivated by my desires, and my behavior as directly governed by the decision, is precisely what leads to the thought that as my words became more shrill, it was my resentment speaking, not I.[5]

Velleman takes my yelling at my friend to be neither a full-fledged action nor an autonomous action. Common sense holds that I deserve blame for my rudeness, and for many other deeds that would be, on similar grounds, regarded as nonautonomous by Velleman. Thus, Velleman's theory seems to be a CAT, presenting us with a theory of autonomy that does not aim to make autonomous actions coextensive with actions for which we are morally responsible. In a footnote, Velleman says that he does not mean to deny that I am morally responsible for the incident, but he suggests that there is still an obvious connection between his view of autonomy and moral responsibility by claiming that I have a duty to be vigilant about "unconsidered intentions" and actively prevent them from running loose, and so I am blameworthy not for yelling, but for failing to prevent myself from getting into the state in which I find myself.[6] I, the agent, have autonomously failed to keep good watch over my resentment. Velleman's footnote is thus an example of the way in which an indirect responsibility claim can be used to defend the idea that there is an obvious connection between a CAT and moral responsibility.

Unfortunately, Velleman's indirect strategy is *not* obviously successful: It faces some substantial philosophical objections. My first objection to Velleman's indirectness claim is one that I have handled in detail elsewhere, so I will state it briefly.[7] It involves the complexities of cases in which we seem praiseworthy, rather than blameworthy, for nonautonomous action. Suppose we change Velleman's case so as to shift from talk of blame to talk of praise. Imagine that the "accumulated grievances" that crystallized in my mind into a decision to break off my friendship involve my friend's increasingly immoral behavior (and the increasing moral dubiousness of being allied with him), which I have been consciously ignoring or downplaying or underestimating. There are occasions on which such a breakup marks a pivotal moral step for a person and hence warrants moral praise. It may still be occasion for moral praise even though, as I walk away from the meeting, I tell myself that I should have done it long ago and that ideally it would have been better if I had done it in a more dignified and planned manner. What justifies this praise? No story about a duty of vigilance can easily explain it, for in the story as told I have failed to be vigilant over the moral qualities of my friendships, and yet I am praiseworthy for breaking off the friendship nonetheless.

Furthermore, even in cases of blame, the "vigilance" thesis needs clarification and defense. There are many cases like the one described by Velleman. People succumb to rage, temptation, or visceral inhibition – adulterers, impulsive aggressors, akratic procrastinators, and so on – and often say things that suggest alienation, surprise, and akrasia: "I don't know what got into me," and "the Devil made me do it." Though we usually "know what they mean," just as we know what Velleman means when he says, "It was my resentment speaking, not I," we usually hold them blameworthy. Are all of these cases of indirect responsibility? What, in such cases, is the course of action for which the sinner is *directly* responsible?

Velleman is at least partly right: There are some cases in which "being vigilant" seems to be the answer, cases in which we hold people blameworthy for failing, as it were, to check their mental brakes. If, for example, I know that drinking a large espresso or missing a dose of lithium is likely to make me irritable, and I have yelled at my friend as a result of neglecting to watch my coffee or lithium intake, it is quite plausible to say that my guilt consists in my negligence. Even if no such stark mechanism is in operation, it may have been that, as I felt my blood pressure go up, I should have taken a deep breath and counted to ten. But things become less clear at this point. It is quite possible to imagine a scenario in which no such "count-to-ten" measures were available to me, or no effective ones anyway. It is also sometimes the case that the agent could not be expected to know of such measures in time to use them (perhaps powerful aggressive urges have never appeared in me before, and when such an urge appears it takes me by such surprise that I do not notice it until I am already screaming). There are also many cases in which the agent has already taken such measures and in general tried as hard as she could not to follow her "outlaw" desires, but her attempts and measures fail. In many such cases, we still blame the nonautonomous aggressor (or the akratic adulterer, procrastinator, etc.). Yet in these cases, there is no clear argument anymore that there has been a blameworthy failure of vigilance.

In lieu of the simple "vigilance" thesis, or as a supplement to it, one might suggest that the autonomous course of action for which the agent is blameworthy must be some sort of failure that resulted in her current state of weakness of will, resulted in the fact that trying "as hard as she can" is not trying very hard. Thus, the agent must be blameworthy for having failed to perform some character-building action or having knowingly performed some character-eroding action. This view would have similar problems to the vigilance view when it comes to cases of nonautonomous behavior that are praiseworthy (as in the cases of Huckleberry Finn and Oskar Schindler).[8] Other than that, the main problem I see with the character development view has to do with the fact that it necessitates a picture of human life in which we have an incredible amount of control over our characters – an amount of control that most parents only wish they could have over the development of their children's characters. How often do we knowingly and autonomously perform character-building or character-ruining actions? To be sure, occasionally we do. Mr. Tucker, a character in Christopher Buckley's satire *The White House Mess*, knows that entering the White House is likely to turn him into what he calls "a jerk." Yet, he chooses to enter the White House, and his moral character is in fact harmed in the ways in which he predicted it would be. From Balzac's Eugène Rastignac to Trudeau's Michael Doonesbury, in fact, fictional characters can be found who make clear-eyed decisions in favor of courses of action that will gain them money or power but will harm their integrity or compassion. I do not doubt that such decisions occur in real life. But instances of such decisions are rare – considerably rarer than the autonomy-oriented moral psychologist needs. Successful, intentional character-building or character-ruining actions performed by a person upon himself are even rarer than successful New Year's resolutions. It is the exception, rather than the rule, that a person's character is substantially self-made, which is why a self-made good character is so impressive in the first place.[9] In many cases in which people lack self-control with respect to some of their desires (or when they simply do not have strong enough "good" desires to combat the "bad" ones), this weakness is primarily the result of early upbringing and unintentional psychological reinforcement (and by the time one may think about changing one's character, it is already at least half-shaped). To the extent that agents contribute to the creation of their weaknesses by means of their autonomous actions, it is usually not in the straightforward way Tucker influenced his own character. Tucker knew about the way his White House job was likely to affect his character. Quite often, however, an agent chooses her character-shaping actions without any knowledge of the way in which they are likely to shape her character, and she does so in circumstances in which she could hardly be expected to know better (any parent trying to shape the character of a child knows how hard it is to make such predictions). One is not usually in a position to predict whether one's choice of a job, school, marriage partner, friend, or area of domicile will affect one's moral character in some fashion, not to mention the many choices that initially appear too insignificant to fuss about. Thus, it is quite unlikely that what nonautonomous blameworthy agents are to blame for is generally some autonomous failure of character building.

There is also a type of case in which there are independent reasons to believe that we are blameworthy in virtue of *having* a certain desire or motivational factor to the extent that we act on it at all, not in virtue of failing to control it (whether through vigilance, character building, or any other autonomous course of action). These are cases in which we act on sinister motives, where our reasons for action are in essential, rather than accidental, conflict with morality. Sexual desire, hunger, desire for money, and other traditional "temptations" are not, by themselves, sinister – they do not essentially conflict with morality, though in the wrong set of circumstances they can lead one to do something immoral. Thus, if, for example, there are cases in which almost any human being, regardless of emotional makeup, would be moved by sexual desire – a motive that is morally neutral by itself – to the point of committing adultery, we may reasonably say that some adulterers, under such circumstances, are blameworthy not so much for their adulterous action as for leading themselves into those circumstances in the first place, or some similar failure of vigilance. Things are different, however, if our nonautonomous sinner acts not from a neutral desire but out of a malevolent motive, such as sadism or racial hatred. If I lash out at my friend because I relish the suffering of my fellow human beings, I am blameworthy even if I have done all in my power to control and eradicate my sadism. Just compare "Sorry, I haven't eaten for days and so I couldn't help eating your special chocolate" to "Sorry, I haven't seen a person in tears for days and so I couldn't help eating your special chocolate." Something similar seems to be true for "slips" motivated by serious racial prejudice. As Hursthouse hints, the confession "I am utterly disgusted by Asian people, but I am doing my best to control it" is far better than wholehearted racism, but it is also a far cry from the confession of a morally perfect agent.[10] The ego-dystonic racist who thinks that there is a lot to improve in her moral character, that she could be a better person, is, after all, correct in her assessment: She *could* be a better person than she is. The same, I take it, holds for the "recovering" sadist.

It might be objected that heaping condemnation upon people such as the visceral racist or sadist makes the world a worse place, in that obsession with the blameworthiness of one's visceral feelings and desires tends to backfire.[11] As long as a person knows that her visceral or unconscious desires are bad, the argument might proceed, tormenting her and censuring her for desires that she does not endorse may only lead to counterproductive results – no one, after all, can cope with being condemned or condemning herself all the time, and encouraging people to dwell too much on the badness of their visceral desires is likely to result in the activation of psychological defenses that are likely to interfere with their mending their ways. I mention this objection because I am at least partially in agreement with those who fear that attacking an involuntary sinner who already is trying to mend her ways is often a counterproductive – and therefore the wrong – thing to do. It may even be cruel, or at least unforgiving in a context in which the virtuous agent would be forgiving. I would like to point out, however, that my view to the effect that the inadvertent sinner is blameworthy does not imply that punishing her – even verbally – is a good thing for society to do or that obsessing over her sins is the right thing for her to do. As I argue elsewhere, to say that one is blame*worthy* is not to say that one *should be blamed.*[12] In some circumstances, blame may be warranted without an expression of blame being morally desirable.

These are some considerations that make the claim that all responsibility for actions that are deemed nonautonomous by a prominent CAT is indirect and derivative from responsibility for prior autonomous actions is a claim that needs clarification and defense. If Velleman wants to say that, on his view, autonomy grounds moral responsibility, he will have to argue at length for this conclusion and make clear how it is supposed to ground it. The same is true for many other CATs.

II. CATS AND OTHER ANIMALS

As an alternative strategy, one might argue that there is a clear enough relationship between CATs and moral responsibility for a different reason: CATs capture things that distinguish persons from other creatures; and as only persons are morally responsible, CATs tell us what it is to be a responsible agent – a creature capable of morally accountable action.

It is true that human beings are the only morally responsible creatures we know at the moment and that, typically, CATs identify mental conditions that only a human being is likely to have. CATs focus on forms of inner hierarchy and/or inner struggle that seem to exist in all normal adult humans and in no other creatures. But this is not enough to trivially or obviously yield the conclusion that CATs are relevant to moral responsibility. It is not enough because (1) many mental abilities are uniquely human, and not all of them are clearly relevant to moral responsibility; and (2) it seems prima facie possible to explain a lot of things about the nonresponsibility of animals without appealing to any CAT.

Let me start from the second point. In *Leviathan*, Hobbes succinctly gives the following view:

> To make covenants with brute beasts is impossible, because not understanding our speech, they understand not, nor accept of any translation of right, nor can translate any right to another: and without mutual acceptation, there is no covenant.[13]

Hobbes is only speaking here of contracts.[14] But if we wish to explain why animals are not moral subjects, it may be an interesting exercise to see how far such commonsense facts as animals not understanding our speech can take us, before we have reached anything quite as complicated as autonomy or identification. The exasperating fact that your cat cannot understand your request that she be careful in handling your computer keyboard from now on counts for a lot when you remind yourself that she is exempt from moral responsibility for knocking it off the table again. Now expand the Hobbesian notion of "not understanding our speech" and speak simply about things that animals, given their intellectual capacities, do not understand. Consider another situation in which we are tempted to blame a nonhuman animal but think better of it: A child discovers that the family dog destroyed her dinosaur-shaped toy. She becomes angry; "But it's *my favorite dinosaur*!" she screams. We may well imagine a parent explaining to her that "He's only a dog, darling. He does not understand that it's your favorite dinosaur." The dog does not understand *mine, favorite,* or *dinosaur,* not even in the murky, visceral way in which a small child does. Similarly, the dog's mind presumably cannot grasp – nor can it track, the way even unsophisticated people can – such things as increasing utility, respecting persons, or even friendship. As Hobbes hints, even if some proto-versions of these notions exist in the animal's mind, these are not concepts that it can sophisticatedly apply to humans. Thus, even if this animal can act for reasons, to some extent, it cannot respond to *moral reasons,* which makes it very hard to regard the animal as blameworthy. To judge a dog vicious for not responding to moral reasons would be similar to judging a dog boorish for not being able to appreciate Mahler. Dwelling on this banal list of things that dogs cannot understand shows us the possibility that what prevents dogs from being moral subjects may or may not have to do with things like having second-order desires (or whatever your favorite notions of autonomy and identification involve). The connection is far from obvious; and even if it exists, it needs explaining.

One could argue, of course, that the dog's lack of autonomy is somehow part of the cause of the dog's incomprehension of property and its inability to track moral reasons. This, however, seems unnecessary speculation. Dogs are also incapable of high aesthetic appreciation, and they cannot appreciate the wisdom of a quarterback's decisions when they watch football either. We do not feel any particular need to say that a dog's failure to appreciate Beethoven or to judge Michigan's offensive line has to do with its lack of autonomy; and our tendency not to fault dogs for not responding to moral reasons appears analogous to our tendency not to judge them critically as boorish or as poor judges of football games. Which leads us to the point I made earlier: There are many abilities that are unique to human beings and to human brains. Human beings can read novels, watch television, use tools, fall in love; human beings have second-order desires, internal conflicts, and so on. Maybe all of these things can be traced to one property called "autonomy," or maybe they have little in common except for requiring a high-caliber brain or the ability to reflect. Presumably, some of these things have to do with moral responsibility, and some do not. Which of them are relevant to moral responsibility and how they relate to each other are fascinating questions, but one cannot assume without argument that just because something is a unique property of humans, it is also the backbone of moral responsibility.

III. CATS AND APPLIED ETHICS

Perhaps the closest thing we have to a pretheoretical notion of autonomy is the notion of autonomy as used in applied ethics, especially medical ethics. Talk of personal choice and of minding one's own business is central to the folk value theory of the United States, and so is the idea of informed choice, of being an educated consumer. Discussions of paternalism and autonomy in medicine are to a large extent driven by intuitions about these things.

But just as the classes of autonomous actions defined by various CATs appear to be much smaller than the class of actions for which agents are morally responsible, the classes of autonomous actions defined by CATs appear much smaller than the class of actions that, say, a patient has the right to perform without paternalistic intervention actions that are "one's own business." *The Field Guide to Psychiatric Assessment and Treatment* discusses the conditions under which a person in need of medical treatment – whether psychiatric or otherwise – should be regarded as competent for the purpose of medical decision making.[15] If a patient is judged incompetent according to these guidelines, paternalistic interventions might be indicated in her case that would not be allowed in the case of a patient who is judged competent. To establish competence, the *Guide* tells us, is to establish that a patient has the following four abilities with regards to her medical needs:

- to understand the relevant facts
- to appreciate their relevance to her personal situation
- to rationally manipulate the information to arrive at a choice
- to communicate that choice

One striking thing about this list is that it has no self-explanatory connection to Frankfurt's or Velleman's theory of autonomy and likewise no such connection to other CATs. There is nothing in the guidelines about hierarchies of mental states, alienation, a subjective sense of passivity or activity, mental conflict, or wholeheartedness. Furthermore, it is not clear how a clinician would find guidance in these CATs. Many treatment decisions made by patients that are not autonomous by CAT standards will be left to the discretion of the patient according to these guidelines, and it is far from clear that this is an error on the part of the guidelines. People typically judged to lack autonomy by CATs include unwilling addicts, compulsives, and people who are torn by inner conflicts. Such people will typically fit the *Guide*'s requirements for autonomy and in such cases are allowed to refuse treatment. And should it be otherwise? Substantial argument seems required here.

Naturally, there could be some connections between some CATs and good competence guidelines. Perhaps, for example, a CAT that places a lot of importance on reflection and rationality can tell us something about the significance of rationally manipulating information. But again, such a claim would have to be researched, elaborated, and defended. It would be substantial, not the stuff of footnotes. As in the case of explaining what exempts dogs from blame, a CAT-oriented explanation of the intuitions underlying the competence guidelines may have to compete with simpler explanations, such as explanations in terms of cognitive limitations that do not speculate that something deeper, like "structure of will," needs to be behind them. (Note that even if CATs describe essentially human characteristics and only humans have a moral status that precludes paternalism, this still does not directly establish a connection between CATs and paternalism for the same reason I outlined when discussing the plurality of essentially human qualities in the previous section.)

It can also be pointed out that there are some very important uses of the word "autonomy" in medical ethics that are clearly not the same as the use of the word in moral psychology and agency theory. For example, one is supposed to "increase the autonomy" of a patient, or increase her ability to "make autonomous decisions," by making sure not to withhold essential information from her and to provide her with additional information if she asks for it. I agree that paternalistic withholding of information from patients is generally wrong and that supplying patients with as much information as they desire is generally right. I doubt, however, that anyone wishes to claim, or that any CAT entails, that an *ill-informed* decision cannot be an instance of autonomous *agency*. Some may wish to claim that an *irrational* decision cannot be an instance of autonomous agency, but being ill informed – either because you have been deceived or simply because the relevant information is not available to you at the time when you have to decide – is not the same as being irrational. Columbus's decision to sail west may have been very uninformed, but not necessarily irrational and not at odds, for example, with the criteria for autonomy proposed by Frankfurt, Velleman, and Ekstrom. Giving a patient more information may also make her more "autonomous" in the sense of making her less dependent on other people – the way one is more autonomous if one can fix one's own car than if one cannot. Few, though, think that being unable to fix one's own car represents a defect of *agency*, and again Frankfurt, Ekstrom, or Velleman do not hold anything of the sort.

IV. IMPLICATIONS FOR COMPLEX AUTONOMY THEORIST

Imagine a defender of a Complex Autonomy Theory responding by saying that her main purpose in developing her CAT was not to explain moral responsibility nor to aid applied ethics, nor that, having heard my arguments, she now renounces any claim that her view has direct implications for moral responsibility. (Frankfurt, for one, has explained in many a conference question period that his latest theories simply are not theories of moral responsibility.) If a CAT is not meant to say anything about moral responsibility or applied ethics, if moral responsibility or applied ethics are not said to be the subject of the CAT, it seems as if what I say has no impact on it. It obviously does not have one type of impact: If a certain CAT never claims to be relevant to moral responsibility or applied ethics, it is no criticism of it that it would not serve as a good foundation for a theory of moral responsibility or of patients' rights. This would be like criticizing a metaphysician for not doing, say, ethics.

But other kinds of caution are indicated if one is to develop a theory of autonomy that is not committed to any claims about moral responsibility or the limits of permissible paternalism. Moral responsibility and the limits of permissible paternalism are subjects about which we have plenty of pretheoretical intuitions, however disorderly they may be. They are subjects about which we are forced to think fairly explicitly, even if not clearly, by personal decisions and by judges and legislators. Divorcing discussion of autonomy from these pretheoretical intuitions makes it more of a challenge to remain clear on the question of what, exactly, we are discussing and debating when we are discussing and debating autonomy or identification. Consider, for example, the following paragraph from Frankfurt:

> Thus Agamemnon at Aulis is destroyed by an inescapable conflict between two equally defining elements of his own nature: his love for his daughter and his being devoted to the welfare of his men. When he is forced to sacrifice one of these, he is thereby able to betray himself. Rarely, if ever, do tragedies of this sort have sequels. Since the volitional unity of the tragic hero has been irreparably ruptured, there is a sense in which the person he had been no longer exists. Hence, there can be no continuation of his story.[16]

The literal-minded (or, in this case, literary-minded) reader might point out that there are *several* sequels to the tragedy of Agamemnon. He leads his men to war and victory (see Homer) and returns home, where he is killed by his wife, who wishes to punish him for sacrificing their daughter (see Aeschylus). But Frankfurt only says that there is *a sense* in which Agamemnon no longer exists, allowing for other senses in which he keeps existing. Still, if one is interested in moral responsibility, one may reasonably ask to hear more about the exact sense in which the Agamemnon who killed his daughter no longer exists after the killing. Does it make sense to punish the returning Agamemnon? After all, the person who decided to kill his daughter "no longer exists" in some sense.

Obviously, Frankfurt does not wish to hold a view implying any such counterintuitive claim about Agamemnon's moral responsibility or about the moral responsibility of anyone whose "volitional unity has been irreparably ruptured." But if he does not mean any such thing, what *does* he mean? Does Frankfurt, in saying that Agamemnon no longer exists, merely want to tell us that death (and subsequent replacement by a different person) is often a good *metaphor* for the state of having betrayed the object of a true love, as such an act changes the traitor deeply? We already know that, insofar as we already use such expressions as "The person I was in the 1960s doesn't exist anymore" or "Breaking up with her would destroy me." One would assume that Frankfurt wishes to make a stronger claim than the claim that "destruction" makes a good metaphor for Agamemnon's psychological predicament – but a stronger claim that does not have counterintuitive implications for moral responsibility (and does not imply, for instance, that post-*Iliad* Agamemnon is not entitled to the property of the presacrifice Agamemnon unless the latter made an appropriate will). I do not doubt that there may be such a claim, but Frankfurt does not make it easy for us to understand what claim he wishes to make.

Velleman, in "Identification and Identity," argues that Frankfurt is wrong.[17] Agamemnon does not destroy himself as an agent. Frankfurt, in "Rationality and the Unthinkable," seems to hold that some actions that would not be regarded as autonomous by Velleman (akratic actions that are surprising for the actor) can be autonomous, because they follow from the agent's volitional essence (see his discussion of Lord Fawn).[18] Whatever the precise nature of either view, it is reasonable to pose some important questions.

Suppose that one philosopher, such as Frankfurt, argues that Agamemnon destroys himself as an agent, while another, such as Velleman, argues that he does not. On the other hand, in the case of my akratically breaking up with a friend, Frankfurt holds that my action may be autonomous (if it came from a deep enough place in my volitional structure), while Velleman holds that it is not autonomous (because it took place without what he calls "my active participation"). Suppose further that *neither* philosopher is committed to anything about Agamemnon's, or my, status with regard to moral responsibility or about our status as competent persons as far as medicine or the law are concerned. How am I to judge whether to prefer Velleman's theory or Frankfurt's? Frankfurt and Velleman seem to disagree. What exactly are they disagreeing about? What intuitions, exactly, are they trying to capture such that one of them might capture them better than the other? I have argued before (following Velleman himself, to some extent) that Frankfurt and Velleman are talking about different things, which can be called "autonomy" and "authenticity."[19] Ekstrom, in this volume, says that, *contra* Velleman and me, Frankfurt and Velleman *are* arguing about the same thing. They have conflicting substantive views of something – autonomy – and while Velleman's view implies that autonomy is somewhat similar to what we normally call "self-control," Frankfurt's view implies that autonomy diverges wildly from self-control as colloquially understood and is more similar to what some romantic people would call "authenticity." But I now believe that if we cannot think of autonomy as related in traditional ways to moral responsibility and the limits of paternalism, even the metadisagreement of Ekstrom and myself does not have a clear subject matter. Does Ekstrom merely doubt the usefulness of my preferred definitional scheme, or does she join the Velleman-Frankfurt argument with a third, broader view of what autonomy is?

In other words, if one's view of autonomy is not meant to be about moral responsibility or the limits of permissible paternalism, and so is not tied in a clear way to intuitions about these topics, it seems important that one make it clear what one's view is about, what sort of intuitions it attempts to capture. I do not think that "intuitions about when we feel, in some sense, that we are not really ourselves" is by itself an answer, however. Once we agree that such statements as "It's my resentment speaking, not I" and "Agamemnon is no longer Agamemnon" are not fundamentally about moral responsibility or permissible paternalism, then nothing tells us that all of the intuitions that express themselves in paradoxical expressions about a person not really being himself or herself are of a piece. All kinds of things can cause a person who owns a house to say "I don't really have a home," a person who is gainfully employed to say that "I don't have a real job," or a person well versed in geography to say that "Calgary is not really a city." The feeling that you do not have a home can strike you because you travel too much, because the people who live with you are so hostile that you feel more comfortable when you are away from them, or because you are not emotionally attached to the place you are in. "I don't have a real job" can be said by a person who likes her job so much that she cannot believe she is being paid for it, a person who feels that she should be making a lot more money, or a person who longs for a more stable and conventional way of life in lieu of her impossibly adventurous one. Similarly, statements like "This is not really me talking" and "This is not really him talking," if they are neither literal nor about moral responsibility, are just as likely to come from different intuitive sources as they are to be about one thing called "autonomy."

So theories of autonomy that are not straightforwardly related to intuitions about moral responsibility and applied ethics should be clear as to what they actually are about. They could well be about important things. For example, some ways of talking about how we can make our lives more autonomous appear to revive, within the analytical tradition, the search for peace of mind (*ataraxia*) or the good life (*eudaimonia*), or at any rate, for something that could alleviate, to some degree, our sense of being helpless before the slings and arrows of fortune and the mental turmoil they create. This may not have much to do with moral responsibility or the limits of paternalism, but it has always been one of the things meant by "freedom" and taken to be important.

Notes

I would like to thank Laura Waddell Ekstrom, Timothy Schroeder, Perry Mandanis, and James Stacey Taylor for help with this chapter.

1. John Martin Fischer and Mark Ravizza, *Responsibility and Control: A Theory of Moral Responsibility* (New York: Cambridge University Press, 1998).
2. Harry Frankfurt, "Freedom of the Will and the Concept of a Person," and "Identification and Externality," both in Frankfurt, ed., *The Importance of What We Care About* (Cambridge: Cambridge University Press, 1988): 11–25, 58–68.
3. Frankfurt, "Identification and Wholeheartedness," in Frankfurt, ed., *The Importance of What We Care About,* 159–176. See also his "Autonomy, Necessity, and Love," in Frankfurt, ed., *Necessity, Volition, and Love* (Cambridge: Cambridge University Press, 1999): 129–141.
4. Laura Waddell Ekstrom, "Autonomy and Personal Integration," this volume.
5. J. David Velleman, "What Happens When Someone Acts?" *Mind* 101 (1992): 464–465; reprinted in J. David Velleman, *The Possibility of Practical Reason* (Oxford: Oxford University Press, 2000): 123–143.
6. Ibid., 465 n. 12.
7. Nomy Arpaly, *Unprincipled Virtue* (New York: Oxford University Press, 2002): chap. 4.
8. I discuss these cases in my *Unprincipled Virtue,* chaps. 1, 3, and in "Moral Worth," *Journal of Philosophy* 99 (2002): 223–245.
9. The claim that we have little control over the development of our character is made and defended by George Sher, "Blame for Traits," *Noûs* 35 (2001): 146–161.
10. Rosalind Hursthouse, "Virtue Ethics and the Emotions," in Daniel Statman, ed., *Virtue Ethics* (Edinburgh: Edinburgh University Press, 1997): 99–118.
11. Thanks to J. David Velleman for bringing this objection to my attention.
12. Arpaly, "Hamlet and the Utilitarians," *Philosophical Studies* 99 (2000): 45–57.
13. Thomas Hobbes, *Leviathan,* Edwin Curley, ed. (Indianapolis: Hackett Publishing, 1994): chap. 14, p. 22.

14. Though the ability to make contracts and being a moral subject are very similar things for him.
15. M. Bauer, *The Field Guide to Psychiatric Assessment and Treatment* (Philadelphia: Lippincott/Williams and Wilkins, 2003).
16. Frankfurt, "Autonomy, Necessity, and Love," 139 n. 8.
17. Velleman, "Identification and Identity," in Sarah Buss and Lee Overton, eds., *Contours of Agency: Essays on Themes from Harry Frankfurt* (Cambridge, MA: MIT Press, 2003): 91–123.
18. Frankfurt, "Rationality and the Unthinkable," in Frankfurt, ed., *The Importance of What We Care About*, 183–184.
19. See my *Unprincipled Virtue*, chap. 4.

PART II

AUTONOMY, FREEDOM, AND MORAL RESPONSIBILITY

8

Autonomy and Free Agency

Marina A. L. Oshana

INTRODUCTION

In this chapter, I want to explore questions about the kind of freedom personal or agential autonomy is said to require. In particular, I want to address: (1) our ordinary pretheoretical intuitions about autonomy; (2) whether autonomy demands freedom to do otherwise, an issue of concern to philosophers who regard autonomous agency as central to responsible agency; (3) whether autonomy is guaranteed by the satisfaction of positive and negative freedom; and (4) the sense in which autonomy requires the freedom to "create oneself." I will begin by offering a brief examination of the concept of autonomy at issue. In Section II, I will explore the question of whether personal autonomy is a phenomenon that depends upon the resolution of our metaphysical status relative to the truth or falsity of determinism. Section III will take up the question of positive and negative freedom, while the issue of self-creation will be the subject matter of Section IV.

I. THE CONCEPT OF AUTONOMY

Autonomy literally means "self-law" or "self-rule," and an autonomous person is one who directs or determines the course of her own life. Having a right to autonomy, or de jure autonomy, will not suffice for actual self-rule. Although a person's behavior and motivations can be traced to a variety of factors, to describe a person as autonomous is to claim that the person exercises de facto control over the choices and actions relevant to the direction of her life. This calls for agential power and authority in the form of psychological freedom – mastery of one's will – as well as power and authority within central social roles and arrangements. One component of agential power and authority is self-control.[1] Autonomy requires that a person generally be disposed to act on her own behalf and that she have the developed capacity to do so.

Equally important, the autonomous agent must be permitted to act on her own behalf.[2] The autonomous person does not allow, and is not party to roles that allow, the influence of others to overshadow or usurp her own judgment. Dedication to a system of belief, to a cause, to an institution, or to another person might equally frustrate the authority autonomy demands. There is obviously some degree to which autonomy requires that persons be committed to their own self-governance, and I am not prepared to specify the level of this commitment. But someone who is only accidentally self-governing and/or who regrets his self-ruled status and who wishes to surrender himself to the authority of another is unlikely to experience more than episodes, of diminishing frequency and significance, of de facto autonomy. In a nutshell, an autonomous individual must not *in fact* be affected by other persons, by social institutions, or by natural circumstances in ways that render him incapable of self-control and of living a self-directed life.

II. CAUSAL DETERMINISM AND AUTONOMY

It is commonly held that the acts for which people are morally responsible are those they perform as self-governed agents. So it is natural to ask whether moral responsibility requires that agents be free in the sense that they act autonomously – that is, whether the acts for which they are held responsible are those they have performed autonomously (or, less strongly, have performed under conditions conducive to autonomy). And if the freedom required for moral responsibility is incompatible with causal determinism, the question arises whether the variety of freedom required for autonomy is compatible with a state of affairs that is causally determined. Causal determinism is the thesis that every state of the universe, including our intentional expressions of will – our actions and choices – is causally necessitated by some prior state or states of the world together with the laws of nature. It is the view that, given the past together with the laws of nature, there is at any instant exactly one possible future; only one actual state of affairs can, at any given point, obtain.[3] If at any instant there is more than one possible future, then indeterminism is true.[4]

Given that the thesis of causal determinism is plausible (and I think it is), the varieties of freedom relevant to autonomy are freedom of the will and freedom of action. Autonomous agents are, if nothing else, agents and as such must be empowered to deliberate about action and to author action. And it is arguable that an autonomous person must be free to change the values and motivations about which she deliberates and to alter her life activities if she so chooses. The notions of deliberation and change imply a capacity for control, and this capacity appears to be intrinsically connected with freedom of will and of action.

Freedom of will can be characterized as the freedom one experiences vis-à-vis such states as intending, willing, attempting, and selecting that serve as impetus to action. Narrowly construed, freedom of action is the freedom to act, and a person who enjoys freedom of action is, at least, free from (internally or externally induced) physical and psychological restraint. In this narrow sense, freedom of action is obviously central to autonomy. For little sense can be made of the freedom autonomy demands if we claim that a person is self-governing and self-controlling but is incapable of initiating action. So there must be a broader configuration of freedom that is the concern of autonomy. More broadly, both freedom of will and freedom of action are explicated in terms of a capacity or power to will or to act given the presence of two or more equally realizable alternatives. Freedom of action is the freedom to function, to provoke and to execute physical movement. To acknowledge freedom of action is to acknowledge that a person faced with a choice between doing X or doing Y can do either X or Y. To say that an individual has freedom of will is to say that when faced with choosing "between two or more mutually incompatible courses of action," the individual has the power to choose either of these.[5] Because both varieties of freedom require that, given the very conditions that obtain, a person is able to do or to will otherwise than she actually does, both are varieties of freedom incompatible with determinism and impossible to realize if determinism should be true.[6]

Neither variety of freedom is sufficient for autonomy, nor are they jointly sufficient. Having the will one wants and translating that will into action need not effectively enable a person to determine her own way of life. Consider the situation of the residents of B. F. Skinner's fictional utopia, *Walden Two*.[7] They are free to act and to will whatever they please. And, unlike most of us, the object of their will is rarely if ever unsatisfied. But this just is the case because, whatever we may say of them as actors, they lack de facto control over the content of their wills and over the configuration of social arrangements that make the realization of their wills possible. As the *Walden Two* example shows, simply enjoying freedom of will or freedom of action will not tell us what we need to know about the manner in which a person develops the ability to will or to act. Does the person with free will, for example, will freely? Does freedom of action ensure that one acts freely? The person who is free to choose X or Y or to do X or Y may nonetheless not be free to decide that X and Y are the choices she wants, as any instance of action under subversive influence will show. Freedom of will and freedom of action will not supply the self-control or self-rule autonomy demands.

Is either variety of freedom necessary for autonomy? The (perhaps surprising) answer is no, although *why* the agent lacks these species of freedom will be relevant for autonomy. A person may be self-governing even where the person cannot will or do otherwise than she in fact does. Consider freedom of will. Suppose I lack freedom of will with respect to certain motivational states, such as a desire to abandon my mother to a life of poverty. I am constrained by the will I have; it is "volitionally necessitated" that, insofar as I remain myself and the circumstances persist, I shall never act in such a way as to desert my mother financially. This fact does not undermine the self-managed quality of my will to assist my mother. Indeed, insofar as my willing is an expression of my own agency and reflects who I am and what I support, I cannot will to withhold assistance for reasons that are consonant with self-government.[8] This would not be the case if, for example, the intention to help my mother was prompted by the coercive threat of another or if my will originated from covert influences inaccessible to review and assessment on my part. In those cases, *I* would not be free to change my values and motives even if the metaphysical freedom to do so remains. But the inability to will otherwise is not, by itself, enough to signal a lack of autonomy or a diminution of autonomy just as the ability to will otherwise is not always indicative of self-rule. As far as freedom of will is concerned, autonomy requires that what the agent wills (or cannot help but will) must not suffer frustration emanating from the attempt of other persons to will for or through the agent or from obstacles originating in one's psychophysiology. This is particularly true when the forces confronting the agent are forces the agent resists.

Similarly, whether freedom of action is needed for autonomy will depend on why the person lacks freedom of action and what this lack signals for the person's authority over herself. Suppose I am not free to run a three-minute mile, or move to Paris, or appear for a lecture on time. The first two are closed to me because of physical limitations and by personal as well as monetary constraints, respectively. The last may be closed to me by simple bad luck – say, I am stuck in congested traffic. In the first two cases, my ability to control my actions by means of my own authority remains intact. In addition, it is not as if I must run a three-minute mile or reside in Paris if I am to live a self-governed life, although either might have been necessary had my occupation been that of professional athlete or avant-garde French film scholar. But when I am at the mercy of traffic, the result is that the control needed in order to carry out a task central to the administration of my life is abridged. Where either freedom of action or freedom of the will is absent, it is not their absence *simpliciter* that becomes decisive in determining a person's autonomy, but the reasons why the person cannot will or do otherwise and what this implies: Did a calamity of nature or technology preempt agential authority by compelling a particular turn of events? Was the agent threatened? Is she a compulsive neurotic? Is there a counterfactual intervener behind the scenes, ready to step in and usurp control of the agent should the agent exhibit signs of independent judgment contrary to the will of the intervener? What consequence did this have on agential power and authority?

The freedom-relevant conditions for autonomy are twofold: One condition assesses the manner in which a person comes to plan and to make certain decisions relevant to the direction of her life, opting for one course of action rather than another. Does the person exhibit a capacity for reflection and self-discovery? Is she self-aware? Is she a competent social navigator?[9] The second condition pertains to the reasons for which the person decides and acts as she does. Is it because she was lacking other robust options? Were her actions an expression of this lack? That persons are or are not autonomous is not founded on metaphysical facts about persons but rather is based on a confluence of social and psychological skills, the exercise of these skills, and the sociorelational position that persons occupy and in which persons function.

Freedom of will and freedom of action call for freedom to do otherwise. If I am correct, neither is needed for autonomy. What autonomy requires is the freedom to direct the actions central to the administration of one's life and thus the freedom to deliberate about and to change one's values and motivations and to alter one's life if one so chooses. But this freedom might be obtainable independent of the truth or falsity of determinism. Autonomy may well be "agnostic" between compatibilism and incompatibilism.[10]

To see that the conditions for personal autonomy can be satisfied even where there are good reasons for believing that determinism is true, remember that autonomy requires that certain properties hold of the actual situation in which a person finds himself. Among these is the ability to decide between putative alternative motives or courses of action. Now suppose that determinism is true. If determinism is true, then it is determined that the personally autonomous individual will make a choice, or will pursue a certain life, or will act in a certain way. Lacking metaphysical freedom, the determined individual can control neither the past nor the laws of nature.

An account of autonomy that speaks to our ordinary intuitions about those persons whom we regard as in charge of their lives does not preclude fixity of the laws of nature and the past, any more than it necessitates such fixity. As Alfred Mele notes, "[D]eterminists are in a position to distinguish among different causal routes to the collection of values (and 'characters') agents have at a time."[11] So let us conceive of two individuals, Arthur and Barbara, whose lives are equally determined but who nonetheless differ in the following way. Arthur is autonomous (or at least will be capable of autonomy) because it will be determined for him to meet the conditions for autonomy (including that of interacting with other individuals in a certain way). Barbara, by contrast, is not autonomous (or will lack the capacity for autonomy) because she will be determined not to meet these conditions. Autonomy would then just require that social and psychological conditions of a particular variety were present and that certain autonomy-undermining phenomena – including social roles, institutions, and relations of a given variety – were absent. In Arthur's case, the proposition "Arthur is determined to choose" is consistent with the proposition "choices relevant to self-governance are available to Arthur in the determined state of affairs." The range of options required for self-determination might not include metaphysical freedom to do otherwise. All that may be necessary is that the social situation in which the individual finds himself coupled with facts about the state of the agent's psychology are autonomy friendly.[12]

Taking pains to restrict his discussion to the phenomenon of actual psychological autonomy, Mele would explain the difference in Arthur's and Barbara's psychological self-governance by appealing to a "modest agent-internal indeterminism" that allows agents "ample control" over their decisions and choices. Even if determinism is true, it is also the case that our decisions and actions are influenced by considerations – beliefs, desires, and the like – that simply "come to mind" without our being in control of their doing so. These become relevant to the agent's deliberations, "opening up alternative deliberative outcomes":

Considerations that come indeterministically to mind (like considerations that deterministically come to mind) are nothing more than input to deliberation. Their coming to mind has at most an indirect effect on what the agent decides, an effect that is mediated by the agent's assessment of them. They do not settle matters. Moreover, not only do agents have the opportunity to assess these considerations, they also have the opportunity to search for additional relevant considerations before they decide, thereby increasing the probability that other relevant considerations will indeterministically come to mind.... [G]iven a suitable indeterminism regarding what comes to mind in the assessment process, it is not causally determined what assessment the agent will reach.[13]

Arguably, the most influential attempt to provide a compatibilist analysis of free agency and, derivatively, of autonomy is Harry Frankfurt's explication of the psychology of responsible persons who act freely. Indeed, Frankfurt's effort to discover the kind of freedom relevant for responsibility leads him to a conception of free will that he himself likens to self-control or autonomy.[14] His famous counterexamples to the Principle of Alternate Possibilities (and the numerous Frankfurt-style counterexamples generated in light of Frankfurt's work) are intended to show that, intuitively, an agent who has no options for choice or for action can be morally responsible. There are no restrictions on the manner in which freedom of action and freedom of the will can be curtailed while preserving the sort of freedom necessary for responsibility and, Frankfurt believes, for self-determination, as this quotation makes plain:

What is at stake... is not a matter of the causal origins of the states of affairs in question, but [a person's] activity or passivity with respect to those states of affairs. A person is active with respect to his own desires when he identifies himself with them, and he is active with respect to what he does when what he does is the outcome of his identification of himself with the desire that moves him in doing it. Without such identification the person is a passive bystander to his desires and to what he does, regardless of whether the causes of his desires and of what he does are the work of another agent or of impersonal external forces or of processes internal to his own body.... To the extent that a person identifies himself with the springs of his actions, he takes responsibility for those actions and acquires moral responsibility for them; moreover, the questions of *how* the actions and his identification with their springs are caused is [*sic*] irrelevant to the questions of whether he performs the actions freely or is morally responsible for performing them.[15]

A third type of freedom has emerged as relevant to moral responsibility and so, perhaps, to autonomy. This is *acting freely*. Frankfurt's view is that acting freely suffices for acting autonomously, and this is a compatibilist species of freedom, one that is indifferent to the question of whether the agent could have done or could have willed otherwise.[16] Even supposing that the agent could have had a different will and could have acted differently, the critical fact for deciding autonomy is that the agent would not have wanted his will to be any different. It is little importance for agent autonomy, says Frankfurt, that a person was free of will and of action (in the sense that various possibilities were available to the person). What is important is that the person wanted – perhaps capriciously and imprudently – to do the action in question; this "wanting" was volitionally strong enough that the agent would not have done otherwise even if no constraints on his ability to do otherwise were present; and, most importantly, the actual chain of causes leading up to action did not include intervention by an element rejected by the actor.

If he is correct, the conclusions Frankfurt reaches suggest three things. One is that moral responsibility could just be a matter of a person's attitude to what may or may not be a causally determined situation. A second is that acting freely, as the relevant sense of freedom for responsibility, is largely compatible with the presence of a social intervener, as long as the intervener behaves in a particular manner. The third is that acting freely is sufficient for autonomy. Here Frankfurt is mistaken. His mistake is due to conflating autonomous agency, a global phenomenon, with autonomous choice and action, which can be highly localized and restrictive. That Frankfurt is concerned with the global phenomenon is evident from the fact that his project consists in an exploration of what must be true of persons in order for them to be the sort of entities accessible to the attitudes and actions that we take toward uniquely responsible agents. Frankfurt is not concerned to delineate the state of affairs that exists when an attribution of responsibility arises, for presumably there will be occasions when it makes sense to say of a wanton, or an unwilling addict, or a child, or a slave that each is answerable for his conduct. It is, rather, the general conditions for free agency – an effort to distinguish between the autonomous and the nonautonomous agent and (more ambitiously) to articulate the concept of personhood operating at the center – that commands Frankfurt's attention.

Frankfurt-style counterexamples to the Principle of Alternate Possibilities illustrate the differences that exist between moral responsibility and personal autonomy. It is true that the phenomenon of acting freely is tested against the actual, rather than an alternate, state of affairs and focuses on the conditions that are actually, rather than counterfactually, present and available to the agent. Similarly, the phenomenon of personal autonomy can be described in a way that makes the actual situation that obtains the one that is important for assessments of autonomy. But the conditions that must actually be met for these two states are quite dissimilar.

According to Frankfurt, acting freely calls for nothing more than the presence of a certain attitude of identification (or, in his later works, satisfaction) and assent on the part of the agent, in conjunction with a stable psychological history, regardless of the nature of the factor that "determines" the agent to act. In addition, Frankfurt purports to show that a person's responsible agency, predicated on the person's free agency or local ability to be self-governing can be manipulated by others, and in objectionable ways, while having no effect on the person's autonomy, as when an isolated incident of manipulation produces a permanent alteration in the subject.[17] But the conditions for personal autonomy are differently satisfied. It is plausible that a person can be responsible for her actions even when she is not autonomous. For example, I can be responsible for failing to shelter and clothe my children, even if I lack autonomy. I can be responsible if I would recognize the legitimate moral expectation that I do this and if I could care for my children on the basis of this recognition, even while I am threatened with punishment from my master or my God, should I refuse to do so. I have argued elsewhere that what we are saying when we attribute autonomy to actors in situations of this sort is that they exhibited "local" autonomy, or autonomy with respect to the execution of individual acts.[18] So personal autonomy as a dispositional or global phenomenon is not necessary for responsibility, and the phenomenon of acting freely as described above is not sufficient for self-determination.

If a person is to act not just freely but to be autonomous while so acting, it is not enough that the person has the will that he wants. It is also essential that what the person does is done by his own lights, under his ownership. What might salvage Frankfurt-style accounts in a way that comports with autonomy would be to stipulate that the chain of events leading up to what the agent does is suitably "reasons-responsive."[19]

Whether or not reasons-responsiveness is a feature of action is determined by a counterfactual sensitivity to reasons for action that is possessed by the mechanism from which a person's actions originate. Normal practical reasoning and deliberation are typical of mechanisms that respond to reasons for and against action, while physical realizations of the central nervous system such as the unmanageable urges of drug addiction are examples of mechanisms that are not reasons-responsive. The idea is that instead of seeking evidence of autonomous agency in the presence of alternative courses of action available to the actor, we can look to the dispositional nature of the mechanism from which the putatively autonomous agent in fact acts. If the agent is provided with sufficient reason to do otherwise, when everything else is held fixed, and the agent would be able to appreciate reasons to do otherwise and would be disposed to respond to these reasons, we have all the evidence we need of free agency.[20] If, on the other hand, the agent is incapable of appreciating what she has grounds to do because of the type of mechanism from which her motives for action ensue, the agent is not well placed to endorse and to bestow authenticity on her reasons for action.

Return now to the question of my autonomy with respect to my inability to abandon my mother to poverty. According to the freedom as responsiveness to reasons explanation, I am autonomous when my actions follow from my decisions, my decisions from my deliberations, and my deliberations from a normal, unimpaired mechanism of practical deliberation, one that would respond appropriately to reasons to do otherwise, even though it does not occurrently do so. The question, then, is whether reasons-responsiveness adequately grounds agent autonomy. Provided that, in the actual sequence, the mechanism on which the agent acts is appropriately reasons-responsive, is autonomy assured?

I think not. While the reasons-responsiveness account supplies an element of agential control absent from Frankfurt's models (while continuing to disengage the question of the compatibility of freedom to do otherwise with causal determinism from the question of the relationship between agential autonomy and causal determinism), responsiveness of the requisite sort says nothing about the social circumstances in which the actor functions nor about the genesis of the deliberative mechanism. It is conceivable that my reasons for assisting my parent emerge from and reflect an unimpaired mechanism of practical deliberation or from a natural, unsullied emotional attachment – I would not choose otherwise, though the source of my choice is responsive to adaptive incentives – at the same time that I act under (social/political) conditions of restraint antithetical to autonomy. In this case, we might say that I exhibit local autonomy with respect to my decision, though I fail to live a self-governed life.[21]

III. AUTONOMY AND LIBERTY

Traditionally, theorists have approached the topic of personal liberty by offering either a negative or a positive analysis of the term. Negative freedom is the libertarian ideal. A person is said to be free in a negative sense when his choices and activities are minimally impeded by other persons, institutions, or other obstacles to will and action. Advocates of negative freedom include John Locke, Jeremy Bentham, John Stuart Mill, and Alexis de Tocqueville, all of whom agree

> that there ought to exist a certain minimum area of personal freedom which must on no account be violated; for if it is overstepped, the individual will find himself in an area too narrow for even that minimum development of his natural faculties which alone make it possible to pursue, and even to conceive, the various ends which men hold good or right or sacred. It follows that a frontier must be drawn between the area of private life and that of public authority.[22]

There are numerous ways in which to understand a positive analysis of freedom. Generally, it is understood as liberty of the sort associated with the psychological resources for self-governance. Bernard Berofsky charges that positive freedom consists of "a variety of cognitive, emotional, and character traits which a person must possess if he is to be... autonomous,"[23] such as intellectual and physical competences. Such traits, he states, are "invariant to environment."[24] More narrowly, Isaiah Berlin defines positive freedom as self-mastery, particularly mastery of the individual by the individual's rational self. According to Berlin, the central issue for positive freedom is who, or what, determines the individual to live a certain way. Positive freedom

> derives from the wish to be self-directed and not acted upon by an external nature or by other men as if I were a thing, or an animal, or a slave incapable of playing a human role, that is, of conceiving goals and policies of my own and realizing them.[25]

That a positive analysis of freedom such as Berlin provides is believed to depend on some understanding of personal autonomy is evident from Berlin's suggestion that positive freedom can be achieved by retreating into the "inner citadel," the realm of psychological autonomy. In this manner, the individual overcomes obstacles such as "the resistance of nature, [the] ungoverned passions... irrational institutions, [and]... the opposing wills or behaviour of others."[26] Despite Berlin's claim that positive freedom is anchored in that aspect of person we label the "rational self," the condition of personal autonomy cannot be described in terms of some essential component of the individual in virtue of which the individual is self-directing.[27] At any rate, I find it too difficult to delineate an aspect of the individual such as rationality that can lay a legitimate and noncontentious claim to the core of the agent. Berlin's definition of positive freedom is unduly narrow because it offers only one suggestion for filling the lacuna left by negative freedom.

Nonetheless, both positive and negative freedom appear necessary for autonomy. The necessary element negative freedom contributes to autonomy is that certain impediments (such as psychological infirmities, physical barriers, coercion, and manipulation) are precluded from the life of the agent. The person whose chronic lack of confidence prompts him to doubt his own judgment against those of his friends suffers obstacles to what he is free to desire and to do, and for this reason he is unlikely to be autonomous. The person who is legally free to vote, but whose attempts to do so are confounded by obstacles such as barriers to the voting station, misinformation, intimidation, or confusing ballots finds his negative freedom and thus his autonomy impaired despite enjoying positive freedom of a sort. The same can be said of the individual who is entitled de jure to worship freely but who is prevented for any number of similar reasons from doing so.[28]

By itself, of course, negative freedom is inadequate to capture many of our deepest intuitions about autonomy. Equally necessary for autonomy is positive freedom. Although negative freedom indicates that a person's "actions are not *blocked* or *compelled* by other's domineering wills"[29] or by obstacles emanating in the person's psychophysiology, it discloses nothing about the specific state of affairs that exists once obstacles of an obvious sort are removed. As Berlin reminds us, it is possible that a "liberal-minded despot," even one who "encouraged the wildest inequalities," "would allow his subjects a large measure of personal [negative] freedom."[30] Subjects might be availed of protection from interference with their liberties. They might move about freely and express themselves openly or have legal action taken against them and return the favor against others. But lacking the authority to manage their lives, these persons can be described as self-governing only in an attenuated sense.[31] Because negative freedom from interference entails nothing about who or what might actually control an individual's actions and choices and stipulates nothing about the condition of a person's psychology, it is compatible with an absence of positive freedom and self-government.[32]

Even in concert, there are conditions specifically required for autonomy that neither variety of freedom may supply.[33] Consider, for example, the clear-headed religious devotee. Although the devotee is master of his will – his actions are not impeded or compelled, and he possesses the intellectual, physical, and emotional resources for self-government – the administration of his life is given over almost entirely to the judgments and recommendations of others. Having abandoned himself to a system of belief (or to a cause, to an institution, or to another person), this individual must rely on the beneficence of others for the sustenance of his person, and as a result faces a situation that is inimical to autonomy. Lacking ownership of the resources needed for de facto control of his life, he lacks autonomy. Still, the religious devotee may be amply equipped with the psychological resources to assume authority, and he is not blocked from doing so by others or by social and legal barriers.

That negative freedom and positive freedom are inadequate for autonomy is signaled by the fact that the distinction between negative and positive freedom is not always clear. As Berofsky notes, "The same environmental condition can be regarded as a grand opportunity for one person, shrugged off by another as a minor annoyance, and treated by the third as an absolute barrier."[34] Racism and sexism, or wealth and celebrity, or physical prowess and physical disability are instructive paradigms. Moreover, "one and the same internal factor can be called either positive or negative. . . . Is intelligence a component of [positive] freedom or is stupidity a barrier to action and, therefore, a component of negative freedom?"[35] Given this intersection, it is hard to specify an amalgam of these freedoms that would provide boundaries for the sort of freedom autonomy requires. As a consequence, I suspect not even an acceptably detailed account of positive freedom conjoined with negative freedom will suffice for self-determination.

By any measure, an account of personal autonomy requires that we answer the questions posed by both a negative and a positive theory of freedom. These are, respectively, "What am I free to do?" and "By what or by whom am I ruled?" Both bear importantly on the idea of self-determination. But the notion of liberty is often conflated, wrongly I think, with the idea of personal autonomy. To be autonomous is to be self-governing, and while autonomy calls for the presence of certain freedoms, autonomy is a "thicker" concept, descriptive of a condition persons enjoy in virtue of certain liberties but not guaranteed by the latter. To be free is to enjoy the power to decide or to act; it is to have the wherewithal to realize one's will. Autonomy, on the other hand, concerns authority over and ownership of the affective and cognitive states as well as the social roles and relationships that provoke action and that sustain action.

Autonomy guarantees that will and action exist under the de facto authority and de jure entitlement of the agent. Autonomy, more than negative and positive freedom, calls for the presence of certain social, political, and economic arrangements.

IV. THE FREEDOM TO MAKE ONESELF

Autonomous agents are sometimes spoken of as atomistic, self-created individuals, dependent on none but themselves and insulated from the influence and guidance of others. The ideally autonomous individual is someone who does not defer to the directives of other persons, who is free to reject traditions, values, principles of belief, and motives for action not her own making. The autonomous individual is impervious to constraints that cement friendships; she does not settle for tradition, nor is she the progeny of her culture. An autonomous agent is directed entirely by her own lights, bound by no constraints other than those she imposes on herself. Because self-definition is the focal point of liberty, this may be a good thing.

But this conception of autonomy is problematic, and not because of the idea that an autonomous individual is, loosely speaking, sovereign over her decisions and actions. The image of human beings as self-directed creatures is attractive to members of a liberal society, such as ours, because it captures an ideal of personal freedom and self-definition that we valorize. The story is problematic because it reserves the term "autonomous agent" for entities that bear little resemblance to human beings.

It is also a picture of persons that has been soundly criticized.[36] In defense of autonomy, let me say (as others have said) that it is a mistake to believe self-determination calls for the radically impossible act of self-creation and that it should be rejected on this account. This is a picture that ignores the social nature of persons and discounts the importance of interpersonal relationships. Who persons are, how they define themselves, and the content of their motivations, values, and commitments are essentially fashioned by connections to other people, to cultural norms, rituals, tradition, and enterprises. We cannot reconfigure these phenomena at will. Indeed, given their enormous centrality to our lives, they are phenomena that might even elude our scrutiny, our attempts to direct a critical lens upon them and render them self-made. So central are these phenomena to who we are that we may lack the ability to partition ourselves from them. The radical individual unmoved by the merits of social cooperation and unburdened by the obligations that accompany social participation is, critics charge, unlike the way persons in fact are and unlike how persons should aspire to be. The picture is flawed on descriptive as well as normative grounds.

The fact that the autonomous individual must be free to step back, to question and judge these phenomena and, if she decides, to opt out of them does not mean she is socially unsituated, or is free in the sense that she is self-constituted, where the self is defined prior to and independent of social roles and relations. Among the philosophers who press this point is Gerald Dworkin, who finds the interpretation of autonomy as radical self-creation misguided. In his "Autonomy and Behavior Control," Dworkin writes:

> We all know that persons have a history. They develop socially and psychologically in a given environment with a given set of biological endowments. They mature slowly and are heavily influenced by their parents, siblings, peers, and culture. What sense does it make to speak of their convictions, motivations, principles, and so forth as "self-selected"? This presupposes a notion of the self as isolated from the influences just enumerated, and, what is almost as foolish, *that the self which chooses does so arbitrarily*. For to the extent that the self uses canons of reason, principles of induction, judgments of probability, etc., these also have either been acquired from others or ... are innate. We can no more choose *ab initio* than we can jump out of our skins. To insist on this position is to make autonomy impossible.[37]

Joel Feinberg agrees. He notes that though it is natural to think of the autonomous person as "self-made," the idea of self-creation cannot and should not be taken literally so as to make a person's character the product solely of one's doing, *ex nihilo* into something. A conception of autonomy need not demand either metaphysical or cultural independence as a requisite for authentic self-ownership. Instead, Feinberg contends that "[a] common-sense account of self-creation ... can be given, provided we avoid the mistake of thinking that there can be no self-determination unless the self that does the determining is already formed."[38]

The core idea Feinberg advances is that people progress from infancy to adulthood in a continuous fashion. As the individual matures, his contributions to, and responsibility for, his personality and personal circumstances increase, and do so in increasingly significant ways. But "there is no point before which the child himself has no part in his own shaping and after which he is the sole responsible maker of his own character and life plan. Such a radical discontinuity is simply not part of anyone's personal history."[39] With the exception of persons who have been "severely manipulated, indoctrinated, and coerced throughout childhood," we are all self-created in giving ourselves the imprint of one's own character. This point, Feinberg notes, is frequently overlooked by philosophers "whose conception of autonomy is unrealistically inflated."[40]

Even a person's character as "authentic" cannot be entirely a function of the person's independent design. For in order to be authentic with regard to one's motivations and principles, a person must possess an undeveloped but recognizable character and rudimentary convictions that antedate and inform the activity of critical reflection. "Some principles, and especially the commitment to reasonable self-criticism itself, must be 'implanted' in a child if she is to have a reasonable opportunity of playing a part in the direction of her own growth."[41] What a person identifies with or repudiates is determined by who the person already is. An individual's more general evaluative commitments are invariably premised on aspects of the self such as race, gender, and sexual orientation. The effect of wholehearted identification or authenticity one experiences relative to one's cognitive and conative states, to one's physicality and to one's social attachments, depends largely on the self-conception brought to the process of reflective appraisal.[42]

Most obviously, autonomy does not require that a person's desires or values have developed under conditions over which he has metaphysically complete control, where complete control means control in the absence of any variety of factors, such as concern for and attachment to others, that might affect the desires, values, and projects of the agent. More to the point, autonomy does not entail that the individual be an island of independence, distanced in a radical way from the company of others. Indeed, the opposite is the case. Insofar as the freedom to make oneself is definitive of agent autonomy, it is a freedom that transpires within the social milieu.

CONCLUSION

What are we to say, then, about the variety of freedom autonomy calls for? We can say that autonomy requires the freedom to oversee states of affairs and events vital to the administration of one's life. The autonomous agent must have the power to deliberate about and to change her values and motivations and to alter significant relations in her life if she so chooses. But the ability to do this is, I have argued, agnostic about the truth or falsity of determinism. Our standard beliefs about those persons whom we regard as in control of their lives neither rule out fixity of the laws of nature and the past nor necessitate such fixity.

If a person is to be autonomous, more than freedom is called for. To be free is to possess the power to decide or to act, but autonomy deals with agential authority over those decisions and actions. Unlike acting freely and unlike positive or negative freedom, autonomy guarantees the agent de facto authority over her will and her circumstances. Finally, while all competent human beings are self-created in that each gives himself the imprint of his own character, autonomy does not demand that the individual be remote from the influence of others.

Notes

1. Alfred Mele contrasts self-controlled conduct with akratic behavior. Unlike persons who act akratically, self-controlled persons are significantly motivated "to conduct themselves as they judge best" and have "a robust capacity" to do this "in the face of (actual or anticipated) competing motivations" – *Autonomous Agents: From Self-Control to Autonomy* (New York: Oxford University Press, 1995): 6. Still, Mele argues, correctly, that even ideal or perfect self-control will not suffice for autonomy if the principles and values that regulate and guide critical reflection are products of "mind control" (ibid., chap. 7; and his "Autonomy, Self-Control, and Weakness of Will," in Robert Kane, ed., *The Oxford Handbook of Free Will* (New York: Oxford University Press, 2002): 534.
2. This is a descriptive claim. The normative or prescriptive claim that autonomous agents should be allowed to act in this fashion is one that calls for independent argument. I offer such an argument in "How Much Should We Value Autonomy?" *Social Philosophy & Policy* 20 (2003): 99–126.
3. Two very different but equally careful and provocative analyses of free will and determinism from an incompatibilist perspective are provided in Peter van Inwagen, *An Essay on Free Will* (Oxford: Oxford University Press, 1983); and Robert Kane, *The Significance of Free Will* (New York: Oxford University Press, 1998).
4. Van Inwagen (*An Essay on Free Will*, 3–5, 135–137) discusses the difference between the thesis of determinism and the thesis of universal causation (which holds that every event or state of affairs has a cause) and so between the notions of "determined" and "caused." He argues that the Principle of Universal Causation does not entail determinism and that indeterminism – the denial of determinism – need not entail the denial of causation because an act can be both undetermined and caused. If true, the denial of determinism need not produce a state of causal disorder or causal unpredictability.
5. Van Inwagen, *An Essay on Free Will*, 8. Employing the concept of possible worlds, van Inwagen interprets talk of an agent's ability – in terms of which he explicates the notion of free will – as "access-talk": A person is able to do something, or has it within his power to "bring about an event satisfying a certain description," if he has access to some world, other than the actual world, in which he performs that action or in which an event satisfying that

description occurs. Thus stated, one need not be empowered to will or to bring about states that are mutually incompatible, and this may make a difference to the compatibilist for purposes of assessing autonomy.

6. Freedom of action is not necessary for freedom of the will: A person can have free will to the extent that she retains some choice over which of her desires shall be her motive to action, while being deprived of her ability to "translate her will into action." Harry Frankfurt states, "When an agent is aware that there are certain things he is not free to do, this doubtless affects his desires and limits the range of choices he can make. But suppose that someone, without being aware of it, has in fact lost or been deprived of his freedom of action. Even though he is no longer free to do what he wants to do, his will may remain as free as it was before. Despite the fact that he is not free to translate those desires into actions or to act according to the determinations of his will, he may still form those desires and make those determinations as freely as if his freedom of action had not been impaired." See Frankfurt, "Freedom of the Will and the Concept of a Person," *Journal of Philosophy* 68 (1971): 14–15.
7. See B. F. Skinner, *Walden Two* (New York: Macmillan, 1962).
8. It is arguable that without certain volitionally necessary characteristics that provide parameters for choice and action, agential autonomy is impossible. The concept of volitional necessity is developed by Harry Frankfurt, who argues that a person's essential nature or identity as an agent is constituted by certain ineliminable characteristics of a person's will. These volitionally necessary aspects of agency undergird agential autonomy. See Frankfurt, "On the Necessity of Ideals," in his *Necessity, Volition, and Love* (Cambridge: Cambridge University Press, 1999). For a different argument that yields a similar conclusion, see Alfred Mele's discussion of autonomy and unsheddable pro-attitudes in *Autonomous Agents*, 147–173. Gary Watson questions the concept in "Volitional Necessity," in Sarah Buss and Lee Overton, eds., *Contours of Agency: Essays on Themes from Harry Frankfurt* (Cambridge, MA: MIT Press, 2002): 129–159.
9. Satisfaction of the first condition means that one is "sensitive to environmental circumstances so as to allow oneself as much elbow room as possible." See Daniel Dennett, *Elbow Room: The Varieties of Free-Will Worth Wanting* (Cambridge, MA: MIT Press, Bradford Books, 1984). This requirement suggests that autonomous agents must be self-aware and able to avoid situations that undermine the pursuit of their life plans. It also implies that they are rational in the sense described by Robert Young: "[B]eing rational can be seen as significant [to autonomy] in the following two positive ways. First, it brings coherence into the relationship between a person's general purposes and his or her particular actions. Some degree of understanding of this relationship will be needed to ensure that actions performed on particular occasions do not seriously thwart or impede more dispositional concerns. Second, and more importantly, perhaps, rationality equips a person to assess critically the advice tendered by others, an increasingly important safeguard given the extent to which we are reliant on the testimony of others about matters of great moment like health, welfare, education, economic and political affairs and so

on." Young, *Personal Autonomy: Beyond Negative and Positive Liberty* (New York: St. Martin's, 1986): 13.

10. Bernard Berofsky notes: "We are all limited and, perhaps, our lives are completely determined. But there are crucial differences in the manner in which our earlier life bears on our later life. The possibly deterministic process that has brought us to our current state may have independence and authenticity depending on the character of our *current* interactions." See Berofsky, *Liberation from Self: A Theory of Personal Autonomy* (Cambridge: Cambridge University Press, 1995): 3. For a discussion of "agnostic autonomism," see Mele, *Autonomous Agents*, 250–253.
11. Mele, "Autonomy, Self-Control, and Weakness of Will," 542.
12. Harry Frankfurt makes a similar point when he states, "My conception of freedom of the will appears to be neutral with regard to the problem of determinism. It seems conceivable that it should be causally determined that a person is free to want what he wants to want. If this is conceivable, then it might be causally determined that a person enjoys a free will. There is no more than an innocuous appearance of paradox in the proposition that it is determined, ineluctably and by forces beyond their control, that certain people have free wills and that others do not." Frankfurt, "Freedom of the Will and the Concept of a Person," in his *The Importance of What We Care About* (Cambridge: Cambridge University Press, 1988): 25.
13. Ibid., 544–545. Absent elaboration, the distinct situations of Arthur and Barbara cannot be characterized to the satisfaction of the libertarian who requires "both indeterminism and significant control at the moment of choice." Mele contends that this requirement spawns its own set of problems: If we attribute to Arthur and not to Barbara some measure of agential control that is not the upshot of plain dumb luck, then we must, so it seems, claim that Arthur's autonomy is determined just as it is determined that Barbara is denied autonomy. Robert Kane offers a meticulous libertarian tactic for explaining this difference of control in *The Significance of Free Will.*
14. See Frankfurt's "Coercion and Moral Responsibility" and "Three Concepts of Free Action," both reprinted in Frankfurt, *The Importance of What We Care About*, 26–46, 47–57. Also see Frankfurt, *Necessity, Volition, and Love.*
15. Frankfurt, "Three Concepts of Free Action, 54.
16. For an analysis of free agency that sidesteps the question of freedom to do otherwise by focusing on the notion of intention, see Donald Davidson, "Freedom to Act," in Davidson, *Essays on Actions and Events* (Oxford: Clarendon Press, 1980): 63–81, esp. 74–75.
17. See Frankfurt, "Three Concepts of Free Action," 52–53. As an aside, I do not see why Frankfurt is willing to allow that an *isolated* incident of manipulation, particularly where it produces permanent alteration in the subject, constitutes a qualitatively lesser assault of free agency than would interference on a continual basis. Perhaps Frankfurt envisions the production of an entirely new entity that goes on to assume the characteristics of a responsible agent. (I thank James Stacey Taylor for raising this point.) Unless Frankfurt requires that episodes of interference are erratic in content or yield an incoherent psychology, continual interference need not be incompatible with

the continuity of cognition and the uninterrupted flow of phenomenal experience he requires for responsibility.

18. Even a slave might be a responsible agent and be held accountable for his behavior. We might, for example, charge that the slave ought rightly to account for those of his acts that transpire under all of the conditions for free agency discussed above. A slave might be responsible for the affection and nurturance he provides his children, if we can assume his capacities to love and nurture have not been obliterated or misshapen by his situation. See Marina Oshana, "Ascriptions of Responsibility," *American Philosophical Quarterly* 34 (1997): 71–83.
19. In characterizing the morally responsible agent as reasons-responsive, I have appropriated a term coined by John Martin Fischer and Mark Ravizza to describe the character of a mechanism or process of reasoning that might lead a person to act. The most sustained discussion of responsiveness to reasons as a test for responsible agency is found in Fischer and Ravizza, *Responsibility and Control: A Theory of Moral Responsibility* (Cambridge: Cambridge University Press, 1998).
20. I am not sure that there is an important or useful difference between a mechanism-based approach and an agent-based approach to responsiveness where the question of responsibility is concerned. Fischer claims that the distinction strengthens the argument that responsibility does not require that the agent be free to do otherwise. Even if there is no counterfactual state in which the agent could do otherwise than she actually does, what matters is that the mechanism from which the behavior at issue emerges is capable of responding differently in the face of new reasons. But if the mechanism can respond differently, then surely it would do so counterfactually, and then surely the agent would counterfactually act otherwise. In fact, in certain contexts it may not be correct to say the agent is responsible even while the mechanism that issues in action is reasons-responsive. This may be the case, for example, with mechanisms of hypnosis that are moderately responsive.
21. The rejoinder, of course, is to ask what additional value autonomy *simpliciter* provides if local autonomy of a sufficiently extensive scope is had. For a discussion of this concern, see my "How Much Should We Value Autonomy?"
22. Berlin, "Two Concepts of Liberty," in his *Four Essays on Liberty* (Oxford: Oxford University Press, 1969): 124.
23. Bernard Berofsky, *Liberation from Self*, 43.
24. Ibid.
25. Berlin, "Two Concepts of Liberty," 131.
26. Ibid., 146.
27. This point has been made by numerous philosophers: "On an alternative, holistic view of human beings, the 'self' of self-control is identified with the whole person rather than with reason.... Self-control can be exercised in support of better judgments partially based on a person's appetites or emotional commitments." Mele, "Autonomy, Self-Control, and Weakness of Will," 532.

28. Of course, while negative freedom is necessary for autonomy, the degree to which and the circumstances under which a person must be negatively free in order to be autonomous vary. The simple fact that I am not free to do certain things is not enough to deny my autonomy. Were there no laws against public nudity, I might choose to go about naked. But the fact that I am prevented from doing so does not make me nonautonomous. There are a host of things I cannot do, and I can be autonomous in spite of the fact that I am not free to do them: Being autonomous is not simply a matter of living as you see fit, but of living in a way that exemplifies self-ownership in the vital areas of one's life.
29. Berlin, "Two Concepts of Liberty," 146.
30. Ibid., 129.
31. Berlin concludes: "Freedom in this sense is not, at any rate logically, connected with . . . self-government." "Two Concepts of Liberty," 130.
32. Similarly, in the United States and like-minded democratic societies, "[t]he removal of social and legal barriers . . . to achieve racial equality may be regarded as inconsequential so long as the skills for taking advantage of new opportunities are absent." But as is true of its negative counterpart, positive freedom is not sufficient for autonomy: "[T]he attainment of parity of ability may be regarded as inconsequential if a pervasive pattern of discrimination persists." Berofsky, *Liberation from Self*, 42.
33. As Gerald Dworkin reminds us in recounting a story of John Locke, a person may possess both negative and positive freedom and yet fail to be self-determining. The story concerns the imprisoned individual who is a victim of deception. Because the doors to his cell have been unlocked, the prisoner is negatively free to leave, for no barriers stand in his way, and he is positively free because the decision to depart is his own. But because his jailers have convinced him that he is locked in, the prisoner is limited with respect to his assessment of the opportunities available to him and so is not in control of his choices. Dworkin, *The Theory and Practice of Autonomy* (New York: Cambridge University Press, 1988): 14, 105.
34. Berofsky, *Liberation from Self*, 42.
35. Ibid., 42–43.
36. For instance, see Michael Sandel in *Liberalism and the Limits of Justice* (Cambridge: Cambridge University Press, 1982); Charles Taylor, *Sources of the Self* (Cambridge, MA: Harvard University Press, 1989): esp. Part I; and Seyla Benhabib, *Situating the Self: Gender, Community and Postmodernism in Contemporary Ethics* (New York: Routledge, 1992).
37. Dworkin, "Autonomy and Behavior Control," *Hastings Center Report* 6 (1976): 24.
38. Feinberg, *Harm to Self*, vol. 3 of *The Moral Limits of the Criminal Law* (New York: Oxford University Press, 1986): 34. Also see Bernard Berofsky's account of objectivity as a feature of his "liberation view of autonomy" in *Liberation from Self*, chap. 8.
39. Feinberg, *Harm to Self*, 34.
40. Ibid., 33.
41. Ibid.

42. Autonomous choice and action is supported by an antecedent nexus of moral, cognitive, conative, social, and cultural factors that enable the person's life plans to be unequivocally his own. Harry Frankfurt contents that without this support, we are "vacant of identifiable tendencies and constraint, . . . unable to deliberate or to make conscientious decisions." Frankfurt, "Rationality and the Unthinkable," 178.

9

The Relationship between Autonomous and Morally Responsible Agency

Michael McKenna

What is the relationship between the concepts of autonomous and morally responsible agency? For those who acknowledge the legitimacy of each, the assumption has been that the connection is quite tight: Either it is thought that they entail each other or, more conservatively, that autonomous agency is necessary for morally responsible agency. I shall argue that, on one reasonable account of autonomy, neither is necessary for the other. My argument turns upon establishing two theses: First, the epistemic condition for autonomous agency involves *less* than what is required for morally responsible agency. Second, the control condition for autonomous agency involves *more* than what is required for morally responsible agency. If the first thesis is correct, it is possible for a person to satisfy all of the conditions for autonomous agency and yet fail to satisfy the more demanding epistemic condition for morally responsible agency. This would prove that morally responsible agency is not necessary for autonomous agency. If the second thesis is correct, it is possible for a person to satisfy all of the conditions for morally responsible agency and yet fail to satisfy the more demanding control condition for autonomous agency. This would prove that autonomous agency is not necessary for morally responsible agency.

I. TWO CONCEPTS: AUTONOMOUS AGENCY AND MORALLY RESPONSIBLE AGENCY

To begin, let us treat autonomous agency in terms of *self-rule*, and let us assume that it is not a necessary condition of personhood but merely demarcates a special class of persons. Parsed accordingly, it is possible that some persons are nonautonomous. In the absence of any skeptical challenge (regarding, for instance, the threat of causal determinism), let us further assume that an adequate account of autonomy does more than merely capture a metaphysical possibility. Instead, it picks out an attainable condition of actual persons.

Turning to morally responsible agency, let us understand it in terms of accountability for guiding conduct in accord with the demands of morality. Morally responsible agents are persons who can properly be held morally accountable for what they do. Moral demands can justly be placed upon them and moral expectations reasonably had of them. They are the objects of moral praise and blame. They are capable of accounting for their behavior within the sphere of (moral) reason-giving, can appreciate the force of excuses, justifications, mitigating considerations, and the like. On one attractive view, the Strawsonian view, they are the appropriate objects of the morally reactive attitudes, including guilt, resentment, gratitude, and moral indignation and approbation.[1] As with autonomous agency, let us assume that morally responsible agency is not a necessary condition of personhood, but merely demarcates a special class of persons. Similarly parsed, it is possible that some persons are not morally responsible agents. And of course, as with the case of autonomous agency, an adequate account of morally responsible agency should not place the bar too high; setting aside special skeptical considerations (about for instance, the compatibility of free will and determinism), it should show how ordinary functioning humans might attain the status of morally responsible agents.

One striking difference between the concepts of autonomous and morally responsible agency is that, unlike the former, theorizing about the latter can be structured in light of a rich stockpile of intuitive judgments mined from ordinary thought and talk. By contrast, autonomous agency seems almost exclusively a term of art largely unrecognized outside of philosophical discourse. While it is nearly impossible to pick up the Sunday paper and find an article devoted to the autonomy of some agent's conduct, it is by contrast almost impossible to pick up the Sunday paper and *not* be struck by an article devoted to why some agent *is* responsible for something or other.[2] Perhaps there are some pretheoretical, intuitive resources to aid in theorizing about self-ruling agency; but if so, they are certainly far more scarce than those informing accounts of morally responsible agency.[3] In developing my arguments, I will therefore examine the concept of autonomous agency by initially considering cases designed to test our intuitions about morally responsible agency (where our intuitive resources are richer). Leaning upon our judgments about moral responsibility, I'll then apply these same cases to autonomous agency, seeking points of similarity and difference.

Another difference between the two concepts is that, within the discipline of philosophy, there is at least *some* consensus as to what moral responsibility is. By contrast, as Nomy Arpaly observes, there is no univocal sense of autonomy at work in philosophical theorizing.[4] Instead, there are many different senses, and writers often unwittingly shift between them. In deference to Arpaly's observations, I shall settle on one core notion of autonomy. I shall take seriously the expression "self-rule" by asking what is involved in an *agent* guiding her conduct by the light of *rules*, and not just any rules, but rules that are *hers*.[5] I do not, however, mean to place stock in any particular interpretation of what is meant by "rule." In approaching the topic of autonomy, Harry Frankfurt's advice is telling:

> The term "autonomy" derives from two Greek words: one meaning "self," and the other meaning "reason" or "principle" or "law." This fact is sometimes regarded as supporting the Kantian notion that "autonomy of the will is the property the will has of being a law to itself." The relation between autonomy and law cannot be established, however, by consulting a dictionary. Whether being self-governed necessarily involves following general principles or rules of action is a philosophical question, not an etymological one.[6]

Perhaps the content of "rule" is to be unpacked by commitment to a principle, a value, a goal, or, as Frankfurt has suggested, a guiding passion such as love. However it is understood, the concept of autonomous agency as I shall treat it in this chapter requires that the "rules" have *some* content as a guide to effective agency.

II. CONTROL CONDITIONS

It is reasonable to assume that morally responsible agency requires two sorts of conditions: an epistemic and a control condition.[7] Persons who are morally responsible agents have the ability to understand both the moral and nonmoral considerations bearing upon the contexts in which they act; they also have the ability to guide their conduct in light of those considerations. In thinking about these matters, it is important to bear in mind that questions about morally responsible agency differ from questions about an agent's moral responsibility for some bit of conduct. Special circumstances might show why a person is not morally responsible for some bit of conduct (in the sense of being praiseworthy or blameworthy for it) without thereby showing that the person is not a morally responsible agent.[8] Still, thinking about special cases in which a morally responsible agent is not responsible for her action (in the sense of being blameworthy or praiseworthy for it) can point to more general conditions upon morally responsible agency itself. This is how I shall proceed.

Consider the control condition. It is this condition, understood in terms of the freedom of the will, that has been the focus of so much philosophical attention. Let us take a case of compulsion, an uncontroversial case in which a morally responsible agent is not responsible for a specific bit of conduct because she lacks free will with respect to it. So consider Jane, who is a perfectly competent morally responsible agent in many spheres of her life. Unfortunately, Jane experiences a literally irresistible desire for a certain drug when and only when it is made immediately available to her. Imagine that Jane bears no responsibility for her addiction. She acquired it from a regimen of narcotics administered to her while in a coma after a near fatal accident (an accident for which she also bears no responsibility). Through no fault of her own, someone presents Jane with the opportunity to take this drug. Jane experiences a literally irresistible desire, and, though unwilling, she takes it. Presumably, Jane was not morally responsible for taking the drug (in the sense of being blameworthy). Jane's inability to control her conduct explains why she was not morally responsible for taking the drug. This sort of example helps to confirm the need for a more general control condition on morally responsible agency itself.

Can we say something similar for autonomous agency? It seems so. Drawing upon the example above, let us grant that Jane is overall an autonomous agent as well as a morally responsible agent. Now consider the case in terms of autonomy instead of moral responsibility. Was Jane self-ruling in unwillingly taking the drug as a result of an irresistible desire? Certainly not. Jane was not autonomous in taking the drug because she was not in control of her conduct. By parity of reasoning, this suggests that autonomous agency, like morally responsible agency, requires a control condition of some sort. It would be premature to conclude that the sort of control required for autonomous agency is the same sort as that required for morally responsible agency, though it would not be surprising if it turned out that way.

III. EPISTEMIC CONDITIONS

Turning to the epistemic condition, consider the following example: The perfectly competent morally responsible agent Tal arrives at Daphne's house and discovers her unconscious and in immediate need of a drug known as The Good Stuff. Urgently searching through Daphne's medicine cabinet, Tal finds a bottle marked "The Good Stuff." He takes from it the prescribed dose and gives it to Daphne. Unfortunately, Daphne's fumbling pharmacist has accidentally given Daphne the wrong drug, The Bad Stuff, a drug that will kill people with Daphne's condition. Daphne dies. Tal had no reason to be suspicious of Daphne's pharmacist and had very good reason to believe that the bottle in her medicine cabinet marked "The Good Stuff" actually contained The Good Stuff and not The Bad Stuff. Was Tal blameworthy for giving Daphne that drug? It seems not, because he could not have been expected to know that it would kill her. In fact, it looks as if Tal is praiseworthy for his effort, despite the fact that what Tal did killed Daphne. In this case, special epistemic factors alter the sort of evaluation one would normally be inclined to make in the absence of these factors. This sort of example helps to confirm the need for a more general epistemic condition on morally responsible agency itself.

Now consider the case in terms of autonomy instead of moral responsibility. Can we say something similar for autonomous agency? It does not look like it. Grant that Tal is an autonomous agent as well as a morally responsible agent. Suppose that, when he was searching for a drug to aid Daphne, Tal was consciously acting from a principle that he endorsed. For the sake of simplicity, suppose the principle is something like: *Always attempt to help those who are suffering innocently.* Was Tal self-ruling in administering the drug to Daphne? It seems so. However we unpack the notion of "rule" in "self-rule," there is no reason to think that Tal was not ruling himself in acting as he did. The special epistemic factors that *do* alter the appropriate sort of evaluation of Tal's moral responsibility (he is praiseworthy, not blameworthy) do not alter in any manner one's assessment of whether Tal was acting according to his own guiding principle of action (always attempt to help those who are suffering innocently). This suggests that there is some sort of disparity between the epistemic conditions for morally responsible agency and autonomous agency.

But perhaps intuitions differ about cases like that of Tal and Daphne. Consider a simple example of deception from Alfred Mele's *Autonomous Agency*:

> Connie is deliberating about how best to invest her money. A respected investment firm has provided her with detailed information about a wide range of options. Connie has good reason to believe that the information is accurate and

> no reason to be suspicious of the firm. She deliberates on the basis of the relevant values and desires of hers together with the information provided and rationally concludes that a certain investment policy would be best for her at this time. As it happens, however, Connie was systematically deceived by the firm. Their figures were contrived, assembled with the design of leading any rational agent with Connie's interests to decide on an investment policy that would maximize benefit to the firm at the investor's expense.[9]

In investing her money, did Connie act autonomously? Was she ruling herself in acting as she did? Mele thinks not. To drive home his point, Mele imagines an extraordinary case of deception involving a futuristic king, King George. George, though ideally self-controlled, gets all of his information about the state of his kingdom throughout his entire life only through a staff who systematically deceive him. Let us suppose for now that George's staff do not deceive him in ways that affect the values and principles that he endorses; they only manipulate the information pertinent to how he applies his values and principles. His staff arrange things so that, the better George deliberates, the worse off his kingdom becomes by the standards that George himself endorses. George, as Mele describes him, is "heteronomous in a significant sphere of his life."[10] He is "*informationally cut off from ruling autonomously*."[11] Mele holds that the reasons for judging that neither Connie nor King George acts autonomously do not require that Connie or King George are deceived by others or serve others' ends. Both Connie and King George, Mele reasons, would be just as nonautonomous if there were some nonintentional cause of their misinformation. Mele's view is that Connie and King George act nonautonomously because Connie and King George, owing to their epistemic predicament, have no control over the success of their efforts to achieve their ends.[12] But to this extent, the cases of Connie and George are like the case of Tal.

Should we reconsider the case of Tal and, consistent with Mele's intuitions about the cases of Connie and King George, conclude that Tal acted nonautonomously in giving Daphne the drug? If so, our intuitions regarding autonomy would track our intuitions regarding moral responsibility. Just as Tal's epistemic limitations pointed toward a general epistemic condition on morally responsible agency, so would those same limitations point toward a comparable epistemic condition on autonomous agency. But it seems to me that Mele is wrong to conclude that Connie and King George do not act autonomously in investing or ruling as they do. Like Tal, Connie and King George can be understood to be ruling themselves in acting as they do. That is, they can be understood *to act in light of rules that they themselves accept as their own.*[13] What seems to go wrong with all of their efforts is that some epistemic shortcoming results in a misfiring or a deviation in the expected outcome of the actions that they do autonomously perform.[14]

IV. DIFFERENTIATING BETWEEN EPISTEMIC CONDITIONS

So we have a disparity in the case of Tal and Daphne between how we understand Tal's moral responsibility as opposed to how we understand his autonomy. Although it seems that epistemic factors affect our assessment of Tal's moral responsibility for giving Daphne the drug, it does not affect our assessment of Tal's autonomy. Should we therefore conclude that autonomous agency does not require an epistemic condition, but morally responsible agency does? If so, then autonomous agency would be more like freely willed agency than like morally responsible agency. Some theorists have treated the notion of autonomy in just this way. Indeed, some have treated it as tantamount to free will – or as a component of it.

Perhaps careful investigation will reveal that self-ruling agency just is, or is a component of, freely willing agency.[15] If so, it would be correct to conclude that autonomous action does not involve a significant epistemic component because freely willed action does not.[16] A dramatically misinformed person such as King George could act of his own free will. But even if it did turn out that autonomous agency required no significant epistemic condition, it would be entirely unwarranted to draw *that* conclusion simply on the basis of examples like the one involving Tal and Daphne. What we can conclude about that case, as well as cases like those involving Connie and King George, is that *if* there is an epistemic constraint on autonomous agency, it differs from the sort of epistemic constraint pertinent to morally responsible agency.

It seems to me that autonomous agency *does* require some sort of epistemic condition, but the condition is restricted to matters relevant to the rules (values, governing principles, goals, passions, whatever) that serve as the basis for an agent's ruling herself. To be self-ruling, there must be some content to the basis upon which one rules, and it is possible that epistemic factors could in some way pollute the formation, evaluation, or retention of those rules. This would help to explain why the epistemic factors polluting Tal's ability to function effectively as a morally responsible agent did not pollute Tal's autonomy; poor information about what drug was in the bottle has no bearing upon the rules or principles by the light of which Tal might govern his own conduct. To confirm my thesis, it would be useful to find an example in which an autonomous agent acts nonautonomously owing to the relevant sort of epistemic glitch, that is, a glitch that impedes an agent's assessment of the rules according to which she rules herself.[17] Imagine, for instance, that in Mele's case of King George, his advisors provide him with information that distorts his own assessment of the values and principles upon which he acts. I shall not pursue this here, nor shall I attempt to develop an account of the epistemic condition on autonomous agency. I wish only to suggest that it is reasonable to presume that there *is* an epistemic condition on autonomous agency, and the case of Tal and Daphne suggests that it is *not* the same condition as the epistemic condition on morally responsible agency. Furthermore, the case of Tal and Daphne suggests that satisfaction of the epistemic condition on morally responsible agency is not necessary for satisfaction of the epistemic condition on autonomous agency; Tal was not morally responsible for his action (in the sense of being blameworthy), but he did act autonomously.[18]

V. CONTROL CONDITIONS, FRANKFURT EXAMPLES, AND ALTERNATIVE POSSIBILITIES

So far, we have reason to think that there is some sort of disparity between the epistemic conditions on morally responsible and autonomous agency. Let us return to the issue of control. Recall that reflection on a simple case – Jane taking a drug due to an irresistible desire – suggested that morally responsible agency and autonomous agency each require some sort of control condition and that the conditions treat this sort of case similarly. How similar might these conditions be? How closely do the two conditions track each other? Indeed, are they two conditions, or is there only one? If they are distinct, is one necessary for the other?

One controversial issue within the free-will and moral-responsibility debate turns upon whether alternative possibilities are necessary for the sort of freedom or control pertinent to morally responsible agency. Harry Frankfurt has argued that certain sorts of examples confirm that they are not. Consider this classic Frankfurt example:

The morally responsible agent Jones plans to kill Smith. Unbeknownst to Jones, Black very much wants Jones to kill Smith, and though Black would much prefer Jones to kill Smith on his own, Black has arranged things so that he can manipulate Jones into killing Smith should Jones show any indication that he will do other than kill Smith. As it happens, Jones kills Smith on his own. Black never intervenes. Jones exercises his morally responsible agency just as he would have had Black's presence been subtracted from the scenario.

This sort of example has been used to elicit the judgment that Jones acted of his own free will and was morally responsible (in the sense of being blameworthy) for having killed Smith, despite the fact that, due to Black's presence, Jones could not have done otherwise.[19]

Although there is a great deal of controversy as to whether Frankfurt's argument is sound, the following seems by contrast relatively uncontroversial: If one does find Frankfurt's argument compelling as applied to moral responsibility, one should find the argument equally compelling as applied to autonomy. If one is prepared to say that when Jones acted on his own, Black's presence eliminated all Jones's alternatives and yet Jones was morally responsible for killing Smith (in the sense of being blameworthy), then one should be equally prepared to say the same as regards Jones's acting autonomously.[20]

Elsewhere, I have argued that a modified sort of Frankfurt example does show that freedom involving alternative possibilities is not necessary for moral responsibility.[21] I believe that the only serious threat to Frankfurt's argument is the one posed by Carl Ginet, Robert Kane, and David Widerker,[22] who each independently challenged Frankfurt by asking how Black could reliably rule out all alternative possibilities prior to the execution of Jones's freely willed action. This seems possible only if it is granted that Jones was causally determined to so act. If Jones was determined, then Frankfurt's argument begs the question against the incompatibilist; if he was not, then any evidence Black would have to predict Jones's future course of action would be consistent with his acting otherwise up until the moment at which he does exercise his free will.

I believe that Ginet, Kane, and Widerker can be answered by constructing examples in which many alternative courses of action remain open to an agent, but in which all of these alternatives are insignificant as regards the deliberative and moral context in which the agent acts. The examples need only arrange things so that deliberatively significant alternatives are closed down and only insignificant ones are left open. So, for instance, imagine that nothing impedes the manner in which Jones does decide to shoot Smith and that Jones does shoot Smith on his own, just as Frankfurt would have it. But suppose that circumstances are arranged so that Jones cannot make the following decision: "I will not shoot Smith."[23] All the same, perhaps it is open to Jones not to decide to shoot Smith, but suppose that this is only open to him in scenarios that he himself would regard as deliberatively insignificant, options he would dismiss as irrelevant to his own assessment of what he should or should not do. In such cases, he comes to no decision about whether to shoot Smith, but instead he simply puts his gun down and begins to chew on his fist, or make "nyuck nyuck" noises like one of the Three Stooges, or dance around while patting the top of his head, or recite nursery rhymes, or several of these things at once. Or suppose he simply puts down his gun and heads home to roast a chicken. In this sort of modified Frankfurt example, there are many alternatives open to the agent – or at least nothing doing the work of an intervener like Black is closing these options off to Jones.

Ginet, Kane, and Widerker cannot object that the ensuring conditions within the above example presuppose that the agent is determined. Still, all of Jones's deliberatively and morally significant alternatives are closed off. I have argued that this sort of example is sufficient to unseat the demand for alternative possibilities as a condition of moral responsibility. To argue otherwise would be to argue that part of what grounds our judgment that Jones is responsible for shooting Smith is the existence of a set of deliberatively *insignificant* alternatives. And these alternatives, I have argued, are not sufficiently robust to aid in explaining why it is that we judge that Jones is responsible for shooting Smith when he does so on his own.

VI. CONTROL CONDITIONS, COMPATIBILISM, AND THE THREAT OF GLOBAL MANIPULATION

Let us grant, in light of Frankfurt's argument, that the control conditions both for morally responsible and for autonomous agency do not require alternative possibilities.[24] Following John Martin Fischer, call the sort of control that an agent does possess in a Frankfurt example "guidance control," which is in contrast to what Fischer calls "regulative control," the latter involving alternative possibilities. Call those theorists convinced by Frankfurt's argument "source theorists." Source theorists maintain that guidance control is the only sort required for morally responsible agency (and for autonomous agency) because this sort of control is not concerned with alternative possibilities, but instead with the source of an agent's conduct. How is guidance control to be analyzed by source theorists, as regards both moral responsibility and autonomy? Will continued inquiry reveal that there just is no place where the conditions for responsible and autonomous agency peel apart?

Various theories of guidance control have been developed by source theorists. I shall not argue on behalf of any one of them here.[25] What unifies them is an effort to reveal a properly functioning sort of causal integration amongst elements in the (moral) psychology of competent agency. When an agent's actions arise from the favored sort of causally integrated structure, then an agent exercises control over them. A proper source theorist account of guidance control would organize our intuitions regarding cases like the above case of Jane's taking a drug due to an irresistible desire. The account would show how it is that Jane was not in control of her conduct and hence not morally responsible (in the sense of being blameworthy) with respect to it.

Focusing first on morally responsible agency, suppose that one of the theories now circulating, or a close hybrid of it, nails down what guidance control comes to. Let us just call that theory, "The Right One." One controversy among source theorists concerns whether The Right One requires that there be an indeterministic break somewhere in the causal etiology of a freely willed action. *Source compatibilists* deny that there must be. They hold that, independent of any requirement of indeterminism, The Right One is sufficient to capture the freedom-relevant condition for morally responsible agency. *Source incompatibilists*, on the other hand, are perfectly happy to entertain a source compatibilist account, but they will treat that version as necessary but not sufficient. According to the source incompatibilists, for The Right One to be the right one, at least one necessary condition must be appended to the compatibilist's account: The relevant process must arise from (or temporally coincide with) a suitably structured event indeterministic causal process.

Source incompatibilists have a number of argumentative strategies with which to press their case against the source compatibilist's account of The Right One.[26] One of these strategies appeals to manipulation cases, those in which an agent is manipulated by a demon or a neurologist to achieve that relevant compatibilist-friendly causally integrated psychological structure.[27] When such an agent then acts from that structure, our intuitive judgment is supposed to be that she does not act freely and is not morally responsible for so acting. Then the incompatibilist will argue that a deterministic history is in no relevant manner any different from such manipulation; it just takes longer. There is no crafty demon or neurologist pulling the strings; instead, the mere unfolding of nature is pulling them. All the same, if one sort of "manipulating" undermines control, so does the other.[28]

Some source compatibilists are committed to the view that moral responsibility, and hence the control condition for it, are current time slice notions. According to these *current time slice source compatibilists,* the history giving rise to the current state of a morally responsible agent is irrelevant to her status as such an agent – except insofar as that history might help to reveal a current defect in her agential capacities. If an agent's history does reveal such a defect, that would *only be* by way of showing that she does not currently satisfy the relevant psychic structure as required by The Right One.[29] Given this, it seems that the current time slice source compatibilists must accept that certain sorts of manipulation cases involve agents who indeed do act freely and are morally responsible for what they do. Acknowledging this, Harry Frankfurt writes:

> What we need most essentially to look at is, rather, certain aspects of the psychic structure that is coincident with the person's behavior. . . .
>
> A manipulator may succeed, through his interventions, in providing a person not merely with particular feelings and thoughts but with a new character. That person is then morally responsible for the choices and the conduct to which having this character leads. We are inevitably fashioned and sustained, after all, by circumstances over which we have no control. The causes to which we are subject may also change us radically, without thereby bringing it about that we are not morally responsible agents. It is irrelevant whether those causes are operating by virtue of the natural forces that shape our environment or whether they operate through the deliberate manipulative designs of other human agents.[30]

If Frankfurt is correct, then the current time slice source compatibilist is saddled with a view that appears to conflict with intuition, because many would hold that a fully manipulated person, fabricated at an instant and determined to act as she does, is not morally responsible for what she does at a next moment in time.

Other source compatibilists have attempted to evade the problem of manipulation cases by developing a historical condition that is to be appended to the relevant current time slice features figuring in an account of The Right One. On a historical account, unless the relevant historical conditions are met, an agent might satisfy all of the compatibilist-friendly current time slice conditions and yet fail to be free or morally responsible in acting as she does. These *historical source compatibilists* have attempted to show both that their historical constraints are not satisfied in manipulation cases and that they can be satisfied even if determinism is true.[31]

I wish to defend source compatibilism, both for morally responsible and for autonomous agency, but I am skeptical that any source compatibilist account, historical or current time slice, will be fully immune to some sort of manipulation case. My reason is a purely formal one connected to the thesis of compatibilism. Compatibilism is committed to the thesis that morally responsible agents, or instead autonomous agents, can emerge from causal sources external to them. Make the conditions for such agents as fancy and as historical as one wishes, isn't it possible that instead of imagining that they arise over time in the typical fashion – the unfolding of event-deterministic causes due to the chugging along of nature – some fancy cosmic demon or crafty neurologist fabricates those causal inputs over a similar duration of time?[32] Short of some ad hoc and question-begging condition appended to any compatibilist's historical condition, how could there not be some deviant causal routes to satisfying the relevant conditions?

I believe the compatibilist must simply bite the bullet here. The compatibilist's best strategy, it seems to me, is not to show how a suitably determined agent differs so very much from a globally manipulated agent. It is rather to show how similar they are. The compatibilist needs to make clear that once the manipulation is so qualified that all an agent's current time slice compatibilist-friendly structures are properly installed through a process of manipulation, then the role of the manipulator begins to shrink into the background; we are simply left with a normal person who happened to be brought into existence in a very peculiar manner.[33]

Consider Derk Pereboom's use of global manipulation cases in his defense of incompatibilism.[34] Pereboom wishes to start with manipulation cases, fix upon the hidden causes that seem to corrupt any appearance of responsibility, and then show how such cases are like standard cases of naturally occurring determination. Once the unseen causes of a naturally determined agent are revealed, Pereboom argues, then our reaction to the agent should be like our reaction to the discovery that a seemingly normally functioning agent has been globally manipulated. The compatibilist should meet Pereboom's challenge with two moves. First, she should work in the other direction, *from* a (possible) naturally determined agent *to* a globally manipulated one. Second, she should fix, not upon hidden causes, but upon the sorts of agential properties that typically serve as a basis for ascribing responsibility. Once it is established that actions issuing from a (possibly) naturally determined agent invite certain sorts of evaluations in terms of responsibility, one can then hold that actions issuing from an appropriately manipulated agent should be evaluated no differently. The nature of the hidden causes, it can thereby be argued, are not relevant to the sort of psychic structure on the basis of which an agent's responsibility is assessed.[35]

VII. HISTORICAL OR CURRENT TIME SLICE CONTROL CONDITIONS?

I have argued that historical source compatibilism fares no better against manipulation cases than does current time slice source compatibilism. If so, both sorts of compatibilists have to accept the counterintuitive consequence that a manipulated agent could satisfy their favored accounts of The Right One and, hence, be morally responsible for her conduct or autonomous with respect to it. On my proposal, what a compatibilist of any stripe ought to do is argue that a manipulated agent, if manipulated in the appropriate sort of way, simply is a morally responsible (or autonomous) agent, fully accountable for her conduct (or self-ruling over it), just like any other competent agent. Therefore, in responding to the challenge posed by manipulation cases, source compatibilists will find no *theoretical* motive for characterizing control as a historical and not as a current time slice notion.

Still, how *ought* the pertinent sort of control be characterized? In keeping with the passage from Frankfurt quoted above, I believe that morally responsible agency *is* a current time slice notion. Although I cannot fully defend this position here, my argument for a current time slice view has to do with the purpose of our moral-responsibility practices as highlighted in P. F. Strawson's work. I take it that our practices center around the following concern, one that is basic to theorizing about all of these issues: When a (putatively) morally responsible agent acts, *what is the quality of her will*?[36] What does it indicate about her and her regard for the moral expectations (the obligations and other demands) placed upon her within the moral community? If the loci of pretheoretical concern is fundamentally about the moral quality of a person's will when she acts, then our fundamental theoretical focus ought to be on her nature at the time of her conduct.

Setting aside global manipulation cases, there are at least three different sorts of arguments one might construct for the thesis that morally responsible agency and the control condition for it *are* historical notions. One is that certain standard and uncontroversial judgments about an agent's responsibility *do* rely upon historical considerations. For instance, if a morally responsible agent gets very drunk of her own free will and later, having lost control, kills someone with her car, we are prepared to hold her responsible for the killing even though, at the time she acted, she had no control over her conduct.[37] But a current time slice theorist can handle such cases by endorsing an innocuous and uncontroversial historical tracing principle. All that is needed is one that permits tracing back to some point at which an agent does exercise her control in acting. This, however, does not give us reason to think that the exercising of those very agential capacities constitutive of control require *further* historical constraints.

Another sort of argument for historicism about moral responsibility turns upon the effect that histories of extremely unfortunate formative circumstances have upon our judgments of responsibility. Consider a case involving a person with such a history. Imagine that later in life the person performs horrendous, evil actions. Further, grant that the person's formative circumstances played a relevant causal role in the evil character traits that gave rise to her terrible actions. Even if all of the current time slice compatibilist-friendly causal structures might have been in place when she performed the evil acts, doesn't her extremely unfortunate history give us reason to alter our judgment regarding her responsibility?[38] These cases can be divided into two categories. First, there are those cases in which the agents' histories give us very good reason to think that in fact, though the glitch might be subtle and therefore hard to detect, these persons do suffer some current impairment in their ability to act. Hence, they do not satisfy the requisite current time slice conditions as specified by The Right One. The second group of cases can be handled by arguing that these persons' unfortunate histories do not give us a reason to think that they are not morally responsible in any way for their conduct. Rather, their unfortunate histories elicit from us distinct responses (independently of those associated with our blaming them), on the basis of which we might feel that other sorts of empathetic responses are *also* appropriate in dealing with them. This might be so even if these two sets of judgments are psychologically hard for us to sustain.[39]

There are also less fantastical "local" manipulation cases, such as when an agent is hypnotized or brainwashed and then acts in a manner that appears to satisfy the relevant current time slice compatibilist-friendly structure. In such a case, the hypnotizing or brainwashing artificially induces some desire, belief, intention, second-order desire, etc. How might the current time slice theorist handle these? Either the manipulation short-circuits an agent's own compatibilist-friendly psychological structure by making the relevant desires (or whatever) wholly irresistible, or the manipulation merely introduces into the agent's mental economy a resistible consideration that it is up to the agent to assess and act upon if she judges it best to do so.[40] If it is the latter sort of case, then the manipulation does no more through some rather bizarre causal pathway than what is done to a person in the course of any day in which unexpected enticements present themselves as reasons to pursue unexpected courses of action.[41] (Consider mundane cases, such as a chance invitation for an act of infidelity or an unexpected opportunity to sneak a couple slices of baloney into the running shoes of one's enemy.)

Morally responsible agency and the control condition for it are current time slice notions. My reason for favoring a current time slice analysis of these notions is linked to the fundamental purpose of our moral responsibility practices, which focuses primarily upon the way a (competent) person's will is when she acts, not how it came to be that way. As for the arguments on behalf of a historical view, I have argued that three fashionable arguments for such a view are unconvincing.

VIII. DIFFERENTIATING CONTROL CONDITIONS

Finally, we are nearing a point at which the control condition for morally responsible agency and the control condition for autonomous agency peel apart. Although, on the view I defend, the control condition for morally responsible agency does not require a historical component, I shall argue that the control condition for autonomous agency does. Of course, there are fashionable current time slice accounts of autonomy, such as Frankfurt's. He maintains that a person acts autonomously when the volitional source of her action derives from essential features of her own will, features with which she identifies most deeply.[42] Clearly, a person could come to have this sort of volitional structure through any sort of historical process. But current time slice accounts of autonomy such as Frankfurt's do not fully capture the few ordinary, pretheoretical ideas we do seem to have about autonomy when we think about it in terms of self-rule. Granted, in keeping with a current time slice view of autonomy, we do recognize characters whom we think of as stalwart individuals, people prepared to remain committed to their convictions, paths, passions, or values, regardless of the external pressures put on them. Think of a character like Zorba the Greek. *He* assesses what is right or wrong for himself. Such a person, we sometimes say, is a rock. Or, instead, we say that he has fiber; he settles for himself how to proceed. These character traits do indeed fix only on current time slice characteristics of a person. But there are also expressions such as "picking oneself up by one's bootstraps" or being a "self-made" person, and these are distinctly historical notions. In particular, when what a person "made" of herself is at least in part based upon her own principles and values, our attention is rightly drawn to the history of her life. Perhaps she came to endorse through years of reflection values or principles accepted within her moral community. Maybe she "discovered" them through philosophical inquiry, or maybe, like an artisan, she shaped for herself those values and principles. When we think about self-ruling persons in this way, we are interested to learn if a putatively autonomous person simply passively, maybe unreflectively, accepted the values and principles that circumstances had offered to her.[43] Or did she instead critically assess those values and principles, maybe even forge them for herself?

I propose the following necessary historical condition for autonomous agency:

> *HA*: A person acts with guidance control of the sort required for autonomous agency only if she acts on the basis of values or principles that she herself has endorsed through a process of critical evaluation.

While fairly demanding as a condition of autonomous agency, HA is still relatively thin. For instance, what counts as "a process of critical evaluation"? Furthermore, is there any restriction to the content of the values or principles (or passions) that might inform an agent? Could "Always trust men in white coats" count as such a principle? These and other such questions suggest that further refinement of HA would be required to add needed substance to it. Still, as it stands, HA is certainly not a mild constraint on autonomous agency. For instance, HA appears to be stronger than the sort of negative historical condition Alfred Mele entertains. According to Mele, so long as an agent acts from values and principles that did *not* bypass at some earlier time her ability to critically evaluate them, she acts autonomously (granting that all other conditions for autonomy are in place).[44] This might be so even if those values or principles are for that agent practically unsheddable at the time at which she acts.[45] It is consistent with Mele's view that a person be handed, maybe by her upbringing, a set of values, and though she never did critically assess them, she would be autonomous when later she acted on them. Why? Because she *could have* critically evaluated them; it is just that she did not. On the view I advance here, an autonomous person *must* take an active role in the formation of the values and principles that serve to shape her later self.[46] If not, she is, in a sense, a passive bystander to the person she subsequently becomes.[47] To emphasize the point: This strongly historical account of source control for autonomous agency requires not merely that an autonomous agent possess the capacities for critically evaluating her values and principles. *It requires that she actually have exercised them.*[48]

Hence, a person might have the *potential* to be an autonomous agent, and yet she might never have exercised her critical capacities of evaluation in such a way as to make any of the values and principles upon which she acts her own.[49]

One perfectly fair objection to this account of autonomous agency is that the historical condition HA sets an unreasonably high bar. If, instead, autonomous agency is understood as *both* a threshold and a scalar notion admitting of degrees, then perhaps what HA captures is a fairly advanced level of autonomous agency. Persons who merely passively and uncritically accepted their societies' values and principles might count as autonomous agents, having surpassed the relevant threshold, even though they would fail to satisfy HA. Those able to satisfy the condition specified in HA would simply be "more" autonomous; they would be persons who made more of their capacity for self-ruling agency. It might be that it is better to think of autonomous agency as a scaler notion whose threshold is much less demanding than HA. But the weaker the notion becomes – the closer the threshold conditions come to a condition requiring merely the *capacity* to endorse values or principles – the more autonomous agency begins to look like morally responsible agency. As it converges on the contours of morally responsible agency, the theoretical motive we have to acknowledge it as a distinct sort of concept diminishes.[50] Hence, I propose that if we do wish to unpack the concept of autonomous agency by taking seriously the expression "self-rule," we shoot for a fairly robust notion that takes seriously the notion of a rule that is one's own.

IX. CONCLUSION: THE INDEPENDENCE OF MORALLY RESPONSIBLE AND AUTONOMOUS AGENCY

Let us collect our results. Morally responsible agency clearly requires an epistemic condition. This was illustrated in the case of Tal and Daphne. But the case of Tal and Daphne did not indicate that autonomous agency required a *similar sort* of epistemic condition. Under the assumption that autonomous agency does require *some sort* of epistemic constraint, we concluded that satisfaction of the epistemic condition for morally responsible agency is not necessary for satisfaction of the epistemic condition for autonomous agency. This suggests that autonomous agency does not require morally responsible agency. An agent could satisfy all of the conditions for autonomous agency, and she could also satisfy all of the conditions for morally responsible agency but one, the very one not required for autonomous agency. She might thereby lack the relevant epistemic capacity distinctive of morally responsible but not of autonomous agency.

These results, that an agent might be an autonomous but yet not a morally responsible agent, accord with Alfred Mele's treatment of autonomous agency. Mele writes:

> In his *Nicomachean Ethics,* Aristotle mentions hypothetical gods for whom the moral virtues are otiose (bk. 10.7). Perhaps we can imagine, in a similar vein, a universe whose only inhabitants are self-sufficient, divine beings who devote their lives to various solitary intellectual activities as they judge best, and want nothing from one another. Having no need or desire whose satisfaction requires interactions with other beings, they act in total isolation from one another. Such gods may be self-ruled or self-governed individuals. Even so, they may be utterly *amoral,* on some conceptions of morality.[51]

With Mele's thought experiment, the gods simply want nothing from others. But imagine just the same beings revised as follows: If they were to want anything from others and were "moral conflicts" to arise, they would have no ability to understand what morality required of them. Still, in all other aspects of their lives, in their many solitary pursuits, they might be self-ruling agents. In a similar vein, a sociopath might be incapable of moral understanding altogether, including an understanding of the morality of the values and principles that she embraces, and yet she might still remain an autonomous person to the extent that she does guide her life and act by a set of amoral values and principles that she herself embraces.[52] Perhaps she embraces a set of deeply held aesthetic or intellectual values but still is incapable of moral understanding. She would be, it seems, an autonomous agent, albeit not a morally responsible one.

Given the above considerations, it looks as if morally responsible agency is not necessary for autonomous agency. But what of the opposite? Is autonomous agency necessary for morally responsible agency? Looking to the control conditions for both autonomous and morally responsible agency and drawing upon Frankfurt examples, I argued that both require only guidance control, a sort of control that does not involve alternative possibilities. Embracing a source compatibilist approach to both, I then asked whether either was a distinctively historical notion. Incompatibilist challenges involving manipulation cases loomed large, and it appeared as if adopting a historicist source compatibilist account of guidance control would be an advantage in defending compatibilism. But in the end, I argued, a historical approach fares no better than a current time slice approach. Either, I argued, had to accept and explain away the unpalatable prospect that a manipulated agent could satisfy a compatibilist account of The Right One (a view that nails down what guidance control actually comes to).

Setting aside the fact that the manipulation cases did not ultimately provide compatibilists with a theoretical motive for endorsing a historical account of guidance control, I argued that, as a condition for morally responsible agency, guidance control is better construed as a current time slice notion. My argument turned upon what seems central to our moral-responsibility practices – the current moral quality of an agent's will when she does act. By contrast, on the view of autonomy I sketched, guidance control is to be understood as a historical notion. This is because, if acting autonomously requires acting from values or principles that an agent has come to embrace and accept as her own through a process of critical evaluation, then autonomous agency requires that an agent actually go through this process and shape for herself the central values and principles that will inform her conduct in life. This requires a certain kind of history, a history in which an agent takes quite an active role in the person she becomes.

Because autonomous agency includes historical requirements that morally responsible agency does not, it is possible that some morally responsible agents might fail to satisfy these fairly demanding historical conditions.[53] A morally responsible agent might never have come to evaluate and reflect upon the values and principles that inform her manner of exercising control over her conduct and thus her life. And on the view I have sketched, she would be a nonautonomous agent, albeit a morally responsible one. Although it might nevertheless be true that she would have the *capacity* to be an autonomous agent, having never taken the step to shape for herself the values and principles according to which she might live, her status as an autonomous agent would remain a mere possibility.

In conclusion, morally responsible agency is not required for autonomous agency, nor, as I have cast it, is autonomous agency required for morally responsible agency.[54] The relationship between them is entirely contingent; while the circumstances giving rise to each might make it likely that a person winding up as one would also wind up as the other, she needn't. Some persons might well be autonomous agents and not morally responsible; others might be morally responsible agents but not autonomous.[55] Naturally, it would seem to be a mark of a flourishing person that she is both. Perhaps it is for this reason that many have thought the connection between them is much tighter than I have argued that it is.

X. APPENDIX

Can we construct a case in which epistemic factors pollute an autonomous agent's ability to act autonomously? Consider the case of the philosophy professor Larry the Utilitarian Liar. Larry has reflected deeply for years on the role of truth telling and lying in one's personal life. After great philosophical effort, having studied Kant on lying, having struggled through Mill's version of utilitarianism, looking at all the new-fangled utilitarian moves, Larry settles on the reasoning of the bullet-biting straight-act utilitarian J. J. C. Smart. Larry is firmly convinced that he should lie any and every time doing so will maximize the most good. In fact, realizing that he is so good at lying, Larry has structured a good chunk of his academic life around optimizing his opportunities to lie for the benefit of the happiness he might bring to other academics and administrators. Larry attends all sorts of academic conferences where people talk about all kinds of pointless stuff (stuff that will never harm anyone), like "deconstruction" and "collapsing a duality in which the *is* and the *is not* disappear." Seeking to help these poor lost souls feel good about their work, Larry feigns great interest and gushes with enthusiasm for the "great insight" found in these discussions.

One day, just after convincingly telling the dean how insightful a recent committee meeting was, Larry notices a slight disfigurement. His nose has started to swell. He immediately goes to his doctor, Dr. Geppetto. Dr. Geppetto realizes that Larry merely has a slight inflammatory infection that will clear up in a few days, maybe even in a few hours; but being a bit of a prankster and aware of Larry's lying ways, Dr. Geppetto tells Larry in a very serious tone, "Larry, I am afraid that you have a very rare condition, a condition affecting the synapses connecting the moral decision-making part of your brain and your olfactory center. Larry, you have Pinocchio-itis. Every time you lie, your nose will grow."

Larry is extremely dubious, and he resolves that upon leaving Dr. Geppetto's office he will immediately find a new doctor. But still committed to his lying ways and concerned to make sure he makes Dr. Geppetto feel very good about himself, Larry replies, "Well, doctor, thank you for that insightful diagnosis. As peculiar as it sounds, I trust that you have zeroed in on my problem. I intend to stop all lying immediately." Just then, as chance would have it, Larry's nose grows another size larger. Though slightly unnerved, Larry dismisses this as a mere coincidence. But then, as he leaves the doctor's office, Larry remarks to the receptionist, speaking untruthfully, "I like what you have done with your hair." Again, as chance would have it, Larry's nose grows another size larger. Within a few hours, Larry has lied several more times; and each time, by sheer coincidence, Larry's nose grows even larger.

Larry becomes terrified. Is this utilitarian policy of lying causing him personal disfigurement? If so, is it worth it? He becomes paranoid. Is this some sort of revenge brought upon him by a Kantian demon? Larry comes to believe that his deeply held principle of lying when it will optimize the most good is wrong, and he resolves not only not to lie, but to be as truthful as he can be. In fact, he resolves that he really should always tell people what he *really* thinks. He resolves that he will guide his conduct by the light of this principle. Heading back to campus, led by his now enormous schnozzle, Larry passes the dean, who asks Larry if he is looking forward to tomorrow's committee meeting. Larry replies, "No more than I am my next root canal." As chance would have it, Larry's inflammatory condition begins to clear up, and just then his nose shrinks one size. Several more such coincidences transpire, and Larry becomes convinced that telling people what he really thinks will keep him from becoming disfigured. By the day's end, Larry's nose is almost back to normal, even though he has also offended most every co-worker and friend with whom he has spoken.

The combination of Dr. Geppetto's trickery and the chance swelling and shrinking of Larry's nose has led Larry to adopt for himself a principle of conduct that is misinformed. Does Larry act autonomously in speaking honestly to the dean and others? It seems not. The epistemic basis for Larry's embracing a principle of extreme honesty is polluted, and it appears to undermine the judgment that, in speaking honestly, Larry is self-ruling. The rules according to which Larry rules himself would not be rules Larry himself would embrace were it not for Larry's misinformation. This suggests that autonomous agency requires some epistemic condition.

Notes

I would like to thank Bernie Berofsky, Craig Duncan, Christopher Fitzmartin, Carl Ginet, Ish Haji, Eric Hiddleston, Sean McKeever, Al Mele, Hans Muller, Derk Pereboom, John Phillips, Steve Schwartz, David Silver, James Stacey Taylor, and Manuel Vargas for their generous advice and helpful comments on this chapter. I presented a version at the 2003 Binghamton-Cornell-Syracuse Philosophy Triangle conference. I am especially grateful to my commentator, Seth Shabo, who offered many keen insights. Thanks are also due to members of the audience, especially Harold Hodes, Terrence Irwin, Sydney Shoemaker, and Tamar Szabo Gendler. I would also like to thank Ithaca College; the final draft of this chapter was written with funding from an Ithaca College 2003 Faculty Summer Research Grant.

Near the completion of this chapter, just before it went to the publisher, I happened to read Nomy Arpaly's imaginative *Unprincipled Virtue* (New York: Oxford University Press, 2003). I was delighted to find that, at various points, we draw similar conclusions, though not parallel ones. Although I did work back through my penultimate draft so as to credit her at various points, I should say that, had I read her work before I wrote this chapter, I might have structured it differently. Readers interested in the terrain I cover should see Arpaly's outstanding book.

1. See P. F. Strawson, "Freedom and Resentment," in Strawson, *Freedom and Resentment and Other Essays* (New York: Harper & Row 1974): 1–25. For a development of the Strawsonian account of moral responsibility, see John Martin Fischer and Mark Ravizza, "Introduction," in Fischer and Ravizza, eds., *Perspectives on Moral Responsibility* (Ithaca, NY: Cornell University Press, 1993): 1–41; and their *Responsibility and Control: An Essay on Moral Responsibility* (Cambridge: Cambridge University Press, 1998): 5–8; R. Jay Wallace, *Responsibility and the Moral Sentiments* (Cambridge, MA: Harvard University Press, 1994); and Gary Watson, "Responsibility and the Limits of Evil: Variations on a Strawsonian Theme," in Ferdinand Schoeman, ed., *Responsibility, Character, and the Emotions: New Essays in Moral Psychology* (Cambridge: Cambridge University Press, 1987): 256–286.
2. Also, with the notion of criminal sanity, the legal system draws a parallel distinction between morally responsible agents and those persons who are not. Furthermore, our literary history is filled with stories about morally responsible agents, sometimes the sad lives of those who are not, and the special circumstances some responsible agents get into that exonerate them, excuse them, mitigate the blame that might be heaped upon them, magnify the praise they heroically merit, etc. Think of the stories of Agamemnon, Oedipus, the Elephant Man, Uncle Tom, Lenny from *Of Mice and Men,* Boo Radley in *To Kill a Mockingbird,* Blanche from *A Streetcar Named Desire,* and countless others.
3. The paucity of intuitive resources certainly warrants some skepticism about the notion. If it is entirely a fabrication of philosophical theorizing, then it might not be worth the philosophical attention it has received. (Nomy Arpaly makes similar remarks in *Unprincipled Virtue,* 117, 129–130.) I shall argue, however, that there are *some* intuitive resources that give content to this term of art and that it does help to pick out a distinctive sort of agency.
4. Arpaly, *Unprincipled Virtue,* 117–148.
5. The notion of autonomy that I shall work with does not fit naturally into any of the eight different notions of autonomy that Arpaly distinguishes. It is closest to what she calls "agent autonomy," but, unlike mine, her characterization of agent autonomy does not place emphasis on the notion of *rule* and is treated as synonymous with the sort of self-control distinctive of persons (*Unprincipled Virtue,* 118).
6. Harry Frankfurt, "Autonomy, Necessity, and Love," in Frankfurt, ed., *Necessity, Volition, and Love* (Cambridge: Cambridge University Press, 1999): 131

7. These conditions find their origins in Aristotle's conditions on the voluntary in Terrence Irwin, trans., *Nicomachean Ethics* (Indianapolis: Hackett, 1985): 1109b30–1111b5. Fischer and Ravizza develop these Aristotelian conditions as applied to moral responsibility in *Responsibility and Control*, 12–14.
8. In speaking of cases in which an agent is not morally responsible for some specific course of action, I'll speak only of cases involving disputed blameworthiness. This is purely for ease of expression, which involves the risk of misleading. Consider a judgment that a bank teller is not morally responsible for handing over money at gunpoint. While not blameworthy for handing over the money (due to the coercive threat), she might actually have been praiseworthy for acting as she did.
9. Alfred Mele, *Autonomous Agents* (New York: Oxford University Press, 1995): 179–180.
10. Ibid., 180.
11. Ibid., 181.
12. Ibid.
13. One might object here that the cases of Connie and King George differ from the case of Tal. In the case of Tal, unlike the cases of Connie and King George, no other being (no other heter) is controlling him. Hence, we can conclude that Tal acts autonomously even though Connie and King George do not. Of course, if this were so, the case of Tal would still serve to help show that the epistemic conditions for autonomous agency differ from those required for morally responsible agency. But parsing the cases this way would be a mistake. What is happening here, I think, is that there are two different notions of autonomy at work, one pertinent to normative questions regarding the moral value of a person's conduct, another pertinent to an account of a certain sort of effective agency. (Naturally, there could be some overlap, though the notions are distinct.) What leads one to think that Connie and King George do not act autonomously is that they are the victims of a sort of manipulation in the service of others, and this conflicts with important normative principles. Hence, it *is* natural to think that their autonomy is in some way impugned. If, however, we are interested in action-theoretic questions about whether certain sorts of persons have the capacity to guide their own conduct in light of rules that they themselves endorse, it is hard to see how the sorts of epistemic pollutants presented to Connie and King George could foul up their having acted in such a manner. (For a similar point, see Arpaly, *Unprincipled Virtue*, 120–121.) What was fouled up was the expected results of their so acting. It is the latter notion of autonomous agency that I am interested in, not the former.
14. Mele's intuitions regarding Connie and King George appear to turn upon thinking about autonomous agency in terms of an agent's effectiveness to achieve her ends, ends that themselves involve considerations external to the state of the agent. When something fouls up a clean path between an agent and the agent's ability to shape the world, then the agent's autonomy is placed in jeopardy. Mele writes:

    [A] sufficient condition of S's being informationally cut off from autonomous action in a domain in which S has intrinsic pro-attitudes is that S has no control over *the success of his efforts to achieve his ends in the domain*, owing to his informational condition (Mele, *Autonomous Agents*, 181; my emphasis).

On the view I am suggesting, autonomous agency is a less external property of persons. Its scope comes to an end at the moment in which an agent performs simple mental actions, such as deciding or choosing. The *effectiveness* of a person's autonomous agency (to shape the external world properly) can be threatened without it *thereby* threatening autonomous agency itself. (For one possible explanation of the difference between Mele's notion of autonomy and mine, at least with respect to the cases of Connie and King George, see note 13.)

15. For a discussion of autonomy that treats it as tantamount to free will, see Thomas Hurka's "Why Value Autonomy?" *Social Theory and Practice* 13 (1987): 361–382. See also George Sher's discussion of this view in *Beyond Neutrality* (New York: Cambridge University Press, 1997): 45–48. For a discussion of free will that treats autonomy as a constituent of free will, see Gary Watson's "Free Action and Free Will," 145.
16. I say "a significant epistemic component" because it might be required for controlled or freely willed agency that an agent know or have good reason to believe that she is an agent. But this sort of thin epistemic condition is not the sort at issue in discussions of autonomy and moral responsibility.
17. For an attempt, see the Appendix in this chapter.
18. The inference here is not the fallacious one that Tal is not a morally responsible agent because Tal is not blameworthy for some bit of conduct. Rather, it is based upon the methodology suggested in the first paragraph of Section 2. A case like the one involving Tal is *suggestive* of a general condition of morally responsible agency. A specific epistemic glitch affected the nature of Tal's responsibility for some bit of conduct, and this *suggests* that a more general epistemic limitation on agency would undermine a person's status as a morally responsible agent.
19. Harry Frankfurt, "Alternate Possibilities and Moral Responsibility," *Journal of Philosophy* 66 (1969): 829–839.
20. If, however, one remains *unconvinced* by Frankfurt's arguments and *does* defend alternative possibilities as a condition of moral responsibility, it is not clear that she should also embrace an alternative-possibilities condition on autonomous agency. Might one not govern herself even if she has no alternatives to what she actually does? Joseph Raz thinks not; he maintains that alternatives are required for autonomy – Joseph Raz, *The Morality of Freedom* (Oxford: Clarendon Press, 1986): 375. But Gary Watson, in discussing the free-will problem, identifies issues about the actual source of one's conduct – self-determination – with autonomy and maintains that it is only one of two necessary constituents of free will, the other having to do with alternative-possibilities freedom (Watson, "Free Action and Free Will," 145). I will not pursue these possibilities here because I shall consider these issues under the assumption that Frankfurt's argument succeeds as applied to both morally responsible and autonomous agency.
21. Michael McKenna, "Robustness, Control, and the Demand for Morally Significant Alternatives," in David Widerker and Michael McKenna, eds., *Moral*

Responsibility and Alternative Possibilities (Aldershot, England: Ashgate Press, 2002): 201–218.

22. Carl Ginet, "In Defense of the Principle of Alternative Possibilities: Why I Don't Find Frankfurt's Argument Convincing," *Philosophical Perspectives* 10 (1996): 403–417; Robert Kane, *The Significance of Free Will* (Oxford: Oxford University Press, 1996): 142–144; and David Widerker, "Libertarianism and Frankfurt's Attack on the Principle of Alternative Possibilities," *Philosophical Review* 104 (1995): 247–261.
23. Maybe this is so because the neural pathways constitutive of this decision, or corresponding with it, are closed down due to a brain lesion or some other malfunction.
24. For other defenses of Frankfurt's argument against the Ginet/Kane/Widerker line, see Ishtiyaque Haji, *Moral Appraisability* (New York: Oxford University Press, 1998): 38–39; David P. Hunt, "Moral Responsibility and Unavoidable Action," *Philosophical Studies* 97 (2000): 195–227: Alfred Mele and David Robb, "Rescuing Frankfurt-Style Cases," *Philosophical Studies* 97 (2000): 195–227; Derk Pereboom, *Living Without Free Will* (Cambridge: Cambridge University Press, 2001): 18–28; "Alternative Possibilities and Causal Histories," *Philosophical Perspectives* 14 (2000): 119–138; and Eleonore Stump, "Libertarian Freedom and the Principle of Alternative Possibilities," in Daniel Howard-Snyder and Jeff Jordan, eds., *Faith, Freedom, and Rationality* (Lanham, MD: Rowman & Littlefield, 1996): 73–88.
25. Harry Frankfurt understands it in terms of a kind of harmony between hierarchically ordered psychic elements in the production of a person's actions. When an agent acts from an effective desire (one that is causally responsible for producing action), and when she also identifies at high-order level with that effective desire, then she acts of her own free will; that is, she acts with guidance control ("Freedom and the Will and the Concept of a Person," *Journal of Philosophy* 68 [1971]: 5–20). John Martin Fischer and Mark Ravizza have analyzed guidance control in terms of the reasons-responsiveness of an agent's own springs of action. Whatever it is in the causal etiology of action that gives rise to it, if it is of a sort that is sensitive to reasons (would respond differently with different sorts of reasons presented to it), and if it is properly integrated within the agent (by way of her taking ownership of it), then the agent acts with guidance control (*Responsibility and Control*, 28–91). Ishtiyaque Haji has also developed a reasons-responsive theory of guidance control and analyzed it in terms of the responsiveness of the (proximal) desires issuing in action (*Moral Appraisability*, 65–85). And to mention just one more theory, Alfred Mele has suggested (but not unequivocally endorsed) a notion of guidance control for autonomy that is developed primarily in terms of the action-theoretic characteristics that enable properly functioning persons to act non-akraticly and in accord with their own best judgments (*Autonomous Agents*, 112–127).
26. See my "Source Incompatibilism, Ultimacy, and the Transfer of Non-responsibility," *American Philosophical Quarterly* 38 (2001): 37–52.
27. See, e.g., Don Locke, "Three Concepts of Free Action: I," *Proceedings of the Aristotelian Society*, suppl., 49 (1975): 95–112; and Richard Taylor, *Metaphysics* (Englewood Cliffs, NJ: Prentice Hall, 1974): 45–46.

28. The two best recent variations on this incompatibilist style of argument are Robert Kane's in *The Significance of Free Will*, 65–71; and Derk Pereboom in *Living Without Free Will*, 110–117, and "Determinism al Dente," *Noûs* 29 (1995): 21–45.
29. In *Responsibility and Control*, Fischer and Ravizza explain such cases by appeal to the notion of *epistemically historical phenomena*, phenomena that concern history only insofar is it helps gain epistemic access to some current time slice phenomena (187–190).
30. Harry Frankfurt, "Reply to John Martin Fischer," in Sarah Buss and Lee Overton, eds., *Contours of Agency: Essays on Themes from Harry Frankfurt* (Cambridge, MA: MIT Press, 2002): 27–28.
31. For instance, Fischer and Ravizza argue that an agent must *take* responsibility for her mechanisms of action, and she must do so on the basis of the appropriate sort of evidence as to the effectiveness of her agency (*Responsibility and Control*, 207–239). Given that an agent does satisfy these historical conditions, then when she acts from the appropriate sort of causally integrated structure, she acts with regulative control and is morally responsible. This process of taking responsibility, Fischer and Ravizza argue, cannot arise via a process of manipulation. Alternatively, Alfred Mele argues that an agent is *not* autonomous if she acts upon currently unsheddable values or principles that bypassed at an earlier time an agent's critical abilities to evaluate them and thereby retain or discard them (*Autonomous Agents*, 172–173). This might be so even if, in terms of current time slice characteristics, such an agent is an optimally self-controlled agent (in the sense that she always acts according to her own best judgments even when her strongest desire is not in accord with it).
32. As applied to Fischer and Ravizza's historicist account (see note 31), whatever the details come to, could not a manipulator fabricate the relevant evidence on the basis of which an agent comes to take responsibility for her mechanisms of action? Or on Mele's account (see note 31), as an alternative to a manipulator "bypassing" an agent's means of critical evaluation, couldn't a manipulator manipulate – just the way a deterministic history does – the means in which an agent critically evaluated the principles and values that subsequently became unsheddable features of her stable character? These objections to Fischer and Ravizza's and also Mele's historical conditions are carefully developed in Tomis Kapitan's "Autonomy and Manipulated Freedom," *Philosophical Perspectives* 14 (2000): 81–103.
33. For a similar reply to global manipulation cases, see Kapitan, "Autonomy and Manipulated Freedom." See also Richard Double's *The Non-Reality of Free Will* (New York: Oxford University Press, 1991): 36–37.
34. Pereboom, *Living Without Free Will*, 110–117.
35. Thanks to both Bernie Berofsky and Derk Pereboom for helping me to formulate this argument.
36. In *Unprincipled Virtue*, Nomy Arpaly shares my affinity for a Quality of Will thesis as it pertains to issues of moral responsibility.
37. Fischer and Ravizza, *Responsibility and Control*, 195.
38. See Gary Watson, "Responsibility and the Limits of Evil."

39. I have replied to Gary Watson in this fashion in "The Limits of Evil and the Role of Moral Address: A Defense of Strawsonian Compatibilism," *Journal of Ethics* 2 (1998): 123–142.
40. In arguing for incompatibilism, Derk Pereboom develops a local manipulation case in "Determinism al Dente." Defending the compatibilist against it in *Moral Appraisability*, Ishtiyaque Haji replied to Pereboom (23–24). My manner of handling local manipulation cases accords with Haji's. For Pereboom's reply, see *Living Without Free Will*, 117–120. For further reflections upon the distinction between resistible and irresistible desires as it pertains to issues of autonomy and responsibility, see James Stacey Taylor's "Willing Addicts, Unwilling Addicts, and Freedom of the Will," unpublished manuscript.
41. Arpaly makes a similar point, though she focuses on more dramatic shifts in a person's character, such as shifting from being a party animal to a workaholic (Arpaly, *Unprincipled Virtue*, 127).
42. See Frankfurt, "Autonomy, Necessity, and Love."
43. Terry Irwin pressed the following provocative objection: Can't we imagine that autonomous agency is analogous to the way that a state might govern itself? Suppose that a state is "set free" from the mother country that once ruled it. From the moment of its first governing acts, does it not at that moment rule itself? And isn't this sufficient for a current time slice account of autonomy for a state? Why, then, not for a person? Two replies: First, if in those initial acts of "governing" the state just set free has no resources on the basis of which to formulate and reflect upon the procedures by which it governs itself, it merely draws upon the structures set in place by its mother state; it is unclear that the rules it acts upon are its own rules in any meaningful sense, though it might be acting "on its own." (Thanks to Harold Hodes for suggesting this reply.) Second, even granting that there is such a legitimate current time slice notion of autonomy as it applies to a person, that notion, it seems to me, just does not capture some of the very few intuitions that seem to inform our thinking about a self-ruling person. Some of those intuitions are about persons who have come to rule themselves by values and principles that they have taken the time to critically evaluate and endorse or maybe even shape for themselves. What I am proposing is a historical account of autonomy that captures those intuitions.
44. In fairness to Mele, his historical condition is meant to be appended to an agent that is "ideally self-controlled." (See *Autonomous Agents*, 121–122.) It seems unlikely, though not impossible, that an ideally self-controlled agent might have acquired values or principles that she never critically evaluated.
45. Mele, *Autonomous Agents*, 172–173.
46. Arpaly entertains a similar view of autonomy (Arpaly, *Unprincipled Virtue*, 128), though she does not endorse it as I do. Instead, regarding it unfavorably, she suggests that it is a version of what she calls "heroic autonomy."
47. An irony of my view is that a nonautonomous person who comes to be autonomous by initiating a process of critically evaluating her own values and principles cannot initially engage in this process autonomously. But is this that surprising? How far is it from the struggles of youth?

48. There is conceptual space here for the idea that a person might be autonomous in one sphere of her life, but not in another. She might, for instance, have cultivated a rich set of values and principles regarding her aesthetic life or instead her athletic or culinary life, while never having devoted any attention to her moral commitments.
49. Such a person is more than what Frankfurt might call a wanton, because she might well identify at higher-order levels of reflection with her own motivations, life plans, or what-have-you; but she would indeed be less than an autonomous agent. Perhaps this result is offensive. Maybe in speaking of persons who are more than wantons but less than autonomous agents, I am doing no more than putting a saccharine coating upon that odious distinction Nietzsche drew between the masters and the herd. But I do not think so. For one thing, on the view I have sketched, many persons who are not autonomous agents certainly could be because they might well have the capacity to set out and settle for themselves what values and principles ought to inform their lives. But also, those persons who are not autonomous agents might not be just because their lives have taken the sorts of turns that would not necessarily prompt one to have to put much energy into deciding for themselves what values and principles to live by. And if it turned out that the sorts of environments that tended to create such circumstances also created relatively decent folks, it would not seem to be such a great loss if most of the people in it were not autonomous in the manner I have set out here.
50. Thanks to Carl Ginet for this suggestion. Some of Arpaly's remarks are also suggestive of a similar point (Arpaly, *Unprincipled Virtue*, 126).
51. Mele, *Autonomous Agents*, 3.
52. I grant that skeptical worries are reasonable at this juncture. For instance, a sociopath who allegedly understands some amoral aesthetic principle but not any moral principles might lack a full appreciation for the aesthetic principle because the content of the principle might have moral assumptions built into it. On the other hand, one might question the plausibility that a sociopath who could fully understand some amoral values would really be unable to understand the moral ones.
53. Arpaly draws similar conclusions when reflecting upon a similar sort of autonomous agency (Arpaly, *Unprincipled Virtue*, 124, 128).
54. Marina Oshana argues for a similar result in "The Misguided Marriage of Responsibility and Autonomy," *Journal of Ethics* 6 (2002): 261–280. But her specific claims about autonomy and responsibility differ considerably from those I defend here. Most significant is that Oshana opts for a very modest notion of autonomous agency, treating it merely as self-directed agency. On the view I develop here, autonomous agency requires a much more robust treatment involving an actual endorsement of rules (where "rule" is meant to be liberally construed). Given that she and I are working with sufficiently different notions of autonomy, it is unclear whether our views conflict.
55. It is worth noting that the circumstances in which a person might be both an autonomous but not a morally responsible agent are relatively rare. There are not that many amoral gods kicking around, nor are there that many autonomous sociopaths. By contrast, given the fairly high bar for achieving

the status of autonomous agents, there likely are more than a few morally responsible agents around who are not autonomous agents. But it is worth bearing in mind that it is of course often only a luxury that allows one the opportunity to dally over the quality of her own values and principles. People who need to do things like feed their hungry children haven't the time for such internal manicuring of their lovely selves. When one is inclined to get all puffed up about the autonomous individual, the self-made man, and what not, it is worth keeping such obvious truisms in mind.

10

Alternative Possibilities, Personal Autonomy, and Moral Responsibility

Ishtiyaque Haji

INTRODUCTION

The Principle of Alternative Possibilities (PAP) – a person is morally responsible for performing an action only if she could have done otherwise – captures the pervasive outlook that to be morally responsible for one's conduct one must have had, at suitable junctures along the causal pathway to the conduct, alternative options. This principle has been the cynosure of interest in discussions on free will and moral responsibility because there are impressive reasons to think that determinism – the doctrine that, at any instant, there is exactly one physically possible future – rules out alternative possibilities and is, hence, if PAP is true, incompatible with responsibility.

It is plausible to assume that, if there is a requirement of alternative possibilities for responsibility, there must be an analogous requirement for personal autonomy, at least when the notion of *being autonomous* is identified, roughly, with that of *being self-governing*. For, intuitively, just as it is initially taxing to see how one's actions could reveal one's moral worth if one lacked the sort of control involving alternative possibilities over those actions, so it is hard to see how one could be self-directing in one's life if one did not have genuine options. In addition, libertarians have insisted with considerable plausibility that an agent is morally responsible for her behavior only if she is the ultimate source of her activity; she must initiate or originate her conduct. Further, libertarians have, by and large, also been friendly toward the requirement – perhaps a variation of the previous one – that if a person is responsible for an action, that action is the causal product of, among other things, values, desires, and beliefs that are "truly her own" or "authentic"; the action is not, for example, the result of brainwashing or other varieties of undesirable manipulation. But it has been claimed that if our world is determined, neither the condition of "buck-stopping" origination nor that of authenticity can be met because our springs of action ultimately derive from events that long preceded our births.[1] If we take these two conditions seriously, then, once again, it is highly credible to assume that autonomy requires analogous conditions. For surely autonomy seems to be compromised when, for instance, one is the puppet of a surreptitious manipulator because either one is no longer in the driver's seat – ultimate origination is subverted – or one's motivational repertoire is no longer one's own – authenticity of one's springs of action is in question. Some of the very requirements favored by libertarians for responsibility, then, seem just as compelling as requirements for autonomy. For the most part, attention in this chapter is confined to the requirement of alternative possibilities. Indeed, like others, Marina Oshana explicitly endorses, in a recent piece, a cousin of PAP (call it "PAPA") to the effect that a person is autonomous only if she has relevant options.[2]

PAP, however naturally compelling, has been threatened by various considerations, including intriguing Frankfurt-type examples. These examples contain a fail-safe mechanism that plays no role in the etiology of the agent's behavior but ensures that the agent reasons, chooses, and acts in just the way in which he does while blocking off all his other options. If such examples do in fact subvert PAP, one might wonder why they do not similarly subvert PAPA.

In what follows, I begin with a summary of a nontraditional Frankfurt-type example that Michael McKenna has recently advanced to circumvent certain libertarian concerns directed against standard so-called "prior-sign" Frankfurt-type cases.[3] I argue that this newly designed example should not pacify libertarians because it encounters special difficulties in the arena of responsibility. But these difficulties are not forthcoming when the example is directed against PAPA. Despite this, however, it is not obvious that the example impugns PAPA, given Oshana's contention that "socio-relational external" constraints need to be met for autonomous agency.

I then appeal to a "global" Frankfurt-type case in which, though an agent acts "on her own" on each occasion of choice, she could never have done otherwise, and I argue that such cases cast preliminary doubt on PAPA. I end with the suggestion that whether there is a requirement of alternative possibilities for either personal autonomy or moral responsibility can profitably be explored by focusing on why it has been thought alternative possibilities are vital constituents of autonomy or free action. I direct attention primarily to the rationale that alternative possibilities enhance the control one exercises in acting autonomously or in freely performing mental or other actions. I conclude that this rationale leaves much to be desired.

I. A CHALLENGE TO PRIOR-SIGN FRANKFURT-TYPE EXAMPLES

As an illustration of a prior-sign Frankfurt-type example, imagine that Mindy believes that, in her circumstances, it is wrong for her to lie to prevent embarrassment. But in spite of this, she decides to lie and lies anyway. As she has no excuse or justification for lying, it seems she is deserving of blame for lying. Unbeknownst to Mindy, though, she could not have refrained from lying owing to the presence of Countess Vena, who has the power to read and control Mindy's mind. The Countess wields this power partly in virtue of possessing the following knowledge. Had Mindy been about to refrain from lying, she would have displayed some involuntary sign, a signature neurological pattern, N*, in her brain; whereas, if she had been about to lie, she would have displayed a different neurological pattern, N. Had Vena detected N*, she would have interceded in Mindy's deliberations via direct stimulation of Mindy's brain and, in this way, would have caused Mindy to lie. But Vena detects N, the reliable sign for Vena that she need not show her hand at all. As Mindy lies on her own, in the absence of any intervention on Vena's part, it seems highly reasonable that Mindy acts freely and is morally blameworthy for lying, despite not having alternative possibilities with regard to her pertinent decision and action. Thus, it has been thought that prior-sign Frankfurt-type cases provide powerful reason to believe that alternative possibilities are not required for blameworthiness or responsibility in general.[4]

One objection to prior-sign examples is couched in terms of a dilemma. If N is an infallible sign that Mindy will behave as the Countess wishes, this is because it must be that the occurrence of the sign – the relevant triggering event or state – deterministically causes the behavior in consideration. But then the example begs the question against those who believe that determinism is incompatible with moral responsibility. If, though, the triggering event – the occurrence of N – is not an infallible indicator that Mindy will behave as the Countess desires, then even after displaying N, Mindy can act contrary to the Countess's wishes and thus has alternative possibilities after all.[5]

II. McKenna's Limited-Blockage Strategy

Addressing this dilemma, McKenna directs his remarks to traditional incompatibilists who claim that "the freedom-relevant condition for moral responsibility involves alternate possibilities"[6] and not, for example, to source incompatibilists who worry that – if an agent's behavior is produced by factors that do not originate in her and over which she has no control, as would be the case if determinism were true – the agent is not responsible for any of her behavior.

In outline, McKenna's "Limited-Blockage Strategy" exploits the thought that only *some* kinds of alternatives – "deliberatively (and morally) significant" ones – are relevant to moral responsibility and that PAP should be amended to encapsulate this idea. The reformulated principle (PSA), in broad strokes, says that a person is morally responsible for performing an action only if she could have performed some deliberatively significant alternative instead. McKenna proposes that traditional incompatibilists should endorse PSA (and not PAP) as the principle of alternative possibilities pertinent to responsibility. But McKenna argues that PSA is false. In a "PSA situation," analogous to the Frankfurt-type situation in which Mindy finds herself, all deliberatively significant alternatives are closed off, save for the one the agent performs. Deliberatively insignificant alternatives, however, are left open. When the agent performs the pertinent deed – lying, for instance, to avoid embarrassment – she acts with libertarian free will, for she could have done otherwise and she is morally responsible for her deed. But she could not have performed any other deliberatively significant alternative. McKenna, then, responds to the second horn of the dilemma while accepting the first.

To appreciate the Limited-Blockage Strategy, let's start with the notion of a deliberatively (and morally) significant alternative. McKenna attempts to clarify this notion by advancing examples with these recurring features. Suppose, pondering an issue that calls for a response in his situation, an agent must settle on a course of action. In many such instances, there will be a range of alternatives simply not relevant to the agent's reasoning concerning the pertinent issue. If these alternatives (or a subset of them) are not germane to apt moral deliberation in which the agent might engage to decide on what to do, the alternatives are deliberatively (and morally) insignificant. Deliberatively (and morally) significant alternatives, in contrast, *are* important to the moral musings of the agent, given her situation and concerns. McKenna proposes that such alternatives figure or aid "in the ground upon which it is judged that an agent is morally responsible for what she has done"[7] and are "relevant to *competent moral deliberation and agency*."[8]

In one of McKenna's examples, *Needed Medication*,

> Tal arrives at Daphne's house and discovers Daphne unconscious and in immediate need of a drug known as *The Good Stuff.* Unknown to Tal, Daphne has stored The Good Stuff in an aspirin jar. Grant that it is actually open to Tal to walk to the medicine cabinet and retrieve for Daphne, from the jar marked "aspirin," The Good Stuff that Daphne needs to survive. It cannot be morally expected of Tal that he consider the option of fetching The Good Stuff from the aspirin jar even though this option is not causally closed to Tal. This mundane epistemic constraint on moral deliberation surely suggests that the range of morally significant options relevant to evaluating an agent's moral responsibility should be restricted in some manner.[9]

Differentiating between objective and subjective moral obligation will be useful. Roughly, just as we should distinguish between its being true that something, *p*, is the case and believing that *p* is the case, so we should distinguish between what one objectively ought overall to do – one's objective moral obligation – and what one thinks one objectively ought to do – one's subjective moral obligation. More precisely, agent, *s*, has a subjective moral obligation at a certain time, *t*, to do an action, *a*, at time, *t**, if and only if *s* believes that, as of *t*, *s* (objectively) ought overall (and not just prima facie) to do *a* at *t**. The concept of subjective moral obligation is, thus, explicated in terms of objective moral obligation. As *Needed Medication* highlights, if we are concerned with a person's subjective moral obligations, we may have to take into account what he knows or believes would happen if he were to do one thing or another, and that if moral obligation is in the forefront in deliberative contexts, it is frequently subjective moral obligation that is so.[10]

Needed Medication confirms that a deliberatively insignificant moral alternative can be one that it is objectively morally obligatory for an agent in her circumstances. We can reasonably assume that it is objectively (but not subjectively) obligatory for Tal to retrieve The Good Stuff from the aspirin jar. Having failed to save Daphne and having been apprised of the whereabouts of The Good Stuff, suppose anguished Tal utters the following to himself: "If I had only known better! I should have given Daphne some of the pills from the aspirin jar." Surely, if "should" here expresses moral obligation, as it seemingly does or certainly may, it expresses objective moral obligation.

McKenna suggests that PAP is too inclusive – it can be satisfied even if the only alternatives of an agent are deliberatively insignificant ones. He offers, instead, a principle (confined, he says, for ease of presentation, to blameworthiness) incorporating what he believes are plausible deliberative constraints that restrict relevant alternatives to deliberatively significant ones:

PSA: An agent *S* is morally blameworthy for performing action *A* at *t* only if she had within her control at *t* performing an alternative action *B* such that (1) performing *B* at *t* was morally less bad than performing *A* at *t*, and (2) it would have been reasonable for *S* to have considered performing *B* at *t* as an alternative to performing *A* at *t* given *S*'s agent-relative deliberative circumstances.[11]

McKenna proposes that "it is PSA and not PAP that ought to serve as the incompatibilist demand for alternative possibilities."[12]

However, McKenna argues that "Brain Malfunction," a sort of Frankfurt-type example, undercuts PSA. The example's leading character, Casper, can either press a button marked "Good" or one marked "Bad." If he presses button Bad, he will immediately make it the case that one million dollars is deposited into his bank account. The transaction will be untraceable. If he presses button Good, he will immediately make it the case that an entire village of people in the Amazon is cured of an otherwise fatal disease. Both buttons cannot be selected, and this opportunity will not present itself again. He has ten seconds to decide. Greedily, Casper presses button Bad. Unbeknownst to him, though, at the time at which he decided to press this button, Casper had a small lesion on his brain that blocked the neural pathway constitutive of (or correlated with) a decision to push button Good. McKenna comments:

[A]ssume that Casper exercises whatever brand of libertarian free will one might prefer and that the presence of the lesion plays no role in the etiology of Casper's decision to press the Bad button. . . . Casper was free during the crucial interval of time *not* to decide to press the Bad button. Casper could have simply ceased deliberating and turned his attention to other affairs . . . [such as deciding] to comb his hair slow and cool like James Dean. . . . All that Casper could not do is decide to press the Good button. All other paths remained open. According to the libertarian defending PAP, Casper acted freely in deciding to press the Bad button. Brain Malfunction is *not* a counterexample to PAP. . . . The problem with PAP as it applies to Brain Malfunction is that when Casper pressed the Bad button, none of the other alternatives to pressing the Good button were regarded by Casper to be deliberatively significant. Casper concerned himself with the options he reasonably took to inform the decision before him. Brain Malfunction is, however, a counterexample to PSA.[13]

It is a counterexample because Casper is blameworthy for pressing button Bad even though it is false that he could have performed some other deliberatively significant, better alternative instead.

Although I concur that responsibility does not require alternative possibilities, I disagree that the Limited-Blockage Strategy corroborates this. *Pace* McKenna, there are weighty reasons for traditional incompatibilists to resist PSA. "Killer-1" is a case that provides intuitive grounds to reject this principle irrespective of whether one is a compatibilist or an incompatibilist. The case's villain, Deadly, plans on settling an old score by killing an unsuspecting patient. He knows that injecting the patient with drug A will prove fatal and that injecting with B will ensure a cure. Deadly arranges for the syringe filled with A to be delivered to the patient's room. Owing to some confusion and luckily for the patient, the syringe containing A is switched with one containing B. Although he believes that it is morally wrong for him to give A, Deadly is determined to execute his vile plan. He injects the patient with B, all the while thinking that he is administering a fatal dose of A.

Stipulate that Deadly's deliberatively significant ("open") alternatives in this case are to give A (a1) and to give B (a2). Assume that all other (seemingly) deliberatively significant alternatives are blocked by some mechanism or neural defect and that all open alternatives in addition to (a1) and (a2) are deliberatively insignificant. Deadly, it seems, is blameworthy for doing (a2) because, among other things, he freely does (a2) in light of the belief that he does wrong by doing (a2). Strictly, Deadly is blameworthy for doing something he believed to be wrong; in his situation, this happens to be giving B. Because Deadly was attempting to do something he took to be wrong but that by sheer luck turned out to be obligatory, *he* is surely to be negatively appraised even though his *act* is positively appraised. However, (a1) fails to satisfy the first clause of PSA because it is false that this alternative is morally less bad than (a2). Had A been given, the innocent patient would have died. Hence, if PSA were true, then, contrary to good judgment, Deadly would not be blameworthy for performing (a2).

One objection to this case is that Deadly's deliberatively significant alternatives are *not* (a1) and (a2) but are really the following: Give what Deadly takes to be A (a1*), and give what Deadly takes to be B (a2*). Deadly, it may be added, is blameworthy for performing (a1*). But even if this is the correct conceptualization of Deadly's pertinent alternatives, (a2*) – the alternative that, if performed, would amount to Deadly's giving A – also fails to satisfy PSA's first clause. Hence, contrary to intuitive judgment, PSA would once again generate the result that Deadly is not to blame for doing (a1*).

Another objection is that though Deadly is blameworthy for *his attempt to kill the patient* (a3), he is *not* blameworthy for *giving B* (a2). This is largely because blameworthiness requires wrongness – one can be blameworthy for doing something only if that thing is wrong – and although (a3) is morally wrong, (a2) is morally obligatory. To meet this objection, let's revise the case. Assume that Deadly is squeamish about needles and under normal circumstances is psychologically incapable of thrusting a needle into anyone. It is only under the special circumstances in which he has the purpose or intention of killing his bitter foe, Lucky, that he can force the injection containing what he believes to be A into Lucky.[14] Suppose Deadly executes his intention to inject Lucky with what he takes to be A in light of the belief that he is doing wrong. It so happens that had he not thrust the needle into Lucky when he did, Lucky would have died. Unbeknownst to Deadly and fortunately for Lucky, Deadly's deed actually prevents Lucky's death. Under these circumstances, it appears that this state of affairs is obligatory for Deadly *if* it is, for a proponent of the Limited-Blockage Strategy, a legitimate alternative:

(AT): Deadly's injecting Lucky with what he believes is A for the purpose or with the intention of killing Lucky.

For the view that we morally ought always, as of a time, to do what we do in the best worlds accessible to us as of that time, given a suitably flexible reading of "best," is commandingly plausible.[15] It appears that in all the bests accessible to Deadly (just prior to his administering A or B), he gives what he believes is A. Moreover, in these worlds he gives A with the purpose or intention of killing Lucky, for without the relevant purpose or intention, Deadly could not have thrust the needle into Lucky.

Notice that (a3) – Deadly's attempt to kill the patient – is true in any world in which (AT) is true. Indeed, it might plausibly be claimed that Deadly's attempt to kill Lucky just is his injecting Lucky with what he takes to be A for the purpose or with the intention of killing Lucky. So (AT) entails (a3).

Next, consider this eminently reasonable principle:

(Prerequisites): If agent, *S*, cannot bring about *p* without bringing about *q* (perhaps because *q* is a logical or causal consequence of *p*), and if *S* can refrain from doing *q*, then if *S* morally ought to bring about *p*, *S* morally ought also to bring about *q*.[16]

Because (AT) is obligatory for Deadly and (AT) entails (a3), it follows from these facts and (Prerequisites) that, contrary to the objection, (a3) is obligatory and not wrong for Deadly.

This objection concerning Deadly's attempt, though mistaken, unearths something notable about Brain Malfunction. Suppose we grant that Deadly is blameworthy for attempting to kill Lucky and, hence, that his attempting to kill Lucky is a deliberatively and morally significant alternative (given the dialectical context). Consequently, it should be granted that in Brain Malfunction, Casper's attempting to press button Bad is also a deliberatively and morally significant alternative. This attempt would consist, roughly, in Casper's pressing button Bad with the purpose of securing personal gain. It seems that Casper could not press button Bad without attempting to press this button. But then, against McKenna's assertion, Brain Malfunction is *not* a case in which all the deliberatively and morally significant alternatives with the exception of the one Casper performs are blocked.

One might retract the claim that Deadly is blameworthy for attempting to kill the patient (as this attempt, in the refined case, is not itself wrong) and opt, instead, for the view that Deadly is blameworthy for *doing something he believes to be wrong* (ao). This is, again, because blameworthiness requires wrongness and (ao) *is* wrong, or so it might be contended. But this objection also has several shortcomings. For one thing, in all the best worlds accessible to him just before he gives any medicine, Deadly does what he believes is wrong (he gives B). Hence, (ao) is obligatory and not wrong for Deadly *if* it is in fact an alternative for Deadly. This result, for another thing, reveals a second deep problem with this objection. We have assumed, credibly, that (a2) – giving B – is obligatory for Deadly. But how, then, can (ao) be obligatory for Deadly as well if (ao) and (a2) are *alternatives*? The right response is that the two are *not* alternatives because it is reasonable to assume that alternatives are incompatible in this sense: It is not the case that there are any two members of an agent's alternative set that are such that their agent is able to perform both of them together.[17] This incompatibility requirement is violated by (ao) and (a2). Thus, the objection is incoherent.

What of the claim, finally, that blameworthiness requires wrongness? If it is true, then Deadly cannot be blameworthy for *Deadly's giving B*, or for *Deadly's attempting to kill the patient*, or for *Deadly's doing what he believes is wrong*, because none of these states of affairs *is* wrong. The dictum that blameworthiness requires (objective) wrongness can be clarified by introducing what I have dubbed the "Objective View" of blameworthiness and its praiseworthiness analogue:

Objective View: One is praiseworthy for an act only if one had an objective (overall) moral obligation to perform it or it was (overall) permissible for one to perform it, that is, praiseworthiness requires that one have done something (objectively) obligatory or permissible (O1); and one is blameworthy for an act only if one had an objective (overall) obligation not to perform it, that is, blameworthiness requires that one have done something (objectively) wrong (O2).

I have elsewhere argued that the Objective View is false;[18] but even if, in particular, its blame component (O2) is true, there is trouble for the Limited-Blockage Strategy. To explain, consider "Killer-2," a case that gives incompatibilists who accept the view that blameworthiness requires wrongness good reason to renounce PSA. Joy is hospitalized; and this time around, Lee Thal wants to murder this patient. He knows that giving A to Joy will kill her and that giving B will cure her but with serious side effects. There is another drug, C, that, if administered, will cure Joy quickly and safely with none of the nasty repercussions of B. But Thal knows nothing whatsoever about C, although C is readily available in the hospital. Assume that the only deliberatively significant alternative open to Thal is to give A (t1). His other (apparent) deliberatively significant alternative is to give B (t2), but this alternative is closed due to "neuronal blockage" of which Thal is unaware. Alternative (t3), give C, is open as well, but t3 is deliberatively insignificant. Of the alternatives exhaustive of Thal's options, t3 is best and obligatory, whereas (t1) is worst and wrong. Apparent option (t2), then, is better than (t1) but not as good as (t3); and if Thal could perform (t2), (t2) would be wrong to boot. Suppose Thal gives A in light of the belief that he is doing wrong in giving A and thereby kills Joy. He is, it appears, blameworthy for giving A.

If blameworthiness requires wrongness, then deliberatively insignificant alternative (t3) certainly *does* play a role in "grounding ascriptions of responsibility." For which alternative in an agent's alternative set is wrong or obligatory depends on the (deontically pertinent) values of the members of that set. (Or, more accurately, the primary moral deontic status of an agent's alternatives – whether they are right, wrong, or obligatory – depends upon the values of the worlds then accessible to the agent; but the values of these, in turn, will depend, in some measure, on the values of the alternatives the agent performs in those worlds.) So, for example, if accessible to Thal at time *t* are worlds in which he does (t1), (t2), and (t3), then (t3) is obligatory and (t1) and (t2) are wrong. If no (t2) or (t3) worlds are accessible to Thal at *t*, but worlds in which Thal gives A and worlds in which he gives A* (A* kills much more slowly and painfully than does A) are the only ones accessible to him at *t*, then (t1) is obligatory for Thal at *t*.

It might be objected that Thal can have no *real* obligation to do something like giving C in this example because having such an obligation requires having knowledge that Thal cannot reasonably be expected to have. Hence, it is false that Thal is objectively obligated to give C. At best, it may be true that, had Thal acquired the requisite knowledge, it would have been the case that Thal ought (objectively) to have given C. The view, however, that objective obligation requires relevant knowledge one can reasonably be expected to have is highly controversial. Indeed, this view seems to garner plausibility only at the expense of ignoring the distinction between subjective and objective moral obligation. Suppose I ought to return some books by a certain date because of a previous promise but completely forget about my moral obligation to do so. Suppose, as a result of forgetting, I simply don't believe that I ought to return the books, and given other urgent matters to which I now have to attend, I cannot reasonably be expected to remember my promise. Even if there is a sense in which I cannot return the books – I don't believe I have any reason to return them – it seems I can still have an obligation to do so. If what we overall ought to do is "objective" in one aspect in which truth is – what's true can obtain independently of what we believe is true – then the view that lack of relevant knowledge is not obligation-subversive is inviting. In this and other relevantly similar cases, the distinction between objective and subjective moral obligation, in fact, goes some way toward *explaining* our moral ambivalence concerning the cases. There *is* a sense in which we can rightly claim that Thal has no obligation to give C: He has no subjective obligation to give C. Consistent with this judgment, though, we also want to claim that, given the facts of the case, Thal should have returned the books – he has an objective moral obligation to do so.

"Objectivists" might also emphasize that there is a requirement of alternative possibilities for obligation, right, and wrong. That is, no one can perform an act that is morally obligatory, right, or wrong, if one could not have performed some alternative instead.[19] The ability to perform a *deliberatively insignificant alternative*, in a Frankfurt-type situation of concern to McKenna, ensures that the deliberatively significant alternative that the agent does perform instantiates one or more of the primary deontic properties of obligatoriness, rightness, or wrongness.

There is, then, substantial reason for an incompatibilist who is an objectivist about blameworthiness to reject PSA because the view that deliberatively insignificant alternatives are not pertinent to grounding ascriptions of moral responsibility primarily motivates PSA.

Suppose (o2) – the view that blameworthiness requires wrongness – is false and that it is to be replaced by the view, roughly, that blameworthiness requires belief in what is wrong. The kernel of this alternative view – the "Subjective View" – is that one is morally blameworthy for something only if one does it in light of the belief that one is doing moral wrong.[20] Then though it is false that (in Killer-2) deliberatively insignificant alternative (t3) – the option that is best – is relevant to competent moral deliberation and agency, (t3), once again, *does* aid in the ground upon which it is judged that an agent is morally responsible for what he has done. For the germane ground of interest is concerned with the freedom-relevant or control dimension of responsibility (and not, for example, with the epistemic dimension). Traditional incompatibilists insist that an agent exercises the right sort of freedom required for moral responsibility in performing an action if he exerts "active" control in bringing it about, and he has an open alternative that is such that he would have exerted active control in bringing it about had he performed it instead. To be morally responsible, the agent must be able to make it the case that what pathway the world takes is "up to him"; he must be able to ensure that one or another pathway is followed in accordance with what he judges best and chooses. The incompatibilist who is a "Subjectivist" is *not* limited to the view that responsibility requires that what *morally* significant pathway the world takes must be up to the agent. For this type of incompatibilist may allow that an agent can, for example, be blameworthy even for an amoral state of affairs (one that lacks a primary deontic property). Such an incompatibilist simply insists that what pathway, *moral or otherwise*, the world takes must be up to the agent. Hence, from the perspective of this sort of incompatibilist, even a deliberatively insignificant alternative can be relevant to ascriptions of responsibility. This is because the availability of such an alternative confirms that the leeway requirement of libertarian freedom is satisfied.

Regardless, then, of being Subjectivists or Objectivists about blameworthiness, incompatibilists have reason to jettison PSA.

III. FROM RESPONSIBILITY TO AUTONOMY

As we have seen, McKenna's Limited-Blockage Strategy exploits the idea that only some kinds of alternatives – deliberatively and morally significant ones – are relevant to moral responsibility and that a principle seeking to capture the thought that alternative possibilities are required for responsibility should be sensitive to this idea. Similarly, in analyzing the concept of personal autonomy, Oshana has lately proposed that being autonomous requires that an agent have a range of specific sorts of option.

Oshana claims that personal autonomy is a sociorelational phenomenon in that "autonomy is a condition of persons constituted, in large part, by the external, social relations people find themselves in (or the absence of certain social relations)."[21] She contrasts this "externalist" conception with "internalist" (or "psychological") ones according to which "ascriptions of personal autonomy . . . depend only on the structural and/or historical character of a person's psychological states and dispositions, and on an agent's judgments about them."[22] Several conditions, she theorizes, require satisfaction for agent autonomy, the one of fundamental interest to us being the condition of relevant options:

> The self-governing individual must have access to an adequate assortment of options. It is not enough that a person acknowledges the state of affairs in which she finds herself as one she would consent to even if she were lacking any other options, for the fact that a person finds her choice acceptable does not mean that an acceptable range of choices was hers. An assortment is not adequate if a person can only choose nonautonomy. Thus the option to choose nonsubservience must be available to the agent. Nor is an assortment adequate if the agent's choices are all dictated by duress (economic, emotional, etc.) or by bodily needs. The social climate must be sensitive to the fact that humans are not brute creatures; they are individuals whose physical and emotional well-being depends on the ability to engage the body and mind variously and creatively. Moreover, these options must be "real" – they must be options that a person can, in fact hope to achieve, and they must be relevant to the development of her life.[23]

Recall that PSA says, in short, that an agent is morally responsible for performing an action only if she could have performed some deliberatively and morally significant, better alternative instead. What would Oshana's analogous principle of alternative options concerning autonomy be? Perhaps

PAPA: A person is autonomous only if she has access (during the course of her life) to an adequate assortment of options.

In the passage last cited, Oshana claims that an assortment of choices is inadequate if one can only choose "nonautonomy," as would be the case, for instance, if one had only the alternatives of choosing to become a slave or a monk or if one's choices were all dictated by duress or bodily needs. This negative characterization of an adequate assortment of options (or "autonomy-relevant options") will suffice for our purposes if we assume that autonomy-relevant options are not inadequate options. The crux of Oshana's condition of relevant options, then, is that, even if one has options, one need not be autonomous because only *autonomy-relevant* options are required for autonomy. This is strikingly analogous to McKenna's view that, should there be a requirement of alternative possibilities for moral responsibility, only *deliberatively significant* alternatives are pertinent.

The argument against McKenna's proposal that an incompatibilist should accept PSA as the PAP-like principle pertinent to responsibility appealed to the distinction between the Objective View and the Subjective View of blameworthiness. I claimed that if the Objective View is true, then the availability of deliberatively insignificant alternatives – in a case in which these are the only open alternatives other than the deliberatively significant alternative that the agent performs – *is* relevant to the grounding of ascriptions of responsibility because of various deontic considerations. But these sorts of consideration, or at least relevantly analogous sorts, do not arise in connection with appraisals of agent autonomy. For the Objective View's principle (O2), the principle that blameworthiness requires wrongness, has no analogue concerning autonomy.

I argued that if the Subjective View of blameworthiness is true (and the Objective View is false), deliberatively insignificant alternatives yet again are crucial to the truth of judgments of moral responsibility, at least from the perspective of incompatibilists who are "standard" libertarians. Regarding the freedom requirements of moral responsibility, this is because libertarians partial to the Subjective View are not limited to the position that what *morally* significant pathway the world takes must be up to the agent. This is because an agent, according to subjectivists, can be blameworthy even for an amoral state of affairs. Rather, libertarians of this bent may simply insist that what pathway, moral or otherwise, the world takes must be up to the agent if the agent is to be responsible for her behavior.

On Oshana's conception of autonomy, an agent *cannot* be autonomous in the absence of having autonomy-relevant options. Even if the agent has several nonautonomy-relevant options, these will not be significant to the truth of judgments of autonomy. It may be helpful to think of Oshana's position as one entailing that, to be an autonomous agent, what *autonomy-relevant pathway* the world takes must be up to the agent.

Hence, a libertarian about autonomy – or more generally, a theorist who believes that autonomy is incompatible with unfreedom to do otherwise – can insist that an agent has "autonomy-grounding control" only if she has autonomy-relevant options. Whereas deliberatively insignificant options may well be germane to the truth of judgments of moral responsibility (from the perspective of libertarians who accept the Subjective View), nonautonomy options are not relevant to the truth of judgments of autonomy.

In summary, it seems that an analogous objection to the objection previously advanced against the claim that incompatibilists should accept the view that responsibility requires deliberatively significant alternatives cannot be directed against Oshana's proposal that autonomy requires autonomy-relevant options. Indeed, Oshana may maintain that there is no Frankfurt-type counterexample against PAPA analogous to the Frankfurt-type counterexample against PSA that McKenna develops. If all autonomy-relevant options are blocked, an agent cannot be autonomous, because being autonomous, Oshana maintains, is not solely a function of a person's psychological condition but is partly contingent on external social factors. These external factors, in turn, must be conducive to providing autonomy-relevant options.

Global Frankfurt-type cases, however, do seem to threaten Oshana's stance. Imagine that Jill is an autonomous person. Her external environment is hospitable to autonomy, and on each occasion of choice she chooses an option from among autonomy-relevant alternatives. Imagine, further, that Jill* is a psychological twin of Jill on a twin earth. Her external environment mirrors that of Jill's, and so do the choices that she makes. However, assume that, unlike Jill, she could not on *any* occasion have done other than what she actually did because of a Frankfurt-type device in her brain. It just happens, by cosmic coincidence, that Jill* does exactly what the global Frankfurt-style counterfactual intervener desires that she do whenever she performs any action. Although Jill*, just like Jill, believes that she has autonomy-relevant options, this belief is false. Hence, if Jill is autonomous, the verdict that Jill* is autonomous as well should have powerful pull.[24]

The externalist might resolutely maintain that although Jill* may believe and feel she is autonomous, she is really not so because she lacks autonomy-relevant alternatives. This sort of response parallels one traditional incompatibilists might advance against those who believe that alternative possibilities are not required for responsibility – to wit, there *must* be indeterminism at appropriate loci along actional trajectories to make room for alternative future pathways if an agent is to be morally responsible for her behavior. Such incompatibilists might tenaciously uphold the view that, in addition to control, leeway is a constituent of the freedom-relevant dimension of responsibility. It might be asserted that an agent is morally responsible for some action (mental or otherwise) only if she exercised active (or proximal) control in performing it *and* she could have done otherwise.[25]

Whether this response is promising turns principally on whether there are plausible considerations to support the proposal that responsibility requires leeway (in addition to active control). It will be instructive to explore this issue briefly prior to reverting to autonomy. One avenue of support for this proposal appeals to the view that, in comparison to the active control that an agent would exercise in deterministically performing an action, leeway *enhances* such control. Responsibility, it is further claimed, requires such enhanced control; and because of its dependence on alternative possibilities, such control is unavailable in a deterministic world. But if the sort of active control at issue is, at bottom, causal control, then it is questionable whether leeway does indeed augment this sort of responsibility-grounding control. Here, I can only give a thumbnail sketch of some of my reservations.

According to an event-causal libertarian view that eschews agent or other forms (if there are any) of substance causation, the sort of causal control that an agent exercises in performing an action, such as a decision, is of the same kind and degree that the agent would have exercised had she acted in accordance with the specifications of the best rival compatibilist view. The sole difference between these two views is that the former allows for leeway: Given exactly the same past and the natural laws, one could have decided or done otherwise. On either view, the decision made or overt action performed is causally produced by apt agent-involving events such as the agent's having prior reasons to make the decision and forming an appropriate intention. An agent's active control in making the decision consists in that decision's being nondeviantly caused in this way. The event-causal libertarian insists that, if decisions are nondeterministically caused, everything prior to the decision that one actually made might have been exactly the same and yet one could have made an alternative decision instead. Had one made some alternative decision, it, too, would have been causally produced by appropriate agent-involving events.

It should be fairly evident that the alternative possibilities an event-causal libertarian view allows for cannot enhance the active (causal) control that an agent exercises in performing whatever action (mental or otherwise) she actually performs. Its being the case that the agent would have exercised active control in doing what she would have done had she done otherwise does not, in any evident way, contribute to the enhancement of the active control that the agent *did* exercise in performing the action that she did. Hence, the mere chance that an agent could have acted differently cannot, in any way, affect the active control that the agent exerted in doing what she did.[26]

Even if an event-causal libertarian view allows for an agent's having active control in performing some action, it fails to allow for a different brand of control. This is the control, roughly, that one has in virtue of being able to *determine* which of two or more open alternatives one performs (on the provision that one's decisions or overt actions are nondeterministically caused). It has been proposed by Randolph Clarke that supplementing an appropriate version of an event-causal libertarian view with agent causation will provide the requisite control. Very briefly, on Clarke's view, a free decision is nondeterministically caused by suitable agent-involving events *and* also coproduced by the agent's substance causing it. Clarke hypothesizes that, as a matter of nomological necessity, whichever of the open decisions the agent makes, that decision will be made, and it will be caused by the agent's having the reasons that favor it (together with other mental events) only if the agent substance causes that decision. Augmentation of the nondeterministic causation of the decision with the substance causation of it by its agent secures for the agent the exercise of further positive powers. These powers influence causally which of the open alternative courses of action (mental or otherwise) that an event-causal libertarian view permits will become actual.[27]

Once again, though, it is improbable that this sort of "hybrid" theory, with its nondeterministic event-causal component and its agent-causal one, sheds any light on why leeway enhances the active control that one exercises in performing an action. For, even as Clarke acknowledges, if an event such as making a decision can be coproduced by being agent caused and nondeterministically event caused, it should be possible for the event to be coproduced by being agent caused and deterministically caused.[28] Suppose, then, that Sue's decision is both agent caused (by Sue) and appropriately deterministically event caused by her having various reasons and an apposite intention to make up her mind. Sue exerts the same sort and degree of active control in making her decision as she would have exerted had her decision been nondeterministically caused by the reasons the having of which deterministically caused that decision. We can suppose as well (nothing about the case invalidates this supposition) that, in agent-causing this decision, Sue agent-caused it in just the manner in which she would have (with the same kind and degree of active control) in a scenario as much as possible like the one under consideration, save for the difference that, in the counterfactual scenario, her decision was nondeterministically caused.

In both of the indicated agent-causal scenarios (the actual non-libertarian one and the counterfactual libertarian one), Sue exerts the same kind and degree of active control in making the decision. Hence, if the kind and degree of active control that Sue would have exerted in the libertarian scenario would have sufficed for her deciding freely, then we should conclude that Sue decides freely in the deterministic (or nonlibertarian) scenario as well. Therefore, it is dubious that leeway is a necessary condition of responsibility or that leeway enhances the active control that one exercises in performing an action for which one is responsible.

On a second avenue of thought, one cannot be the ultimate originator of one's actions without having open alternatives. It might further be contended that being the ultimate originator of one's actions contributes to the active control that one has in performing actions for which one is responsible. The conception of ultimate origination at issue will largely dictate the persuasiveness of this line of reasoning. According to one popular conception, one is the ultimate originator (or initiator) of one's action only if one has ultimate control over that action. Ultimate control involves the lack of deterministic causal influence upon one's action of agent-external events. As Alfred Mele explains, for an agent to have ultimate control over, for instance, his making some decision, it should not be the case that there are minimally causally sufficient conditions – conditions that do not include any event or state internal to the agent – for the agent's making this decision. Hence, agents could have ultimate control over their actions only if determinism is false.[29]

However, as Clarke stresses, because this conception of ultimate control is wholly negative – it is merely the absence of any deterministic causation in actional trajectories – it ensures that the agent has alternatives *without* securing for the agent additional powers to influence causally which alternatives left open by nondeterministic causation of the agent's having of reasons, and so forth, will be made actual. In short, this conception of ultimate control ensures that the agent has alternatives *without* securing for the agent any greater degree of active control than the degree of such control that the agent would have had had her action been deterministically caused.[30]

Libertarians might propose that ultimacy per se, independently of considerations of active control, contributes to freedom. Just as active control is a constituent of the freedom-relevant dimension of responsibility, so, on this proposal, is ultimate origination. Both the libertarian and nonlibertarian hybrid (agent-causal) views previously described imply that agents (because they are substances) are uncaused causes of some of their actions. However, the nonlibertarian variant seems to provide for only a tempered version of ultimate origination. This is because, on this view, each event that is agent-caused is made inevitable by events that existed long before the agent in question did. It is only the libertarian hybrid view that provides for agents' robustly originating their actions.[31]

There is a concern, however, with this proposal. Why is the sort of robust origination, available on the libertarian hybrid view, of such significance to the freedom dimension of moral responsibility when the sort of origination secured by the nonlibertarian hybrid view is not? After all, a reasonable assumption is that, if origination is to make a difference to attributions of responsibility, it must do so *because* it has a bearing on active control (call this the "Control-Influencing Assumption"). The degree and kind of active control provided for by either of these hybrid views are equivalent. Hence, the difference in the kind of origination seems not to have any impact on active control. But then, if the Control-Influencing Assumption is correct, one might be reluctant to side with the proposal under scrutiny.

One possibility of escape, of course, is to reject the Control-Influencing Assumption. The epistemic dimension of responsibility is a bona fide dimension, and its being such a dimension appears to be independent of whether epistemic considerations affect active control. Perhaps one should say similar things about ultimate origination. But this sort of move runs into a problem. Epistemic considerations, when relevant, are relevant to assessments of responsibility because they bear on an apt evaluation of the agent in relation to certain episodes that occur in that agent's life. When an agent acts "from" relevant ignorance, it is fairly evident, for instance, that she does not express ill or good will, depending upon the case, toward another in performing her action. It is difficult to see how considerations of origination have this sort of bearing. How can it be that one's moral worth, for example, is augmented, say, when praiseworthy (or diminished, say, when blameworthy) vis-à-vis a certain act, if one is a "robust" originator (as on a libertarian dualistic view) but not similarly affected if one is a "tempered" originator (as on a nonlibertarian dualistic view)?

Summing up, incompatibilists who are libertarians might claim that, in addition to active control, leeway is an independent constituent of the freedom-relevant dimension of responsibility. I have argued, though, that this proposal is not without difficulty.

Reverting to autonomy, we were entertaining the suggestion on the part of the externalist that, despite pressure from global Frankfurt-type cases, autonomy-relevant alternatives are a crucial constituent of personal autonomy. But whether this suggestion is plausible depends, vitally, on whether the externalist can supply good grounds in its support. Our digression on what bearing, if any, leeway has on responsibility-grounding control is succor for the view that it is not evident what these grounds could be. Autonomy-relevant options, for instance, do not augment the control that the agent exercises in autonomously selecting choices, and they need not, as global Frankfurt-type cases confirm, influence, in a manner detrimental to autonomy, the "external" social conditions in which the agent finds herself.

In conclusion, appropriately developed Frankfurt-type examples provide strong but not knock-down grounds to reject the view that alternative possibilities are required either for moral responsibility or for personal autonomy. The case against a requirement of alternative possibilities for responsibility or autonomy can, I suggest, be strengthened by exploring why exactly it has been thought that leeway contributes either to the freedom-relevant dimension of responsibility or to some dimension of autonomy.

Notes

I thank an anonymous reader for Cambridge University Press for comments on an early draft.

1. See, e.g., Galen Strawson, *Freedom and Belief* (Oxford: Oxford University Press, 1986); Robert Kane, *The Significance of Free Will* (New York: Oxford University Press, 1996); Robert Kane, "Free Will, Responsibility, and Will-Setting," *Philosophical Topics* 24 (1996): 67–90; Derk Pereboom, *Living Without Free Will* (Cambridge: Cambridge University Press, 2001); and Derk Pereboom, "Determinism al Dente," *Noûs* 29 (1995): 21–45.
2. Marina A. L. Oshana, "Personal Autonomy and Society," *Journal of Social Philosophy* 29 (1998): 81–102; and "The Autonomy Bogeyman," *Journal of Value Inquiry* 35 (2001): 209–226. Joseph Raz also believes that autonomy requires alternative possibilities. See his *The Morality of Freedom* (Oxford: Clarendon Press, 1986).

3. Michael McKenna, "Robustness, Control, and the Demand for Morally Significant Alternatives: Frankfurt Examples with Oodles and Oodles of Alternatives," in Michael McKenna and David Widerker, eds., *Freedom, Responsibility, Agency: Essays on the Importance of Alternative Possibilities* (Aldershot, England: Ashgate, 2003): 201–217.
4. See, e.g., Harry G. Frankfurt, "Alternate Possibilities and Moral Responsibility," *Journal of Philosophy* 66 (1969): 829–839; John Martin Fischer, *The Metaphysics of Free Will* (Cambridge, MA: Blackwell, 1994): chaps. 1–5; Alfred Mele, *Autonomous Agents: From Self-Control to Autonomy* (New York: Oxford University Press, 1995): chaps. 9–10; and Michael J. Zimmerman, "The Moral Significance of Alternate Possibilities," in McKenna and Widerker, eds., *Freedom, Responsibility, and Agency*, 201–213.
5. See Carl Ginet, "In Defense of the Principle of Alternative Possibilities: Why I Don't Find Frankfurt's Argument Convincing," *Philosophical Perspectives* 10 (1996): 403–417; Robert Kane, *The Significance of Free Will*, 142–144; and David Widerker, "Libertarianism and Frankfurt's Attack on the Principle of Alternative Possibilities," *Philosophical Review* 104 (1995): 247–261, and "Libertarian Freedom and the Avoidability of Decisions," *Faith and Philosophy* 12 (1995): 113–118.
6. McKenna, "Robustness, Control, and the Demand for Morally Significant Alternatives," 201.
7. Ibid., 213. See also 206–207.
8. Ibid., 207.
9. Ibid., 208.
10. On this point, see, e.g., Fred Feldman, *Doing the Best We Can* (Dordrecht: D. Reidel, 1986): 46; and Michael J. Zimmerman, *An Essay on Moral Responsibility* (Totowa, NJ: Rowman & Littlefield, 1988): 95–96.
11. McKenna, "Robustness, Control, and the Demand for Morally Significant Alternatives," 209. The notion of being *morally bad* is multiply ambiguous. PSA does not, e.g., discriminate between being overall or intrinsically or instrumentally morally bad. In what follows, I shall assume that it is either the first or the second of these notions that McKenna has in mind. The pertinent examples that invoke this notion can be understood as ones in which "morally bad" refers either to overall moral badness or intrinsic moral badness.
12. Ibid., 210.
13. Ibid.
14. For other examples involving similar psychological capacity or incapacity, see Alfred Mele's *Springs of Action: Understanding Intentional Behavior* (New York: Oxford University Press, 1992): 87–88.
15. See Feldman's *Doing the Best We Can*; and Michael J. Zimmerman's *The Concept of Moral Obligation* (Cambridge: Cambridge University Press, 1996).
16. See Zimmerman's *The Concept of Moral Obligation* and Feldman's "A Simpler Solution to the Paradoxes of Deontic Logic," *Philosophical Perspectives* 4: 309–341, for a discussion of (Prerequisites).
17. On alternatives, see, e.g., Lars Bergstrom, "On the Formulation and Application of Utilitarianism," *Noûs* 10 (1976): 221–244; and his "Utilitarianism

and Alternative Actions," *Noûs* 5 (1971): 237–252. See also Lennart Aqvist, "Improved Formulations of Act Utilitarianism," *Noûs* 3 (1969): 299–323.

18. See my "An Epistemic Dimension of Appraisability," *Philosophy and Phenomenological Research* 57 (1997): 423–444; *Moral Appraisability: Puzzles, Proposals, and Perplexities* (New York: Oxford University Press, 1998): chaps. 8–9; and *Deontic Morality and Control* (Cambridge: Cambridge University Press, 2002). See also Zimmerman, *An Essay on Moral Responsibility*; "The Moral Significance of Alternate Possibilities"; and "A Plea for Accuses," *American Philosophical Quarterly* 34 (1997): 229–243.
19. See my "Control Requirements for Moral Appraisals: An Asymmetry," *Journal of Ethics* 4 (2000): 351–356; and *Deontic Morality and Control.* See also Zimmerman's "The Moral Significance of Alternate Possibilities." Regarding the requirement of alternative possibilities for moral wrongness, a correlate of the "ought" implies "can" principle, **K**, is that if it is (overall and not just prima facie) obligatory for one to refrain from performing an action, then one can refrain from performing that action (i.e., "ought not" implies "can avoid"). Another stock deontic principle (principle **OW**) says that it is (overall) obligatory for one to do something if and only if it is (overall) wrong for one to refrain from doing it. An implicate of this principle is that if it is wrong for one to perform some action, then it is obligatory for one to refrain from performing that action. This implicate, together with the correlate of **K** that "ought not" implies "can avoid," generates the conclusion that if it is wrong for one to perform an action, then one can refrain from performing it.
20. For elaboration, see my "An Epistemic Dimension of Appraisability"; and *Moral Appraisability*, chap. 9.
21. Oshana, "Personal Autonomy and Society," 81.
22. Ibid., 83.
23. Ibid., 94. Oshana cautions that she is "relying on the intuition that we can speak meaningfully about having options for actions, even though we may be undecided about the truth of determinism and the Principle of Alternative Possibilities" ("Personal Autonomy and Society," 102 n. 36).
24. On thoughts on the bearing of global Frankfurt-type cases on whether moral responsibility requires autonomy, see Mele's *Autonomous Agents*, 139–142. For further explorations of the relation between autonomy and moral responsibility, see Oshana's "The Misguided Marriage of Responsibility and Autonomy," *Journal of Ethics* 6 (2002): 261–280.
25. Randolph Clarke uses the label "active control" in "Modest Libertarianism," *Philosophical Perspectives* 14 (2000): 21–45; and in *Libertarian Accounts of Free Will* (New York: Oxford University Press, 2003).
26. See Clarke's "Modest Libertarianism" and "Agent Causation and Event Causation in the Production of Free Action," *Philosophical Topics* 24 (1996): 19–48.
27. See Clarke's "Agent Causation and Event Causation in the Production of Free Action"; and *Libertarian Accounts of Free Will*, chaps. 7–9. Clarke argues that the notion of agent causation is intelligible, but he doubts whether it is

possible for persons to agent-cause events (see his *Libertarian Accounts of Free Will*, chap. 10).

28. Clarke, *Libertarian Accounts of Free Will*, chap. 9.
29. See Mele's *Autonomous Agents*, 211. See also Kane's *The Significance of Free Will*, 72–73.
30. Clarke, *Libertarian Accounts of Free Will*, chap. 6.
31. Clarke, in correspondence, suggested this sort of response to me.

11

Freedom within Reason

Susan Wolf

Perhaps no problem in philosophy is easier to motivate than the problem of free will, for it is not just philosophers occupied with academic puzzles but thoughtful people of all sorts who can be struck and upset by the thought that the direction of their lives might be determined by things wholly beyond their control. In earlier times, this thought was perhaps chiefly connected with the contemplation of the idea of divine predestination. Today, the worry that there is no such thing as free will might as easily arise from other sources. Free will seems to be threatened not only by what may be called divine determinism, but also by psychological determinism – that is, by the view of human psychology that holds that one's interests and beliefs and values, and consequently one's decisions for action, are wholly a product of one's heredity and environment. Moreover, the very reality of our status as valuing, deliberating agents whose thoughts, desires, and wills are effective in guiding our behavior can be called into question by the scientific perspective that views human beings as wholly physical creatures whose behavior, like the behavior of all other natural objects, can be completely explained in terms of the interaction of atomic or subatomic particles.

I have said that we are "upset" by the thought that we may not have free will. But, to quote *Mad Magazine*, "Why worry?" What difference does it make if we lack free will? Because people differ in the aspects of the free-will problem that concern them and because philosophical discussions of this issue vary accordingly, it is best to be explicit about the specific worries one cares to address. Some people, I think, are shaken up primarily because in ordinary day-to-day life we assume that we do have free will, and the recognition that we might be wrong about this would imply that we are living an illusion. That is, in day-to-day life we see ourselves – at least in good circumstances of psychic health and political liberty – as "calling the shots" about our own lives, as making our own decisions about where, and how, and with whom to live, as choosing whether to eat a peach, go to Italy, rob a bank, become a hairdresser. If we lack free will, it means we are not calling the shots – our lives are in the hands, rather, of God or physics or the past, and reflection on this makes us feel like fools, duped by superficial appearances. Others are less concerned about being duped than about the lack of freedom itself. They fear the absence of power and of ultimate control. If their lives or their individual acts are not theirs to create in whatever image they choose, this seems to rob their lives of significance, their acts of any meaning. My own concern, somewhat more specific than this, has to do with issues of responsibility. Among the things that we feel to be licensed by the ordinary assumption that we are in control of our lives and our acts is the appropriateness of holding ourselves and each other responsible for how we live and what we do. We blame, resent, feel indignant toward those who act in ways they ought not to; we praise, admire, feel grateful to those who act well . . . or better than the rest of us. We form these attitudes, at least so it appears, only on the assumption that those who acted badly could have acted better, that those who acted especially well did not have to do what they did. Our attitudes and affections rest on the assumption that what people do expresses and reveals qualities that are especially and deeply attributable to them. If free will is an illusion and we are not calling the shots, then these attitudes appear to be inappropriate and unjustifiable, and so do the practices of reward and punishment, of credit- and discredit-giving that reflect and express these attitudes. To imagine a world without these attitudes and the practices related to them is to imagine an extraordinarily different world, a world much colder, much bleaker, much less human. Were we thoroughly and consistently to eradicate from our lives all traces of the assumption that we are responsible beings, we would have to see ourselves as well as other people not as persons but as objects. Such a feat might well be impossible to achieve. At any rate, most of us would not want to achieve it. So we have reason to hope that the world is not such as to make that perspective the only rational option. We have reason to hope, that is, that the metaphysical truth about the world and our relation to it is not such as to imply that we are not responsible beings.

What *does* the world imply about our status as responsible beings? This is the fifty million dollar question – not only because there may be relevant facts about the world that are beyond our grasp, but because our understanding of the concept of responsibility is so murky as to leave it unclear what facts about the world would be relevant. It is the latter aspect of the question to which philosophers may hope to provide illumination and with which I will be concerned here.

Though we begin with a murky and possibly confused understanding of the concept of responsibility, we tend to have plenty of intuitions about who is and isn't responsible in individual cases. Indeed, reflection on individual cases and the implications that follow from them is one of the most common paths to the philosophical worries about freedom and responsibility that I have been discussing. Although we go through life with the background assumption that, barring special circumstances, we – that is, adult human beings of normal intelligence and emotional stability – are responsible for what we do, reflection on the incidents and circumstances in which we withdraw our attributions of responsibility leads to puzzlement about whether and, if so, how any of us can ever be responsible for anything at all.

Imagine, for example, that while you are standing in a hallway, minding your own business, someone walking by jostles you or steps on your foot, without even stopping to apologize. Other things being equal, you are apt to blame and resent him for his behavior – you hold him responsible for his behavior, and his behavior was bad. But you are apt to withdraw your blame and your attribution of responsibility if you subsequently discover that the man was pushed into you or unwittingly hypnotized by someone else. Similarly, you will withdraw your resentment if you should learn that the man had been in the midst of an epileptic seizure or a hallucinatory episode in which you appeared to him as someone or something else.[1]

Why do we hold people responsible in ordinary circumstances but not in the special sorts of cases just described? A first attempt to articulate the difference might suggest that, in ordinary circumstances, we assume that a person's actions or behavior *originates* in the person himself; he *initiates* the chain of events; the action is *up to him.* But when a person is pushed or hypnotized, he is not the initiator but rather a link in a chain. To be sure, he is the one who bumps into you, but there is something else, behind him, as it were, causing him or compelling him to do so. Importantly, it is irrelevant to the issue of his responsibility whether the force behind him takes the form of another human or otherwise conscious agent. A wind, a seizure, or a psychotic delusion can as easily take the control of his movements out of his hands or his mind.

So it seems that we hold an agent responsible for an action when, and only when, his actions originate from within himself, when nothing beyond or behind his self is forcing him to act as he does. I shall use the word "autonomy" to refer to this condition. That is, I shall say that a person is autonomous when, and only when, his actions are governed by his self, and there is nothing behind or beyond his self, making it govern actions the way he does.[2] The Autonomy View of responsibility, then, is the view that beings are responsible just insofar as they are autonomous. If their actions are governed by things external to their selves or if their selves are themselves governed by things external to them, then they are not responsible for the actions that ensue.

The Autonomy View seems to me the most natural and intuitive view of what responsibility requires. As I have suggested, it seems to follow directly from a first attempt to articulate what lies behind our individual intuitive judgments about responsibility. But the Autonomy View is problematic for at least two reasons.

The first is that if responsibility does require autonomy, it is questionable whether any of us is ever responsible for anything. For autonomy requires that our actions be governed by our selves and that our selves not be governed by anything beyond our control. Now, it is undeniable that many of our actions are governed by our selves – that is, they result from our own decisions and choices. Moreover, it is fairly rare that these decisions and choices are overtly caused or determined by such obviously external forces as a gunman or a hypnotist or the wind or a seizure. But neither do our choices or decisions or selves arise spontaneously out of nothing. Though the factors that shape who we are and what we value, and consequently that shape how we respond to the circumstances that confront us, are rarely so easy to point to as they are in the examples of what I called "special circumstances," it is plausible that such factors are always operative nonetheless, calling into doubt the assumption that even the strongest candidates for autonomous action really are as autonomous as they appear.

The second problem with the autonomy view is perhaps more purely philosophical. It is that even if autonomous action is possible, even if we are, most or all of the time, autonomous agents, it remains disturbingly opaque why or how this should make us responsible agents. That is, it seems easy enough to grasp why nonautonomous agents might *not* be responsible for what they do. If their actions are governed by their selves, but their selves are governed by something outside their control, then it is not really they who are calling the shots; they are not in ultimate control.

But if being autonomous means that instead of one's self being a product of external forces, one's self is a spontaneous, undetermined entity, it is hard to see why one should be any more responsible for the decisions, choices, and actions that flow out of *that.* One is in no more control of a self that has arisen out of nothing than one is if one's self has arisen out of something. An undetermined self seems no more responsible than a determined self.

In light of the serious difficulties faced by the Autonomy View, some philosophers have taken a different approach. Noting that autonomy appears at once impossible and of uncertain value in the vindication of our sense of ourselves as responsible agents, they have tried to develop an account of responsibility for which autonomy is not required. These philosophers argue that the intuitions and the reasoning that lead us to think that determinism of any sort is incompatible with free will is confused and mistaken. Rather, they say, the conditions that need to be satisfied in order for us to be generally responsible are ones that we have good reason to think are commonly met.

We may organize our sense of the problem of free will (understood in terms of its connection to responsibility) around what I shall call "the dilemma of autonomy." That is, beginning with the strong appearance that free will and responsibility require autonomy, we may try to attack or resolve the problem along one of two paths. On the one hand, we may hold fast to the appearance and overcome the problems with the Autonomy View to which I have already referred. Alternatively, we may tackle the appearance, trying at once to break the tendency to see freedom as involving independence from all external causes and to provide a positive account of what freedom does involve, given that it doesn't involve that. Because supporters of the Autonomy View typically regard their position as committed to the incompatibility of free will with any sort of determinism, they are often labeled "incompatibilists" in academic philosophy; supporters of the alternate approach typically believe free will to be compatible with at least some forms of determinism, and so they are called compatibilists.

My own view, which I shall be sketching below, falls strictly in the second category – it holds that autonomy is not necessary for the kind of freedom required by responsibility. However, the positive account of freedom and responsibility I endorse is so different from what most people in this category take to be sufficient that few philosophers who have identified themselves with the compatibilist tradition show much sympathy for my view. (Regrettably, philosophers in the incompatibilist tradition show little sympathy for my view as well. My only hope is that, if the criticisms from both directions balance equally, this will count as a point in favor of my view to those who are so far uncommitted to one tradition or the other.)

I have already described the problem confronted by the Autonomy View. The difficulties encountered by nonautonomous views will present themselves in due course. Specifically, I shall present what seems to me the most compelling version of a nonautonomous account of free will (my own account excluded) in a way that I hope will bring out both the insights and the problems that I believe are endemic to such accounts.

I have mentioned that one of the tasks confronting a proponent of a nonautonomous view is that of showing that the reasoning that leads us to think responsibility requires autonomy is mistaken. To see how this is done, let us return to our example of the various ways in which special circumstances lead us to exempt people from responsibility and blame. Earlier, reflecting on the case of the person who had been pushed or hypnotized or seized by epilepsy or delusions, I offered the suggestion that such a person was not responsible because, although he was the one who bumped into you, his behavior was ultimately determined by someone or something that was ultimately beyond his control. The problem we immediately confronted, however, was that this more general description could arguably be applied to all human agents, not just to those who are unusually beset by domineering people or oppressive circumstances.

Taking a more fine-grained approach to these examples, however, we may find a somewhat less general description that locates the source of their unfreedom in something that distinguishes their situations from ours: Specifically, a difference between a person who is pushed and someone who bumps into another person intentionally is that in the latter case but not in the former the person's behavior is determined by his will. Hypnotism is not quite like being pushed, for the hypnotist typically works *on* the will rather than circumvents it. But of the person acting under hypnosis, we can say that, though he moves according to his will, his will is not determined by his own desires.

These reflections suggest an account of freedom much more moderate in its requirements than the autonomy view: namely, one according to which a person is free and responsible for his behavior when, and only when, his behavior can be governed by his will and his will can be governed by his desires. Note that this account of freedom would exclude the victims of physical force and hypnosis (and also the victims of some sorts of mental and physical disorders), without excluding us. For most of us, most of the time, can and do act as we choose – we decide to walk or stand, to eat or refrain from eating, to attend a lecture or go to the movies. Moreover, we decide what to do on the basis of our desires – *our* desires and not the desires of a hypnotist or gunman.

As an account of freedom and responsibility, the idea that freedom consists in the ability to do what one wants goes back at least as far as the eighteenth-century philosopher David Hume. But in the form so far presented, it suffers from being both too broad and too vague. It is too broad because it can apply to lower animals and young children as easily as it can apply to adults. An unharnessed horse in an unfenced field may be able to do what it wants to do, and so perhaps can a one-year-old with a lenient, perhaps too lenient, caretaker. Though there is indeed a sense in which it is natural and appropriate to call such individuals free, this is not the kind of freedom that licenses us to hold the agents in question responsible for their actions.

The account is too vague because it does not differentiate between relevantly different desires. There are many desires that we would prefer to be without – a desire for nicotine or even chocolate, a desire to sleep with one's best friend's spouse, or, to borrow an example from Gary Watson, to smash one's opponent's face with a squash racquet after suffering an ignominious defeat.[3] Sometimes such desires are a result of circumstances beyond the agent's control, and sometimes they are so irresistibly powerful as to give the agent no choice but to try to satisfy them. (Consider, for example, the heroin addict or the compulsive handwasher.) Taken literally, such cases are ones in which the agent acts on the basis of desires he has. But in another sense, the agent does not want to act on those desires – he does not even want to have those desires and would resist them if he could. According to the nonautonomous account of freedom and responsibility I've offered, a person is free whenever he acts on the basis of his desires. But these examples suggest that there are cases in which a person can be overwhelmed *by* his desires. The mere fact that one acts according to one's will and one wills according to one's desires, then, does not seem sufficient to guarantee the freedom necessary for responsibility.

In recent years, a number of philosophers have developed more sophisticated versions of the account just described in ways that rid that account of the difficulties just mentioned. Specifically, they have called attention to the complexity of the motivational systems of mature human beings, noting particularly that not all of our desires, interests, and dispositions are on the same level.[4] Some of our desires, as we have seen, are desires we would just as soon be without. We find them in us – whether as a result of biology or conditioning – but we do not value them or identify with them. Other desires, or, more generally, other features of our character, we cherish – we claim them for our own, whether we have cultivated them by design or approved them after we had come to see them as parts of us, and we would go to considerable length, not just to satisfy these desires, but to preserve them. These latter desires may be referred to as comprising our systems of *value*. These are what we think of as constituting our deepest selves.

In light of the distinction between values and other "mere" desires, or between one's whole, partly superficial, partly alienated self and one's deeper or real self, we can improve on the earlier proposal to understand freedom in terms of the ability to do what one wants. The kind of freedom necessary for responsibility, it might be suggested, is the freedom to do what one *really* wants – that is, the freedom to do what one's core, deep, or real self wants, which may be different from what one's strongest desires would urge upon one. To put it another way, the freedom necessary for responsibility on this account consists in the ability not just to behave in accordance with one's will and to will in accord with one's desires, but more specifically in the ability to govern one's will (and so one's actions) in accordance with the specific set of desires that constitute one's system of values.

In my book, I referred to this view as the Real Self View.[5] It has much to commend it – among other things, that it explains in a satisfying way not just why people are exempted from responsibility in the special circumstances that were on our initial list, but also why lower animals and young children are not suitable candidates for responsibility. For lower animals and young children do not yet have real selves – unlike mature human beings, their desires are all on one level, and they seem fairly pictured as tossed around by whatever desires have been given to them.

Despite the appeal of the Real Self View, however, it has a serious flaw. What makes the Real Self View a distinctively nonautonomous account of free will is its insistence that one's status as a free and responsible being lies not in whether but in how one's actions are determined. Specifically, freedom and responsibility are held to depend solely on whether one's behavior can be governed by the dictates of one's real self – never mind where one's real self came from or why it came to dictate the behavior that it does. But it is not at all clear that we should never mind where one's real self comes from in evaluating one's status as a free and responsible agent.

An example will bring the problem more sharply into focus. Consider someone who was raised in an unusually sheltered environment, by authoritarian albeit loving parents, in a community in which open debate and reflection are discouraged. As an adult, the man has as complex a psychology as most, with a system of values as well as other mere desires. But because the community and the family in which he was raised are deeply racist, he also grows up to be a racist, and his racism is reflected in his values. We may assume that he is aware of his racist values and approves of them. They are among his values, and, insofar as his actions exhibit racism or even directly promote it, he happily claims responsibility for them. He regards them as expressions of his real self.

In fact, the man's racist values *are* part of his real self. For one's real self just is one's collection of values, of features with which one identifies and approves – that is how the notion of a real self was defined. Despite this, however, it seems to me highly questionable that the man is responsible – and thus blameworthy – for his racist activities. For although these activities are governed by his values, his life – at least so I am imagining – had no room in it for questioning, for coming to see the reasons why racism is wrong. He didn't have a chance to not be a racist, and so it seems unfair to blame him for acting out and expressing a racism he had no choice but to have. Indeed, it seems to me that this case is not significantly relevantly different from the case of the child or even the compulsive handwasher. For, although the man himself sees his racism in a different light from the way the child sees his urges or the handwasher his compulsion – the racist I am imagining is proud of his racism and wishes to claim responsibility for it – the fact is that he is just as "tossed around" with respect to his racism as the others are by their desires. He, like these others, is helplessly moved to act in accordance with a desire that he did not choose to acquire.

Obviously, my characterization of the racist is structurally similar to stories we might tell of others who, due to the values of their communities, could not but be Nazis or sexists or snobs. Only slightly less obvious is its similarity to stories of victims of different sorts of deprived childhoods, people who, due to abuse or neglect or exposure to nothing but violent, uncaring people, inevitably develop real selves that care little for human life and love and much for physical power or wealth.

In general terms, the case of the racist exemplifies those cases in which an agent's behavior is determined by the agent's values (or real self), but the agent's values (real self) are themselves inescapably determined by forces external to the agent's control. The flaw in the Real Self View is that it takes such cases to be unproblematic cases of responsible behavior. Many people share my view that these may not be cases of responsible behavior at all. Even if they are cases of responsible behavior, we must be given some explanation of why they are – of why an agent is more responsible for actions that are governable by his values than he is for actions that are governed by his nonvalued desires, if his values are no more within his control and are no more products of his choice than are the mere desires for which he is recognized not to be responsible.

Thus, I conclude that the Real Self View is unsatisfactory. What is particularly troublesome, however, is that the objection that led to this conclusion seems to force us straight back to the Autonomy View, a view that we have seen is riddled with problems of its own. If the racist, the Nazi, the victim of the deprived childhood are not responsible for their behavior because their behavior is governed by values that are shaped by forces beyond their control, aren't we all deprived responsibility on the same grounds? After all, we are as much a product of our cultures as these individuals are of theirs. Is there any way to solve the problem of the Real Self View without returning to the problems of the Autonomy View? I think that there is – that there is a way between the Scylla and Charybdis of the traditional responses to the problem of free will and responsibility.

To see the way out, it is useful to notice a feature common to the cases that pose a problem for the Real Self View. The cases of the racist, the Nazi, and the victim of the deprived childhood are all cases of people whose behavior and whose values are faulty, deficient, bad. They are cases of people, who, were they responsible for their actions, would thereby be blameworthy. Reflecting on the supposition that they could not help but have those values, then, inclines us to exempt them not just of responsibility, but of blame.

If we turn our attention to cases of good action and admirable behavior, however, we find somewhat different intuitions applying to these cases. Consider for a moment, not the racist or the Nazi, but an abolitionist or a member of the French Resistance or the woman in my former home city who single-handedly set up soup kitchens and shelters for Baltimore's homeless. When we reflect on the sources of these people's values or of their courage and commitment and integrity, we are not so concerned or upset by the thought that they are products of their environments. Perhaps one of our heroes was especially moved by a parent, another by a teacher or a neighbor or a priest. Perhaps the trauma of losing a sibling at an early age, witnessing a lynch mob, or battling cancer and surviving was instrumental in the development of their dedication to relieve suffering or to make the world a better place. Of course, these people didn't choose to have wise and inspiring role models. They couldn't help but experience or witness the tragedies that molded their characters. But it seems crazy that this should be a reason to withhold the praise or credit that we initially judge them to deserve.

When we focus on these positive cases, it seems bizarre to regard it as a condition of responsibility that the values on which one acts be formed independently of one's environment – what better way can there be to form one's values than to listen to and observe and reflect on the views of the people one encounters and on the experiences one has?

Focusing on cases of good-acting agents suggests that it is no obstacle to responsibility that one acts on values that themselves have been formed by forces external to the agent's control. Reflecting on bad-acting agents, however, seemed to lead us to the opposite conclusion. Are these intuitions simply contradictory, or is there a relevant distinction between these sets of cases that can make sense of our different attitudes?

Let me describe one proposal that I believe to be mistaken before offering the one that I endorse.

It might be noted that when we look at cases of bad-acting agents, our tendency to exempt them from responsibility (and thus from blame) rests heavily on our imagining cases in which it is posited that the agent could not but have become vicious or disturbed. Their environments (or, as it may be, their physiologies) leave them no choice whatsoever; their characters and consequent behaviors are inevitable, irresistible, determined absolutely by forces beyond their control. When we understand similar cases somewhat differently – noting perhaps that not all Germans in the 1930s approved of the Nazis or that not all ghetto children become criminals, we are less likely to exempt the individuals in question from blame.

When we reflect upon the good-acting agents we do not similarly focus on the narrowness of their options. Even when one traces a person's courage or altruism to a specific influence or source, we are not apt to think of it as an overpowering influence, one that could not have been resisted. One might suspect, then, that we are not comparing truly analogous pairs of cases: We exempt the bad-acting agent from responsibility, one might suppose, because we think he was shaped absolutely and irresistibly by forces beyond his control. We do not exempt the good-acting agent because we covertly, perhaps even unconsciously, imagine the agent as one who was encouraged by good influences, but who was not compelled to become good. Rather, we assume that the decision to accept these influences was more truly up to him.

This suggestion would effectively bring us back to the Autonomy View. For it contains the idea that however much an agent is shaped by physical or cultural influences, responsibility requires that the agent must ultimately decide whether to submit to these influences and that this decision must be in the hands of a self even deeper than the real self of the Real Self View, a self independent of all external influences.

I believe this suggestion is mistaken. There is no such ultrareal or superdeep self, independent of all external influences, arising from nothing; and even if there were, it is hard to see why a being with such a self would be any more responsible than a being without it. But the attractions of this view can be analyzed as a misplaced attempt to put one's finger on a different view.

This other view I call the Reason View. The title of this chapter (and my book) comes from it. According to this view, the relevant difference between the good-acting agents, shaped, say, by inspiring role models, whom we view as responsible and praiseworthy, and the bad-acting agents, shaped, say, by horrible role models or by the absence of role models or by brutal and impoverished upbringing, whom we exempt from responsibility and blame, is that the former have been led through reason, perception, good sense, and good data to adopt their values and live by them, while the latter have been shaped in ways that have kept reason and truth out.

In other words, I think that there is something to the image of the good and praiseworthy person as one who is not merely passively molded by good influences but who actively chooses and affirms them. But I believe that this image is misidentified when it is thought to involve an autonomous metaphysically independent chooser. What matters rather is that the agent's embrace of these good values be an expression of her understanding that they are good, of her appreciation, that is, of the reasons that make these values preferable to others. It is by being rationally persuaded that these values are good ones that the agent makes them her own in a way for which she is responsible. But there is no analogous story to be told of the agent who acquires bad values from his culture. We cannot say that the racist is responsible for his racism if it results from his understanding of what is good about racism – for there *is* nothing good about racism for him to understand. Nor can we say that the racist is responsible for his racism if it results from his understanding about what is bad about racism – for no sane person chooses values because he understands them to be bad.

Insofar as a person is shaped by his culture to adopt bad values, then, it is in the nature of the case that he is shaped by forces of unreason. Our tendency to excuse those whom we think could not help but develop bad values or perverse ideals, then, is due to our seeing them as having been pushed blindly along a path that, through no fault of their own, they could not recognize as undesirable or wrong. Their vision was inescapably distorted, their power to question or simply to see was helplessly limited or blocked. Those whom we think are responsible for developing good values may be no less strongly influenced by their backgrounds than the people with bad values whom we exempt from blame, but the development of their values invoked and made use of, rather than interfered with, these agents' powers of reason and perception. If their values are formed, or revised or affirmed, in accordance with their reason and perception, then they have exercised all the powers of self-determination it is sensible to want, or at least all the powers of self-determination that our status as responsible agents requires.

We are attracted by the view that responsibility requires autonomy – that it requires, in other words, the ability to resist all external forces, the power to choose either one's own character or one's acts independently of anything outside one's control because we think of "external forces" as inimical to our powers as agents. "External forces" suggests violence, or at least something brute and blind; things or circumstances "beyond one's control" suggest accidents or hardships one would have preferred to avoid. But in fact, of course, education is as external a force as indoctrination, and exposure to intelligent discussion of new ideas is as little within one's control as exposure to bullets. In other words, the sources of our freedom are as external as are the forces that inhibit and interfere with it. Realizing this should lead us to see that what is required for freedom and responsibility is not independence from external forces. It is not, in other words, the metaphysical property of autonomy. Rather, we require independence from specifically bad forces in the world – forces that either interfere with or deprive us of the ability to act on our values or disrupt and prevent us from forming our values in the light of reason and truth. Moreover, we are in other respects positively dependent on the world for our freedom and responsibility – for we are dependent on the world, both on our biology and on our environment, for giving us both the abilities and the opportunities to transcend the status of lower animals and young children and become responsible agents.

According to the Reason View, then, the freedom necessary for responsibility is a freedom within reason. This is more freedom than is required by the Real Self View – for it requires that the responsible agent not only be free to govern her actions in accordance with her values, but that she be free to form or revise her values (or, if you like, to revise her Real Self) in accordance with what reason and truth would suggest. It is less freedom than is required by the Autonomy View – for it neither requires nor values an agent's freedom from those aspects of the world that provide us with the faculties of thought and perception and the data on which these faculties can operate to yield an appreciation of what the world is and can be like.

Before closing, let me make a few remarks that may prevent some misunderstandings.

The development of my view about responsibility laid stress on a disanalogy between good-acting and bad-acting agents. As we have seen, my view accepts the intuition that if a bad-acting agent "never had a chance" to do or to want to do something better than what he does, then he is not fairly held responsible and blameworthy for his acting badly. At the same time, I have argued that a good-acting agent, whose decision to align herself with good values is as strongly a product of her background as the former agent's choices are a consequence of his, may nonetheless deserve credit for her behavior. In audiences to whom I have presented my view in other forms before, this asymmetry has been the source of both misinterpretation and criticism.

Specifically, some people have understood my view to be too free to give praise – to imply, in particular, that anyone who acts well and does so on the basis of values she has gained from her culture or her upbringing can fairly be held responsible and praiseworthy for it. Still more have been concerned with the thought that my view automatically excuses virtually all criminals and exempts from blame anyone whose wrongful behavior can be traced to bad influences in his culture or upbringing. But these inferences rest on a misunderstanding.

Although I believe that there is an important disanalogy between good-acting agents and bad-acting agents, the disanalogy is quite specific: It is that a good-acting agent may have been irresistibly drawn to accept good values as a result of the exercise of good reason, whereas this can never be said of the agent who acts in a blameworthy way. It may be precisely because a person holds the values of her society up to reflection and questioning that she has no choice but ultimately to affirm (or reject) them. But if a man is irresistibly led to affirm bad values, this can only be because he was deprived of the ability to appreciate the reasons why those values are bad. This stress on the ability to appreciate reasons – reasons why one set of values deserves affirmation, while another set ought to be reconsidered and revised – is all-important. It is the possession or lack of this ability, and not the desirable or undesirable nature of the acts or the values themselves, that, on my account, makes the difference between responsible and nonresponsible agency.

Thus, according to the Reason View, a person who does the right thing for the wrong reasons deserves no more praise than a person who doesn't do the right thing at all. Moreover, a person who does the right thing on the basis of values she doesn't understand (a person whose acceptance of good values, in other words, is as blind and unreasoned as the acceptance of the racist's values in our earlier example) is as little responsible for what she does as those whose paths lead to more objectionable behavior.

Moreover, a person who does the wrong thing, though it must be for bad reasons, is not necessarily exempt from responsibility and blame. It is crucial to establish whether the person in question had reasons to act better available to him. In the cases I dwelt on, we imagined people who could not but have acquired bad values or false beliefs and so could not but have made bad decisions on the basis of them. But it is a real and difficult question how often such cases occur. If a person acts badly despite his ability to appreciate the reasons for acting better, then he is fully responsible and blameworthy for his choice. If, therefore, as some people believe, almost anyone is able to tell good values from bad (whatever her cultural or subcultural background), then almost anyone will be blameworthy should she choose a bad path.

Understanding the Reason View in more detail and seeing how it is to be applied in practice may quell some of the doubts that a cruder understanding of the view may call to mind. But it will not quell all of them. Even if one doesn't overestimate the practical significance of the Reason View's acknowledged disanalogy between good and bad, one may find the associated asymmetry between the conditions of praise and blame conceptually disconcerting. The Reason View admits that two people who are equally products of their respective heredities and environments may nonetheless not be equally responsible agents. And this may seem at once unfair and rationally arbitrary. There is something powerfully compelling about the thought that insofar as we are all products of our environments or of our physiologies or our genes, then we should all be in the same boat with respect to our status as responsible agents. Indeed, this thought, though rejected by the Reason View, is affirmed by both of its otherwise contrasting opponents. The Autonomy View insists that no responsible agent can be purely a product of external forces, while the Real Self View regards such external determinism as nowhere posing a threat.

That the Reason View takes issue with both its traditional alternatives with respect to this question marks what may be its most distinctive and controversial feature. Specifically, it marks the fact that according to the Reason View, the problem of free will and responsibility is not as purely nor as fundamentally a metaphysical problem as it has traditionally seemed to be. Proponents of the Autonomy View have felt that responsible agents need to be metaphysically distinctive from the rest of the world – they have felt that responsibility requires contracausal powers, the ability to stand back from the physical and psychological forces in the world, to be removed from the world at the same time as being able to act upon it. Proponents of the Real Self View have argued that no such special powers are necessary, that, to the contrary, the powers possessed by normal mature human agents, such as the power to form values and to deliberate and act in accordance with them, are sufficient for responsibility. Both views have taken the question at least to be "How much metaphysical power is necessary?" How free from external forces does a responsible agent have to be?

According to the Reason View, however, the difference between responsible and nonresponsible agents is not fundamentally metaphysical – it is normative. What we need in order to be responsible is not the power to form and revise our values independently of the world, but rather the power to form and revise our values well rather than badly, in light of an understanding of the world and of what is important and worthwhile in it. The freedom needed for responsibility involves the freedom to see things aright – the freedom, if you will, to appreciate the True and the Good.

There is no privileged perspective from which one can pronounce whether or to what extent we have this freedom. There can be no guarantee that one does, or that one can, see things aright, that one has, as it were, mentally grasped the True and the Good. And so, if the Reason View is right, there can be no guarantee that we are fully and in every respect free and responsible agents. At the same time, I see no reason to doubt that these powers are at least partly open to us. The ability to understand and appreciate the world poses no obvious conflict with our status as metaphysically ordinary parts of the physical universe, as products both of physics and the past.

The Reason View, then, may be thought to be more pessimistic than some views that take our status as free and responsible agents as more or less guaranteed. But it is less pessimistic than others, according to which the conditions of responsibility are so strong as to be wildly unlikely, or impossible, or even incoherent. Moreover, the Reason View offers the hope that insofar as we are not free, we can do something about it. For, on this view, Reason, broadly construed to include powers of imagination and perception as well as logical thought, opens the path to freedom. The more we are able to understand and correctly and sensitively evaluate our world, the more responsible we are able to be in acting within and upon it. Insofar as we want to promote freedom and responsibility, then, both across the population and within ourselves, we can do so by promoting as well as by exercising faculties of reason, perception, and reflection, by encouraging as well as by cultivating open and active minds and attitudes of alertness and sensitivity to the world. These are what we need if we are to have the freedom and the ability to see things aright. If we have this freedom and the associated freedom to form our values accordingly, and if in addition we have the freedom to govern our actions in accordance with the values we form, then we have all the freedom that responsibility requires.

Notes

1. A similar example is found in P. F. Strawson, "Freedom and Resentment," *Proceedings of the British Academy* 48 (1962): 1–25. This chapter is much indebted to that article.
2. This metaphysical use of the term "autonomy" derives from Immanuel Kant. It is an important question, which I shall not pursue here, how this relates to the use of the term in political theory.
3. Gary Watson, "Free Agency," *Journal of Philosophy* 72 (1975): 205–220.
4. See, e.g., Harry Frankfurt, "Freedom of the Will and the Concept of a Person," *Journal of Philosophy* 68 (1971): 5–20; and Watson, "Free Agency."
5. Susan Wolf, *Freedom within Reason* (New York: Oxford University Press, 1990).

PART III

THE EXPANDING ROLE OF PERSONAL AUTONOMY

12

Procedural Autonomy and Liberal Legitimacy

John Christman

A crucial issue in discussions of the nature of individual autonomy concerns whether a person can be properly called autonomous if her value commitments contain (or fail to contain) certain substantive ideals, that is, whether "autonomy" can be conceptualized without reference to such ideals. If not, the question is whether such a "content-neutral" or "procedural" conception of autonomy – one which is defined without including substantive values to which the autonomous person must be committed – will suffice in the theoretical and practical settings in which we want the concept to operate. At the same time, debates over the acceptability and foundations of liberalism have included protracted discussions about whether and how state neutrality can be maintained in the principles and mode of justification of liberal institutions. Debates about public reason, for example, have pitted perfectionists against proceduralists in asking whether it is plausible to expect participants to bracket reference to substantive, comprehensive values in affirming the basic framework of justice, as political liberalism demands.[1] That is, can the processes of public reason that provide the grounds of legitimacy for liberal justice be fashioned in ways that do not rely upon particular substantive values in their architecture.

These debates are clearly isomorphic in an interesting way and speak to questions of the nature of commitment, obligation, and independence. In this chapter, I want to consider certain aspects of these debates and to explore this parallelism. In both cases, I think, the question revolves around how autonomy is meant to function in our moral and political vocabulary. It surrounds the question of whether, in particular, autonomy is meant to *neutrally* pick out the conditions of independent agency around which broadly applicable political principles are built (and meant to apply across the full terrain of pluralistic value systems) or whether autonomy-based liberalism merely presents one ideal among others grounding a particular sectarian political morality. As one can see, these questions go to the heart of the foundations and scope of the modernist liberal project.

Because such issues extend beyond the scope of a single chapter (not to mention the particular powers of its author), I want only to make some selective observations about these debates. I will first look at the concept of autonomy and the disagreements in some of the recent literature concerning whether the concept should be seen in a purely proceduralist light or not. I will then turn to arguments about liberalism and the role of public reason in the legitimation of liberal principles. I will argue (albeit in a piecemeal manner) that insofar as autonomy is meant to serve as the "marker" of citizenship for institutions of the liberal state, then it ought to be construed procedurally rather than as containing substantive value requirements.

I. THE CONCEPT OF AUTONOMY

Autonomy is meant to manifest self-government, the ability of the person to guide her life from her own perspective, rather than be manipulated by others or be forced into a particular path by surreptitious or irresistible forces.[2] In the recent philosophical literature, autonomy has been conceived as embodying a variety of conditions, which I would group under the following headings: cognitive (and normative) *competence*, on the one hand – rationality, self-control, freedom from psychosis and other pathologies, and the like – and the condition of *authenticity*, on the other hand. This latter often includes the requirement of critical self-reflection, either actual or hypothetical, on the factor relative to which the person is autonomous. In standard hierarchical accounts, autonomy obtains when the person engages in (or has the capacity to engage in) second-order reflection on first-order desires and identify with the latter, in some sense of "identify."

Competence conditions for autonomy are those, such as rationality and other sorts of decision-making competence, that indicate that the agent is able to function adequately in judgments and choice. An autonomous agent must be at least minimally rational in the sense of having a belief and desire set that does not contain manifest inconsistencies. Manifest inconsistencies are those that would involve manifest conflicts among beliefs (or values, etc.) if brought to consciousness. A related requirement is that the agent not suffer from self-deception: The autonomous person cannot be under the influence of desires or motives that are part of mere "cover stories" for other, incompatible and more deeply held, desires and motives.[3]

Authenticity conditions, on the other hand, go beyond this to pick out the requirement that the desires and motives that move an agent to action are, in some sense, her true, authentic desires and motives. Such conditions capture the requirement that autonomous agents act on their own, rather than from artificial, external, or manipulated motives. Authenticity of characteristics (desires, values, and the like) is usually cashed out in terms of the capacity for self-reflection: the ability to subject particular aspects of oneself to critical scrutiny and for that scrutiny not to result in internal division and conflict. Also, as I have argued elsewhere, autonomy must be seen in light of a person's history – the various conditions that have gone into the shaping of her present character.[4] Moreover, the reflection required of autonomous agents must be piecemeal, requiring that agents reflect on particular aspects of their character without ever presupposing the ability to look at oneself from a completely disembodied perspective. Finally, such reflection should be hypothetical, in that few of us have reflected on all those aspects of ourselves that, nevertheless, are thoroughly authentic and freely formed.

If such piecemeal reflection in light of one's history were to take place or has taken place, the person is autonomous only if she is not deeply *alienated* from the characteristic in question. To be alienated from some aspect of oneself is to experience strong negative affect relative to that characteristic – to disapprove in some manner – and to resist whatever motivational force it may have (as with a desire, for example). If I reflect on some addiction that I have – one that is not authentic in this sense – I view it as distanced from me, as something about which I feel regret or dismay and that is less than fully motivating (relative to nonalienated desires).[5]

This condition of nonalienation is suggested here as a replacement for the condition of "identification" that other theorists have defended.[6] On some models, the autonomous person is one who, upon reflection, identifies with her desires and values. It has been pointed out, however, that identification is an implausible condition for autonomy: In one sense, it is too weak a requirement because many *in*authentic aspects of myself are ones that I, regrettably, identify with in the sense that I must admit they are, in fact, *me* (my addictions for example); in another sense of identify, however, the requirement is too strong, in that I will not identify with many of my own imperfections (authentic though they may be) in the sense that I don't approve of them all told.[7]

Nonalienation, however, is a less stringent condition, but it is one that captures the intuition that a person who, upon reflection, feels no affinity with certain aspects of herself, wants to change or, if that is not feasible, distance herself from them and feels a diluted sense of motivation relative to them is not autonomous. Therefore, a person is not autonomous relative to those aspects of herself that would produce such feelings of alienation were she to reflect on them in light of how they came about. Moreover, nonalienation adds an affective element to autonomy, in contrast to the picture of the disengaged cognizer characteristic of traditional views.

Finally, the reflective endorsement of our various desires and character traits constitutive of autonomy must be "effective" in a substantive sense. That is, the hypothetical self-endorsing reflection we imagine here must be such that it is not the product of social and psychological conditions that prevent adequate appraisal of oneself in general. This includes the ability to assess the various aspects of one's being, and the freedom from those factors and conditions that we know independently systematically disrupt introspection. A person whose reflections are clearly and directly shaped by rage, drugs, the programings of a kidnapper, conditions that forbid consideration of anything but a narrow range of options, and the like cannot be said to be "adequately" considering her condition. A general test for such a requirement might be this: A person reflects adequately if she is able to realistically imagine choosing otherwise were she in a position to value sincerely that alternative position.[8] That is, her reflective abilities must contain sufficient flexibility that she could imagine responding appropriately to alternative reasons (where "appropriately" and "reasons" are understood from her own point of view).[9] Such a requirement needs much more description and defense, of course, but a fully worked-out notion of "adequate reflectiveness" could, in principle, be articulated that did not rest on specific contents concerning the values and norms a person is moved by in her reflections, but that rules out cases where reflective self-endorsement simply replicates the oppressive social conditions that autonomous living is meant to stand against.

The view of autonomy sketched here is meant as an example of the "content-neutral" view promoted by proceduralist theorists. This position is motivated by several considerations that will be considered below, but a fundamental point concerns the nature of value and commitment. Specifically, the proceduralist approach to autonomy can be seen to rest on the claim that values and commitments are valid for a person when she can autonomously come to see their import. But only if autonomy is understood as defined independently of such values can this view of commitment hold. I will return to this point below.

The Anti-Proceduralist Challenge

The view of autonomy outlined here is simply an example of a broader approach to the concept in which it is claimed that a person is autonomous (either *tout court* or relative to a certain characteristic) when she has developed in a way that is "procedurally independent." This means that, irrespective of the "content" of these processes – of the values, desires, or characteristics embraced by the agent – a person is autonomous when she adopts traits in the proper manner or if she reflectively identifies with the characteristic. Such an account is what Gerald Dworkin has called "content-neutral."[10]

This implies, of course, that a person can be autonomous yet committed strongly to a value system or rule structure that severely limits her choices. A deeply religious devotee, a military recruit, a person committed to a traditional role of obedience and self-deprecation, all would count as autonomous if the decisions to become such a person could meet the procedural conditions set out by the models. This has led some theorists to object to the procedural notion of autonomy and insist on more substantive conditions. These objections, which I will spell out in a moment, can be grouped under two headings: One set claims that the autonomous person must (and this is a conceptual "must") have certain value commitments in order to count as autonomous. Such value commitments include, for example, a regard for her own status as a morally worthy (and trust worthy) agent and reliable decision maker.[11] Another objection is that, to be autonomous, the agent must enjoy substantive independence as well as procedural independence. This means that the person must have, at every stage in her life, certain open options in order to count as autonomous and that a severely restricted person fails to so count even if she entered into these restrictions freely and wholeheartedly (and meets all the other conditions of procedural independence). These two lines of argument are connected, of course, in that they both reject procedural models as insufficient, claiming that the procedurally independent person who has (in the first case) low regard for her own value and (in the second case) few real options for action and decision is not autonomous no matter how "voluntarily" she comes into that condition.[12]

Let me expand on these objections. Paul Benson, for example, argues that autonomy conceptually involves the agent's "taking ownership" of her action. This agential ownership implies an individual authority to speak and answer for action. In this way, autonomy includes normatively substantive conditions: Only a person who considers herself the authority in her actions, who regards herself as worthy to answer for her actions by norms she herself accepts, is autonomous. This is a substantive normative requirement of autonomy that goes beyond purely procedural conditions concerning internal self-endorsement, self-development, or personal integration.[13]

Also, Joseph Raz has argued that autonomy must involve what he calls "adequacy of options." A person must face a significant range of minimally valuable options in order to count as autonomous. This is crucial for his argument that a pluralist society (which provides such contrasting options and life paths) is required by autonomy-based liberalism.[14] But by what criteria are we to gauge the "adequacy" of such options? Raz does not give a precise formula, but his claim is that a person whose choices are severely constrained, or who has options but would have to pay unacceptably high costs for rejecting all but one, is not autonomous in a way that connects to well-being (a significant connection for Raz).[15]

This connects with others who have been critical of "content-neutral" accounts of autonomy for implying that severely restricted agents – albeit ones who embrace such restrictions in ways that conform to the proceduralist accounts – should be labeled autonomous. A person who lacks significant choice over important areas of her life, who does not regard herself as the final source of judgments about the value of her commitments, is not, for these critics, autonomous no matter how reflective and informed were her decisions to enter into such a state.[16] Examples of such "happy slaves" are rife in the literature. Simply imagine a person who, from sincere conviction, allows herself to enter into a condition where another person or authority completely controls her options, commands her obedience, and is the ultimate source of value questions for her.

Clearly, we would have to describe such examples in great detail, taking special account of the cultural, political, and historical context, to determine precise intuitions here, and some have tried to do so,[17] but I hope to sidestep such subtleties here to make a different point. That is, the question of whether a voluntarily self-restrained person is autonomous will turn, not on free-floating intuitions about concepts, but rather on the role that the concept of autonomy will play in theoretical and practical contexts. No matter how focused we might be on a particular case of voluntary self-restraint, the question of whether such a person exhibits autonomy for us will turn on the question of what is implied by that attribution.

To see this, consider that the type of person typically imagined in such cases chooses, at some time (t1) to enter certain conditions of severe restraint and obedience and does so in ways that we assume here are minimally rational (given her other beliefs), reflectively endorsed, and thus "authentic" in the proceduralist sense. Subsequent to t1, we all agree that her options will be severely restricted, and her regard for herself as the "ultimate" source of value judgments is forsaken. We must imagine also that the value orientation to which this decision fits is, for her, a rational and reflectively acceptable orientation and that the condition of strict obedience over time is a fundamental part of that orientation. The phrase "over time" here is significant, in that for procedural conditions to be met in some robust manner, we must demand that the reflective endorsement of the decision to enter into the constrained condition remains, in some way, available to the agent. Proceduralists might demand, for example, that the person must be given the option every few years or so to leave the constrained conditions in order to ensure that the reflective embrace of it is genuine (not because such constraint is intrinsically incompatible with autonomy, but because of the demands of adequate reflection of the sort sketched earlier). For the purposes of our discussion, let us consider that the person is severely constrained from t1 to t10, where t10 merely marks the point where an agent would have to be able to revisit the initial decision (to be constrained) in order for that decision to be considered procedurally authentic.

What we now must decide is the following: Is the person autonomous at t1 but then gives up her autonomy at t2–t10? Or is the person autonomous from t1 to t10 as part of an authentic value orientation *involving* the constraints in question? Now I will venture some considerations on behalf of calling such a person autonomous, but my main claim here is that such intuitive considerations are never conclusive and that one cannot answer this question simply on the intuitive merits of cases; one will have to widen the context to see what work we are asking the concept to do.

But how could one ever claim that a person is autonomous who is so severely limited in her choices and options that she cannot choose (without great cost) to reject her present circumstances or to disobey some authority figure (our agent after t1)? This depends, of course, on how such "constraints" are described. To label someone a happy "slave" is already to convey a judgment about the acceptability of her condition and its relation to human freedom. But what some call "slavery," others call deep devotion to the rightful orders of a superior. Do the young recruits in the U.S. military, who are subjected to the emotionally violent and unrelenting authority of superior officers, who must obey even the most personal and intrusive orders, count as nonautonomous? Or are they simply enduring a process that is part of a larger, fully autonomous life plan? Does the acceptance of one's own "inferiority" in certain decision-making realms in the practice of certain religious devotions count as the abnegation of one's own agency or the willful acceptance of a valued moral framework?

Similarly, how must we understand the requirement that the autonomous person must enjoy a range of choices that are somehow objectively stipulated? Does this include the option to move about? To change living situations? Engage in physical activity of a certain sort? For each such set of options, there are clearly cases of life plans for which they are irrelevant, where agents are "constrained" only in the sense that modification and rejection of their chosen life path is highly costly. But as I have argued elsewhere,[18] having options to alter one's condition is only significant if one is *alienated* from such conditions. All of us are "constrained" by our physicality, our social history (which predates us), our previous commitments (whose rejection now would be highly costly), our value commitments, and the like. These constraints in no way diminish our agency or autonomy – despite the great difficulty in altering them – because we are thoroughly embedded in them and oriented by them.[19] This implies that the range and significance of options of the sort relevant to autonomy is a function of the value perspective that guides reflective agency, not an externally stipulated set of options. But my main point is that the very *description* of options as "open" or "constrained" (or whether the language of "options" is appropriate at all) is what may be contested in competing value orientations. What for some may be an overall framework that provides meaning to life paths may, to another, be abdicating one's authority to think for oneself.

Autonomy clearly relates to the quality of independence and freedom. The issue here, however, is whether such independence and other related values are constitutive parts of the condition of being autonomous or merely concomitant values that are associated with it. Proceduralists take the latter view in saying that while virtually all autonomous persons are *in fact* independent in a substantive way, and a crucial part of the reason we value autonomy is that we value such freedom, we nevertheless *define* autonomy in a way that does not require such substantive freedom.

But as I said, it is not my concern to defend the proceduralist model against all such criticisms (which would have to be set out much more carefully than I have done here). Clearly, those who defend substantive notions of autonomy can plausibly claim that, in some sense, a person who has engaged in a life project that involves forsaking her independence of choice or asks her to consider her judgment on important matters as less valuable than some external source of authority has given up what we might well call her "autonomy" (albeit reflectively and, *ex hypothesi*, for what counts for her as good reason). But to use "autonomy" in this way is to convey a substantive judgment about various lifestyles and value orientations; it is to dictate an *ideal* for individuals to relate to or reject. To say that autonomous persons are those with self-trust and open options (specified philosophically rather than derived from the agent's own reflective value orientation) is to use the label "autonomous" as a *competitor* in the clash of value orientations at stake here. The person who wishes to follow her spiritual leader in all matters of faith and value, and who gives up easy options of exit, has rejected what these theorists are calling "autonomy" in favor of what she takes as more important: a life of obedience and spiritual devotion.

I want to suggest, moreover, that insofar as autonomy is used in certain political contexts, in particular as fundamental to the specification of who is the subject of justice and what the basic interests of such subjects are, reserving autonomy to only those with substantive independence has certain theoretical and practical costs that may well not be worth paying. In addition, we will see that viewing autonomy narrowly in the way that substantive theorists insist upon makes it more difficult to show how being autonomous can be part of the ground of political *commitment* of a sort that is crucial for (some understandings of) principles of justice.

II. LIBERALISM AND PERFECTIONISM

The liberal approach to social justice has many faces, and any overarching characterization of it will be contentious. Some urge that the central tenet of liberalism is a commitment to the priority of liberty;[20] others claim it is, more generally, a commitment to the priority of the right over controversial conceptions of the good,[21] while still others focus on the conception of interests at the heart of liberalism, specifically the fundamental interest we all have in pursuing the good in our own way (from the inside, as it were).[22] A crucial division among liberal thinkers that has settled into place in recent years is the distinction between "perfectionist" and "political" liberalism. Defenders of the former view contend that justice demands the postulation of particular values – ones such as autonomy, tolerance, equality, and liberty – that guide institutions and shape policy. These values are claimed to gain their validity *objectively*, that is, independently (in principle) of their actual endorsement by those whose lives are affected by the institutions guided by them. In other words, for perfectionist theorists, constitutional structures must be put in place that guarantee the protection of such values even against the will of those members of the population who live under them but who also reject them.

Political liberalism, on the other hand, rejects the possibility of determining specific values or comprehensive moral views that apply broadly in a deeply pluralistic world. Divisions concerning value claims of all sort – especially relating to the relative weights, meanings, and final specification of particular values – divide populations in all modern societies, so that justice can only amount to a political consensus about principles needed to guide social policy in the face of such ultimate disagreement.[23] Political institutions cannot claim legitimacy, on this approach, if they are justified by values that members of the population can reasonably reject (where "reasonably" is a term to be unpacked). Even if those values are, in some sense, *valid* (objectively), they represent an unacceptable imposition on the consciences of well-meaning citizens who, perhaps out of narrowness of vision but not in unreasonable ways, do not accept them.

Political liberalism, then, rests fundamentally on a principle of legitimacy, which can be stated in this way: "[I]n a closed society of free and equal citizens maintaining diverse moral views, political power is legitimate only when such citizens may reasonably be expected to endorse it."[24] This is a procedural account of legitimacy, according to which political power is acceptable because of its grounding pedigree, not its content.

But this means that this process of endowing institutions with legitimacy and, more importantly, of legitimizing the principles that justify those institutions, must be spelled out in some detail. Rawls's version of political liberalism relies heavily on the structure of public reason as the forum by which basic constitutional principles are endorsed or rejected.[25] Jürgen Habermas, on the other hand, postulates democratic processes that mirror unconstrained speech situations allowing for free communication among rational agents.[26] Other democratic theorists insist on the constitutive role of democratic deliberation in formulating, refining, and possibly rejecting dominant principles.[27] For views such as these, legitimacy is bestowed by virtue of procedures that either make no crucial reference to substantive values or make such references only provisionally, as part of the political process of establishing consensus.[28]

Also, in many of its guises liberal theory is said to be fundamentally committed to a principle of *neutrality* in the justification of principles of justice. That is, public principles must rest on considerations that do not take any one comprehensive moral view – any one conception of the good – as paramount or superior to others.[29] Such a commitment is complex and controversial, but the liberal commitment to neutrality stems from the demands of liberal legitimacy combined with the acknowledgment of pluralism: Only if principles are justified neutrally can they possibly gain allegiance from the disparate subpopulations in society whose identity congeals around conflicting value frameworks. The liberal commitment to the equality of moral status of all individuals and groups, along with the acceptance of permanent pluralism, entails this kind of constraint.

However, perfectionists have challenged this picture on the grounds that state power cannot be justified consistently to a population who hold reasonable, indeed *true*, beliefs about fundamental value questions. For such people, state policy justified in this "neutral" manner produces results that conflict with their own favored view; as such, they are being asked to bracket their commitment to such a view in favor of social allegiance, toleration, reciprocity, and other fundamental elements in the liberal conception of justice.

Steven Wall, for example, argues from a perfectionist standpoint that "political authorities should take an active role in creating and maintaining social conditions that best enable their subjects to lead valuable and worthwhile lives."[30] What counts as a worthwhile life is variable, of course, but nothing in the liberal program implies that we must be skeptical about the truth of at least some such value claims. Rawls, for example, specifically argues that particular comprehensive views must not only be considered "reasonable" in the public justification of principles of justice, they may well also be *true*. No element in the liberal program for the ("neutral") justification of principles can imply that some particular reasonable value framework is unjustified. This implies that *if* there are objectively determinable values and some citizens reasonably commit themselves to such values, liberalism appears to have no argument for why its meliorist neutralism should hold sway over such particular values when they conflict.

And conflict is unavoidable. For example, if there is a "truth of the matter" on questions such as whether an early-term fetus is a moral person with the right not to be killed, and liberal theory has explicitly ruled out justifying a social policy with reference to the truth value of such a view, then any allegedly "neutral" policy on abortion will in fact conflict with one side or another on such a question. Because at least one such side may (*ex hypothesi*) hold not only reasonable but *sound* views about such value questions, then liberalism must deny the validity of such a view in its justification of principles; that is, it must compete with such a position rather than provide an impartial framework within which it is considered.

Now one way to soften the blow of these challenges is to look more closely at the demand of *acceptance* in the liberal standard of legitimate power. Political liberalism rests on the principle of legitimacy that demands that each citizen be able to *affirm*, *consent to*, or *authorize* the basic constitutional essentials of her government.[31] However, one could well claim that the demand that citizens positively embrace the principles that structure state institutions is too stringent, for many have not considered the matter sufficiently, or would not grasp the philosophical language in which those principles are expressed, or the like.[32] A better test for legitimacy, then, is that (reasonable) citizens do not actively *reject* the basic principles of justice.[33] Moreover, the way in which many either embrace or reject the organizing principles of their government may better be expressed in language that permits the *affective* component of their reaction. If I am deeply religious and the basic principles of my society contain elements that explicitly denigrate my religion, my inability to accept those principles will rest on a reaction that is as much visceral as it is cognitive or calculating.

Though even in such a case, my rejection cannot merely be a subjective, psychological reaction that no one else could ever understand. For such a response to ground the rejection of (otherwise) shared principles, it must involve judgments that I can expect others to grasp at some level, considerations that can be made effectively *public*. For this reason, I propose that the test for legitimacy of political principles should be the following: Principles are legitimate only if the (reasonable) citizens to whom they apply would not be *understandably alienated* from them. To be "understandably" alienated is to definitively reject the principles, but in ways one can share with others and reasonably expect them to understand (though not necessarily accept), and that can be generalized to other cases. To be "alienated" from such principles is (as in the case of autonomy) to vehemently reject them, resist their motivating force, and actively disavow them. This is a weaker condition than that one fails to "affirm" such justifications or principles.

Much more needs to be said about such a reformulation of the liberal principle of legitimacy, but it may go some way toward mollifying critics of liberalism who rightly point to the ongoing *dissensus* in modern democracies among reasonable groups concerning the principles and procedures that structure government power. Nevertheless, those critical of proceduralist political views would surely insist that cultural and moral *difference* is so entrenched and multifaceted that the standards of legitimacy set out by liberal politics will not be met for a wide variety of populations, especially those who hold views (religious, cultural, and otherwise) that they regard as grounded in an objective worldview.

But more must be said here about the structure of the political liberal standard of legitimacy in order to further negotiate the perfectionist critique. Rawls, for example, claims that the citizens to whom the legitimacy test applies must be "reasonable." Reasonableness, however, is a *normative* position, not an epistemological one. That is, to be reasonable, for Rawls, is to be willing to accept fair terms of cooperation for one's society, to acknowledge and accept the fact of reasonable pluralism, which means that one comes to understand (via the "burdens of judgment") the various ways that reasonable people can come to adopt opposing values and also that, despite one's own justified commitment to one's own moral views, one is not willing to utilize undue coercion to impose them on others.[34] This is a hefty set of normative commitments, and they only apply to those who already accept the ideals of tolerance, reciprocity, freedom, and equality that liberal justice embodies.

But notice, this is a *presupposition* of liberal legitimacy for Rawls. He thinks that, in fact, such values are already operative in the public political culture of modern constitutional democracies and hence that citizens to which liberal justice is meant to apply already *are* reasonable in his sense. He is not arguing that such principles are (metaphysically) valid or objectively justified. Their presence in the political consciousness of the population is taken as a social-psychological *fact*.

Clearly, there are instances where this level of moral commitment to tolerance is not held. If persons or groups view their (for example) religious commitments as outweighing any commitment to pluralism and tolerance that underlie secular political institutions, then liberal justice simply cannot obtain, on this view. Some have taken this to mean that liberalism implies that its principles can be forcibly *imposed* on such unreasonable people or groups.[35] But this need not be the liberal position, and it doesn't follow strictly from its conditions of legitimacy. Those conditions merely state the requirements for legitimacy; if those conditions fail to obtain, political power (relative to the unreasonable groups) is *not* legitimate. This says nothing about what alternative recourse concerning "unreasonable" people *is* legitimate.

Let us return, then, to the specific challenges raised by perfectionists to the project of political (procedural) liberalism. First, we must look closely at the conditions of legitimacy being imagined here. The particularly poignant objection that such a challenge raises for liberalism is that citizens hold views for reasons that they validly see as objective (in some cases, it is conceded) and that this validity obtains independent of general intersubjective acceptance of them. What liberalism paradoxically demands, perfectionists argue, is that public political principles must be accepted by people in ways that conflict with the manner in which they embrace their other moral values. That is, even when citizens affirm the value of, say, tolerance, they will often do so for reasons that *they take to be* objective and hence valid independent of others' acceptance of this value; but liberalism demands that they affirm this principle, not because of its objective status, but because of its role in the legitimation of principles for co-citizens. Proceduralist liberalism, then, demands allegiance from people for reasons different from those that actually ground their political commitments.

One response to this position is to object to the perfectionist conception of *moral* validity. The perfectionist position being considered here assumes at least a minimal "externalism" about the validity of moral values, in that it assumes that values (principles, rules) can apply even if those persons to whom they apply do not and would not see them as valid. The defender of proceduralism may respond by claiming that such a view of moral obligation is *generally* deficient, that moral values can only apply to those who, in principle, could accept their validity.[36]

This is, of course, a weighty and complex matter, and many have discussed it both in the context of moral principle as well as that of epistemology and practical reason.[37] But we need not take this route directly. There is a long-standing recognition of a difference between the status of people's moral commitments and that of their political views, at least in the following regard: Principles that apply to social institutions, interpersonal relations, and other aspects of public culture necessarily contain provisions that constrain, coerce, modify behavior, redefine social roles, and force compliance. The reasons I might have for believing in (for example) a set of religious teachings take on a special character when those teachings include requirements for the forceful constraint of other co-citizens. The liberal view includes a presumption that power is always suspect and that only when it can be justified must it be tolerated. That is, no reason, however valid for an individual, can count as a reason for others to be constrained or guided by it unless it can be a *reason for them.* Intersubjective validity of the sort envisioned is necessary for this.

The motivation for this move is that without this condition of legitimacy, the application and enforcement of principles is a function merely of *power* – the force of those who happen to have superior ability to enforce their view of the good. Whether such a view of the good is valid as a moral claim, its enforcement can only be successfully carried out if there are sufficient numbers or sufficient might available to enable such enforcement. Therefore, social enforcement of principles is the result of pure power unless those affected by the principle can, in some fashion, accept the reasons for it. This is a view of social life that is fundamentally modernist and emerges first (in this manner) in Rousseau and later in Kant in a more purified form.[38]

Moreover, interactions among people in social environments have innumerable aspects, not all of which can be described as physical, dyadic interaction.[39] We occupy roles, live in symbolically mediated cultural settings, work and live in natural or artificial environments whose features shape the quality of that activity, and so on. Lives are shaped, framed, and constructed out of the complex, multifaceted fabric of social life. What matters is how the rule-bound institutions of that social life operate to shape that life. My claim here is that the reasons for constructing such institutions must be such that those living under them can understand and accept those reasons from their own point of view (or at least not be "understandably alienated" from them).

Consider the person who reflectively rejects the objective standard that lies behind (let us assume) a valid perfectionist principle. Political policies that can only be justified with reference to such a principle would therefore have to be imposed upon this person without such justification counting as a reason for her. That is, even if the value upon which this imposition is based is valid (externally), its enforcement would be enacted without recourse to a justification that the victim of that enforcement could access. (Recall that the moderate externalism to which perfectionist politics is committed implies that values can be valid even if the person to whom they apply could not in principle accept them.) Whether this person "obeys" the enforced imposition of this principle will depend on whether the power lying behind that enforcement is effective, if there is enough *might* to make it *right.* But relying on the superior force of one side in an argument is not sufficient for justifying the enactment of the implications of that argument.[40]

This clearly is not a conclusive argument against the perfectionist position, but it does state a view that earmarks the modernist, liberal approach to politics. Unless the exercise of power can be justified in ways accessible to those living under its purview, it is nothing but an arbitrary show of force.[41] In this way, nonperfectionist liberal justice rests on a basic respect for *autonomy*: Only when the person's capacity to embrace aspects of her situation (principles, social conditions, personal characteristics) in an authentic (and minimally competent) manner can justice obtain.[42] Only with such a commitment to respect for autonomy can social institutions and political power operate without displays of arbitrary force.

However, as in the first section of this paper, I do not want to advance conclusive arguments on the proceduralist side of the debate here. Rather, I want to highlight how the particular set of disagreements, which go to the heart of the shape and plausibility of the modernist liberal project, I believe, rests on particular understandings of commitment, political power, and the validity of principles behind the exercise of that power.

III. THE CONVERGENCE OF DEBATE

In the first section of this chapter, I discussed the debate over the concept of autonomy that centered on that notion's relation to objective values. I argued, in admittedly only a preliminary way, that demanding substantive value commitments in the conditions of autonomy, including the requirement of substantive independence, might be a mistake. Though in the end, I admitted that that question comes down to a clash of intuitions about whether persons described (contentiously) as "happy slaves" ought to be labeled autonomous. I claimed there that further reflection on the *intuitive* character of the concept of autonomy would not be fruitful. We need to know how the concept is functioning – what practical or theoretical work it is doing – in order to analyze further its most plausible conditions. Autonomy has been crucial in the design of liberal principles of justice, of course, and it is here that I would think that its function and structure should be explored.

As I noted, there are many conceptions of liberal justice, and many of them avoid direct or fundamental reference to autonomy. Those versions of liberalism that do refer to autonomy, however, use that notion to describe the citizen whose perspective and interests are used to derive and shape principles of justice.[43] That is, autonomy is a "marker" that designates those types of agents who will be bound by the principles that shape the basic institutions of a society. In the process of legitimation of those principles, it is the perspective of the autonomous agent that is envisioned for the possible consent that is basic to that process. Moreover, the postulation of social goods needed to formulate principles of distributive justice (for Rawls, the social primary goods) are defined according to the basic interests of the autonomous agent.[44]

Therefore, the considerations just adduced concerning the perfectionist challenge to liberalism – and the arguments brought out to deflect that challenge – bear directly on the question of the value neutrality of the concept of autonomy itself. For if by "autonomous" we mean only those persons who have particular value commitments – say, to relations of independence of a certain sort – then the principles of justice that shape social institutions will automatically rule out the perspective of those who reject those values. This perspective will not be considered and rejected in the mechanisms of public reason; rather, the viewpoint will not even be *considered*. Such "persons" will be viewed like children or the insane, as "unreasonable" and politically irrelevant. Such exclusion is clearly dangerous and should be accepted only with trepidation.

The question of whether and how to consider *anti*liberal viewpoints in a liberal forum (or claims against justice in just institutions) is complex and well discussed. The claim I am making here is merely that insofar as "autonomy" is used to describe the perspective and interests of the citizen of just institutions, and those institutions gain legitimacy only when such citizens accept them or do not vehemently reject them, then the concept of autonomy at work in that process ought not to contain, as a conceptual requirement, stipulations about the substantive values of the person in question. That is, claims of the sort considered earlier – that to be autonomous should mean that one lives in conditions of independence (with open options) and that one *values* such independence – imply that the question of what *counts* as independence is foreclosed in the process of public reason constitutive of political legitimacy. If only autonomous citizens take part in the public deliberations marking the legitimacy of a regime and to be autonomous is to believe in a certain sort of independence, then those deeply committed to lifestyles and value systems at odds with that conception of independence will not even *get a hearing* in the public debate. Such exclusion is, as I said, dangerous and problematic within the confines of a system of justice committed to openness and free debate.

This is hardly to settle the matter on this multifaceted constellation of issues. But I at least hope to have accomplished the task of bringing together two bodies of theoretical literature that have mostly remained apart: the question of the conceptual structure of autonomy and the foundations of (liberal) justice.[45] These questions are strongly connected, in that the relation between agency and value and the issue of whether so-called objective (perfectionist) values must be postulated as a background condition for both agency (autonomy) and justice can be shown to converge. Given the wide variety of interpretive frameworks within which such "objective" values as (negative) freedom, self-reliance, independence, and the like are postulated, we should hesitate before concluding that only certain of them can be used to demarcate the citizens whose lives will be shaped by our public institutions. The widest array of viewpoints, value conceptions, and moral orientations should be represented in these processes in order to prevent the dangerous and often violent practices of exclusion that Western constitutional democracies have been known to enact in the name of expanding the purview of particular value frameworks and moral conceptions.

Notes

1. For a general discussion of political liberalism, see, e.g., John Rawls, *Political Liberalism* (New York: Columbia University Press, 1993); Donald Moon, *Constructing Community: Moral Pluralism and Tragic Conflicts* (Princeton: Princeton University Press, 1993); and Gerald Gaus, *Justificatory Liberalism* (New York: Oxford University Press, 1996). For a perfectionist critique of liberalism, see Steven Wall, *Liberalism, Perfectionism, and Restraint* (Cambridge: Cambridge University Press, 1998).
2. Writers who have analyzed the concept of autonomy in detail include Gerald Dworkin, *The Theory and Practice of Autonomy* (Cambridge: Cambridge University Press, 1988); Alfred Mele, *Autonomous Agents* (New York: Oxford University Press, 1995); Diana T. Meyers, *Self, Society and Personal Choice* (New York: Columbia University Press, 1989); and Bernard Berofsky, *Liberation from Self* (Cambridge: Cambridge University Press, 1995). For recent surveys of such literature, see Thomas May, "The Concept of Autonomy" *American Philosophical Quarterly* 31 (1994): 133–144; Catriona Mackenzie and Natalie Stoljar, eds., *Relational Autonomy: Feminist Perspectives on Autonomy, Agency, and the Social Self* (New York: Oxford University Press, 2000); my "Autonomy in Moral and Political Philosophy," *The Stanford Encyclopedia of Philosophy* (http://plato.stanford.edu/contents.html); and John Christman, ed., *The Inner Citadel: Essays on Individual Autonomy* (New York: Oxford University Press, 1989).
3. Other competence-related conditions can be mentioned: The autonomous person cannot suffer from those neuroses that have the effect of debilitating

other autonomy-related decision-making functions. The severely paranoid person, or the agoraphobic, or the person living with bulimia or anorexia nervosa cannot be thought to be autonomous (at least relative to those areas of her life affected by the conditions). Similarly, various affective deficiencies disrupt autonomy (in ways usually not noted in the literature on this concept). A person who is chronically unable to call forth or suppress certain emotions – to call forth love and care or suppress anger and rage – when they are appropriate to the person's own occurrent projects and decisions, may not be acting autonomously.

4. Christman, "Autonomy and Personal History," *Canadian Journal of Philosophy* 21 (1991): 1–24. See also my "Defending Personal Autonomy: Reply to Professor Mele," *Canadian Journal of Philosophy* 23 (1993): 281–290.
5. The concept of self-alienation is analyzed in a different form in certain areas of psychoanalytic theory: See, e.g., Karen Horney, *Our Inner Conflicts: A Constructive Theory of Neurosis* (New York: Norton, 1945).
6. See, e.g., Harry Frankfurt, "Freedom of the Will and the Concept of the Person," in Frankfurt, *The Importance of What We Care About* (Cambridge: Cambridge University Press, 1988): 11–25.
7. Also, the narrowness of seeing autonomy as merely a function of the operation of *desires* should be noted. A more useful approach would see autonomy as involving judgments about any aspect of the self or character that guides choice or constitutes the personality. Therefore, emotional states, habits, capacities, and even physical states – what I will label "characteristics" or "traits" – should be included in the purview of self-appraisal that autonomy involves. See, e.g., Richard Double, "Two Types of Autonomy Accounts," *Canadian Journal of Philosophy* 22 (1992): 65–80.
8. A development of an idea similar to this (though not couched in the context of a proceduralist conception of autonomy) can be found in Catriona Mackenzie, "Imagining Oneself Otherwise," in Stoljar and Mackenzie, eds. *Relational Autonomy*, 124–150. This condition also resembles the requirement of "reasons-responsiveness" that some have argued is necessary for moral responsibility. See, e.g., John Martin Fisher and Mark Ravizza, *Responsibility and Control: A Theory of Moral Responsibility* (New York: Cambridge University Press, 1998).
9. Cf. Joseph Raz, *The Morality of Freedom* (Oxford: Oxford University Press, 1986): 372–377, where he argues that autonomy requires an adequate range of options, as I discuss below. Notice, however, that the requirement I am proposing is importantly different: I am not claiming that an autonomous person must face actual open options, but only that in order to be able to reflect adequately she must be able to imagine alternative choices under (counterfactually) optimal conditions. Moreover, these alternative choices are defined subjectively, on my view, not, as with Raz, from a purely philosophical, external viewpoint. For discussion of a similar point, see my "Liberalism, Autonomy, and Self-Transformation," *Social Theory and Practice* 27 (2001): 185–206. (I am grateful to Diana Meyers for discussion of this point.)
10. See Dworkin, *The Theory and Practice of Autonomy*, 8–9.

11. See Paul Benson, "Autonomy and Self-Worth," *Journal of Philosophy* 91 (1994): 650–668; Keith Lehrer, *Self-Trust* (New York: Oxford University Press, 1997); and Trudy Govier, "Self-Trust, Autonomy and Self-Esteem," *Hypatia* 8 (1993): 99–119.
12. See, e.g., Sigurdur Kristinsson, "The Limits of Neutrality: Toward a Weakly Substantive Account of Autonomy," *Canadian Journal of Philosophy* 30 (2000): 257–286; Marina Oshana, "Personal Autonomy and Society," *Journal of Social Philosophy* 29 (1998): 81–102; and Natalie Stoljar, "Autonomy and the Feminist Intuition," in Mackenzie and Stoljar, eds., *Relational Autonomy*, 94–111.
13. Paul Benson, "Taking Ownership: Authority and Voice in Autonomous Agency," in John Christman and Joel Anderson, eds., *Autonomy and the Challenges to Liberalism: New Essays* (New York: Cambridge University Press, forthcoming). Benson also includes powerful critiques of purely procedural accounts of autonomy in this paper, ones that motivate his own view. I cannot take up these critiques here. For a partial response, see my "Relational Autonomy, Liberal Individualism, and the Social Constitution of Selves," *Philosophical Studies* 117 (2004): 143–164.
14. Raz, *The Morality of Freedom*, chaps. 14–15.
15. Ibid., 369–378.
16. See, e.g., Raz, *The Morality of Freedom*, 370–375, and Oshana, "Personal Autonomy and Society," 86–93.
17. See, e.g., Oshana, "Personal Autonomy and Society."
18. Christman, "Liberalism, Autonomy, and Self-Transformation," 185–206.
19. For a similar point, see Charles Taylor, "What Is Wrong with Negative Liberty?" in *Philosophy and the Human Sciences, Philosophical Papers*, vol. 2 (Cambridge: Cambridge University Press, 1985): 211–229; and *The Ethics of Authenticity* (Cambridge, MA: Harvard University Press, 1991): 31–41.
20. See Gerald Gaus, *Justificatory Liberalism* (New York: Oxford University Press, 1996).
21. For discussion, see my *Social and Political Philosophy: A Contemporary Introduction* (London: Routledge, 2002): chap. 4.
22. See Will Kymlicka, *Liberalism, Community and Culture* (Oxford: Oxford University Press, 1989): 9–20.
23. See, e.g., John Rawls, *Political Liberalism* (New York: Columbia University Press, 1993); Charles Larmore, *Patterns of Moral Complexity* (Cambridge: Cambridge University Press, 1987); and John Gray, *Post-Liberalism: Studies in Political Thought* (New York: Routledge, 1993). Cf. also Jeremy Waldron, *Law and Disagreement* (Oxford: Oxford University Press, 2001).
24. Rawls, *Political Liberalism*, 217.
25. See Rawls, "The Idea of Public Reason Revisited," in *The Law of Peoples* (Cambridge, MA: Harvard University Press, 2001): 129–180.
26. Jürgen Habermas, *Between Facts and Norms* (Cambridge, MA: MIT Press, 1994).
27. See, e.g., Iris Marion Young, *Inclusion and Democracy* (Oxford: Oxford University Press, 2002), although she is not here defending a proceduralist liberal view.

28. E.g., on Rawls's view, substantive conceptions of the good must be postulated as part of the "model conceptions" that build principles of justice. The social primary goods, e.g., are postulated as indices of social standing necessary to formulate principles of distributive justice (not as metaphysically grounded values objectively applicable to all). See Rawls, *Political Liberalism*, 180.
29. For general discussion of this issue, see my *Social and Political Philosophy*, 98–103.
30. See Wall, *Liberalism, Perfectionism and Restraint*, 22.
31. See Rawls, *Political Liberalism*, 218; and Thomas Nagel, *Equality and Partiality* (New York: Oxford University Press, 1991).
32. For discussion of this point, see, e.g., Bert van den Brink, "Liberalism Without Agreement: Political Autonomy and Agonistic Citizenship," in Christman and Anderson, eds., *Autonomy and the Challenges to Liberalism*; see also Marilyn Friedman, "John Rawls and the Political Conception of Unreasonable People," in Virginia Davion and Clark Wolf, eds., *The Idea of Political Liberalism: Essays on Rawls* (Lanham, MD: Rowman & Littlefield, 2000): 16–33; and Jeremy Waldron, *Liberal Rights: Collected Papers, 1981–91* (Cambridge: Cambridge University Press, 1993): 35–62.
33. This is similar to Thomas Scanlon's view that something is morally wrong/unjust if it cannot be justified to others on grounds they cannot reasonably *reject*. See his "Contractualism and Utilitarianism," in Amartya Sen and Bernard Williams, eds., *Utilitarianism and Beyond* (Cambridge: Cambridge University Press, 1982): 103–128; and *What We Owe to Each Other* (Cambridge, MA: Harvard University Press, 1998).
34. Rawls, *Political Liberalism*, 59–70.
35. See Friedman, "John Rawls and the Political Conception of Unreasonable People."
36. For an argument along such lines, see Gerald Gaus, "Liberal Neutrality: A Compelling Radical Principle," in Steven Wall and George Klosko, eds., *Perfectionism and Neutrality: Essays in Liberal Theory* (Lanham, MD: Rowman & Littlefield, 2003): 137–165.
37. See, e.g., Gaus, *Justificatory Liberalism*.
38. For an interesting discussion of Kant's views relating to this point, see Jeremy Waldron, *The Dignity of Legislation* (Cambridge: Cambridge University Press, 1999): 36–62.
39. For this reason, we should resist the characterization of liberalism as resting fundamentally on a principle of *noncoercion*. See, e.g., Gerald Gaus, "Liberalism," in *The Stanford Encyclopedia of Philosophy* (http://plato.stanford.edu/contents.html). First, "coercion" is a concept whose meaning cannot be given without an already settled understanding of the validity and applicability of principles of justice. A single physical interaction may be described as either "theft" or "recovering one's property from someone who just stole it," depending on how the applicable property rights are defined. (For a similar argument, see Ronald Dworkin, "What Is Equality? Part III: The Place of Liberty," *Iowa Law Review* 73 (1987): 1–54.) Additionally, as I note in the text, social interaction should not simply be modeled as dyadic physical interactions.

40. This is an important line of argument that Rousseau develops in various works. See, e.g., "Of the Social Contract," in Victor Gourevitch, ed., *The Social Contract and Other Later Political Writings*, Bk. I (Cambridge: Cambridge University Press, 1997), 141–153.
41. This is parallel to the distinction Habermas makes between strategic and communicative interaction. See his *Moral Consciousness and Communicative Action* (Cambridge, MA: MIT Press, 1991): 58.
42. Note that this does not amount to a claim that autonomy has metaphysically grounded objective value, but rather that it must be presupposed in the process of legitimation demanded by justice.
43. For further discussion, see my *Social and Political Philosophy*, chap. 4, and my entry on "Autonomy in Moral and Political Philosophy," in *The Stanford Encyclopedia of Philosophy* (http://plato.stanford.edu/contents.html).
44. See Rawls, *Political Liberalism*, 58.
45. For a further attempt to bring into dialogue these two lines of discussion, see Christman and Anderson, eds., *Autonomy and the Challenges to Liberalism: New Essays*.

13

The Concept of Autonomy in Bioethics

An Unwarranted Fall from Grace

Thomas May

Despite its foundational role in the development of the field of bioethics, the concept of autonomy has recently come under attack from a variety of nonliberal perspectives in bioethics, particularly communitarian, feminist, and "family-based decision-making" perspectives. The attack on the concept of autonomy usually centers on one (or both) of two related criticisms: first, that the concept of autonomy is too narrowly "atomistic," ignoring the social context of personal identity; and second, that a narrow concern with a patient's autonomy rights neglects the social dimensions of healthcare treatment decision making (in particular, the impact of healthcare treatment decisions on a patient's community or family).

Communitarians, for example, argue that the idea of "self" that has developed since Kant is one that views the self as cut off from others,[1] lacking in its appreciation of the social dimensions of identity. Mark Kuczewski, for example, writes, "The Communitarian view of the person sees the self as constituted by social roles, communal practices, and shared deliberative exchanges."[2] Similarly, feminist writers from Carol Gilligan to Virginia Held have argued that the dominant understanding of "self" is based in autonomy and furthermore is a masculine conception, while feminine paradigms emphasize relationships.[3] Susan Wolf describes this feminist critique of contemporary bioethics as related to the grounding of contemporary bioethics in liberal individualism: Feminism, states Wolf, often views liberal individualism as impoverished, encouraging disregard of relational bonds. Thus, states Wolf, "[T]here is some overlap between non-feminist communitarian critiques of autonomy in bioethics and feminist cautions against mistaking autonomy's sufficiency."[4] Recognizing these criticisms, John Hardwig argues that the paradigm of medical decision making should be shifted away from one that places the sole locus of medical decision making on an individual patient's values and rights, toward a paradigm that incorporates the values of the family and others whose interests are affected. States Hardwig: "I am a husband, a father, and still a son, and no one would argue that I should or even responsibly could decide to take a sabbatical, another job, or even a weekend trip *solely* on the basis of what I want for myself."[5]

There are two reasons for the communitarian and feminist desire to bring about autonomy's fall from grace: First, there is a mistaken identification of moral relationships and requirements with political obligations; second, there is a view of autonomy grounded in a particular approach that conceives isolation of the individual as an ideal. Below, I will argue that all of these critiques of autonomy are misguided, leading to an unwarranted fall from grace for the concept of autonomy in bioethics literature.

I. DISTINGUISHING MORAL RELATIONSHIPS FROM POLITICAL REQUIREMENTS

Both communitarian and feminist critiques of autonomy focus on the narrowness of political rights associated with this concept in medicine, then offer critiques grounded in the adequacy of this concept from a moral perspective. Below, I will argue that the salient perspective for bioethics is that of the political. In fact, this political understanding of autonomy is consistent with a much richer and varied moral perspective than seems recognized by the communitarian and feminist perspectives in bioethics. It is important to distinguish the *moral* obligations one has from the *political* boundaries of social decision making. Healthcare decisions often involve issues of profound importance – even life-and-death – and the outcomes of these decisions are thus deeply relevant to the political rights of individuals. As I discuss below, political boundaries place fundamental limits on the social application of moral beliefs.[6] Because medical decision making is by nature social, involving at minimum the interaction of patient and healthcare provider (and, should community or family values be relevant, an even greater number of people), we must recognize the fundamental relevance of the political framework for decision making in medicine. This means that, at times, we must recognize political obligations as taking precedence over moral beliefs when structuring decisions in this social context.

For example, Hardwig argues that the medical decision-making paradigm of autonomy, in treating the paradigm of medical decision making as too narrowly focused on the patient's interests, is anomalous to the paradigm for other important decisions in our lives, as illustrated by the quotation above. It is here that I believe Hardwig is mistaken. The mistake is one of comparing the *moral* requirement to consider the interests of others when our decisions affect them (in the case of deciding to change jobs) with the *political* right not to do so (in the case of medical decision making). Although it is surely true that few would argue that, morally, I *should* make important decisions in a way that ignores the effects of such decisions on my family, it is equally true that, politically, I *could* make such decisions and, indeed, have a *political right* to do so if I choose. To do so would surely indicate that I am not a good husband, father, or son; but the obligations entailed by these relationships, except in extreme cases (such as abuse) that are covered by the liberal "harm principle," are moral, rather than political. Indeed, the political paradigm for such decision making is not different than how Hardwig later describes the autonomy paradigm for medical decision making in a critique of its narrow focus: "Some patients, motivated by a deep and abiding concern for the well-being of their families, will undoubtedly consider the interests of other family members. . . . But not all patients will feel this way."[7] If I were to make medical decisions that affected my family without regard for the decision's impact on those interests, I would surely be judged in a negative manner, just as I would be judged negatively if I were to make decisions about changing jobs, for example, solely on the basis of what I want for myself. But in neither case am I *required* to consider the interests of others. Should I choose, I may accept the negative evaluations that others make of me and act according to my own vision of the good. My right to do so is one of the most fundamentally protected ideals in the U.S. political system, as I discuss below.

Both the cultural history and political institutions of the United States are decidedly focused on liberalism. Liberal societies reject advocacy of substantive value systems at a social level; instead, a plurality of values coexist, and no one of these, for social purposes, is given a privileged position. In place of a privileged moral system or systems, liberalism offers a social system that defines value as determined, in substance or content, by individuals living in that society. Thus, the moral dimension of decision making becomes, for social purposes, in large part political: The political framework of liberalism establishes the paradigm of autonomy because it rejects a privileged perspective that might be *imposed*. Importantly, this does not take a position concerning the ultimate moral worth of a particular perspective, but rather is a political position concerning how to adjudicate between competing frameworks for assessing "the good." Thus, for example, one may recognize Hardwig's *political* right to change jobs without considering his family, while simultaneously judging this to be *morally* bad.

At a *moral* level, the rejection of a privileged perspective leads to a position of *tolerance* in social policy. This policy of tolerance applies, politically, even where there are good *moral* reasons to advocate a substantive position. For example, one argument for liberal tolerance of religious moral perspectives is based on the idea that "even if the state could base its case for partisanship on reliable and well-founded claims to religious knowledge, such claims would be so inherently contentious that the expected costs of basing policy on religious knowledge claims would always outweigh the expected benefits."[8] This fundamental idea of *political* tolerance in social policy is shared by John Rawls, who states: "Briefly, the idea is that in a constitutional democracy the public conception of justice should be, so far as possible, independent of controversial philosophical and religious doctrines. Thus, to formulate such a conception, we apply the principle of toleration to philosophy itself: The public conception of justice is to be political, not metaphysical."[9]

Politically, liberal rights place "boundaries" on the *social application* of personal visions of the good.[10] These boundaries, in turn, limit the extent that we can *require* an individual to realize another person's vision of the good. In short, while we may believe strongly that the good an individual attempts to realize should include promotion of family and community values, we are limited in our ability to *require* that she attempt to promote these values. Imagine, for example, a healthcare professional who believes firmly that morality requires that we address overpopulation and that all persons are morally obliged by this requirement to address overpopulation through abortion procedures once a person has had a given number of children. While her belief concerning overpopulation might lead *her* to seek an abortion, no matter how deeply she holds such moral convictions, she may not impose these convictions on others. The implications of the liberal framework for medical decision making are clear: While we may encourage a patient to decide to accept or reject treatment considering the impact of this decision on community or family, we may not require this. The autonomy right of "informed consent and refusal" allows adult, competent patients to base their decisions on whatever values they choose to structure their lives.

The role of political autonomy rights in healthcare decisions, then, can hardly be overemphasized, so long as our political system remains liberal. Failure to account for these rights neglects the fundamental political boundaries that govern our social interactions. So far as bioethics is concerned with the *practice* of medicine in a *social* (or clinical) context, bioethics *must* take seriously political boundaries. Thus, the *liberal* political framework is vital, and nonnegotiable, as a starting point in our discussion of bioethics decision making in the United States. Be we liberals, communitarians, communists, or other in ideology, the fact is that we find ourselves in a liberal constitutional society. This context governs our social relations. Healthcare, as a social practice, will be bounded by the fundamental political context within which it exists. In short, the role that moral beliefs play in bioethics will be limited, in a social context, by the political rights of individuals. Thus, liberal autonomy rights in healthcare are not subject to rejection on the basis of arguments that nonliberal values are neglected. To give up the paradigm of autonomy in medical decision making is to give up the most basic values underlying the U.S. political system.

Perhaps we should discard the liberal framework, if this framework is indeed impoverished and through this inhibits social progress. Some feminists, for example, regard the liberal framework as harmful because, as Susan Wolf describes this perspective, "By depicting the moral community as a set of atomistic and self-serving individuals, it strips away relationships that are morally central."[11] Mark Kuczewski argues that right-based paradigms inhibit resolution of interminable debates because these paradigms tend to approach conflict through voting, a mechanism that focuses on the expression of individual values and preferences. What resolution of deep conflict requires, Kuczewski argues, is a more communitarian approach rooted in interpersonal consensus achieved through commitment to foundational social values.[12] In both cases, the perceived need to shift from the paradigm of autonomy in medical decision making is rooted in the narrow framework ascribed to autonomous decision making itself: Rejection of the autonomy paradigm by communitarians, feminists, and others centers on concerns about the impoverished view of self promoted by the autonomy paradigm, a view of self as isolated from social relationships. Even Hardwig's critique centers on the idea that the autonomy paradigm does not grant sufficient weight to social relationships. It is the narrow view of self as "atomistic," as cut off from others, that is the deepest criticism levied at the autonomy paradigm.

This ascribed narrowness, however, is based upon a philosophical vision of moral autonomy that does not reflect the framework employed in contemporary political paradigms. Below, I argue that the concept of autonomy employed within the liberal political framework is far richer than the atomistic conception normally criticized.

II. AUTONOMY AS AUTARKEIA

Contemporary discussions of autonomy in moral philosophy normally view the concept as an ideal of self-sufficiency, or "autarkeia." This ideal is one that seeks to eliminate the influence of "external" forces, allowing purity of purpose.[13] Aristotle discusses the concept of self-sufficiency, or autarkeia, in most detail in the context of a city-state, though he does discuss the concept in other contexts.[14] For Aristotle, autarkeia is the primary good and chief aim of a city-state, but it can only be achieved within the context of a city-state. This idea grounds the communitarian insight of the importance of one's social relationships to one's identity: Communitarians emphasize the deep role of social relationships in self-identity.

The problem arises because communitarian writers tend to view the concept of autonomy as directly tied to the Greek ideal of autarkeia. Indeed, the influence of the concept of autarkeia can be seen in many modern conceptions of autonomy. Conceptions of autonomy presented by Joel Feinberg,[15] John Rawls,[16] and Robert Paul Wolff[17] (as well as others) all center around the idea that external influences pose a threat in some form to human autonomy. The fact that current uses of the term "autonomy" reflect the ideal of "autonomy as autarkeia" should come as no surprise. I have argued elsewhere that these contemporary conceptions of autonomy are directly tied to Kantian influence and the ideal of autarkeia.[18] However, although it is clear how this notion has come to prominence, it is not the concept that is applied within the frameworks employed by the political and social systems that we find ourselves in and that, as I discussed above, grounds the value of autonomy.

If the notion of autonomous decision making employed by the political framework described above is directly tied to the ideal of autarkeia, the autonomy paradigm would indeed reflect the type of narrow decision-making paradigm ascribed to it. Consider, for example, Aristotle's development of the concept of autarkeia in the context of the "great-souled man." For this type of man, self-sufficiency consists in choosing what one will pursue without the pressure of need or utility being a relevant determinant of choice. The pursuit of the beautiful and profitless, rather than the profitable and useful, is more proper to a character that is self-sufficient.[19] To choose on the basis of usefulness is to choose in order to fulfill an external purpose. A self-sufficient man does not look beyond himself for this purpose.

The role of self-sufficiency within the concept of autonomy is clear in the work of Immanuel Kant, who discussed autonomy in terms of man's moral character and thus was concerned with man's control over the moral value of his actions. In the *Grounding for the Metaphysics of Morals*, Kant begins by asserting the nature of the good to be identified with the "good will." Intelligence, for example, is only good if it is not employed by an evil will. In this way, the moral value of such things as intelligence are dependent and contingent. The presence of the good will, however, is not dependent on external considerations for its moral value. In order to maintain this moral value, the will should not subjugate itself to contingent, external factors. Thus, we can see the parallels between Kant's vision of moral value tied to the will and Aristotle's ideal of autarkeia for the great-souled man: "Autonomy of the will is the property the will has of being a law to itself (independently of any property of the objects of volition)."[20] Although Immanuel Kant does not focus on the idea of political society in his discussion of autonomy,[21] the underlying emphasis on self-sufficiency and independence from external influences over human flourishing is clearly the central concern for Kant as well.

As communitarians correctly point out, to act in a self-sufficient manner seems a rather austere existence. Such a life would lack many of the things we think of as important parts of a rich life. For example, to act for such purposes as fulfilling the wishes of a loved one *because* it is what the loved one wishes would not meet the requirement of self-sufficiency. Yet such actions are often what we consider the very embodiment of a rich life.[22] In addition, there appears to be a fundamental incompatibility between self-sufficiency and any appeal to authority. However, appeals to various forms of authority are constitutive of the very social relationships that communitarians point to as central elements of life. For example, we appeal to the authority of the physician in medicine, to the scientist in physics, and so forth. Far from being a threat, these appeals to authority seem to broaden the richness of our lives, allowing us to be free from learning these basic skills and to devote our time and efforts to developing competencies in other areas.

The communitarian insight concerning the importance of social relationships to a person's identity is not, in itself, challenged at a fundamental level by advocates of the autonomy paradigm. Joesph Raz, for example, argues that autonomy itself is tied to certain social forms, as even the having of goals is dependent on the social framework one finds oneself in: One cannot choose to be a lawyer, for example, outside a social system grounded in laws and the types of relationships that give rise to lawyers.[23]

The challenge posed to the communitarian paradigm is directed at the role of social relationships in autonomous decision making. As employed within liberal political frameworks, the concept of autonomy does not insist on the isolated, atomistic view of self developed in writings focused on moral value. Rather, the conception of autonomy reflected in liberal political frameworks is itself a concept developed for social application, one that structures decision making by identifying who has ultimate authority for identifying the values that should guide decision making where the values of individuals conflict. In this, it does not *proscribe* decision making based on social bonds, relationships, and consensus: It merely protects against the imposition of these bases for decisions primarily affecting the individual in question. A closer look at the roots of the concept can be helpful in understanding the concept for political purposes.

III. AUTONOMY AS SELF-RULE

John Macken shows that the term "autonomy" was first employed by the Greeks to denote certain rights of a city-state (to manage its own affairs) even when dependent on a mother-city or outside power.[24] Tracing use of the concept of autonomy, Macken finds that even through the Enlightenment "autonomy" was used to refer to the rights of individuals to manage their own affairs within the limits of a larger framework set by law. Such a use of "autonomy" seems at odds with the concept of self-sufficiency, or autarkeia, as developed since Kant. Indeed, the concept of autonomy as originally developed by the Greeks is interesting from more than a historical perspective, as this original notion provides a much richer account of decision making that incorporates the social dimensions found lacking in the idea of "autonomy as autarkeia" and can serve as a model that simultaneously protects the liberal rights central to the political paradigms.

"Autonomy" is derived from the Greek words *autos* and *nomos*, meaning, literally, "self-rule." To gain a better understanding of the proper roots of this term, it is helpful to delve into an understanding of "rulers" in Greek philosophy. In the *Politics*, Aristotle compares citizens to sailors on a ship. The ruler is like the pilot, or helmsman, of the ship. It is no coincidence that Aristotle uses the analogy of a helmsman, for the helmsman of a ship steers the ship within the context of a wide variety of "external" considerations. For example, the helmsman must consider whether it is empirically possible to turn a certain direction, what the weather and currents are like, and so forth. For Aristotle, the ruler acting as helmsman exercises "practical wisdom," a concept that involves determination of virtuous action in relation to the "external" considerations of one's own capabilities and characteristics, as well as the situation at hand.

In this Aristotelian sense, external influences are not viewed as a threat to one's ability to rule, so long as one acts according to practical wisdom rather than some other determinant of behavior (such as allowing desires to steer one to indulge in every pleasure). As helmsman, a ruler steers according to practical wisdom. So long as external influences do not *determine* behavior, but merely affect how one rules – as currents or weather affect a ship's helmsman – they pose no threat to one's ability to *rule* one's own life.

It is this notion of autonomy as helmsman that is employed by the political structures of the United States. Elsewhere, I have argued that the primary *political* function of the concept of autonomy is to serve as a basis for the ascription of responsibility for the determination of action.[25] By rejecting a privileged perspective on the values that should guide decisions, liberalism promotes the autonomy paradigm by reserving for the individual the role of identifying the values that should guide decision making. In this, the liberal structure ascribes responsibility to the individual for her determination of action and develops mechanisms for the regulation of action based on this framework. Thus, the ways in which we interact with others and the variety of ways in which we regulate this behavior (such as cultural norms, religious convictions, hierarchical structures, and legal systems, just to name a few) require an understanding of behavior in terms of autonomous individuals.

Only to the extent that we can recognize persons as autonomous are we able to regulate their behavior within the liberal framework. Rules require a positive effort to comply that cannot be achieved passively; simple coincidence of actual and required behavior is not rule following.[26] The unique feature of rules is that they regulate conduct in a particular way: by specifying the required behavior and expecting the subject to then conform his behavior to this requirement. In a liberal framework, any social pressure designed to secure conformity to a rule must be brought to bear upon an agent within whose power it is to secure conformity. It is this idea that underlies the liberal conception of responsibility and provides the context of political structures: Conformity or lack of conformity to rules is the result of autonomous decisions made by individuals. When this paradigm is threatened, the political structures designed to secure conformity (for example, criminal punishment) do not apply. We can see this clearly in how we approach illegal behaviors by the insane, children, or others not regarded as autonomous: Their behavior is not subject to criminal punishment in the way the behavior of those who are ascribed responsibility for their actions is. In this, the conception of autonomy employed within this framework must be able to understand an individual as autonomous even when acting (or not acting) on the basis of rules, social norms, or any of a wide variety of "external" influences. In short, the concept of autonomy is one of "self-rule" within a context of "external" considerations, much like the concept described by Macken above. If the conception of autonomy were one of isolated self-sufficiency, this framework would not be feasible.

This very role of autonomy within the liberal framework requires that external considerations such as rules, laws, social norms, and other external influences be able to be taken into consideration consistent with an ascription of responsibility based on autonomy. In this, it illustrates how the political conception of autonomy as "helmsman" is much richer than that of autonomy as autarkeia. The helmsman metaphor allows for consideration of a broad array of external considerations consistent with the idea of autonomous decision making. Importantly, this conception of "autonomy as self-rule" allows for appeals to authority in areas of life in which we lack skills and knowledge. We, as the "helmsmen" of our own lives, steer toward various forms of authority in certain facets of life and away from authority in others. We are not self-sufficient, but this does not mean that we do not "rule" our own lives. In this way, the notion of autonomy can be developed as a practical notion for individuals living within the structure of a political and social system.

Perhaps most importantly, the concept of autonomy as helmsman understands the central role of external considerations, including family and social relationships, in steering the course of our lives. In this, it avoids the charge of atomistic isolation of the individual from social relationships and encourages an understanding of autonomous decision making as ultimately made by an individual, but made within a context of social relationships and circumstances.

Notes

1. See Mark G. Kuczewski, "Can Communitarianism End the Shrill and Interminable Public Debates?" in Mark G. Kuczewski and Ronald Polansky, eds., *Bioethics: Ancient Themes in Contemporary Times* (Cambridge, MA: MIT Press, 2000): 181–182.
2. Ibid., 182.
3. See Christine E. Gudorf, "A Feminist Critique of Biomedical Principlism," in Edwin R. DuBose, Ron Hamel, and Laurence J. O'Connell, eds., *A Matter of Principles?* (Valley Forge, PA: Trinity Press International, 1994).
4. Susan M. Wolf, "Introduction: Gender and Feminism in Bioethics," in Wolf, ed., *Feminism and Bioethics* (Oxford: Oxford University Press, 1996): 17.
5. John Hardwig, "What About the Family?" *Hastings Center Report* 20 (1990): 6.
6. See Thomas May, *Bioethics in a Liberal Society: The Political Framework of Bioethics Decision Making* (Baltimore: Johns Hopkins University Press, 2002).
7. Hardwig, "What About the Family?" 8.
8. See Richard Arneson, "Neutrality and Utility," *Canadian Journal of Philosophy* 20 (1990): 215–240.
9. John Rawls, "Justice as Fairness: Political, Not Metaphysical," *Philosophy and Public Affairs* 14 (1985): 223–251.
10. See May, *Bioethics in a Liberal Society.*
11. Wolf, "Introduction," 17.
12. Kuczewski, "Can Communitarianism End the Shrill and Interminable Public Debates?"
13. See Thomas May, "The Concept of Autonomy," *American Philosophical Quarterly* 31 (1994): 133–144.
14. See E. B. Cole, " 'Autarkeia' in Aristotle," *University of Dayton Review* 19 (1988–89): 35–42.
15. Joel Feinberg, *Harm to Self* (Oxford: Oxford University Press, 1986).
16. John Rawls, *A Theory of Justice* (Cambridge, MA: Harvard University Press, 1971).
17. Robert Paul Wolff, *In Defense of Anarchism* (New York: Harper & Row, 1970).
18. See my "The Concept of Autonomy."
19. See Cole, " 'Autarkeia' in Aristotle," 35–42.
20. Immanuel Kant, *Grounding for the Metaphysics of Morals,* James W. Ellington, trans. (Indianapolis: Hackett Publishing, 1981): 44.
21. Ibid.
22. For a good discussion of how many modern notions of practical autonomy are at odds with such behavior, see Gerald Dworkin, *The Theory and Practice of Autonomy* (Cambridge: Cambridge University Press, 1988): 23–25.
23. See Joseph Raz, *The Morality of Freedom* (Oxford: Oxford University Press, 1986).
24. See John Macken, *The Autonomy Theme in the Church Dogmatics* (Cambridge: Cambridge University Press, 1990).
25. See Thomas May, *Autonomy, Authority and Moral Responsibility* (Dordrecht: Kluwer Academic Publishers, 1998).
26. See H. L. A. Hart, *The Concept of Law* (Oxford: Oxford University Press, 1961).

14

Who Deserves Autonomy, and Whose Autonomy Deserves Respect?

Tom L. Beauchamp

"Autonomy," "respect for autonomy," and "rights of autonomy" are different notions. "Respect for autonomy" and "rights of autonomy" are moral notions, but "autonomy" and "autonomous person" are not obviously moral notions. Indeed, they seem more metaphysical than moral. However, this distinction between the metaphysical and the moral has fostered precarious claims such as these: (1) Analysis of autonomy is a conceptual, metaphysical project, not a moral one; (2) a theory of autonomy should not be built on moral notions, but on a theory of mind, self, or person; and (3) the concept of autonomy is intimately connected to the concept of person, which anchors the concept of moral status.

I will be assessing these claims with the objective of determining who qualifies as autonomous and what sort of autonomy deserves our respect. I will argue that moral notions – in particular, respect for autonomy – should affect how we construct theories of autonomous action and the autonomous person. However, theories of autonomy should only be *constrained* by the principle of respect for autonomy, not wholly *determined* by it.

I. CONCEPTS AND THEORIES OF AUTONOMY

Autonomy is generally understood as personal self-governance: personal rule of the self free of controlling interferences by others and free of personal limitations that prevent choice. Two basic conditions of autonomy, therefore, are (1) *liberty* (independence from controlling influences); and (2) *agency* (capacity for intentional action). However, disagreement exists over how to analyze these conditions and over whether additional conditions are needed. Each of these notions is indeterminate until further specified, and each can be used only as a rough guide for philosophers in the construction of a theory of autonomy.[1]

Some available theories of autonomy feature traits of the *autonomous person*, whereas others focus on *autonomous action*. Theories of the autonomous person are theories of a kind of agent. For example, the autonomous person is portrayed in some theories as consistent, independent, in command, resistant to control by authorities, and the source of his or her basic values and beliefs. These theories are often structured in terms of virtues and persistent ideals. My analysis of autonomy is not focused on such traits of the person, but on actions. My interest is on choice rather than general capacities for governance. Until the final section below, I will not be concerned with conditions of personhood. I assume that autonomous persons sometimes fail to act autonomously because of temporary constraints caused by illness or depression, circumstantial ignorance, coercion, or other conditions that restrict options. An autonomous person who signs a contract or consent agreement without understanding the document and without intending to agree to its conditions is qualified to act autonomously, but fails to do so. Similarly, a man who is threatened with death by a thief and who hands over his wallet because he does not wish to suffer the threatened consequences does not act autonomously, even if he is an autonomous person.

Conversely, some persons who are generally incapable of autonomous decision making make some autonomous choices. For example, some patients in mental institutions who are unable to care for themselves and are legally incompetent make autonomous choices such as ringing for a nurse, stating preferences for meals, and making telephone calls to friends. Such persons act autonomously even if they fail critical conditions of the autonomous person.

II. THE ROLE OF THE PRINCIPLE OF RESPECT FOR AUTONOMY

To maintain coherence with fundamental principles of morality, a theory of autonomy should be kept consistent with the substantive assumptions about autonomy implicit in the principle of respect for autonomy. To respect an autonomous agent is to recognize with due appreciation that person's capacities and perspective, including the right to control his or her affairs, to make certain choices, and to take certain actions based on personal values and beliefs. Such agents are entitled to determine their own destiny, and respect requires noninterference with their actions. Respect involves acknowledging decision-making rights and enabling persons to act, whereas disrespect involves attitudes and actions that ignore, insult, or demean others' rights of autonomy. This does not entail that, from the moral point of view, we are to respect only the morally good intentions and actions of agents. Many acts of individual autonomy are morally neutral, yet are owed respect.

Making Theory Conform to Moral Principle

Some theories of autonomy do not presume that a principle of respect for autonomy provides any substantive basis for the theory. They do not mention the principle or attempt to conform the theory to its assumptions. This matter is of the first importance because a theory that distinguishes nonautonomous acts from autonomous ones teaches us what it is that we are to respect and opens up the possibility of disrespecting certain "choices" that are of the most penetrating importance to the agent, on grounds that these choices are nonautonomous. Any theory that leads us to classify acts as not autonomous that are of the greatest importance to us in the basic governance of our affairs is both morally dangerous and conceptually dubious. If, for example, a theory declares *nonautonomous* the acts of average persons in opening a bank account, writing a will, selling a house, or refusing an offered surgical procedure, the theory is unacceptable. To declare such choices nonautonomous is to imply that another person may legitimately serve as guardian and decision maker. On this basis, a will could be invalidated or a surgical procedure authorized against the person's wish.

An instructive example of the moral perils that a theory of autonomy can pose is found in the work of Julian Savulescu on decisions to limit choices for or against life-sustaining treatments. In developing his account, Savulescu realizes that he must set out the conditions of autonomy in just the right way in order to get morally justified outcomes. If he fails in the theory of autonomy, the choices of patients will be inappropriately limited or reversed. Savulescu sharply distinguishes autonomous and nonautonomous acts using a distinction between *mere desires* and *rational desires.* Autonomous actions are only those performed from rational desires. Savulescu argues that healthcare professionals and guardians are only required to respect the actions of a patient that are done from rational desire; an *expressed desire* is not sufficient. He argues that many choices – for example, a Jehovah's Witness's decision to refuse a blood transfusion – can and should be judged not rational, therefore not autonomous, and therefore lacking in moral weight.[2]

The theory of autonomy that I present below presumes the cardinal moral importance of protecting, under the principle of respect for autonomy, everyday choices. I am assuming that everyday choices of ordinary persons are paradigm cases of autonomous choices. A critical test of the adequacy of any theory of autonomy, then, is whether it coheres with the moral requirement that we respect everyday choices such as opening bank accounts, purchasing goods in stores, and authorizing an automobile to be repaired.

I am not asserting either that ordinary persons never fail to choose autonomously or that we are morally required to respect all autonomous choices by not interfering with them. Clearly, certain behaviors "performed" or "willed" by individuals are not autonomous (e.g., giving up one's wallet when coerced and attempting to fly off a balcony when in a drug-induced state); and we are just as certainly not required to respect all choices of thieves, religious zealots who spew hatred, persons who act with conflicts of interest, and the like.

A Typical Example

As an example of the choices of ordinary persons having status as autonomous, consider the refusal of a blood transfusion by a Jehovah's Witness who has never reflectively questioned whether he should be a member of his faith or asked whether he wants to be the kind of person who refuses blood transfusions. Throughout his life, he has been a firmly committed Jehovah's Witness. Now his religious commitments conflict with the healing commitments of healthcare professionals who are urging a transfusion. His life is on the line, and he adheres to the doctrines of his faith.

One could challenge the proposition that this Jehovah's Witness is acting autonomously on grounds that his beliefs are unreflective assumptions instilled by authoritarian dogma or what Savulescu calls irrational desires; but this challenge seems to me conceptually obscure and, as a matter of theory and policy, fraught with danger. That we adopt beliefs and principles deriving from forms of institutional authority does not prevent them from being our beliefs and principles. Individuals autonomously accept moral notions that derive from many forms of cultural tradition and institutional authority. If the Witness's decision can be legitimately invalidated on grounds of acting nonautonomously, so may a great many institutionally guided choices. A theory of autonomy that conflicts with this assumption I hypothesize to be an unacceptable and morally problematic theory.

III. A CONCISE THEORY OF THE CONDITIONS OF AUTONOMOUS ACTION

I will be assuming in this chapter an account of autonomous choice that I have elsewhere set out in terms that I believe to be compatible with the constraints on theory that I just outlined.[3] That is, this account of autonomy is designed to be coherent with the assumptions that I believe we must make when we insist that the choices of ordinary persons be respected. In this account, I analyze autonomous action in terms of normal choosers who act (1) intentionally, (2) with understanding, and (3) without controlling influences. What follows is a brief statement of these conditions, omitting their subtleties.

The Condition of Intentionality

Intentional actions require plans in the form of representations of the series of events proposed for the execution of the action. For an act to be intentional, it must correspond to the actor's conception of the act in question (although a planned outcome might not materialize as projected). Unintended acts, such as a pediatrician's dropping of a newborn infant during delivery, are nonautonomous, but the agent may still be held responsible for what occurs.

The Condition of Understanding

An action is not autonomous if the actor has no appropriate understanding of it. Here we need a way of analyzing the question "Do you understand what you are doing?" Starting with the extreme of *full*, or *complete*, understanding, a person understands an action if the person correctly apprehends all of the propositions that correctly describe the nature of the action and the foreseeable consequences, or possible outcomes, that might follow as a result of performing or not performing the action. This full understanding does not amount to omniscience, because the criterion demands only foreseeability. Less complete understanding occurs by degrees. At extremely low levels of apprehension, no real understanding is present.

Autonomous actions require only a basic understanding of the action, not a full understanding. An account of understanding that required an extremely high level of understanding would be oppressive if made a condition of autonomy. Many years ago, when I decided to become a philosopher, I did not well understand the profession or its demands. However, I did know something about the writings of philosophers; I did know a few graduate students in philosophy; and I did have a reasonably good idea of my abilities as a student of philosophy. To say that my decision to be a philosopher was nonautonomous because I lacked relevant information about the profession would be inaccurate, even if such information was relevant to the choice made.

The Condition of Noncontrol, or Voluntariness

The third of the three conditions constituting autonomy is that a person, like an autonomous political state, must be free of controls exerted either by external sources or by internal states that rob the person of self-directedness. *Influence* and *resistance to influence* are basic concepts for this analysis. Not all influences are controlling. Many influences are resistible, and some are even trivial in their impact on autonomy.

Coercion is the most obvious form of influence involving controls that originate from an external source. Coercion occurs if one person intentionally uses a credible and severe threat of harm or force to control another. For a threat to be credible, either both parties must know that the source of the threat – the police, say – can effect it, or the one making the threat must successfully deceive the person threatened into believing it is credible. Some threats coerce virtually all persons, whereas others coerce only a few persons. Whether coercion occurs depends ultimately on the subjective responses of those at whom coercion is directed.

Coercion entirely compromises autonomy, despite the fact that victims of coercion do make a choice whether or not to submit to the coercer. Coercion is at one end of a continuum of types of influence. At the other end of the continuum are weak forms of influence, such as rational persuasion. In *persuasion*, a person must be convinced to believe something through the merit of reasons advanced by another person. Persuasion never compromises autonomy. Between coercion and persuasion is *manipulation*. The essence of manipulation is getting people to do what the manipulator wants, without recourse to the conditions present in coercion. For example, if a salesperson manages to influence a customer to purchase a product by filling the customer with unfounded fears about a competitive product, the person does what the agent of influence intends and has been manipulated. Informational manipulation encompasses lying, withholding information, and exaggerating so as to mislead. Each of these strategies *limits* another's autonomy, but only certain forms of manipulation deprive a person of autonomous choice. For example, offers of benefits such as a job promotion that requires a person to move to a less desirable location are intended to manipulate, but they do not deprive the person manipulated of autonomy. By contrast, lying that involves withholding critical information can both manipulate and deprive a person of autonomous choice.

Finally, this third condition of noncontrol, or voluntariness, encompasses not only *external* controlling influences but *internal* influences on the person, such as those caused by mental maladies. However, I will not pursue the complexities of this problem here. I will simply assume that an adequate condition of voluntariness must account for both internal and external controlling influences.

Degrees of Autonomy and Substantial Autonomy

The first of the above three conditions of autonomy – intentionality – is not a matter of degree: Acts are either intentional or nonintentional. However, acts can satisfy both the conditions of understanding and absence of controlling influences to a greater or lesser extent. For example, threats can be more or less severe and understanding more or less complete. Actions are autonomous by degrees, as a function of satisfying these conditions to different degrees. For both conditions, a continuum runs from fully present to wholly absent. For example, children exhibit different degrees of understanding at various ages, as well as different capacities of independence and resistance to influence attempts. This claim that actions are autonomous by degrees is an inescapable consequence of a commitment to the view that at least one of the conditions that define autonomy is satisfied by degrees.

For an action to be classified as either autonomous or nonautonomous cut-off points on these continua are required. To fix these points, only a *substantial* satisfaction of the conditions of autonomy is needed, not a full or categorical satisfaction of the conditions. The line between what is substantial and what is insubstantial may seem arbitrary, but thresholds marking substantially autonomous decisions can be carefully fixed in light of specific objectives of decision making, such as deciding about surgery, buying a house, choosing a university to attend, making a contribution to charity, driving a car, or hiring a new employee.

Problems of Adequacy and Completeness

One can and should raise questions about whether the theory I have outlined contains an adequate set of conditions for a theory of autonomy. This theory looks to be what, in other philosophical literature, might be called a theory of free will or free agency. Free agency has often been analyzed in terms of (1) a condition of persons through which intentional actions are willed (a condition absent in contrastive cases, such as dreaming, and unintentional word slips), and (2) the absence of internal and external controls (compulsion, constraint, etc.) that determine the choice of actions. Such a theory of free choice is clearly similar to the one I am proposing for the analysis of autonomy.

If my theory is nothing but a theory of free agency, it may have missed its target of *autonomy*. To test this hypothesis, I now look at a type of theory that proposes one or more conditions different from those that I have proposed.

IV. SPLIT-LEVEL THEORIES OF AUTONOMY

Several philosophers maintain that autonomy consists in the capacity to control and identify with one's first-order desires or preferences by means of higher-level (second-order) desires or preferences through processes of deliberation, reflection, or volition. Harry Frankfurt's theory of the freedom of persons and Gerald Dworkin's theory of autonomy are widely discussed examples. I will more closely follow the language of Dworkin's theory, because Frankfurt's theory of *persons* is not explicitly presented as a theory of *autonomy*.

An autonomous person, in this theory, is one who has the capacity to accept, identify with, or repudiate a lower-order desire or preference, showing the capacity to change (or maintain) one's preference structure or one's configuration of the will. All and only autonomous persons possess such distanced self-reflection, in which second-order mental states have first-order mental states as their intentional objects and considered preferences are formed about first-order preferences and beliefs. For example, a long-distance runner may have a first-order desire to run several hours a day, but also may have a higher-order desire to decrease the time to one hour. If he wants at any given moment to run several hours, then he wants at that moment what he does not truly want. Action from a first-order desire that is not endorsed by a second-order volition is not autonomous and is typical of animal behavior.

Frankfurt argues that it is essential to *being a person* that the second-order desires or volitions be such that the individual "wants a certain desire to be his will."[5] These second-order desires or volitions he calls "second-order volitions." Because they are essential to being a *person*, any individual lacking these volitions is not a person. Dworkin offers a "content-free" definition of *autonomy* as a "second-order capacity of persons to reflect critically upon their first-order preferences, desires, wishes, and so forth and the capacity to accept or attempt to change these in the light of higher-order preferences and values."[6] The language of *capacity* strongly suggests that this theory is one of autonomous *persons*, not a theory of autonomous *actions*.

Problems with the Theory

Several problems haunt this theory. First, there is nothing to prevent a reflective acceptance, preference, concern, or volition at the second level from being caused by and assured by the strength of a first-order desire. The individual's acceptance of or identification with the first-order desire would then be no more than a causal result of an already formed structure of preferences. Frankfurt writes that "whether a person identifies himself with [his or her] passions, or whether they occur as alien forces that remain outside the boundaries of his volitional identity, depends upon what he himself wants his will to be."[7] The problem is that the identification with one's passions may be governed by the strength of the first-order passion, not by an independent identification. If a person's identification (from what "he himself wants his will to be") at any point is itself the result of a process of thoroughgoing conditioning or lower-level passion, then the identification is never sufficiently independent to qualify as autonomous.

For example, the alcoholic with a passion for red wine who identifies with drinking seems nonautonomous if his second-level volition or desire to drink red wine is causally determined by a first-level desire. Suppose the alcoholic forms, as a result of the force of first-order desire, a second-order volition to satisfy his strongest first-order desire, whatever it is. This behavior seems nonautonomous, but looks as if it would satisfy Frankfurt's conditions. Moreover, an alcoholic can reflect at ever higher levels on lower-level desires without achieving autonomy if identification at all levels is causally determined by initial desires.

To make this split-level theory plausible as an account of autonomy, a supplementary theory would have to be added that distinguished influences or desires that rob an individual of autonomy from influences or desires consistent with autonomy.[8] Frankfurt seems to address these problems with the thesis that "truly autonomous choices" require "being satisfied with a certain desire" and having preexisting "stable volitional tendencies."[9] However, I am unconvinced that this analysis rescues the split-level theory.

Second, this theory risks running afoul of the criterion of coherence with the principle of respect for autonomy mentioned earlier. If reflective identification with one's desires or second-order volitions is a necessary condition of autonomous action, then many ordinary actions that are almost universally considered autonomous – such as cheating on one's spouse (when one truly wishes not to be such a person) or selecting tasty snack foods when grocery shopping (when one has never reflected on one's desires for snack foods) – would be rendered *non*autonomous in this theory.

Frankfurt's theory runs this risk in its treatment of persons who have a "wanton" lack of concern about "whether the desires that move him are desires by which he wants to be moved to act." Such an individual, says Frankfurt, is "no different from an animal."[10] Indeed, "insofar as his desires are utterly unreflective, he is to that extent not genuinely a person at all. He is merely a wanton."[11] This theory needs more than a convincing account of second-order desires and volitions; it needs a way to ensure that ordinary choices qualify as autonomous *even when persons have not reflected on their preferences at a higher level and even when they are hesitant to identify with one type of desire rather than another.*

Depending on how "reflection," "volition," and the like are spelled out in this theory, few choosers and few choices might turn out to be autonomous because few would fail to engage in higher-order reflection. Often the agents involved will not have reflected on whether they wish to accept or identify with the motivational structures that underlie such actions. Actors will in some cases be unaware of their motivational or conditioning histories and will have made no reflective identifications. Actions such as standing up during a religious service, lying to one's physician about what one eats, or hiding one's income from the Internal Revenue Service might on this basis turn out to be nonautonomous. The moral price paid in this theory is that individuals who have not reflected on their desires and preferences at a higher level deserve no respect for actions that derive from their most deep-seated commitments, desires, and preferences. There is a danger that they will be classified as no different than animals.[12]

Conversely, if one relaxes the standards of higher-order reflection, then many acts will become autonomous that these theorists wish to exclude from the realm of autonomy. For example, some actions of nonhuman animals will be autonomous. I will return to this problem in the final section below.

Converting the Theory to Nonrepudiated Acceptance

The defender of a split-level theory could shift ground and require as a condition of autonomous action only *nonrepudiation* in the values underlying choice, not *reflective acceptance* of them – a move occasionally suggested, obliquely, by Frankfurt.[13] This position is negative rather than positive: Values, motives, and actions are autonomous if the agent does not reflectively repudiate or abjure them, and they are not autonomous if they are repudiated. This set of repudiated actions would presumably not be large, but it would include important cases of weaknesses of the will, such as acts of taking drugs and acts of infidelity in which the person repudiates the driving desire or value, while nonetheless acting on it: "I was seduced in a weak moment." This position does not seem to make the mistake of rendering nonautonomous most of our ordinary actions that are intentional and informed.

Intriguing illustrations of this thesis come from clinical examples of repudiated phobic and compulsive behavior, such as the repudiation of a compulsive hand washer. I concede the attractiveness of the theory for these examples, but I wish to push beyond them to more commonplace examples of repudiated action to see if the theory remains attractive. What should we say about a corporate executive who sincerely repudiates her characteristic avarice and greed? She repeatedly, but unsuccessfully, tries to become more spiritual and less materialistic in her desires. She goes on being an aggressive corporate executive of the sort that she wishes she were not. Are her actions nonautonomous because repudiated? It seems to me that her repudiation is an insufficient reason to withhold classification of her acts as autonomous. The perpetual dieter who continuously repudiates eating carbohydrates, but goes on eating carbohydrates anyway, is a similar case. These agents may not be acting autonomously, but, if not, nonautonomy seems to derive from some form of involuntariness (e.g., uncontrollable desire), not from a failure to conform to a repudiation of desire.

There are related problems about allowing a person's actions to qualify as autonomous when values and motives are *not* repudiated. For example, in the case of the compulsive hand washer, suppose that, instead of repudiating desires for or the choice of hand washing, the hand washer had never reflectively considered his or her desires or motives. It is implausible to describe compulsive actions of hand washing as autonomous. Again, we have a problem of noncontrol, not nonrepudiation. Similar questions can be raised about Frankfurt's unwilling addict who identifies himself through a second-order volition as desiring not to be an addict, but goes on being one because he is in the hold of the addiction. Frankfurt argues that this addict is a person, not a wanton, but that his actions of drug use are not of his own free will.[14] I agree that he is a person who is not acting freely, but is he acting autonomously? Frankfurt never answers this question, but the analysis strongly suggests (whether this is intended or not) that the addict "acts" unfreely, but autonomously.

It will not be easy to construct a split-level theory using second-order identification or nonrepudiation as a criterion. Such conditions are not clearly needed for a theory of autonomous action or the autonomous person. The condition of noncontrol (as analyzed in Section II above) seems to me a more promising way to fill out a theory of both autonomous choice and the autonomous person.

V. AUTONOMOUS PERSONS AND THE PROBLEM OF MORAL STATUS

Thus far, I have concentrated on autonomous choice, although the most plausible interpretation of split-level theories (and other theories of autonomy) is that they are theories of autonomous persons. Setting aside how best to interpret particular theories, I proceed in this section to *autonomous persons* in order to address questions of *moral status.*

It is often assumed in philosophical literature on persons that they are essentially autonomous; all persons are autonomous, and all autonomous individuals are persons. However, not all theories make such an assumption. Some writers maintain that fetuses, young children, advanced Alzheimer's patients, and even the irreversibly comatose are persons, but ones who lack autonomy. I will not be considering this controversy about persons. My concern is with theories that find autonomy or some feature of autonomy (e.g., intention, rationality, or second-level identification) to be constitutive of personhood. When I use the term "person" hereafter, it refers exclusively to autonomous persons.

I said earlier that a theory with demanding conditions of autonomy (e.g., requiring full understanding, no external or internal constraint on the agent, or second-level reflective identification) will reach the conclusion that many of our presumed choices are not *autonomous* choices. The same problem applies to persons; the more demanding the conditions in a theory of persons, the fewer the number of individuals who satisfy the conditions and therefore the fewer who qualify for a status conferred by being persons. The conditions in the theory can then be built into how we should interpret the principle of respect for autonomy (or, perhaps, respect for persons). As the quality or level of required mental skill is reduced in a theory, the number of individuals who qualify for protection under the principle will increase; and as the quality or level of mental activity is increased (made more demanding), the number of individuals who qualify for protection under the principle will decrease.

If a theory demands a high threshold of mental capacity and a robust personal history of reflective identification with values, then many individuals normally regarded as autonomous will be deemed nonautonomous, or at least many of their preferences and choices will be rendered nonautonomous. For example, many decisions by hospital patients about their care would be classified as nonautonomous.[15] Correlatively, if a theory demands only a very low threshold of mental skills (modest understanding, weak resistance to manipulation, etc.), then many individuals who are normally regarded as nonautonomous will be deemed autonomous – for example, certain nonhuman animals. This problem underlies and motivates my discussion of moral status in this section.

Metaphysical and Moral Theories

Some theories of autonomous persons are *metaphysical*, others *moral*.[16] As I draw the distinction, autonomous persons in a metaphysics of persons are identified by a set of psychological (not moral) properties. Properties found in various theories include intentionality, rationality, self-consciousness (of oneself as existing over time), free will, language acquisition, higher-order volition, and possibly various forms of emotion.[17] The metaphysical goal is to identify a set of psychological properties possessed by all and only autonomous persons. Morally autonomous persons, by contrast, are capable of moral agency. The properties or capacities in a theory of morally autonomous persons distinguish moral persons from all nonmoral entities. In principle, an entity could satisfy all the properties requisite for being a metaphysically autonomous person and lack all the properties requisite for being a morally autonomous person.

Unfortunately, most theories of persons cannot easily be distinguished into one of these two types. These theories are not attentive to the distinction between metaphysical and moral persons. Proponents fasten on the goal of delineating the distinctive properties of persons, whether they turn out to be moral or nonmoral properties. For three decades, and arguably for several centuries, the dominant trend in the literature has been to delineate properties of individuals in a metaphysical account from which conclusions can be drawn about their moral status. Most philosophical accounts attempt to remain faithful to the commonsense concept of person, which is, roughly speaking, identical to the concept of human being. However, there is no warrant for the assumption that only properties distinctive of the human species count toward personhood or autonomy or that species membership has anything to do with moral status. Even if certain properties strongly correlated with membership in the human species qualify humans for moral status more readily than the members of other species, these properties are only contingently connected to being human. The properties could be possessed by members of nonhuman species or by entities outside the sphere of natural species, such as God, computers, robots, chimeras, and genetically manipulated species.[18]

What Have Metaphysical Theories to Do with Moral Theories?

Proponents of metaphysical theories often spread confusion by moving from a metaphysical claim about persons to one about moral status or moral worth. This move can be baffling, because metaphysical properties have no moral implications. A metaphysical-to-moral connection can be made only through a correlative appeal to a moral principle, such as a principle of respect for persons or respect for autonomy. The principle must be defended independently of the metaphysical theory (and given some suitable content and relationship to the theory).

Suppose that X acts autonomously, rationally, self-consciously, and the like. How is moral autonomy or any form of moral status established by this fact? No moral conclusions follow from the presence of these properties. X need not be capable of moral agency or able to differentiate right from wrong; X may lack moral motives and a sense of accountability. X may perform no actions that we can judge morally. X might be a computer, a cunning knave, a dangerous predator, or an evil demon. No matter how elevated our admiration or respect for this entity's mental capacities, these capacities will not amount to and will not establish moral status. Capacities of autonomy, language possession, rationality, self-consciousness, and the like lack intrinsic connection not only to moral status but also to moral properties such as moral agency and moral motivation.

Many philosophers, including Aristotle and Kant, hold that animals have minds but lack such critical human properties as rationality, language use, and dignity. Kant judged that human dignity – which he closely linked to moral autonomy – places humans in a privileged position in the order of nature; humans have properties that confer upon them a moral status not held by nonhuman animals.[19] Whatever the merits of Kant's view in particular, the belief persists generally in philosophy, religion, and popular culture that some special property – perhaps autonomy or a property connected to it – confers a unique moral status or standing on human persons. In philosophy, it is commonly asserted that nonhuman animals lack such properties as self-awareness, a sense of continuity over time, the capacity to will, the capacity to love, and/or autonomy and therefore lack personhood (or its functional equivalent) and moral status.[20]

However, it is more assumed than demonstrated in these theories that nonhuman animals in fact lack the relevant form of self-consciousness, autonomy, or rationality. I have yet to see a philosophical theory that argues the point by reference to available empirical evidence. A typical statement by philosophers is the following thesis of Frankfurt's:

> It is conceptually possible that members of novel or even of familiar non-human species should be persons.... It seems to be peculiarly characteristic of humans, however, that they are able to form what I shall call "second-order desire." ... Many animals appear to have the capacity for what I shall call "first-order desires." ... No animal other than man, however, appears to have the capacity for reflective self-evaluation that is manifested in the formation of second-order desires.[21]

Philosophical theories, including this one, typically ignore striking evidence of types and degrees of self-awareness of nonhuman animals, not to mention the pervasive presence of intentionality in animals and comparative studies of the brain. In some striking studies, language-trained apes appear to make self-references, and many animals learn from the past and then use their knowledge to forge intentional plans of action for hunting, stocking reserve foods, and constructing dwellings, for example.[22] These animals are aware of their bodies and their interests, and they distinguish those bodies and interests from the bodies and interests of others. In play and in social life, they understand assigned functions and either follow designated roles or decide for themselves what roles to play.[23]

Such abilities of nonhuman animals have rarely been taken seriously in contemporary philosophy, and yet they provide plausible reasons to attribute elementary self-consciousness and some degree of autonomy to nonhuman animals. Their abilities seem to admit of degrees of just the properties that I identified above in Section II. Any theory similar to the one I presented there must allow for the possibility (I think inevitability) that some nonhuman animals are at a higher level of autonomy (or, possibly, personhood) than some humans. Some measure of autonomy can be gained or lost over time by both humans and some nonhuman animals, as their critical capacities are gained, enhanced, or lost.

The fact that humans will generally exhibit higher levels of cognitive capacities under these criteria than other species of animals is a contingent fact, not a necessary truth about the human species. A nonhuman animal may overtake a human whenever the human loses a measure of mental abilities after a cataclysmic event or a decline of capacity. If, for example, the primate in training in a language laboratory exceeds the deteriorating Alzheimer's patient on the relevant scale of high-level mental capacities, the primate may achieve a higher level of autonomy (or, perhaps, personhood) and may thereby be positioned to gain a higher moral status, depending on the precise connection allowed in the theory. (Even if animals such as the great apes fail to qualify as autonomous *persons*, it does not follow that they have no capacities of autonomous *choice*.)

Criteria of Morally Autonomous Persons

The category of *morally* autonomous persons is relatively uncomplicated by comparison to the category of *metaphysically* autonomous persons. I will not attempt an account of the necessary and sufficient conditions, but it seems safe to assume, for present purposes, that X is a morally autonomous person if (1) X is capable of making moral judgments about the rightness and wrongness of actions; and (2) X has motives that can be judged morally. These are moral-capacity criteria, not conditions of morally correct action or character. An individual could be both immoral and a morally autonomous person. These criteria also would require, in a deeper analysis than I can provide here, explication in terms of some of the cognitive conditions discussed previously. For example, the capacity to make moral judgments no doubt requires a certain level of the capacity for understanding.

Being a morally autonomous person, unlike being a metaphysically autonomous person, is sufficient for moral status. Moral agents are paradigm bearers of moral status. Moral agents know that we can condemn their motives and actions, blame them for irresponsible actions, and punish them for immoral behavior. Any morally autonomous person is a member of the moral community and qualifies for its benefits, burdens, protections, and punishments. Some of the moral protections afforded by this community may be extended to individuals who fail to qualify as autonomous, but moral status for these individuals will rest on a basis other than autonomy.

Nonhuman animals are not, on current evidence, plausible candidates for classification as morally autonomous persons, though some evidence suggests that the great apes, dolphins, and other animals with similar properties could turn out to be exceptions. I will not defend this view, but I will mention a conclusion of Charles Darwin's that I accept.[24] He denied that animals make moral judgments, but affirmed that some animals display moral emotions and dispositions. Though they do not make genuine judgments of moral blame when they punish their peers for misbehavior, they do display genuine love, affection, and generosity toward their peers. However difficult it is to prove this thesis, it is no less difficult to disprove it.

Finally, if being morally autonomous is the sole basis of moral status (a view I do not hold), then many humans lack moral status – and precisely for the reasons that nonhuman animals do. Fetuses, newborns, psychopaths, severely brain-damaged patients, and various dementia patients are candidate cases. I believe that individuals in these classes do merit moral protections, but that moral protections for them are not grounded in a capacity of autonomy. These humans are in the same situation as many nonhumans: Moral status for them is not grounded in being morally autonomous any more than it is grounded in being metaphysically autonomous. However, this topic of moral status will have to be the subject of another paper aimed at showing that certain *noncognitive* and *nonmoral* properties, such as emotions and affective responses, are sufficient to confer some form of moral status.

CONCLUSION

Theories of autonomy, like many theories in philosophy, develop from pretheoretical, considered judgments. Considerable vagueness surrounds the ordinary concept of autonomy, and philosophical theories of autonomy that attempt to give the notion substance should be welcomed. These theories are interesting in their own right, and practically they may be of assistance in helping us understand what it is that we are to respect when we respect another's autonomy. At the same time, in the development of these theories we should not stray from our pretheoretical judgments about what deserves respect when willed or chosen by another. The moral value of respect for autonomy precedes and is not the product of a philosophical theory, and no theory is acceptable if it conflicts with this value.

Notes

1. Cf. treatments of the concept of autonomy in Joel Feinberg, *Harm to Self*, vol. 3, in *The Moral Limits of the Criminal Law* (New York: Oxford University Press, 1986): chaps. 18–19; and Thomas E. Hill, Jr., *Autonomy and Self-Respect* (Cambridge: Cambridge University Press, 1991): chaps. 1–4. Individual (by contrast to political) autonomy is a recent concept lacking a significant history of philosophical analysis. When the eight-volume *Encyclopedia of Philosophy* (Macmillan) was published in 1967, it offered no indexed mention of "autonomy." (Its sole reference is to "autonomous idiolects"; the entries under "self-determination" are scarcely more informative.) In its current non-Kantian uses, the term came into vogue in philosophy shortly after this *Encyclopedia* went to press.
2. Julian Savulescu, "Rational Desires and the Limitation of Life-Sustaining Treatment," *Bioethics* 8 (1994): 191–222; and Julian Savulescu and Richard Momeyer, "Should Informed Consent Be Based on Rational Beliefs?" *Journal of Medical Ethics* 23 (1997): 282–288. I am not asserting that Savulescu's conclusions could never be warranted; obviously, a Jehovah's Witness could be acting nonautonomously. I am pointing to the profound practical consequences to which a theory of autonomy may be put and suggesting a very different starting point than the one used by Savulescu.
3. Ruth R. Faden and Tom L. Beauchamp, *A History and Theory of Informed Consent* (New York: Oxford University Press, 1986): chap. 7; and Tom L. Beauchamp and James Childress, *Principles of Biomedical Ethics*, 5th ed. (New York: Oxford University Press, 2001): chap. 3. Some writers committed to a feminist perspective have argued that my theory is not entirely compatible with the constraints on theory that I have proposed, or at least that my theory needs adjustments. See Carolyn Ells, "Shifting the Autonomy Debate to Theory as Ideology," *Journal of Medicine and Philosophy* 26 (2001): 417–430; and Anne Donchin, "Autonomy and Interdependence," in C. Mackenzie and N. Stoljar, eds., *Relational Autonomy* (New York: Oxford University Press, 2000): 236–258.
4. Gerald Dworkin, *The Theory and Practice of Autonomy* (New York: Cambridge University Press, 1988): chap. 1–4; and Harry G. Frankfurt, "Freedom of the Will and the Concept of a Person," *Journal of Philosophy* 68 (1971): 5–20, as

reprinted in his *The Importance of What We Care About* (Cambridge: Cambridge University Press, 1988): 11–25. See also Laura W. Ekstrom, "A Coherence Theory of Autonomy," *Philosophy and Phenomenological Research* 53 (1993): 599–616; and Gary Watson, "Free Agency," *Journal of Philosophy* 72 (1975): 205–220. Although it is far from clear that Frankfurt holds a theory of autonomy, see his uses of the language of "autonomy" in his *Necessity, Volition, and Love* (Cambridge: Cambridge University Press, 1999): chap. 9, 11. Frankfurt's early work was on *persons* and *freedom of the will*. In his later work, he seems to regard the earlier work as providing an account of autonomy, which is a reasonable estimate even if it involves some creative reconstruction.

5. Frankfurt, "Freedom of the Will and the Concept of a Person," in his *The Importance of What We Care About*, 16. In his later philosophy, Frankfurt modified his early theory of identification. See his "The Faintest Passion," in *Necessity, Volition, and Love*: 95–107, esp. 105–106.
6. Dworkin, *The Theory and Practice of Autonomy*, 20
7. Frankfurt, "Autonomy, Necessity, and Love," in his *Necessity, Volition, and Love*, 137.
8. Problems of this sort were first called to my attention by Irving Thalberg, "Hierarchical Analyses of Unfree Action," *Canadian Journal of Philosophy* 8 (1978): 211–226.
9. Frankfurt, "The Faintest Passion" and "On the Necessity of Ideals," in his *Necessity, Volition, and Love*, 105, 110.
10. Frankfurt, "Freedom of the Will and the Concept of a Person," 18.
11. Frankfurt, "The Faintest Passion," 105–106.
12. There are more demanding theories than these second-order theories. Some theories require extremely rigorous standards in order to be autonomous or to be persons. For example, they demand that the autonomous individual be authentic, consistent, independent, in command, resistant to control by authorities, and the original source of values, beliefs, rational desires, and life plans. See Stanley Benn, "Freedom, Autonomy and the Concept of a Person," *Proceedings of the Aristotelian Society* 76 (1976): 123–130; Benn, *A Theory of Freedom* (Cambridge: Cambridge University Press, 1988): 3–6, 155ff., 175–183; R. S. Downie and Elizabeth Telfer, "Autonomy," *Philosophy* 46 (1971): 296–301; and Christopher McMahon, "Autonomy and Authority," *Philosophy and Public Affairs* 16 (1987): 303–328.
13. Frankfurt, "The Faintest Passion," 104–105. See esp. the account of satisfaction. A nuanced version of this theory of nonrepudiated acceptance (using the language of *nonresistance*) seems to be held by John Christman, "Autonomy and Personal History," *Canadian Journal of Philosophy* 21 (1991): 1–24, esp. 10 ff.
14. Frankfurt, "Freedom of the Will and the Concept of a Person," 18.
15. See Savulescu, "Rational Desires and the Limitation of Life-Sustaining Treatment," 202ff. (summarized at 221–222).
16. Other philosophers have used this or a similarly worded distinction, but not as I analyze the distinction. See Daniel Dennett, "Conditions of Personhood," in Amelie O. Rorty, ed., *The Identities of Persons* (Berkeley: University of California Press, 1976): 175–196, esp. 176–178; Joel Feinberg and Barbara

Baum Levenbook, "Abortion," in Tom Regan, ed., *Matters of Life and Death: New Introductory Essays in Moral Philosophy*, 3rd ed. (New York: Random House, 1993): 197–213; and Stephen F. Sapontzis, *Morals, Reason, and Animals* (Philadelphia: Temple University Press, 1987): 47 ff.

17. See Michael Tooley, *Abortion and Infanticide* (Oxford: Clarendon Press, 1983); Harry Frankfurt, "On the Necessity of Ideals," 113–115, and "Freedom of the Will and the Concept of a Person," chap. 2, esp. p. 12; Dennett, "Conditions of Personhood," 177–179; Mary Anne Warren, *Moral Status* (Oxford: Oxford University Press, 1997): chap. 1; H. Tristram Engelhardt, Jr., *The Foundations of Bioethics*, 2nd ed. (New York: Oxford University Press, 1996): chaps. 4, 6; Loren Lomasky, *Persons, Rights, and the Moral Community* (Oxford: Oxford University Press, 1987); and Lynne Rudder Baker, *Persons and Bodies* (Cambridge: Cambridge University Press, 2000): chaps. 4, 6.
18. On the relevance and plausibility of robots and physical-mental systems that imitate human traits, see John Pollock, *How to Build a Person* (Cambridge, MA: MIT Press, 1989); and Ausunio Marras, "Pollock on How to Build a Person," *Dialogue* 32 (1993): 595–605.
19. For Kant, a person's dignity – indeed, "sublimity" – comes from being his or her own moral lawgiver, i.e., from being morally autonomous. Kant, *Foundations of the Metaphysics of Morals*, Lewis White Beck, trans. (Indianapolis: Bobbs-Merrill, 1959): 58. Kant added that the dignity deriving from this capacity is of a priceless worth that animals do not have: "[Each person] possesses a dignity (an absolute inner worth) whereby he exacts the respect of all other rational beings.... The humanity in one's person is the object of the respect which he can require of every other human being." Kant, *The Metaphysical Principles of Virtue*, Part I, James W. Ellington, trans., in Kant, *Ethical Philosophy* (Indianapolis: Hackett Publishing, 1983): 97–98.
20. As is asserted, more or less, by Frankfurt in "Autonomy, Necessity, and Love," 131 n. 2, and "Freedom of the Will and the Concept of a Person," 16–17; Allen Buchanan and Dan Brock, *Deciding for Others: The Ethics of Surrogate Decision Making* (Cambridge: Cambridge University Press, 1989): 197–199; John Harris, *The Value of Life* (London: Routledge, 1985): 9–10; and Dworkin, *The Theory and Practice of Autonomy*, esp. chap. 1.
21. Frankfurt, "Freedom of the Will and the Concept of a Person," 12.
22. See Donald R. Griffin, *Animal Minds* (Chicago: University of Chicago Press, 1992); and Rosemary Rodd, *Ethics, Biology, and Animals* (Oxford: Clarendon Press, 1990): esp. chap. 3–4, 10.
23. Cf. Gordon G. Gallup, "Self-Recognition in Primates," *American Psychologist* 32 (1977): 329–338; and David DeGrazia, *Taking Animals Seriously: Mental Life and Moral Status* (New York: Cambridge University Press, 1996): esp. 302.
24. Charles Darwin, *The Descent of Man and Selection in Relation to Sex* (Detroit: Gale Research, 1974): chaps. 3–4.

15

Autonomy, Diminished Life, and the Threshold for Use

R. G. Frey

I. THE EXPOSURE OF THE NONAUTONOMOUS

Normative ethical theories today place enormous stress upon autonomy or agency and treat it as of the utmost significance to the value of human life. Some theorists understand agency as referring to personhood or to moral personality; some take it to involve such things as rationality and action upon reasons, self-awareness, self-critical control of one's desires, the application of norms to conduct, and deliberative choice. Some take it to be about making one's own decisions (in the important affairs of life) and directing one's life or about constructing a life of value for oneself or about adopting and living out a life plan or rational plan of action. On all these views, the effect is to set up agents or autonomous beings as a special or privileged class, against which the lives of nonautonomous beings – such as infants, young children, the irreversibly comatose or those in a permanently vegetative state, those suffering from senile dementia, the severely mentally enfeebled, some of the brain damaged, and animals – are assessed and valued. So privileged is this class that all kinds of notions are invented or assumed – such things as impaired autonomy, potential autonomy, interrupted capacity, unrealized capacity, trusteeship, and proxy agency come to mind – by which to try to squeeze as many beings as possible into it. The fear, obviously, is that, if some human being falls outside the privileged class, the protections that normally extend to one morally may possibly be in doubt. On the other hand, it is normally assumed as a matter of course that animals fall outside that class and that, although we are under some obligation not to be cruel to them, the usual protections that apply, morally, in the case of humans do not apply in the case of animals. After all, we eat and experiment upon them routinely.

Elsewhere, I have argued that this matter is not nearly so clear-cut as may seem evident to many – that, with regard to medical experimentation in particular, though I support the use of animals in medical/scientific research, the case for antivivisectionism is far stronger than most people suppose.[1] I have argued this precisely because the case of nonautonomous humans poses what I take to be a very severe difficulty, to do with the value of the lives of the nonautonomous and with what can ground a difference in treatment between autonomous creatures and creatures who are nonautonomous. Put summarily, though references to my writings on animals often crop up in the animal welfare/animal rights debates, it is in fact something to do with humans – specifically, with humans who lack agency – that is ultimately the focus of my attention, both in those debates and, more generally, in areas of medical ethics to do with the using or taking of a life. I have not been able to find a satisfactory way of distinguishing specifically human lives among all the creatures who make up the class of the nonautonomous.

It is easy to illustrate in a general way the problem I have in mind. In *A Theory of Justice*, in his discussion of the basis of equality, John Rawls indicates that it is in virtue of their moral personality that human beings are to be treated in accordance with his two principles of justice.[2] He defines "moral personality" in terms of two capacities, one to do with having a sense of justice, the other to do with having a conception of the good or a rational plan of life. Immediately, however, the cases of infants and children occur to him; in order to encompass them within the fold of his two principles, therefore, he maintains that we can draw a distinction between *having* a capacity and *realizing* a capacity. Infants and children are thus held to have the basis of moral personhood, even though they have as yet not realized the capacities that constitute it. It then occurs to him as well that there are those who have lost these capacities temporarily, through "misfortune, accident, or mental stress."[3] These, too, he proposes to cover by his distinction between having and realizing the relevant capacities. But what of those who have lost the relevant capacities permanently? Of these individuals, Rawls says that they "may present a problem," that, while he cannot in *A Theory of Justice* examine their cases, "[he assumes] that the account of equality would not be materially affected."[4] It is hard to discern the basis of Rawls's confidence in this matter, for the individuals in question have lost the very basis, in his view, for why they are owed the duties of justice. Of course, a theory of justice is not a theory of morality, and we need not speculate about how morality intersects the treatment of the nonautonomous in Rawls. It is enough to realize that there is a threat to those who fall outside the privileged class, which in Rawls's case is limited to all those who have the two capacities that constitute moral personality; and I take it that all those who are characterized as nonagents or the nonautonomous at the outset of this chapter would fall outside that class.

Does it matter whether infants, seriously defective humans, and animals are autonomous or agents? In what follows, I will suggest that it both does and does not matter. It does not matter where pain and suffering are concerned; it does matter to the value of the lives in question. This latter topic in turn bears upon a discussion of the threshold for using or taking life. Killing and the value of life are linked: If a life had no value, it is hard to see why using or taking it would be wrong. If a life has radically reduced value, however, is not the threshold for using or taking it in turn lowered as well? It is this intuition that ultimately the issue of lack of agency or autonomy bears upon, though it is complicated to articulate exactly how.

Care is needed in discussing these issues about autonomy. Often, today, when we ponder the treatment of animals in medical/scientific experimentation, the philosophical literature juxtaposes the lives of animals with those of nonautonomous humans; the so-called argument from "marginal cases" or "defective humans" turns upon just this juxtaposition. Doubtless, to many, when these terms are used of human lives, there will be thought an insensitivity in the discussion; indeed, the very idea of thinking of human lives in the same breath, as it were, with animal lives may be thought insensitive. Yet, this is precisely the parallel that falls out of the usual emphasis in virtually all normative ethical theories upon autonomy or agency, because the nonautonomous fall, at least at first blush, beyond the protections that extend to the autonomous. In the philosophical literature, this insensitivity, if it is such, is part of the very fabric of the problem of discussing who or what is included in the moral community. To this extent, then, every theorist must face this parallel and say something, for example, about whether distinctions can be drawn among the lives of the nonautonomous and about how these lives are to be treated. I want to address this parallel and say something about the value of the lives involved in such a way as to indicate why I think this issue supersedes all considerations as to who or what is a member of the moral community. Even so, however, problems remain with the nonautonomous. I shall present my discussion in the context of some considerations concerning medical/scientific experimentation.[5]

II. BENEFITS AND USE

All justifications of animal research in medicine and science involve appeals to the benefits that such research confers upon humans; in effect, the benefits conferred upon us by animal research offset the costs to animals that that research purportedly exacts. I have discussed many different aspects of this appeal elsewhere;[6] here, I want to focus upon a single dimension of it.

The dimension I have in mind is this: The benefits that animal research confer could be obtained by conducting that research upon humans. In fact, because there frequently are numerous problems with reliance upon animal models to predict exactly what will occur in humans, it may be thought that the use of humans has an obvious, more rigorous element of reliability about it.

So, anyone who wants to appeal to the benefits of animal research as, either in whole or in part, part of its justification must deploy an additional argument to show why, though we may use animals to the ends of medical and scientific inquiry, we may not use humans to those ends. We may not, for example, infect humans with various carcinogens in order to study the pathology of illnesses, and we may not do this even if certain humans consented to our so infecting them. Thus, the appeal to benefit must have underlying it some further argument that indicates what justifies using animals in medical/scientific research in ways that it would be considered improper to use humans. What this further argument requires from us is some way of distinguishing the human from the animal case. Otherwise, we seem left in an uncomfortable position: If the benefits of medical/scientific research are everything that we are led to believe that they are, then these benefits may be obtained through using either animals or humans in that research, in the absence of anything that indicates which group of beings is to be used. The idea is not that we would use humans instead of animals, but simply that, absent some distinguishing argument, we *could* use humans as well as animals.

III. DIFFERENCES AND THE PROBLEM OF HUMANS

It might be held that we simply cannot use in medical/scientific research creatures who possess certain characteristics, with it being left up to each individual to specify which are their preferred characteristics for distinguishing humans from animals. For example, we might be held to be more intelligent; have more numerous and deeper capacities for pain, distress, and suffering; and be more able to direct our own lives in accordance with some conception of the good or some plan of life than animals. The problem with this attempt to distinguish us from animals, of course, is that not all human beings share in the characteristics picked out to the same degree. So, what do we do about these humans? If animals may be used because they lack the relevant characteristics, what do we do about those humans who lack those characteristics?

Of course, it may be that "side effects" come in at this point: Many or most people would be outraged by our using humans as well as animals. Yet, many if not most of these very same people do not find it wrong to use animals in such research. So what can be the difference? What can make it wrong to use humans but right to use animals, given that both groups lack the characteristics selected as those that are supposed to bar using certain creatures in research?

What is assumed above is that, whatever characteristic or set of characteristics one selects as the relevant one by which to bar use in research, humans will be found who lack the characteristic, or lack it to a degree sufficient to bar their use, or lack it to a degree such that some animals will have it to a greater degree. Numerous primates, for example, give evidence of being more intelligent than severely mentally subnormal humans, of being more sentient, in all of its senses, than anencephalic infants, of being better able to direct their lives than those fully in the grip of senile dementia. Indeed, these things will be true of numerous animal species, depending upon which characteristics are selected and thus which humans are under consideration.

True, humans but no animals have had human parents. But this does not appear to be a characteristic of the sort that we want, because it says nothing about the life being lived, the quality of that life, a creature's intelligence or capacity for pain and suffering, the prospect of directing one's own life, and so on. These seem more like things that could serve to mark off human from animal lives and bar certain kinds of treatment, because they say something about life as it is being lived and about the nature and quality of that life. The nature and quality of life of anencephalic infants, whatever their parentage, seem by all standards currently available to us to be far worse than the lives of many ordinary animal lives. And this seems true as well for those in the final stages of many progressively degenerative diseases, such as amyotrophic lateral sclerosis, AIDS, Huntington's chorea, Alzheimer's disease, and so on.

In short, whatever characteristic we pick, we find humans who lack that characteristic and animals that to a greater or lesser degree have it. The argument from benefit is neutral with respect to whether we obtain the benefits through animals or through animals *and* humans; the problem is that our characteristics appeal does not mark off humans from animals in morally significant ways.

Plainly, recourse to even more cognitive characteristics will make the case even worse. For depending upon how sophisticated a cognitive task one sets for beings to accomplish, even more potential human candidates for inclusion in the protected class will be excluded from it. Whereas if the task is watered down so as to include as many humans as possible, it becomes possible to argue that numerous animals will be able to perform the task in question.

If that is so, however, why not simply conclude that those animals that can perform the cognitive task in question are protected from use? Certainly, we could do this. It would have the effect of extending the ambit of antivivisectionism, of course; but far worse from the human point of view, it would have the effect of protecting some animals while not protecting some humans.

I do not have space for a full examination of all the many kinds of reliance upon the characteristics claim. The nature of the response to this reliance, however, should be clear: This way of trying to justify animal experimentation, in the sense of justifying why we can use animals but never humans, runs into a problem that has nothing to do with animal welfare/animal rights issues at all. Do we embrace antivivisectionism because we can find no way to distinguish the human from the animal case in morally significant ways? (This is what I meant earlier in saying that the case for antivivisectionism is stronger than most people realize; it does represent, after all, a possible option, if to many a somewhat unrealistic one.) Do we use humans who fall outside the protected class in the way we use animals, side effects apart? Or do we protect these humans on some other ground, one that bars inclusion of any animals within the protected class and that can plausibly be held to anchor a difference in treatment? But then what is that ground?

I do not have space to go over the different possible grounds that typically arise in this kind of argument. But I will canvas several, in order to give the flavor of the depth of the problem, as I see it, before turning to the subject of the value of lives, wherein I find the way forward.

IV. POSSESSION OF RIGHTS

One might argue that humans but not animals have moral rights. This line, however, in no way departs from the earlier problem; for no appeal to rights can succeed until and unless one specifies the characteristic(s) in virtue of which humans but not animals have moral rights. Whatever it is, it seems likely that I will find humans who lack that characteristic. Nor is the point affected if one tries to develop theories of negative as opposed to positive rights; for even rights of noninterference have typically been held to provide a sphere of protection around individual, autonomous agents with plans and purposes of their own, thereby enabling them to act upon plans and purposes as they wish, up to the point of interference with others. In essence, these negative rights were to preserve a certain sense of "freedom" of self and of action, and nothing of the kind seems appropriate in the cases of many humans. Nor is the appeal to specifically "human rights" an improvement, because we need to know in virtue of what one has "human" rights, if it is something other than the earlier claim of simply having had human parents. Thus, if a human right not to be tortured turns even in part upon the ability to feel pain, then numerous animals have that characteristic.

V. PARTIALITY TOWARD SPECIES

It might be held that the solution to our problem is really much more apparent: Why can we not simply show partiality for our own kind and thus distinguish, particularly over treatment, between humans and animals? Much here would need to be said on the charge of speciesism and the attempt to understand exactly how that charge is supposed to work. But we do not need to go into that discussion, because there is an obvious dimension to the notion of showing partiality to "our kind" that poses a difficulty. Who gets to specify what that kind is? If I were to seek to show partiality to white, heterosexual males, presumably there would be a complaint. So why are we any more entitled to show partiality over characteristics that isolate species, as opposed to race, sex, and sexual orientation?

Can we claim to stand in a special moral relationship to each and every member of our species and thus, as a result, invoke partiality in favor of members? Although a husband and wife stand in a special relationship to each other, typically we do not all stand in a special relationship to each and every other person. Mere membership in the moral community does not form a special relation; but if it did, because animals are members of the moral community, as I shall maintain, there would still be no basis for distinguishing the two cases.

Usually, a special relationship with someone is something that we step into and, ultimately, can step out of. Species membership is not, of course, like this; indeed, it is not something that is voluntarily acquired and is not even something that we usually think of in moral terms. To have a special relationship that is beyond or outside our choice and control is an unusual view of such a relationship and, indeed, of moral relations generally.

And it is simply a mistake to equate some claim about species as a special moral relation with the claim that we are under some duty to render mutual aid to other humans. Even if we were under some such duty, it does not follow that the ground of that duty lies in membership in the same species.

VI. CLAIMS OF THE JUDAIC/CHRISTIAN ETHIC

Some cultural, religious traditions demarcate the human from the animal case; others do not. Suppose we focus on Christianity: In virtually all its different manifestations, as they have infused our moral thought, it is true that our cultural, social, and moral traditions prohibit us from using humans as we use animals. What underlies this prohibition, I think, are the claims that animals are not members of the moral community and that their lives are of little or no value. Underlying these claims is the Judaic/Christian ethic, which has posited a sharp break between humans and animals, and it is true that these two claims would underwrite such a break. If animals are not members of the moral community, then what we do to them is of no real moral concern; if their lives have little or no value, then the use or loss of those lives, lives that do not fall within the moral community in any event, cannot be of great moral concern. Here, too, of course, we are forced back to the characteristics claim, to that which includes all humans but no animals and that can plausibly anchor a difference in treatment. Yet, increasingly, the scientific context in which we seek for this difference seems to be one, not of a radical break between humans and animals, but rather of a continuum of abilities and capacities. It lies beyond the scope of this chapter to explore these overlapping abilities and capacities, though it is well to bear in mind here, too, that disease can rob humans of these abilities and capacities. The people that Rawls said might pose a problem for his views of equality in truth do not have unrealized capacity or potential ability; the fact is that disease and illness have robbed them of the relevant capacities and abilities altogether. It does not make much sense to treat them as having "potential" abilities, when, for example, in old age disease and illness have robbed them of certain possibilities of action and thought altogether.

To be sure, the attempt to invoke religion into our discussion had a point in an earlier age. The problem with the characteristics claim is that, whatever characteristic we select, we find humans who lack it and animals that have it. We find human lives of radically divergent quality, lives so impaired that, increasingly, those who live them seek relief from them. What the appeal to God did was to confer an equality on all human lives, no matter what characteristics a particular life had or lacked: All human lives were equal in the eyes of God and were sacrosanct. Thus, in a sense, appeal to God solved our problem: There was a ground for not using humans the way we use animals in medicine and science, for there was a characteristic that all humans shared, however drastically reduced their quality of life, but that no animals shared. In essence, we were God's preferred creature.

How persuasive this thought is in our more secular age remains to be seen. Certainly, it will not convince those whose religious faith is much diminished or has disappeared altogether. Nor at this juncture have secular attempts to replace God proved very successful, though notions like "inherent value" and "inherent worth" seem in part designed to replicate what was achieved earlier by claiming of all human lives that they were equal in the eyes of God. For what we find is that attempts to maintain that two lives of radically different quality are nevertheless of the same worth come unstuck on a simple point: If it is not condition or quality that determines its worth, in what does the worth of a life consist? How do we recognize its presence or absence in a life?

Of course, it is obvious that not all human lives have the same quality, and contemporary debates over suicide, the right to die, euthanasia, and physician-assisted suicide all involve aspects of the discussion of widely discrepant and often tragically diminished qualities of life. With equality in the eyes of God in doubt, nothing seems to underpin the claim of the equal worth of all human lives. All we seem left with are lives of different and, at times, radically diminished quality.

VII. MORAL CONSIDERABILITY AND THE VALUE OF A LIFE

So, what now is left us? The main fallback position, I think, will be to endorse the twin claims of the Judaic/Christian ethic – namely, that animals are not members of the moral community, and their lives have little or no value. As I have indicated elsewhere,[7] I think both these claims are false.

Very briefly, a creature is morally considerable or has moral standing if it is an experiential subject, with an unfolding series of experiences that, depending upon their quality, can make the creature's life go well or badly. Such a creature has a welfare that can be positively or negatively affected, depending upon what we do to it, and with a welfare that can be enhanced or diminished, a creature has a quality of life. The most common experimental subject (i.e., rodents), let alone primates, has moral standing: It is an experiential subject with a welfare and a quality of life that our actions with respect to it can affect. This is the case, moreover, whether or not rodents are agents or autonomous beings and whether or not they possess moral rights. Thus, agency and rights are to my mind irrelevant to the issue of moral standing or considerability.

Put differently, experiential subjects that are not human beings are members of the moral community on the same basis that we are, and we do not have to go through the contortions of deriving different senses of autonomy, such as trusteeship, proxy agency, impaired autonomy, or unrealized capacity, in order to account for why they have standing. Agency or autonomy has nothing to do with whether a creature is morally considerable or not.

Rodents, pigs, and chimps are experiential creatures with a welfare and a quality of life, and I see no reason to deny that, as such, they feel pain. In this regard, I can see no difference between knifing a pig and knifing a child. Pain is pain, and species is irrelevant. These are experiential creatures, and pain represents an evil in the lives of all such creatures, most certainly as it lowers a creature's quality of life. I see no way to discriminate morally here over pain.

If, however, pain and suffering count morally, then surely animal lives must count morally as well. For what concerns us about pain and suffering, whether in ourselves or in animals, is how these things impair, diminish, and blight the quality of life. They adversely affect the lives of all creatures that can experience them. It would be foolish to treat a child in agony as having a high or desirable quality of life, and I can see no reason why it would not be foolish to say anything different in the case of experiential animals. They, too, have a welfare and a quality of life. As a result, their lives in my view have value.

Obviously, more needs to be said here, and I have in some of the material referred to above tried to fill in more of this picture of moral standing and the value of lives. Suffice it to say here that I think we are forced to accept that (the "higher") animals have moral standing and that their lives have value and that, therefore, we gain no easy access to animal though not human experimentation through reliance upon these two aspects of the Judaic/Christian ethic.

I do not, of course, maintain that all human lives have the same value. But neither do I maintain that ordinary adult human life has the same value as animal life, and it is this issue of the comparative value of human and animal life that holds the key to the experimentation issue.

VIII. THE COMPARATIVE VALUE OF LIVES

So, where are we? Where pain and suffering are concerned, I can find no difference between the human and animal cases, though, of course, I concede that humans may suffer in some ways that animals do not. Where the value of lives is concerned, I think that animal lives have value and on the same basis that human lives have value. We are all experiential creatures with a welfare and a quality of life that can go up or down, depending upon what is done to us. We cannot use animal lives as if they had no value.

Thus, what we require is a defense of our using animal lives in experiments that includes both an account of what makes a life valuable and, if we are not to use humans in the ways we use animals, a nonspeciesist account of why normal adult human life is more valuable than animal life. In the material referred to above, I have offered such an account.

If in an experiment a life *had to be used and taken* and we could use either a rodent or a man, most would say, other things being equal, that it would be worse to kill the man. What makes it worse is not species membership but our widely shared view that human life is more valuable than animal life. Although the rodent's life has value, it does not have the same value as the man's life, and it is worse to destroy lives of greater rather than lesser value. It is this view that figures throughout the discussion of killing in all domains that involve choosing between lives: Other things being equal, where taking a life is concerned, take the life of lesser value; where saving a life is concerned, save the life of greater value. Where killing is concerned, then, it is this view about the comparative value of human and animal life that, I suggest, dictates using the animal.

Yet, this comparative view of the value of a life will be speciesist, unless something other than species membership confers greater value upon the man's life. If something else can be cited, then we can point to a genuine moral difference between using and killing a rodent and using and killing a man, which difference we can then insert into the argument to justify animal as opposed to human experimentation.

As I have argued in other places, the view that I think best captures this "something else" is a quality-of-life account of the value of a life.[8] The value of a life is a function of its quality, its quality of its richness of content, and its richness of content of its capacities and scope for enrichment. In this regard, the capacities of a creature for a rich life are crucial, and everything that science, experiment, and direct observation teach us indicates that the human and animal cases differ. Animal life has value; the question, however, is whether the life of a rat approaches our own in richness, quality, and thus value, given its capacities for enrichment. Observation, direct acquaintance, and the behavioral sciences give us no reason to think so. The rat's capacities for enrichment are just too limited in number, scope, and variety to make us think differently. Nothing here is speciesist: Normal adult human life is more valuable than animal life, not because of species membership, but because of richness of content.

The inner lives of animals, then, matter to this discussion. That they have inner lives and are experiential beings is, I think, beyond question, certainly in the case of the "higher" animals. I have discussed elsewhere some of the problems associated with gaining access to the subjective experiences of animals and cautioned against concluding that, because we may not be able to know everything of their inner lives, we can know nothing of them. But further elaboration of my views in this regard, which readers can obtain elsewhere in any event, is not my aim here.[9] Suffice it to say that the greater value of normal adult human life explains why it is worse to kill the man than the rodent. It amounts to the destruction of something of greater value, so that, *if an experiment has to be performed and a life taken*, one takes the life of lesser value.

The problem over the use of humans can now be put in a different light: I know of nothing that guarantees that human life will always have a higher quality than animal life. Indeed, given the tragic depths to which some human lives can plummet, it seems quite likely that the quality of some animal lives will exceed those of a number of humans. If we are to use the life of lower quality, then this may well in certain cases work against human lives of radically diminished quality.

Richness of content in our lives is tied to our capacities for enrichment. Where these are impaired or missing, as with the loss of a sense, a life appears less rich than an ordinary adult human life that contains those kinds of experiences that that capacity makes possible. This does not mean that another capacity cannot compensate for this loss, but it does mean that we should have to be convinced of this.

A rich human life goes far beyond a rich cat life. Observation and science seem to tell us that we have capacities that far outstrip anything the cat has. Nothing is settled, of course, by this presumption of argument; but something must be said in the cat's case, by way of compensation, to make us think that the richness of its life approaches that of the normal adult human. Perhaps this can be done, but it seems that one would need to point to a feature (or set of features) of the cat's capacities that transforms its life through that single dimension to the level of richness that is conferred on our lives by all our various capacities.

I concede, of course, that much work needs to be done on the nature and assessment of quality of life. But it would be a mistake to think that this work cannot be done or can never be satisfactorily done or can never be done to any usable end. Talk of quality of life is a ubiquitous feature of medical settings, of medical prognoses, of decisions over the allocation of medical resources, and so on. Some things may be rough and ready, invoking physical and psychological elements, as in contemporary debates in the QALY (Quality Adjusted Life Years) literature. But those in permanently vegetative states and anencephalic infants do not appear to be hard cases, where, arguably, there is no quality of life left to be assessed. Today, if we take many of those who seek physician-assisted suicide at their own word – when, say, amyotrophic lateral sclerosis has destroyed their lives and rendered their continued existence to them a misery – it is they themselves who take the quality of their lives to have plummeted to a degree sufficient to have compromised the value of those lives. So, they seek release from them.

Quality-of-life views of the value of a life, then, give us a nonspeciesist reason for viewing normal adult human life as more valuable than animal life. But they do not give us reason to think that all human lives of whatever quality are more valuable than all animal lives; indeed, it seems obvious that there are some human lives of far lower quality than numerous animal lives. So, if experimentation demands of us morally that we use the life of lesser value, then we face the prospect of having to envisage using these human lives – subject, of course, to the constraints that possible side effects may impose upon us. I do not see how it can be claimed to be moral to use a life of higher value in preference to one of lower value, if lives of lower value are available.

In short, if human lives are not (approximately) equally rich, they are not of equal quality; and if they are not of (approximately) equal quality, they are not of equal value. In fact, some animal lives can be of a richness and quality higher than some human lives, such as the brain dead and anencephalic infants (to take the least controversial examples), and so can be of greater value.

IX. AGENCY AND DIMINISHED VALUE

My aim here, however, is not to expound further on whether animal experimentation is justified; it is to indicate in the above line of argument what role agency or autonomy plays in the attempt to demarcate the human from the animal case.

Does it matter, then, whether seriously impaired humans and animals are autonomous? Where pain and suffering are concerned, it does not matter. It is wrong to burn a child and wrong to burn a cat. The act is wrong because of the pain and suffering it causes; it is irrelevant that they are not agents or autonomous beings. And the act is wrong, by the way, not for reasons of the kind that Kant embraced, not because of the increased prospect of our performing an act of burning an autonomous being; it is wrong because of the suffering it causes in the child and in the cat. But what about where using or killing the seriously defective infant or the cat is concerned? Here, I think, agency or autonomy *does* make a difference, though perhaps not in an obvious way.

Normal adult human life is more valuable than ordinary animal life. The comparative question is whether an animal's life approaches normal adult human life in quality and thus value, given its capacities and the life appropriate to its species, and I have suggested that it does not, given the greater richness and the greater potentialities for enrichment in the human case. Agency or autonomy can help us enhance the value of our lives. There is no necessity in the matter: Autonomy is instrumentally, not intrinsically, valuable. Its value depends upon the uses made of it, and, in the cases of normal adult humans those possible usages significantly enrich a life. To direct one's own life to secure what one wants; to make one's own choices in the significant affairs of life; to assume responsibility over a domain of one's life and thus acquire a certain sense of freedom to act; to decide how one will live and to shape one's life accordingly; these are the sorts of things that can – again, there is no necessity in the matter – open up areas of enrichment in a life, with consequent effects upon that life's quality and value. Autonomy matters, then, because of what it enables us to make of our lives.

Much can be said here, in order to paint exactly how autonomy enables us to add dimensions of richness and value to our lives, far beyond anything that we associate with animals. What agency enables us to do is to fashion a life for ourselves, to live a life shaped by choices that are of our own making and thus reflect how we want to live. The accomplishment of ends so chosen in this regard is one of the great goods of human life and one of the factors that can enrich individual human lives. Moreover, we fashion this life for ourselves in a community of shared moral relations with others, where we live out our lives in a normative understanding of these relationships with others and so see our lives as going well or badly depending upon how these relationships are affected by what we do to others and by what they do to us. When we seek to draw up some comparative stance on the value of our lives versus that of animals, no mere account of the activities we share with animals – eating, sleeping, reproducing – could come anywhere near accounting for the richness of which human lives are possible and which autonomy makes possible.

The point that not all human lives are equally rich, because not all human lives have the same sources of enrichment available to them, will be obvious. With truncated scope for enrichment, the quality of life will suffer, unless one can make up in a single source of enrichment what all the various sources confer on normal adult human life. And while we cannot pronounce on this in the absence of evidence, we shall indeed need evidence. Where we find radically reduced sources of enrichment, the problem seems more acute.

What, then, are we to say of those radically diminished lives at the very extreme of the picture, where we think there is present no quality of life at all, as in the case of those in a permanently vegetative state and where, as in the cases we began with from Rawls, various if not all sources of enrichment have been permanently lost? As the above will indicate, I cannot find anything by which to distinguish their cases from animal cases, but I can find something that makes me think their lives can be less valuable than the lives of some perfectly ordinary animals, which, in turn, affects the case for which life to use, *if a life has to be used,* in experimentation. I cannot, therefore, share Rawls's confidence that something will be found by which to avoid this possible outcome. To be sure, he was talking about a theory of justice, and I am talking about a theory of morality; but the exposure of the nonautonomous is the same in both cases.

Let me stress, then, that on a quality-of-life view of the value of a life of the sort sketched, the human and animal cases are remarkably alike in the role that experiences unfolding in a life play. What the animal case has to contend with, so far as normal adult humans are concerned, is the extent, variety, quality, and depth of experiences that are available to humans through the multiple dimensions of our lives, some of which are made available to us through the exercise of our autonomy. Nothing in all this says that human lives are more valuable than animal lives *because* they are autonomous lives; all autonomy does, *at best*, is to make ranges of experiences available to humans. Even without autonomy, animal lives are valuable, because animals remain experiential creatures; but without autonomy, human lives are not as valuable as they can be, because the full range of the experiences such lives are capable of through the additional capacities that normal adult human lives typically possess is not present.

One might urge that we give up quality-of-life views of the value of a life, give up accounts of richness in terms of a life's content, adopt some abstraction such as inherent value, or endorse God and plead for the equality of all human lives in God's eyes. Yet, it seems odd to do these things in order to put ourselves in a moral position to continue to enjoy the benefits of medicine and science at the expense of animals, some of whose lives will otherwise exceed in value some of ours.

Notes

1. See my "The Ethics of the Search for Benefits: Animal Experimentation in Medicine," in R. Gillon, ed., *Principles of Health Care Ethics* (New York: John Wiley, 1993): 1067–1075; "Medicine, Animal Experimentation, and the Moral Problem of Unfortunate Humans," *Social Philosophy and Policy* 13 (1996): 181–211; "Vivisection, Morals, and Medicine," in H. Kuhse and P. Singer, eds., *Bioethics: An Anthology* (Oxford: Blackwell, 1999): 471–480; and "Moral Community and Animal Research in Medicine," *Ethics and Behavior* 7 (1997): 123–136.
2. John Rawls, *A Theory of Justice* (Oxford: Clarendon Press, 1972): 504 ff.
3. Ibid., 510.
4. Ibid.
5. In this regard, see my "Organs for Transplant: Animals, Moral Standing, and One View of the Ethics of Xenotransplantation," in A. Holland and A. Johnson, eds., *Animal Biotechnology and Ethics* (London: Chapman & Hall, 1997): 190–208; "Justifying Animal Experimentation: The Starting Point," in Ellen Frankel Paul, ed., *Why Animal Experimentation Matters* (Newark, NJ: Transaction, 2001): 250–280; "Animals," in H. LaFollette, ed., *The Oxford Handbook of Practical Ethics* (Oxford: Oxford University Press, 2003): 151–186. I draw upon and restate part of this material – and material from my papers "Lives within the Moral Community" and "The Significance of Agency and Marginal Cases" – in what follows.

6. See the material referred to in notes 1 and 5 above.
7. See my "Medicine, Animal Experimentation, and the Moral Problem of Unfortunate Humans," 181–211; and "Justifying Animal Experimentation: The Starting Point," 250–280. I also here draw upon material from my paper "Moral Standing, the Value of Lives, and Speciesism," in H. LaFollette, ed., *Ethics in Practice* (Oxford: Blackwell, 1997): 139–152. I conclude something slightly different in the present chapter.
8. See notes 1, 5, and 7.
9. Ibid.

Index

For EU product safety concerns, contact us at Calle de José Abascal, 56–1°,
28003 Madrid, Spain or eugpsr@cambridge.org.

www.ingramcontent.com/pod-product-compliance
Ingram Content Group UK Ltd.
Pitfield, Milton Keynes, MK11 3LW, UK
UKHW042145130625
459647UK00011B/1185
* 9 7 8 0 5 2 1 7 3 2 3 4 5 *